12/24/21

To Justin who is an
avid reader in a long
line of avid readers. No
wonder you are so smart!
Keep reading and enjoying it
Love & hugs,
Grandma

ADVANCE PRAISE FOR *DO NOT DISTURB*

"The whole world wanted to believe in the miracle that was Rwanda—a country built from the wreckage and devastation that intertribal violence and ethnic cleansing had caused. The whole world ignored the few voices pointing out the silencing of political opponents through imprisonment, kidnapping or torture. To our shame, our need for Rwanda to succeed far exceeded our desire or ability to see the cost at which that success was bought.

"In this extremely important and profoundly disturbing book, Michela Wrong sets out all the missteps that were ignored, all the flagrant human rights abuses that were overlooked, and all the criminality for which excuses were found, until the new horrors that have been visited upon that country were perpetrated.

"Ms. Wrong is not suggesting that we become Afro-pessimists but telling us that not only is the price of freedom eternal vigilance, but also that we must, in the words of Amilcar Cabral, 'tell no lies, claim no easy victories.'"

—**Archbishop Desmond Tutu**, winner of the Nobel Peace Prize

"A withering assault on the murderous Rwandan regime of Paul Kagame, and a melancholy love song to the lost dreams of the nations of the Great Lakes. Michela Wrong proves once again that she is an intrepid and highly professional researcher of the subject she knows best. It's a major accomplishment, very driven, very impassioned."

—**John le Carré**, author of *Tinker Tailor Soldier Spy*

"Michela Wrong takes her readers on an absorbing political journey, in which Rwandan comrades-in-arms Paul Kagame and Patrick Karegeya steadily mutate into lethal adversaries upon achieving power. The ghosts of other historic mortal fallouts—Stalin and Trotsky, Sankara and Compaore, Robespierre and Danton, Mugabe and Mujuru—haunt this story, but more importantly, it draws our attention to the significant structural problems created by ex-military leaders' participation in the building of post-war democracy and peace."

—**Miles Tendi**, author of *The Army and Politics in Zimbabwe: Mujuru, the Liberation Fighter and Kingmaker*

"An intimate, clear-eyed chronicle of the violence and intrigue at the heart of the Rwandan Patriotic Front's history. This is perilous terrain; Wrong skillfully navigates amid myths and disinformation to splice together the stories of the men who came to rule Rwanda."

—**Jason Stearns**, author of *Dancing in the Glory of Monsters: The Collapse of the Congo and the Great War of Africa*

"In rich, searing prose, backed up by damning evidence and compelling anecdote, Michela Wrong exposes the sinister paradoxes of Kagame's murderous 'donor darling' regime. Her book lays out a roadmap for another collective 'never again' outcry yet to come.

"Focusing on the happy beginning and tragic end of Patrick Karegeya—a spymaster strangled in a South African hotel room by a Mossad-like squad of operatives he helped establish—*Do Not Disturb* is an insightful, scrupulous, stirring yet nuanced account of a reign of terror that set Rwanda and the whole African Great Lakes on fire, using four weapons of mass destruction: the cord, the hoe, the gun, the missile. Like Saturn, the regime is now devouring its children. This masterly investigative book should be widely read."

—**Noel Twagiramungu**, Director, Africa Center for Strategic Progress

"A unique insight into many hitherto little known dark sides of a profoundly criminal regime. Based on firsthand observations and numerous interviews with key players, victims, and witnesses, this book is an indictment of those complicit in ensuring President Kagame's impunity during the last quarter century."

—**Filip Reyntjens**, author of *Political Governance in Post-Genocide Rwanda*

DO NOT
DISTURB

DO NOT DISTURB

THE STORY OF
A POLITICAL MURDER
AND AN AFRICAN REGIME
GONE BAD

MICHELA WRONG

PUBLICAFFAIRS

New York

PublicAffairs
Hachette Book Group
1290 Avenue of the Americas, New York, NY 10104
www.publicaffairsbooks.com
@Public_Affairs

Printed in the United States of America

First Edition: March 2021

Published by PublicAffairs, an imprint of Perseus Books, LLC, a subsidiary of Hachette Book Group, Inc. The PublicAffairs name and logo is a trademark of the Hachette Book Group.

The Hachette Speakers Bureau provides a wide range of authors for speaking events. To find out more, go to www.hachettespeakersbureau.com or call (866) 376-6591.

The publisher is not responsible for websites (or their content) that are not owned by the publisher.

Print book interior design by Jeff Williams.

Library of Congress Control Number: 2020952178

ISBNs: 978-1-61039-842-8 (hardcover), 978-1-61039-843-5 (e-book)

LSC-C

Printing 1, 2021

To Marilda Wrong (née Musacchio),
who made me what I am.

He believes in killing his opponents,
that is the problem I have with them.

There is a long list of people
that have died politically.

I was in a position to know.

—*Patrick Karegeya*

CONTENTS

Contents

THE GUN

THE MISSILE

PRINCIPALS

Ugandans

Amin, Idi (Gen)—former army chief of staff, toppled Obote, president 1971–1979, died in exile in Saudi Arabia in 2003.

Besigye, Kizza—former National Resistance Army (NRA) rebel, Museveni's doctor during Bush War, opposition leader.

Byanyima, Winnie—former National Resistance Movement (NRM) cadre, UNAIDS executive director, married to Kizza Besigye.

Kayihura, Kale (Gen)—former NRA rebel and chief of police.

Kazini, James (Gen)—commander of Uganda People's Defence Force (UPDF), took part in Operation Kitona and Kisangani wars.

Museveni, Yoweri—founder of NRM, president of Uganda since 1986, married to Janet Kataaha.

Obote, Milton—prime minister, then twice president, 1966–1971 and 1980–1985, died in 2005.

Otafiire, Kahinda (Gen)—NRM stalwart, minister of justice.

Mbabazi, Amama—NRM stalwart, former prime minister.

Saleh, Salim (Gen)—Museveni's younger brother, former NRA and then army commander, businessman.

Rwandans

Batenga, David—Patrick Karegeya's nephew, in exile.

Bayingana, Peter—doctor in NRA, founding member of Rwandan Patriotic Front (RPF), killed in 1990.

Bizimungu, Pasteur—fifth president of Rwanda, 1994–2000.

Gafaranga, Apollo Kiririsi—businessman and intelligence informant, wanted for Patrick Karegeya's murder.

Gahima, Gerald—former attorney general, founding member of Rwanda National Congress (RNC) opposition group, in exile.

Gisa, Jeanette, née Urujeni—businesswoman, widow of Fred Rwigyema.

Habyarimana, Emmanuel (Gen)—army officer under Juvénal Habyarimana, joined post-genocide army, former defence minister, in exile.

Habyarimana, Juvénal—third president of Rwanda, 1973–1994, killed in plane crash in 1994.

Himbara, David—economist, former adviser to Paul Kagame, professor of international development, founder of human rights group, in exile.

Higiro, Robert—former RPA rebel, major in Rwanda Defence Force (RDF), UN peacekeeper, human rights activist, in exile.

Kabarebe, James (Gen)—former RPA rebel, Democratic Republic of Congo (DRC) army chief, former Rwandan army chief and defence minister, presidential adviser.

Kagame, Paul—former NRA rebel, sixth president of Rwanda, since 2000.

Kagame, Jeannette, née Nyiramongi—businesswoman, first lady, wife of Paul Kagame.

Kanyarengwe, Alexis—army colonel who helped install Juvénal Habyarimana, vice-chairman and then chairman RPF, died 2006 from an "abrupt paralysing ailment."

Karake, Karenzi (Gen)—former head of Directorate of Military Information (DMI) and National Intelligence and Security Service (NISS), known as "KK."

Karegeya, Patrick—assistant director in Ugandan military intelligence, Rwandan head of external security (ESO) 1994–2004, killed by strangulation in Johannesburg in 2014.

Karegeya, Leah, née Umuganwa—businesswoman, widow of Patrick Karegeya, in exile.

Kayibanda, Gregoire—second president of Rwanda, 1962–1973, killed by starvation in 1973.

Kayonga, Charles (Gen)—former army chief of staff.

Micombero, Jean-Marie—former secretary general at Ministry of Defence, prominent RNC member, in exile.

Munyuza, Dan—former head of DMI and ESO, current chief of police.

Ndahiro, Emmanuel (Dr.)—Kagame's former doctor and adviser, former head of ESO and NISS.

Ntabana, Aime—one of Patrick Karegeya's informants, missing since 2013.

Nyamvumba, Patrick (Gen)—former chief of defence, AU/UN mission to Darfur commander, former minister of internal security.

Nyamwasa, Kayumba (Gen)—former RPF head of military intelligence, commander of gendarmerie, army chief of staff, head of NISS, ambassador to India, founding member of RNC, in exile.

Ndagijimana, Jean-Marie Vianney—foreign minister in first post-genocide Rwandan government, in exile.

Nziza, Jack (Gen)—former director DMI, permanent secretary ministry of defence, now inspector-general of armed forces, known as "The Terminator."

Rudasingwa, Theogene—former RPF general secretary, Kagame's chief of staff, founding member of RNC, in exile.

Rutagengwa, Emile—former RPA rebel and DMI operative, Patrick Karegeya's assistant, in exile.

Rwigyema, Fred (Gen)—former NRA commander, Ugandan army chief, inspirational head of RPF, killed in 1990.

Sebarenzi, Joseph—former parliamentary speaker, in exile.

Sendashonga, Seth—interior minister in first post-genocide government, assassinated in exile in 1998.

Twagiramungu, Faustin—prime minister in first post-genocide government, later opposition leader, in exile.

Zaireans/Congolese

Kabila, Joseph—son of Laurent, president of DRC, 2001–2018.

Kabila, Laurent—revolutionary, leader of Alliance of Democratic Forces for the Liberation of Congo-Zaire, president of DRC, 1997–2001, assassinated in 2001.

Mobutu, Seko Sese—known as "the Leopard," president, 1965–1997, died in 1997.

Tanzanians

Nyerere, Julius—first prime minister of Tanganyika, president of Tanzania, retired in 1985 while remaining hugely influential, died in 1999.

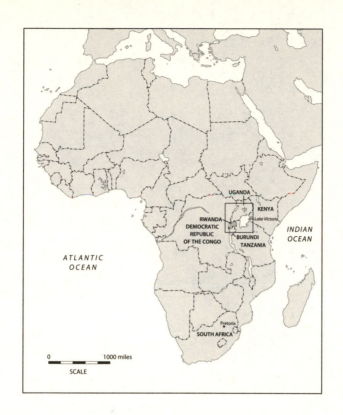

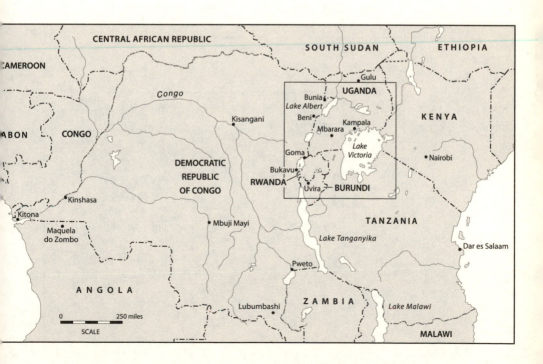

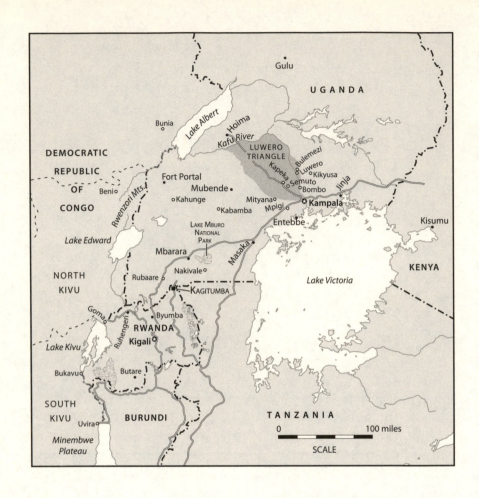

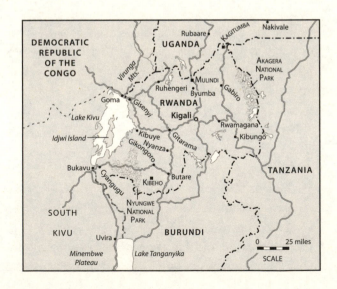

INTRODUCTION

Throughout the writing of this book, I kept thinking about the Epimenides paradox. The one that runs: "'All Cretans are liars,' says Epimenides, the Cretan." It came to mind because Rwandans kept telling me that deceiving others, being economical with the truth, was something their community reveled in, positively prided itself upon.

Especially when dealing with Western outsiders. A proof of superiority, not shame, when successfully achieved. So much so, that the practice had worked itself into the language. *Naïf comme les blancs* (Naive as the white folk), Rwandans will say of someone, in the same way that other cultures will say "as thick as two short planks," or "as dumb as a post."

One of Rwanda's prime ministers, Agathe Uwilingiyimana, shocked the head of a UN peacekeeping force by telling him: "Rwandans are liars and it is a part of their culture. From childhood they are taught to not tell the truth, especially if it can hurt them."[1] She was one of the first victims of the 1994 genocide, murdered by *interahamwe* thugs.

A successor told me the same thing over coffee in a Brussels hotel lobby many years later: "In Rwanda, lying is an art form. When you, as a white journalist, leave a meeting, they will be congratulating themselves: 'We took her for a ride.' Lying is the rule, rather than the exception."

It was an accusation tossed into conversations with Tutsis and Hutus, Rwandans and Ugandans, diplomats and military men, lawyers and journalists. "You spoke to so-and-so? Oh, he's the most terrible liar."

It was not, it seemed, a recent practice. Dip into the history and you quickly stumble upon gleeful deceits. One is the story of German explorer and naturalist Dr. Richard Kandt, who arrived at the gates of the Rwandan royal court in 1898.[2] When Dr. Kandt asked to see the *Mwami,* King Yuhi Musinga, the courtiers did what they always did when presumptuous white men ventured into this land of misty volcanos and rolling green hills: they presented him with a kinsman and awaited his reaction, laughing among themselves at the German's anticipated stupidity.

Dr. Kandt, however, had not only bothered to learn the local language, he had done some research. He knew that the Mwami was a teenager. Expressions changed as he shifted into Kinyarwanda, pointing out that this fully grown "Mwami" must be a fake and asking to see the real king. His eventual reward was to be made Resident in Rwanda, a mediator between the Rwandan Tutsi court and a renascent Germany hungry for an African empire. His house in Kigali is now a national museum, a fitting tribute to one of the first westerners to beat a Rwandan at his own game.

English adventurer Ewart Grogan, a contemporary of Kandt's, after an 1899 trip to "Ruanda-Urundi," as it was then known, railed bitterly against the mendacity of local guides, who would deny the existence of a mountain, he claimed, even when it virtually stared him in the face. "Lies, lies, lies, I was sick to death of them," he wrote. "Of all the liars in Africa, I believe the people of Ruanda are by far the most thorough."[3]

It's not surprising, perhaps, that historically, dissimulation and secrecy became prized in an incestuous court beset with intrigue, where nobles lived in constant fear for their lives. Ritualists relayed messages from a Supreme Being only they could decipher, earthly power rested with a Queen Mother who sat invisible behind a screen, and the aristocracy exerted feudal dominion over the peasantry, obliging each hamlet to spy on its own inhabitants and report back to the throne.

Around the personage of the Mwami, who was never publicly seen to eat or drink, swirled a haze of euphemistic terminology. "The King is seated" indicated he was performing bodily functions; "The King has given his person" was the closest a courtier came to indicating the Mwami might have died. To be elliptical, layered, intellectually opaque—these were signs of good breeding. The crudeness of direct speech was reserved for peasants.

Kinyarwanda itself is a language infused with subtle wisps of meaning, hidden references its intended audience immediately picks up but foreigners miss. "Oh, if only you spoke Kinyarwanda you'd understand, it's as clear as day," a Rwandan will often exclaim in frustration, after translating a politician's content-packed speech, which, when converted into English, appears, disappointingly, to say nothing terribly significant. To the Rwandan's ears, the threats are direct, the promises crystal clear.

Look up the word *ubwenge* in a Kinyarwanda dictionary and the translation reads "wisdom," or "sense." But it can also be translated as "cunning," "deception," a quality Rwandan children are encouraged to develop, seen as the ultimate sign of maturity. It goes hand in hand with the concept of *intwari*, which French historian Gérard Prunier defines as "the quality of impassivity, aloofness, being beyond and above events, implacable." *Intwari* was expected of young Tutsi boys destined to become warriors. Dignity before spontaneity: "In this respect," adds Prunier, "the culture the Rwandans most resemble are the Japanese." But what he is describing also echoes the "stiff upper lip" made famous by English aristocrats, a characteristic associated in both countries with an upper class groomed from birth for leadership and military service in defense of the nation.[4]

As a Rwandan psychologist once told me: "To show emotional reserve is considered a sign of high standing. You do not just pour out your heart in Rwanda. You do not cry. It's the opposite of Western oversharing, a form of stoicism."

A culture that glories in its impenetrability, that sees virtue in misleading: to someone proposing to write a nonfiction account embracing many of the most controversial episodes in Rwandan history, it posed a bit of a challenge.

Two deadly secrets squat at the base of Rwanda's modern history: the circumstances in which the charismatic commander of the rebel Rwandan Patriotic Front (RPF) met his end in 1990; and the question of who shot down the plane carrying the Rwandan president and his Burundian counterpart, a double presidential assassination that set the 1994 genocide in motion. Few contemporary histories are so thoroughly contested. With the passage of the years, a variety of analysts, commissions of inquiry, and investigating magistrates have changed their minds on key points, angrily contradicted one another, or simply given up on the attempt to establish the truth, opting for a bland: "No one will ever know."

The conflicting narratives would be understandable if the events in question dated back thousands of years. The fact that they concern episodes that took place in the last quarter of a century, involving players often still available for interview, highlights the problem posed by the calculated unreliability of key witnesses.

When it came to embroidering the truth, Patrick Karegeya, Rwanda's former head of external intelligence, knew more than most. During one of our most intriguing conversations, he explained some of the characteristics of the political lie. We'd been talking about Muammar Gaddafi, whom Patrick (almost everyone referred to him by his first name) had met several times. For decades, African rebel groups routinely turned to the Libyan leader for arms and funding—and he often obliged. Like many despots, Patrick said, Gaddafi possessed an elephantine memory for faces and names. "He was like a library, he knew everything about Africa, about every African leader. He was not good at analysis, but he knew everything about everyone."[5]

I mentioned that both Mobutu Sese Seko and Haile Selassie possessed similar memories: contemporaries and biographers remarked upon it. What explained that prodigious retention of detail?

"Because he had evil intentions," was Patrick's simple answer. "When you are lying, you focus on the lie you are telling, because you know you need to remember it when you next meet that person. You remember the encounter, because you were lying all that time. Whereas if I try in a year's time to remember this coffee with you, I won't be able to recall when exactly it took place or what we said or did. Because I was just being myself." Deceit, if it is to be sustained, requires focus.

It was said with rueful self-knowledge. In his latter years, Patrick—like many of those interviewed for this book—was trying to undo a knot of his own tying. He and his closest colleagues in the RPF were responsible for a compelling narrative peddled to journalists, diplomats, human rights workers, Western officials, and ordinary Rwandans throughout the 1990s and aughts. They had sold that story with passionate energy, driving aggression, and a sophisticated understanding of their respective audiences' guilt complexes and pressure points.

These were men supremely skilled at seduction, intellectual, emotional, or sexual. American diplomats weary of negotiating with sleazy Great Lakes politicians thrilled at the puritanism of these thin, driven young men in camouflage. NGO workers who were new to Africa's Great Lakes listened to their tales, hearts pounding with sympathy and outrage—initially, at least. Reporters, photographers, and filmmakers became lifelong friends or ended up jumping into bed with them. Intensity, along with imminent danger—and the Great Lakes has always been a dangerous place to live and work—is one of the great aphrodisiacs.

One journalist I know, working for a mainstream news agency, covertly joined the RPF's intelligence payroll; another confessed, many years later, to carrying a top-secret message for the movement to a Congolese minister in Kinshasa: the conflict of interest this represented never crossed his mind. After the genocide, Rwanda could so easily be viewed through the prism of the Holocaust and the pledge of "Never Again." And to the Anglo-Saxon world, at least, it seemed clear who the Good Guys were: the insurgent RPF.

It was a story line that required careful curation by officials like Patrick, and the history of the period is littered with deliberately leaked memos, suppressed reports, and many a daring forgery. The men I spoke to went on to challenge and undermine the account, only to discover—irony of ironies—that they had done their original work rather too well. Having superbly marketed the narrative of the underdog turned moral crusader returning home, they found, when they tried denouncing it, that their listeners preferred the lie to its teller. When Cretan Epimenides tells you not to believe the Cretans, why would a sane person listen?

The debate over the Rwandan narrative has always been polarized between those—often Francophones—who saw the RPF as invaders willing to sacrifice millions in their ruthless quest to return Tutsis to power in Rwanda, and those—usually Anglophones—who saw them as warrior-liberators who, tracing a giant geographical and historical boomerang, overturned one of Africa's most evil regimes.

The level of hatred and contempt felt by each side for the other is astonishing. Perhaps only the Israel-Palestine debate can equal it for venom. The vitriol is in part explained by the stakes involved, the extraordinary amount of blood shed at every stage. Who can contemplate all those hundreds of thousands of dead—not just in Rwanda, but in neighboring Democratic Republic of Congo (DRC)—and remain coolheaded?

As Paul Kagame gradually emerged as one of Africa's uncontestable autocrats, damning evidence kept surfacing of RPF atrocities. At first it could be brushed aside, using the classic justifications of realpolitik: Rwanda was situated in a rough neighborhood, the argument went; its government, trying to restore peace and security to a traumatized society, could not be held to the standards of Sweden or Switzerland.

Then the movement that had seemed to outsiders so united began splintering, and key members quit and ran. The RPF's self-imposed oath of Omertà, rigidly observed up till then, began to crack, and as it did so, people like me who had seen the RPF as implacable, certainly, but a disciplined, highly effective movement with a farsighted leadership and a progressive agenda, felt our certainties begin to tremble.

As examples of RPF human rights abuses and unaccountability accumulated, I was not the only previously supportive journalist who winced, frowned, and was quietly grateful to be writing about other things. My career had taken me elsewhere, Rwanda was no longer my beat. Still, it was painful to accept that I might have unwittingly misled my readers.

On the few occasions when I met up with Patrick Karegeya during these years, I avoided asking him certain questions. Of course, I kick myself for that now. I told myself it was out of politeness. Reminding an exiled spy chief that he had once told the media the exact opposite of what he was now saying seemed, well, rude. The guy was down on his luck, beleaguered in every sense of the word, why rub salt into his wounds? But my concern was also for myself: I didn't want to confront the truth of just how thoroughly I might have got it wrong.

Political philosopher Frantz Fanon captured that disinclination perfectly: "Sometimes people hold a core belief that is very strong. When they are presented with evidence that works against that belief, the new evidence cannot be accepted. It would create a feeling that is extremely uncomfortable, called cognitive dissonance. And because it is so important to protect the core belief, they will rationalise, ignore and even deny anything that doesn't fit in with the core belief."[6]

The greater the effort that goes into forming a belief, the more reluctant those who hold it are to adjust their lenses. The investment a shamefaced outside world poured into Rwanda after the genocide—financial, emotional, intellectual—was enormous, given the country's tiny size and population. No wonder so many are reluctant to reassess.

What I discovered, however, was that whatever the conscious mind decides to engage with—or bypass—one's cognitive process continues to churn heedlessly along in the background. There came a day when, with a near-audible mental *ping*, I realized I no longer believed most of the key "truths" upon which the RPF had built its account, and hadn't for ages. It felt like a relief. Shibboleths can weigh heavy on the soul.

One thing I never doubted, not for a second, was that a genocide had occurred in Rwanda in April 1994. I'd seen the bodies, gagged at the unmistakable aroma that comes off a hurriedly buried mass grave, registered the bloody handprints left on the walls of classrooms and church buildings by Tutsi men, women, and children scrabbling to escape their executioners. Images of that kind are hard to forget.

What I no longer believed was the RPF's explanation of how the country had come to reach that terrible point, or the movement's depiction of itself as not just a morally blameless actor during the buildup to that episode, but the rebel equivalent of a knight in shining armor, cantering in to lance the dragon of ethnic slaughter.

So how *do* you write Rwanda's contemporary history when so many key sources now readily admit they lied at the time? In theory, the answer is: by interviewing all and sundry without fear or favor, comparing and contrasting the various perspectives, and eliminating contradictions in order to come up with something roughly approaching an objective truth.

But that's just not possible in Rwanda. Had I spent months in Kigali interviewing those in power and getting their version of events, I would have struggled to win interviews with leading members of the exiled opposition, understandably wary of government infiltration. And each interview with an exile—meetings I was confident Kigali's intelligence services would swiftly hear about—meant I was less likely to be allowed into Rwanda again. On this story, crossing the battlefront was not going to be possible.

So I chose the side less written about and that seemed to me the most obviously intriguing: the side of those who had once been stalwarts of the RPF, Kagame's closest aides and confidants, who had lost faith in the man and the project and found themselves out in the freezing cold, struggling to make sense of their own personal trajectories.

Their testimonies had had surprisingly little impact by the time I got to them. "They would say that, wouldn't they?"—the dismissive Mandy Rice-Davies line—hovered silently in the air when their allegations came up. To me, it didn't hold much logical water. Were we to assume that men and women who currently depended on Kagame for their livelihoods and security were more likely to be honest than these players, who knew so much and now had so little to lose?

What about their often openly acknowledged track record of deceit? In a trial, a defense team feels it has scored a triumph when it manages to demonstrate a prosecution witness has lied in the past, no matter how trivial the fib. "They lied once," the argument goes, "so they must be lying now."

It's a simplistic view of human nature. People lie for a reason. Discerning the motive—something copious interviewing, comparing what was said then and now, along with plenty of background reading, can yield—surely allows some of the falsehoods to be disentangled from the truth. I spent more than four years attempting to do just that and when I've failed—there are many points of the story when I honestly don't know what happened—I admit to it in the text.

Fear proved to be the biggest hurdle in conducting my research. I've always been a reporter who attributed talk of assassination plots and state monitoring to an exaggerated sense of self-importance on the part of the person concerned. The longer I spent researching this book, however, the more I began to feel that in this case, the worry was entirely logical. As the saying goes: "Just because you're paranoid, doesn't mean they aren't after you."

I might have brushed off warnings that the Kigali government was an enthusiastic practitioner of computer hacking, for example— "Don't ever say anything that matters over email or on your mobile phone," was a mantra among those I spoke to—if I hadn't had a jaw-dropping early experience of my own.

In early 2015, I received an email from Rwanda's high commissioner to London, inviting me to click on a Dropbox link. I cocked my head: the email looked more than a little suspicious. But this was the Rwandan ambassador, I told myself, a man with standing in the community, not some West African con man offering a share in the Prince of Togo's missing fortune. Perhaps the high commissioner had joined the stream of Rwandan diplomats and generals parting ways with his government, I thought, and the link would lead to a leaked revelation, or a confidential appeal for help.

"Dear High Commissioner," I emailed back. "I just received an email that professes to come from you, encouraging me to go to a Dropbox. Could you confirm this is a genuine message? There are various things about it that suggest a possible Nigerian scam." Williams Nkurunziza's answer was immediate and reassuring: "Yes the email is from me. Please check it and revert."

I did, and was rewarded with a steady stream of viruses over the following months. When I showed a computer analyst what I'd downloaded, he examined its particulars and ran an antivirus scan. "That's a phishing email. I'm not even going to click on that website, it looks so dodgy." When I mentioned this incident to a US State Department contact with decades of Great Lakes experience, he shook his head in wonder: "The *high commissioner* did that? They really are completely shameless."

No Rwandan would have been as trusting—as *naïf*—as I'd just been. Those who leave expect to be tracked and take appropriate steps. Hence the laborious protocol dictating how to communicate and meet up with Rwandan exiles.

The standard response to an email sent to a Rwandan you don't already know is silence. Suspicion runs so high, a mutual Rwandan acquaintance must first provide your bona fides. Future communications won't be by email, that's far too easy to track. Since the Rwandan government is on excellent terms with Israel, the United States, and the United Kingdom, it's best to assume not only that Kigali has the equipment for sophisticated cybertracking but also benefits from monitoring by its Western friends. Skype was once popular but is now deemed unsafe. WhatsApp replaced it for a while, only to be abandoned in turn for Signal and Telegram. Text messages are good, but keep the wording vague.

One of my regular correspondents avoids all forms of digital communication and relies on old-fashioned methods, sending me envelopes in the post. Others will never say anything of interest unless speaking face-to-face.

Meetings will always be in a public place. You'll be sent instructions to get to a particular subway or railway station only to receive a last-minute text changing these arrangements. You'll settle at the restaurant indicated and be about to order a coffee when you will receive one more message, telling you the contact is actually in the café next door, sizing you up from a distance, or, unnervingly, sitting right behind you.

"I hope you're being careful," was a refrain I constantly heard. "I hope you're taking precautions," another. "Don't trust him/her/them," the third.

All this does not lend itself to relaxed conversation. I've shared coffees with jittery, uptight Rwandans whose eyes scoured my face, clearly asking themselves if they could trust me or whether I was on Kigali's payroll, even as I, in turn, wondered if they were the personification of a phishing virus, trying to flush out opinions dutifully reported back to HQ. I became wearily accustomed to a "don't use my name and don't say anything that could get me identified" instruction at the end of the encounter.

A relative of Patrick's kindly acted as a guide when I toured western Uganda researching this book. After I'd left the country, he received two anonymous phone calls, one asking him why he was driving white journalists around, the other telling him his life was in danger and he should go underground. Petrified, he did so.

"We all feel monitored, all the time," another relative told me in the Ugandan capital, Kampala. "As far as we're concerned, there's no difference between the Uganda and Rwanda intelligence services, they work so closely together. So I never say anything important over the phone now, just chitchat inanely about makeup and nail varnish, silly girly things like that. My friends must think I've gone insane."

Yet another female relative spotted me by chance at a restaurant and chased me across its parking lot in the dark, clapping her hands to attract my attention, not daring to call out my name. "I'm so sorry I haven't answered your phone calls," she said when she caught up with me. "But we are being watched."

The fear extends well beyond Africa. One evening I was walking alongside a visiting Rwandan student down Great Portland Street in Central London when I noticed a large black man with an expensive camera taking pictures. My reaction was to vaguely wonder whether there was enough light for the camera to focus. My companion's was convulsive and immediate: he bounced away from me, establishing enough distance between us to ensure we couldn't appear in the same shot. He automatically assumed the photographer had been hired by the Rwanda High Commission to capture evidence of him consorting with a controversial writer. We sat together for ten awkward minutes in the glare of a café before he asked if we could move somewhere less exposed, and ended up exchanging our most private views in the darkness of an archway.

I spoke to a Western economist, a man who kept challenging Rwanda's impressive development record but insisted on publishing his articles anonymously. When I urged him to go on the record, he refused. "You have to understand, I have a wife, I have children," he explained. I stared at him, marveling at a level of anxiety that would have seemed in order if he'd been a member of the Mafia turning state's evidence.

It was particularly striking as a few weeks earlier I'd met another development expert specializing in the Great Lakes who felt obliged to avoid the region in which he had built his reputation because he'd been declared persona non grata by the Rwandan government following a disagreement over statistics. "I wouldn't feel safe anywhere in the Great Lakes now," he said.

These conversations took place in London, not downtown Kigali. No one doubts the regime's Mossad-style ability to efficiently reach out and locate its enemies—whether real or suspected—halfway across the world. And as this book makes clear, such fears are justified.

In Boston, I met a Rwandan who planned to change his name by deed poll, so that he could masquerade in the future as African American. Most Rwandans routinely adopt Twitter, Facebook, and Skype handles that give no clue as to their nationality. In the United Kingdom, one of my interviewees confessed he was getting psychiatric help for post-traumatic stress disorder; another's emails, sent from Sweden, showed clear signs of paranoid delusion. If any group has won the right to its nightmares, it is the Rwandan diaspora.

Fear is as infectious as any virus. I've written books before that annoyed ruling regimes, but have never felt quite so personally at risk. If something happened to me, I decided at a certain point, I would at least make sure my material survived. I took to religiously backing up every interview and set of notes, then storing the key USB stick with a friend, in case my apartment was broken into. To prevent cybersnooping, I kept the laptop on which I wrote this manuscript permanently offline, hiding it at the end of each working day under the dirty clothes in a laundry basket.

While I decided early on I would not be able to conduct any useful interviews inside Rwanda, I played briefly, before publication, with the idea of flying to Kigali on a tourist visa, simply to soak up recent sights and sounds. Everyone has a tipping point, and mine came when I learned of the experience of Shaun Abrahams, chief prosecutor in the case brought in South Africa against six men accused of trying to kill General Kayumba Nyamwasa, Rwanda's former army chief of staff, in 2010.

When he was acting director of a Priority Crimes Unit at the National Prosecuting Authority, Abrahams was booked to address a workshop on counterterrorism in the Cape. He's a lively speaker, but the South African think tank organizing the event, at the Erinvale Estate Hotel, was still surprised by the number of Rwandans—both embassy staff and students at the University of Cape Town—signing up for the event. They hadn't expected such enthusiasm.

Then Abrahams received a visit from South African intelligence. "Cancel your attendance," he was told. "You're on Kagame's hit list and they're out to get you at that event." The official could not tell him what exactly was being planned—a beating, a poisoning, a shooting?—but with the seminar scheduled to last three days, all options were open. Abrahams dropped out.[7]

That did it, as far as my own plans were concerned. If one of the most senior officials in the South African judicial system didn't feel safe in his own country, what chances would a solo journalist venturing inside Rwanda itself stand?

The end result of all this surveillance, monitoring, and threat is to lock Rwandan citizens inside individual ghettos, self-censoring every utterance, wary of contact with the outside world. Despite the enormous amount of information already in the public domain, the diaspora—whether Hutu, Tutsi, or Twa—has long stopped expecting outsiders to understand. Rwanda's is a private grief.

In many cases, an awareness of guilt forms part of that introversion, which dovetails so neatly with Rwandans' famous impenetrability. A possible *génocidaire* label—a routine accusation by the Kigali government—hangs over every Hutu by mere dint of their ethnicity. As for the Tutsis who belonged to the RPF during the long march from the Luwero Triangle via Kampala to Kigali and then on to Kinshasa and Kisangani, they know that copious crimes were committed along the way. I took it as read that many of those I spoke to had blood on their hands. To denounce Kagame means admitting what was done and what one was. As the international clamor for universal justice grows in the West and the International Criminal Court spreads its feelers across Africa, exiled RPF members find themselves hog-tied.

Given a landscape as distorted by disinformation, propaganda, and wishful thinking as this one, no one who writes a book about Rwanda can claim to have told the truth and nothing but the truth. All a writer can say is that they made a valiant investigative effort, they did their best. Had I waited another decade, no doubt I could have been more certain of my findings, as time tends to flush out the most egregious inventions. But given the extraordinary attrition rate among members of the RPF elite, I feared that by that stage, there might be few left to comment.

13

Most of the books published to date on Rwanda have rightly focused on the 1994 genocide, that pivotal, hallucinatory moment in twentieth-century history. But this is not a book about the genocide. It's a book about a small, tight-knit elite, but an elite whose vaunting, Shakespearean ambitions happened to shape the destiny of Africa's Great Lakes region. The personality clashes, foibles, and vendettas of that group of men and women have had a vastly disproportionate impact on not only the continent itself, but the way the West views and interacts with modern Africa. This is their story, whether they like it or not.

THE CORD

Patrick Karegeya.

Karegeya family.

General Kayumba
Nyamwasa in South
Africa in 2016.

Michela Wrong.

Rwandan president
Paul Kagame.

*Siphiwe Sibeko,
Getty Images.*

CHAPTER ONE

AN INCIDENT
AT THE MICHELANGELO

A large eye does not mean keen vision.
—Rwandan proverb

The Michelangelo Towers hotel has always been a favorite with Johannesburg's movers and shakers. It's an ugly building, with more than a touch of the ridiculous. South African architects have long been fixated with Renaissance Italy, and the Michelangelo, which gazes across a courtyard to a giant bronze statue of a dancing Nelson Mandela, the Sandton City mall's distinguishing feature, is modeled on a Florentine palazzo. Only this palazzo has the grim solidity and restricted views of a dungeon.

No matter. South African government ministers are regularly spotted being shown into their chauffeur-driven cars by the top-hatted doormen, and the tables in the café restaurant, where a piano lugubriously tinkles, are usually occupied by at least one of the "tenderpreneur" millionaires who benefited from Black Economic Empowerment, whose eyes make the briefest of contacts with those of a well-known newspaper columnist before moving discreetly on.

Visiting African dignitaries, in particular, remain loyal. Back in the days when many were still fresh from guerrilla life, with its forced marches, camp beds, and military rations, the Michelangelo offered them a first taste of the capitalistic indulgences that could be theirs. A certain affection endures.

On the afternoon of January 1, 2014, a customer stood at reception, giving the staff a hard time. Tense and overwrought, David Batenga, a young Rwandan who had made South Africa his home, was trying to cajole the Michelangelo's employees into yielding up the secrets of the guest register.

He was growing increasingly frantic at his inability to contact his uncle, Patrick Karegeya, whom he knew had checked a guest into the Michelangelo three days earlier. Patrick was the kind of man who constantly worked his phones, pinging texts, messages, and emails in relentless succession his nephew's way. Since New Year's Eve, though, there had been only silence. It was out of character. It felt wrong.

Tourists from the Northern Hemisphere tend to flock to South Africa over Christmas and New Year's, hungry for its warmth and light. As schools let out, businesses close, and families head for Durban and Cape Town's endless beaches, Johannesburg and Pretoria fall quiet. The high veldt sits baking in the heat; the jacarandas, jasmine, and bougainvillea lining suburban streets fill the air with sweetness; and each afternoon, clouds clump like cottage cheese on the horizon until a sudden wind whips through the trees. Then rain sluices the gated communities with gelatin-thick sheets of water.

It's a testing time for the divorced, the single, and the exiled. So many parties, so many family get-togethers, each festivity underlining one's solitude. Patrick, born extrovert, joker, and socialite, was on his own again that year. His wife, Leah, who had moved to Knoxville, Tennessee, with their sons, Elvis and Richard, was visiting friends in Washington; his daughter, Portia, was in Montreal. So when he heard that Apollo Kiririsi Gafaranga, a young Rwandan businessman and playboy friend, was flying in, it felt like a relief.

Usually, Apollo went to stay at Patrick's house in Ruimsig, a modern suburb on the outskirts of Johannesburg. But this time, Apollo had made an unprecedented request: he asked his friend to book him a suite at the Michelangelo, explaining that he had a series of meetings planned with Russian, Zimbabwean, and Qatari businessmen. Money was no object, he said. Patrick obliged, and when Apollo flew in on the morning of December 28, Patrick went to meet him.

Patrick had every reason to be careful. Rwanda's former head of external intelligence, he had fled the Central African country in 2007 after a high-profile falling-out with President Paul Kagame and set up an opposition movement. Kagame was widely assumed to be behind the botched assassination attempt on one of Patrick's political allies in South Africa in 2010. It was logical to assume Patrick was on the same hit list, but he refused to take the level of care David Batenga thought appropriate. "Uncle used to say, 'Relax. We're just too paranoid. Start living.'"[1]

But David *did* worry, intensely. His relationship with Patrick was unusually close. The ex–spy chief had been the man who insisted he attend school, in the teeth of bitter resistance from David's father, an old-fashioned Tutsi pastoralist who believed in the prime importance of "cows and land, cows and land—he had plenty of both." Patrick had paid for David's schooling and played a pivotal role in getting him to Durban to study accountancy.

When Patrick fled to South Africa he had initially lived with his nephew, who had unquestioningly taken on the role of chauffeur, fixer, de facto bodyguard, secretary, and confidant. "I literally knew everything about the guy. He was more than an uncle, he was my father, my guardian, my best friend. He was everything to me."

The two men even physically resembled one another. Discount the three-decade gap and David could be a younger version of his uncle; they shared the same surprisingly pale skin—*el-Arabi, mwarabu* (the Arab), or *muzungu* (white man), comrades dubbed Patrick—the same mobile, sardonic mouth and knowing, mischievous eyes.

When David talks about those days, he starts and does not stop. He could be giving evidence to the South African police—as he has done so many, many times—or testifying in court, as he longs to do. Dates, times, appointments, the wheres and whens of meetings and BlackBerry message exchanges—there's a relentlessness to the detail that betrays a brain turning over traumatizing material, trying to sift the significant from the trivial, wondering what could have been done differently.

At lunchtime on the 28th, David drove over to join Apollo and Patrick and together they watched the English Premier League soccer match at the Garden Court Hotel, just off Nelson Mandela Square. Patrick was a Liverpool fan, David supported Arsenal, Apollo wasn't bothered either way. "Uncle said, 'This Hutu guy, he wants to go for a massage.'" David ferried the two to a Chinese massage parlor outside the mall and left them to it.

Truth was, David never felt at ease in Apollo's presence. "I took an instant dislike to him. I didn't like him from day one, and it only grew. If you sit with someone for hours over several days, their character slowly emerges. You could see he loved money." David noted, in particular, the intermittent quality of communications with Apollo when he was in Rwanda. "He'd vanish. Switch off his phone and be off Skype for three, four months in a row. Everything would go dead. And then he would suddenly show his face in South Africa." It made him wonder what exactly Apollo had been up to during the break.

David had shared his doubts with Patrick, but his uncle brushed them off, and if you're a young African man you don't tell an elder he's talking rubbish. Counterintuitively for a former head of intelligence, personal suspicion had never been part of Patrick's emotional makeup. He based his relationships with people on split-second assessments, gut instinct, and once an individual entered the inner circle, they stayed there.

It was a peculiarly un-Rwandan characteristic, but then, Patrick was the least typical of Rwandans. He'd always opened his home, his heart, and his wallet to emotionally damaged, questing young men in need of surrogate father figures, and Apollo, for all his flashy bravado, fitted that category.

There were self-serving reasons for the friendship, too. Apollo was in business with Jeannette Kagame, the president's wife. He regularly shared beers with members of the Rwandan Patriotic Front in the officers' mess in Kigali, where he soaked up political gossip: "What kind of gossip? Oh, the state of the nation," explains David. "Who's in agreement with who. Who's not happy with Kagame. Which investors are in the country. Who is in and out of favor. Which foreign officials are arriving, what RPF relations are like with various rebel movements. He didn't say much but he seemed to know a lot." For an intelligence expert in exile and in opposition, Apollo's chitchat was gold dust.

So David left the two men and returned to the soccer. He spoke to his uncle by phone that afternoon. "'Are you still in the massage?' I asked. Patrick said, 'Yes, we have our feet up, we're drinking coffee.' I said, 'OK, I'll see you guys tomorrow.'" By evening Patrick was safely back at home.

Patrick and Apollo spent the 29th together, and that evening the three men met up again to watch soccer at the News Café in Randburg, an unashamedly macho sports bar. Leaving his uncle to wend his way home, David ran Apollo back to the Michelangelo at 11 p.m.

The 30th was much the same. David, who was juggling his self-appointed role as fixer and fallback driver with his job as an accountant, attended a meeting with some asset managers at the Michelangelo's restaurant. He joined Patrick and Apollo afterward, leaving them there for another business meeting at 3 p.m.: "I called Uncle at 6 p.m. and he said, 'I'm going home and he's going to the hotel.' I checked up on him later: 'Have you reached home?' 'Yes.'"

On the 31st, David called his uncle to tell him he was going to see Kennedy Gihana, the secretary-general of the Rwanda National Congress (RNC), the opposition group Patrick had cofounded. Gihana had survived a mysterious car accident, but had been discharged from the hospital on crutches. David wanted to visit him at home.

Patrick told his nephew he was going to see Apollo at the Michelangelo. "I was invited to a Black-and-White New Year's Eve party that evening, which started at 8 p.m. I rang Uncle and said, 'Are you sharp?'"—South African slang for "cool"—"He said, 'Yes, everything is okay.'" It would be their last exchange.

At a quarter to midnight, David rang his uncle from the party to wish him a Happy New Year. "I phoned all three of his phones. Only two were working, but he didn't pick up." This was unusual. Those who have worked in intelligence rarely go incommunicado. "He was always someone who responded very quickly, within five minutes. But I thought, 'These guys are having fun,'" remembers David. "Patrick loved social events. And there was nothing to indicate anything was wrong."

In Montreal, Patrick's twenty-four-year-old daughter, Portia, seven hours behind, was also watching the clock. The thousands of miles separating father and daughter were never allowed to interrupt a constant conversation. Her WhatsApp account sports a photo of her graduation: Portia, in black gown, has her head on her father's shoulder, while Patrick, arms wrapped around her, is beaming with pride. She was waiting for midnight to strike in South Africa so she could surprise him.

Like David, Portia has near-photographic recall of that period. The day before, father and daughter had chatted via Skype. They had talked about a miniskirt ban in Uganda, and the irony of German race-car driver Michael Schumacher being plunged into a coma after a skiing accident. "I asked him what he had been up to and he said he had come from dinner with a guy from Kigali"—Apollo. Portia cracked a joke, asking, "Do you really trust those guys?" "Argh, I know, but sometimes you have to," Patrick replied.[2]

With her family scattered across two continents, the young law student had been feeling beleaguered. "My dad was stuck in South Africa, my mum and brothers were in the States, I was the only one able to move between any of them. My great fear was that something might happen to someone in the family and we wouldn't be able to get to them."

But Portia had the optimism of youth. "I had decided to write a letter to myself reviewing each year, setting goals. And since this was the first one, I'd decided to do a whole life review. I'd written about the past decade, everything that had gone wrong, stuff that had happened to me. It was so hopeful and happy: isn't that insane? I was telling myself, 'You know, you've been through so much, but things are looking up now.'

"I remember telling Dad, '2014 is going to be the year of the Karegeyas. Things are going to be great. We definitely all have to focus and get our shit together.' And he agreed."

But when midnight struck in South Africa and she sent a message on Skype, Patrick didn't answer. "I always got paranoid when he didn't reply. I'd always send another message immediately afterward." Nothing. She rang David. "Are you sure he's OK?" she asked him. David sought to reassure her, but Portia was not convinced. "I was so uncomfortable that whole time." David himself only half believed his own words. At 1 a.m., he tried ringing Patrick. "My wife was saying, 'Why are you ringing him so much?'" He felt angry with Patrick now, annoyed at the anxiety his uncle was causing those he loved.

Also uneasy was Leah Karegeya, Patrick's wife. She was by nature a worrier, but whenever she shared her fears of the Rwandan regime with her husband, he would shrug and say, "Doesn't Kagame die, too? Do you want to live forever?"

Money was tight that year. The job this upper-class Rwandan had taken to make ends meet—working for a Knoxville agency offering care to America's elderly—yielded nothing like enough. When a relative in Delaware invited her to explore possibilities in the area, she had agreed, flying out after a Christmas Day shift. She had been preparing for a road trip to Washington, where she planned to join her sons for New Year's Day. "I'd been talking to Patrick by Skype, telling him I was scared because I had a two-hour drive to do on my own, through the rain. He never trusted my driving, so he told me, 'Use the GPS and text me when you get there.' And I did, but there was no answer.[3]

"I went to church with my friends to at least see in the New Year in a spiritual mood. I kept checking my phones, but there were no messages. I was getting a bad feeling. We were so used to communicating all the time. Portia called and said, 'Something's strange. Daddy hasn't been in touch.'"

The following morning in Johannesburg, David was distracted. January 1 was his brother-in-law's birthday and a family get-together had been organized. But at 9 a.m. he tried his uncle's phones again. "All his phones were off. I thought he had a hangover, but decided to go round to his house and check." That was when David became seriously alarmed. Patrick was not at home. The bed was made up and the car was not in the parking lot.

He drove to the Michelangelo, left his car in the giant parking lot, and went to reception. The realization that he didn't actually know Apollo's surname made him feel suddenly foolish. "I said, 'I'm here to see a guest. I don't know his last name, but he's a Rwandan.'" The reaction from the receptionist was predictable, but David, like his uncle, knew how to charm.

"They searched the entire computer system, but there was no trace of 'Apollo.'" At a loss, David walked through the Michelangelo's restaurant—nothing—hung around for an hour, then went to the parking lot to leave. "And that's when I see Uncle's car. I tried to open it, but it was locked. That meant either they'd been picked

23

up, or they're in the mall, or they're in the room—so at least I know they're there."

He returned to reception. "I thought, 'Let me check under Patrick's name.' Now that was not sharp, he never booked under his own name." But his uncle, astonishingly, had this time done exactly that.

"They checked—Room 905. I said, 'Now we know, so phone the room.' They called, but no one picked up." The two must be walking around, David concluded. "So I sit down. And I wait and wait and wait. Occasionally I say, 'Can you check?' and they say, 'We can't bother the guest.'"

A "Do Not Disturb" sign dangled from the door handle, and in top hotels, that sign casts something like a spell. Whether they suspect rows of coke are being snorted on the other side of the door, that mini-orgies are being staged, or that professional poker games are in progress, staff are trained never to violate the instruction. Privacy is the top-tier client's prerogative, and entering would mean breaking a professional taboo.

"I become an asshole," remembers David. "I am literally there the entire day, until the evening." By this time, he was consumed by anxiety.

A female member of the staff finally agreed to go up to Room 905 and knock on the door. Once again, there was no answer. "I say, 'Please go in the room.'" But that "Do Not Disturb" sign kept working its magic.

Eventually the hotel manager relented, taking the elevator to the ninth floor with a security guard in tow. They returned to the front desk with a bizarre, partial report. They could see the bed from the door and the legs of someone lying on the bed. The television was on, very loud.

"The guest is sleeping, sir."

"Did you talk to him?"

"No."

"I need to speak to the person who is sleeping."

"We would need to call the police."

"Please do that."

When the police arrived, they went directly to Room 905. "Maybe they thought it was a drugs-related crime. I wait and wait. I get tired. I start standing. All I get from the desk is, 'The police are here. They are working on your case.' I go and watch TV in the restaurant. Finally a woman taps me on the shoulder and I stand up."

Asking David to sit, the hotel employee made what must have been the most unusual announcement of her career:

"Your guest is dead, sir."

"My mind," remembers David, "was revving so fast. I thought it was Apollo who was dead—maybe that was more hope than anything else. I was thinking, 'Could he be a traitor?'"

Then she took David up to Room 905, a hotel room whose bland elegance—the stained wood, the muffling Persian rugs and heavy drapes, the polished mirrors and throw cushions—was designed to convey unobtrusive luxury. Jarringly, inappropriately, the room was crowded with uniformed men, its atmosphere charged with testosterone and shock.

"There must have been twenty cops in there. 'Don't touch anything,' they said. I saw his jeans and socks, and I think I really knew then."

At moments of great drama, events slow down. Flooded with adrenaline, the brain uses the extra time it has somehow been granted to meander, picking up on the quirky and the curious. A man lay on his back on the made bed, David saw, sheets pulled halfway across him. His hands were on either side of his head, suggesting he had been fending off an attacker. The victim's blue-and-white-checked shirt had ridden high above his bare stomach in the struggle, revealing a huge weal across his chest where his skin, normally pale by African standards, had turned livid, deprived of oxygen.

"He was the color of charcoal," says David. "Remember that he had been there twelve hours by then, and the blood had dried." Blood from the victim's eyes, nose, and ears was streaked across his face and had coagulated in the mattress. It had soaked all the way through to the other side, the police found when they flipped it over.

Below the dead man's nose, bloody froth had dried to form a small, pink mustache. David looked at his face, not wanting to believe what he was seeing. "His eyes were closed. For a moment I was thinking, 'It looks like him, but it's not him.'" Finally forced to register that the victim on the bed was not Apollo but his surrogate father, the man he respected above all others, David broke down.

The duvet was on the floor. Patrick's three smartphones had all been taken, but Apollo's travel bag was still there, half-packed with torn and bloodied shirts. Inside the room's safe, a bloodstained towel and a curtain rope were discovered. After turning the volume on the room's television up high, one assailant had probably leaned on Patrick's chest and strangled him with the curtain rope, while another held a towel over his face to muffle any cries. The deed done, the duvet had been thrown over the body, the towel and curtain rope stowed in the safe, and the "Do Not Disturb" sign hooked on the door as the killers left the room.

It had all done the trick. The combination of small touches had bought them more than enough time to reach the airport and make their getaway.

A bottle of wine sat on a table uncorked, with a full glass next to it. Patrick's folded spectacles lay neatly on one of the bedside tables. These were details that would later fuel a theory that Patrick had been drugged—poison is traditionally a Rwandan weapon of choice—before being strangled. A Muslim, Apollo did not touch alcohol, so he would have had the perfect excuse for refusing a glass, leaving Patrick, known to be a man who enjoyed a drink, to serve himself. The spectacles' position suggested that, feeling either suddenly dizzy or unwell, he had taken them off to lie down, a moment of vulnerability his attackers had exploited.

In Montreal, Portia was frantically checking her phone, aware that her life was slipping disastrously out of kilter. "I'd spoken to my mom: 'Why haven't you heard from him?' and she had said, 'Oh, Elvis says he has heard from him'"—but that was a misunderstanding.

"So I was texting David and no one was replying, and then a group message began on WhatsApp with the headline: 'Loss.'" It was being written by David in South Africa.

"I immediately knew. I picked up the landline and called David directly, before he had finished writing. I said, 'What are you saying?'"

Leah learned she was a widow from Jolie, David's wife, almost physically unable to articulate the words. "Portia was calling from Canada while Jolie, in South Africa, kept dropping the phone. She did that once, and again a second time, and the third time I said, 'Is Patrick dead?' just like that. And she burst into tears. After that it was darkness."

During the night, one by one, shocked members of the RNC gathered at the Michelangelo and filed into the room, crammed with armed cops and forensic experts snapping photographs and collecting evidence, to pay their last respects. Some of the Rwandans quietly saluted the corpse. It was always easy to forget with Patrick, but he had been an army colonel, after all, and many were former comrades-in-arms. The impromptu vigil lasted till 4 a.m. In the dissidents' wake trailed reporters and TV crews. "It was a case of everyone who knows a journalist, call a journalist," remembers David.

In this surreal five-star setting, a trap—so carefully prepared that the smart former intelligence chief had never once caught a glimpse of its contours—had been sprung. The pieces of the puzzle now slotted neatly into place. Apollo's request for a hotel room—supposedly for meetings with foreign businessmen—had in fact been designed to extract Patrick from his well-guarded gated community.

"There were three of them—Apollo was number four," says David. "The guys they sent were specialized, army commandos. They were booked into the room across the corridor." Booking that second room—Room 911—was a prerequisite, as only guests with room cards could work the elevators at the Michelangelo. In the process the perpetrators had helpfully provided future investigators with their passport details. "They flew in on Kenya Airways just before midnight the previous day and spent the day patrolling the area, setting things up."

Playing the role of Judas, Apollo, David believes, probably lured Patrick up to the room with the suggestion of a drink. Either the killers were hiding inside Room 905's bathroom, or Apollo and Patrick had gone up to the room alone and then Apollo had let the killers in. The attack's precise details will probably never be known, because while the Michelangelo has CCTV in its lobby, cameras are not installed in either the elevators or the corridors.

The body's location on the bed prompted a rumor that Patrick, always a ladies' man, had gone to Room 905 because Apollo had dangled the possibility of a sexual encounter: a classic honeytrap. But David had detected no suggestion of a woman's presence in the buildup to the murder. It's more likely the bed was simply the natural place on which to pinion a struggling man. Bodies roll off sofas, armchairs topple with a thud.

Had Apollo himself wound the curtain rope around Patrick's throat and held the garrote tight for the agonizingly long minutes it must have taken Patrick to die? Most of those I've spoken to don't believe so. Apollo, by most accounts, was one of those soft boys who never quite achieve true manhood, a spoiled socialite with no military experience, and this was too important a job for an amateur to be allowed to botch. Apollo, Patrick's friends and family agree, was no more than the decoy. It's a chilling image, but most likely Apollo stood and watched as Patrick was overpowered.

He had delivered his side of the deal, which was to get Patrick away from public eyes, out of sight. Patrick, who should have known better, who would usually insist on meeting in cafés and restaurants for precisely this reason, had gone up to that room with all the trusting naivete of a drunk ingenue about to be date raped. Why? Well, because he liked Apollo. The boy was always good for a laugh. The personal trumped the professional every time. Those who plotted the assassination had known Patrick well enough to understand that.

Before they stopped answering David's phone calls, the Hawks, South Africa's police team specializing in organized crime, told David what they suspected. "They killed him between 8:30 and 9:00 p.m." After carrying out the murder, the team was driven away in a car with Burundian diplomatic plates; the professionals flew out that evening, while Apollo boarded a RwandAir flight the following morning. "He took a risk, staying on for that early flight."

The press would later report that the hit squad had flown to Mozambique, where they had been arrested, and that extradition was being sought by the South African authorities. It was all nonsense, disinformation, David believes, fed into the thresher to muddy the perpetrators' tracks. He puts it on a par with the reports—never sourced—that CCTV tapes from the Michelangelo had gone missing, and that someone had tampered with the forensic samples that would have indicated whether Patrick was poisoned. It all went to make a convenient muddle. Convenient for the killers.

What was beyond dispute was that Patrick's watch had been ripped off his wrist, presumably both as trophy and proof of a job well done. In a final lurid and—by its nature—unverifiable detail, RNC members would later hear from their contacts within Rwanda's military elite that the attack had been both photographed and filmed. The first thing the perpetrators had done on landing in Kigali, the contacts said, was to head for the presidential palace to share the footage, an event President Kagame had celebrated by cracking open a bottle of champagne.

The entire incident bore a marked resemblance to the assassination of Hamas military leader Mahmoud al-Mabhouh in a Dubai hotel room in 2010 by a team of Mossad agents. Al-Mabhouh was injected with a muscle relaxant, given a massive electric shock to the head, then suffocated. "The formative influence on Rwandan intelligence is Mossad and this was standard Israeli MO," commented a South African security expert I interviewed. "First you drug them, then you strangle them: the whole incident is totally silent."

David felt crippled by guilt: for allowing Patrick out of his sight, for not heeding his own suspicions regarding Apollo, for not raising the alarm earlier. But with all these regrets came the shocking realization that he himself had narrowly avoided death. Had he stayed with his uncle, the hit squad would have got two for the price of one. "They wanted us together. If I'd gone into the room I'd have died too."

The reaction from the Rwandan government had the schizophrenic quality characteristic of a self-confident regime that doesn't give a fig what outsiders think, while conscious certain public positions need to be adopted for diplomacy's sake.

Hearing the news in London, I rang Rwanda's high commissioner to the United Kingdom, Williams Nkurunziza, for comment. He blandly assured me that any claims of government involvement were "irresponsible and without a basis in fact."

But in Rwanda itself the tone from top officials was one of pure triumphalism. Asked on Twitter about the murder, Foreign Minister Louise Mushikiwabo tweeted, "This man was a self-declared enemy of Gov & my country, U expect pity?" When Patrick's son Elvis angrily intervened, asking if any enemy of the state deserved to be strangled, the minister was unabashed: "It's my Government position: what happens to its enemies should not make it lose sleep."[4]

General James Kabarebe, the defence minister, was the next to pile on. "When you choose to be a dog, you die like a dog, and the cleaners will wipe away the trash so that it does not stink," he told a meeting in Kigali.[5] In Rwanda, villagers dispatch feral dogs, regarded as vermin, by hanging them. A former friend and colleague had been reduced to a thing, an animal, an item of garbage.

As for President Paul Kagame, he chose a National Prayer Breakfast, of all places, to drum home an implacable "you can run but you can't hide" message. Available on YouTube, the speech is quietly bloodcurdling.[6] Kagame, speaking in the Kinyarwanda he knows most diplomats and Western development officials neither understand nor have time to have translated, cannot suppress a triumphant smile. His voice descends to a near whisper as he addresses his quailing audience. "Whoever is against our country will not escape our wrath. The person will face consequences. Even those who are still alive, they will face them."

His delivery slows to the thumping pace of someone reading a horror story to a terrified child. He leans over the podium, hawk face as taut as a fist, bony forefinger extended, pausing strategically and giving a strange, sibilant sigh. "Whoever he or she is, it is a matter of time." The government ministers, dog-collared church men and their well-dressed wives, sycophantically applaud.

Kagame later made a limp attempt to reconcile the two positions—celebratory crowing versus adamant denial of responsibility—telling the *Wall Street Journal*, "Rwanda did not kill this person—and it's a big 'no.' But I add that, I actually wish Rwanda did it. I really wish it."[7] It was a case of having your cake and eating it. Kagame *wanted* his coterie to know exactly who was responsible, since the murder was in part a warning directed at anyone thinking of following Patrick's example. But glorying publicly in an assassination does not translate well on the international stage: lip service had to be paid to the rule of law.

Over the years, I've never met a Rwandan, a foreign diplomat, or a Western politician who didn't believe Kigali was responsible—the only debate was how high up the administrative chain responsibility went. Many episodes in the RPF's narrative may be bitterly contested, but Patrick Karegeya's murder is not one of them.

•

The following days were full of tumult. In the United States and Canada, the Karegeyas struggled to work out how to get to South Africa. "Oh my God, I can't forget that period," says Leah.

"It was such a bad time." Nothing was easy, for—with the exception of Portia, who had a valid Ugandan passport—the family's immigration status was undecided at the time. Leah, Richard, and Elvis had originally flown into the United States on Rwandan passports, but Kigali had then canceled their citizenship, leaving them marooned while a judge decided their status. If they left, they might never be able to return.

Perhaps out of pity for a grief-stricken family, perhaps out of respect for the dead man, with whom many of them had once hobnobbed, officials at the State Department and the South African Foreign Ministry worked together to solve the problem. Leah and the boys were given temporary South African passports and issued with "advance parole" US documents, a one-time-only arrangement allowing individuals without permanent residency to leave and return. It took two weeks of bureaucratic string-pulling, but the miraculous was achieved.

From Kigali, in the meantime, came small, chilling indications that Patrick's killers were making the most of the haul netted during the assassination: the contacts stored on Patrick's smartphones.

A few days after Patrick's death, Portia suddenly saw his name pop up on Skype, showing his phone had been switched on and whoever now possessed it was online. "Someone was using his account, and that could only be the people who had killed him," she said. A distant relative received a call from Patrick's smartphone: picking up, he could have sworn it was Kagame's distinctive, reedy voice on the line. The caller abruptly hung up. Patrick's vast network of friends and supporters was being systematically sounded out by Kigali's intelligence services, every drop of insight into the opposition's membership and activities soaked up.

The family had originally wanted Patrick buried in Mbarara, western Uganda. Uganda's state minister for foreign affairs, Henry Okello Oryem, initially agreed, but a few days later, a ministry spokesman rescinded the offer, saying that since Patrick was a citizen of Rwanda and a resident of South Africa at the time of his death, he could not be buried in Uganda. "The government will consult with the Rwandan embassy about this issue," said spokesman Fred Opolot. "Our position is that we cannot take a unilateral decision since Col Karegeya is not an ordinary Rwandan."[8]

Like Peter at the cock's crow, a second African government, for whom Patrick had both fought as a guerrilla and worked as an intelligence official, had denied him. It felt, to Portia, like a further, malevolent turn of the screw. "I was amazed. Because I know all he wanted was to be buried in Mbarara. My reaction was, 'He's dead! What are you defending?' But when I reflected on it, it all made sense."

In Africa, high-profile funerals are never simply moments of mourning. They are carefully scrutinized get-togethers at which loyalties are broadcast, deals are done, successions prepared. Patrick's interment would provide an opportunity for a mass demonstration of anti-Kagame sentiment, and Uganda, already on strained terms with Rwanda, was anxious not to further alienate a key regional ally.

"If the body had been buried in Mbarara, the whole of Mbarara and Kampala would have gone there to attend the funeral, and the whole of Kigali would have crossed the border to get there too," said one of Patrick's oldest friends. "It would have been the ultimate state funeral. So of course [Ugandan president Yoweri] Museveni refused permission."[9]

On arrival in Johannesburg, Leah and the children could not face a visit to the morgue, but Patrick's old mother, who had flown to join them from Uganda, insisted on going. In her nineties—no one was exactly sure of her age, not even her—Jane Keshoro was almost blind. But she knew how to identify her son. *Karegeya* means "little finger" in Kinyarwanda. Patrick was born with a vestigial sixth finger, a genetic peculiarity passed down through the family, regarded as a sign of good luck. To accept her son's death, Jane needed to touch Patrick's scars, the places where a surplus finger had been removed at birth.

Jolie went with her, and saw what the old woman could not as she tenderly explored her son's hands. "He was completely blue, because he had had no oxygen," recalls Leah. "The body was unrecognizable. That attack was obviously very violent, and they did it very quickly."

The dispute over Patrick's resting place ended on January 19, when he was buried on the outskirts of Johannesburg. Underfunded municipal cemeteries are running out of space in South Africa, overwhelmed by a combination of AIDS deaths and a local aversion to cremation. Alienated by the proliferating vandalism and neglect,

South Africa's moneyed elite is turning instead to the private sector to bury its dead, and private cemeteries such as Fourways Memorial Park are the result.

Even here, the long arm of Paul Kagame made itself chillingly felt, reaching out to freeze spontaneity and stifle compassion. When he had first arrived in South Africa, Patrick had known intelligence chiefs and foreign ministry officials, ambassadors and journalists, Tutsi businessmen and Hutu exiles. A natural extrovert, he had both cultivated old acquaintances and forged new relationships, partly through habit, partly professional instinct: his opposition party needed all the friends it could get. Now the presences were as significant as the absences.

Back in the day, knowing Patrick had been something to brag about; now the association had turned toxic. Every invited guest knew that any media footage recorded at the event would be pored over in Kigali by intelligence. There were certain to be informants among the guests, too, feeding Kagame's regime vital tidbits: who had turned up, what they said, what expressions flitted across their faces during the ceremony.

The most high-profile absentee was South African president Jacob Zuma himself. During the apartheid era, the banned African National Congress (ANC) had relied on friendly heads of state in sub-Saharan Africa as it set about establishing a continent-wide network of covert offices and safe houses. President Museveni had made the exiled movement welcome in Kampala, and as a young ANC intelligence operative, Zuma had repeatedly crossed paths with Patrick at Uganda's Directorate of Military Intelligence (DMI). The two had worked closely together in the early 2000s, when President Nelson Mandela had devised a peace plan for Burundi. Patrick had shuttled with Zuma between Kigali and Bujumbura, finessing the deal. But in these awkward new circumstances, realpolitik trumped personal loyalty.

Thembi Majola, a former South African ambassador whose friendship with Patrick stretched across the decades, remembers agreeing to give a mutual friend, a former journalist, a lift to the funeral. "'Pick me up, we'll go together,' he told me. Then he disappeared for six months." She shakes her head. "When Patrick died only two of his senior South African contacts were at his funeral—the former head of intelligence, Billy Masetlha, and me. Yet Patrick was someone who a lot of people had once called 'my friend.'"[10]

The outcast's funeral still managed to bring Johannesburg traffic grinding to a halt, as the hearse and its accompanying convoy of guests, flanked by police outriders—lights flashing, sirens wailing—made its noisy way to the cemetery, a helicopter clattering overhead.

Funerals vary in timbre, their tone dictated by how and when the individual concerned met their end. This one was marked not by serenity, or resigned acceptance, but by raw outrage and the mutual suspicions that are hallmarks of Rwandan elite society. "We knew the informants were there amongst us," remembers a relative—"in the service, at the reception, expressing condolences, and then reporting every little bit back to Kigali."

As the priest led the congregation through the various steps, members of the family rising one by one to speak at the podium, the key members of the RNC—former army chief of staff General Kayumba Nyamwasa and his wife, Rosette; former ambassador Theogene Rudasingwa; regional chairman Frank Ntwali; lawyer Kennedy Gihana, still on crutches—sat silently, digesting not only what their friend's loss meant for the party, but just how likely they were to suffer the same fate.

"I've lost a father, I've lost a friend, I've lost a role model," David Batenga, who could so easily have been lying in a coffin next to Patrick's, told the congregation. Tears cascaded down Elvis's cheeks as he choked out, "I haven't seen my Dad for the last three years and *this* is what I've come back to." Portia, pale and beautiful in black, found a steady voice long enough to praise her father for the character trait that—above all else—was probably responsible for his death: defiance. "You stood tall and you looked your enemies straight in the eye and you said, 'Try me.'"

As for Leah, she used her moment to address her husband's killers, her direct message jarringly at odds with the soothing organ music and religious pieties. "I want whoever is here and is a spy of Rwanda to go and tell them"—here she lapsed into Kinyarwanda—"'You should be ashamed of what you did.'"

The sense of malevolent eyes tracking the mourners extended all the way to their departure. After Elvis and Richard had boarded their South African Airways flight, bound for the United States, they were approached by the airline's staff and asked to disembark, then forced to fly the following day. A rumor, never confirmed, flickered through family ranks: someone had called the US Department of Homeland Security claiming the two boys were a terrorist threat, and it had called the airline. They could imagine who. "So vindictive," marveled one family member. "You've already had your kill. What more do you want?"

It was Portia who went to the house in Ruimsig to gather her father's few personal effects.

During the seven years in South Africa, Patrick had lived at six different addresses, and the first thing he'd done in each place was to hang a collection of huge framed photographs of his wife and children on the walls. Touring the house, registering the evidence of a life interrupted, Portia was surreally confronted by her own smiling face and those of her brothers.

When you walk into the space of someone who has recently died, humdrum objects become imbued with significance, from the fingerprint smudge on a pair of spectacles to the butter-smeared knife on a draining board. These prosaic items were recently touched by someone who can never touch again, they possess magical powers now, for they have outlived their owner.

"It was very difficult to compute," said Portia. "This was a man who thought he was coming home, that he was coming back. I was walking into his room and seeing the laundry basket with his shirt in it, the toothbrushes, the cupboard full of food."

Next to Patrick's bed, she found a copy of *From Dictatorship to Democracy*, a pragmatic, pocket-book-sized guide to effective nonviolent struggle, written by Professor Gene Sharp, an American political scientist.[11] Hailed as "a treatise on toppling tyrants," it has been consulted by dissidents in Burma and Indonesia, Tibet and Ukraine.

We are not seen by others as we see ourselves. If many regarded Patrick in his prime as a sinister cross between Machiavelli and Talleyrand, he had always viewed himself as a man on an ideological trajectory. The spine of Patrick's copy of *From Dictatorship to Democracy* is cracked, and pen markings—so deep in some places they nearly go through the paper—highlight the passages that struck him as relevant to the regime he had once worked for, believed in, and now opposed.

Citing Aristotle and political scientists such as Karl Deutsch and John Austin, Sharp argues that totalitarianism has a shorter life than other forms of rule and that seemingly impregnable dictatorships in fact depend on a population's tacit acceptance.

Perhaps the most poignant underlinings involve the passages where Sharp considers the risks of standing up to absolutist rule: "None of this means that weakening and destroying dictatorships is easy, nor that every attempt will succeed. It certainly does not mean that the struggle will be free of casualties, for those still serving the dictators are likely to fight back in an effort to force the populace to resume cooperation and obedience." Choking to death on the bed in the Michelangelo, Patrick had become one of those casualties.

A few Bible citations are scrawled on the inside of the book's back cover. An intellectual iconoclast, Patrick had long been that rare thing in Africa: an unabashed atheist. The savagery of the genocide, deposited on a bedrock of existing skepticism, had left its mark. "If God exists, he can't locate Rwanda on a map," he would bitterly quip. His lack of faith disappointed the devout Leah and shocked more conventional African friends. "He told me he thought that when you died, that was it, game over, no afterlife, nothing," one of them told me in wonderment. "How can you live without faith?" Yet before he died, Patrick had started occasionally attending a local church, in part, it seemed, because he had befriended a Presbyterian couple who worshiped there. Perhaps this was the result.

"Isaiah 40:31," reads one scribble. It is the kind of exhortation preachers use to galvanize the doubting and fatigued: "But they that wait upon the LORD shall renew their strength; they shall mount up with wings as eagles; they shall run, and not be weary; and they shall walk, and not faint."

It was a measure of the strain exile had placed on Patrick's shoulders, that this emotionally resilient man, estranged from wife and children, carrying a huge burden of disappointment on his fifty-three-year-old shoulders, all too aware of the terrible risks he ran, should have turned to a long-rejected faith as he approached the end.

CHAPTER TWO

CHRONICLE OF A DEATH FORETOLD

Colonel Dan Munyuza: There's a thing someone could put in his food or his drink, without him noticing. It could take days or months before it has an effect.

Liaison: Really?

Munyuza: It's very effective. Doctors wouldn't even detect it.

Liaison: Okay. There's noth . . .

Munyuza: You could administer it to him . . . like . . . in his favourite soup . . . or his favourite dish that only he likes . . . He'd eat it, then . . .

Munyuza: Are you saying it's possible . . . ?

Liaison: Well first, I'd like to check with (my accomplice).

Munyuza: If he says it's okay . . . let me know. I'll give you the phone number of someone there. . . . You'll meet him, he'll hand it to you . . .

Liaison: Okay.

Munyuza: It looks like water drops, it will go unnoticed in his food.

Liaison: So all I'd have to do would be to dissolve a few drops and have him eat it without . . .

Munyuza: Don't worry. We already used this technique before. . . . It works fine.

—*Imfunsi* [1]

Hearing of a prominent Rwandan murdered in a hotel in Johannesburg, those who only fitfully followed African affairs might well have assumed the regime in Kigali was taking revenge on an exiled *génocidaire*—one of the despicable men who ordered the 1994 massacres in which between 500,000 and 1 million people were killed.

One of the fastest killing sprees in human history, committed with the simplest of instruments—the hoe and the machete—the genocide is the only thing many outsiders know about Rwanda, an event ranking in horror with the Holocaust, the Hiroshima and Nagasaki bombings, and the flattening of Dresden. President Paul Kagame's label as "the man who had halted the genocide" had accorded him near saint-like status in the West.

But this episode did not fit the Hutu-versus-Tutsi prism through which Rwandan events are routinely viewed. Not only was Patrick, a Tutsi, from the same ethnic community as the regime that killed him, but he belonged to a core group of rebel stalwarts who had saved one another's lives, made toasts at each other's weddings, and together toppled Juvénal Habyarimana's extremist regime. If an aura of unchallengeable moral righteousness shimmered around Kagame during his frequent appearances on panels in Davos and at US universities, then, logically speaking, Patrick, presidential consigliere and one of the architects of his accession, should have shared that halo.

Patrick's murder was evidence, instead, of a revolution eating its own. There are echoes of the ice axe buried in Leon Trotsky's brain in his Mexico study at Joseph Stalin's behest, of the burly Georges Danton mounting the steps of the guillotine on Maximilien Robespierre's orders. It joined a list of fratricidal acts in African history that included Mobutu Sese Seko's dispatching of Patrice Lumumba to the rebel province where he was shot, and the coup that left Thomas Sankara dead, and his best friend, Blaise Compaoré, as president of Burkina Faso. It is a story as thoroughly explored in fiction and on the stage—the astonished Caesar crying out "Et tu, Brute?" as his friend buries the knife—as it has been in real life: the tale of comrades who risk all for one another only to fall out with the bitter implacability of disappointed love.

"This was a band of brothers, who all fought alongside one another," a grim-faced US State Department official told me one evening in a bar in Foggy Bottom. "Then one of them—the *primus inter pares*—separates himself from the rest and becomes leader. And now everyone I once knew in Rwanda is either in prison, dead, or in exile."[2]

Perhaps the outcome itself was the least surprising thing about what happened at the Michelangelo. The truly extraordinary thing about Patrick's death was not its climax but the prolonged buildup, in which the wily former intelligence chief and the regime for which he had once worked played a deadly cat-and-mouse game drawing in embassy officials, ambassadors, informers, lowly taxi drivers, and both double and triple agents. In the course of my research I met three people who had each been approached to kill Patrick. Had I pressed on, it was clear I could have located many more. Rarely was a death more thoroughly foretold.

On its side, the regime boasted a sophisticated military and security apparatus, an international network of embassies, and a range of compliant Western and African governments either too sold on the RPF's post-genocide narrative or too in awe of Kagame to kick up a fuss. On his side, Patrick had only two weapons, which were rather harder to quantify: the contacts he had amassed across several continents, and his peculiar gift for friendship.

If Kigali's attempts to eliminate Patrick were multipronged and unrelenting, they were also shockingly crude, a sloppiness that spoke volumes about how little his enemies felt they had to fear from exposure. The system and techniques Patrick had helped create would be undiscriminatingly unleashed upon him. The biter was to be well and truly bit.

•

The contest began—because it was definitely that, a testing of wits—when Patrick took the *subway*, as it was jokingly called, out of Rwanda, crossing the frontier with Uganda by night on November 22, 2007.

He was one week out of prison, where he had spent eighteen months after being found guilty by a military tribunal of insubordination and desertion and stripped of his rank: an ironic punishment, given that he'd earlier tried to quit the army but had seen his request refused. "Amen to that!" he had told his wife and children.

On his release, he'd been driven to the Ministry of Defence in Kigali, where he'd ended up in a long and furious exchange with a panel of four top generals—James Kabarebe, then chief of general staff; Charles Muhire, air force chief of staff; Charles Kayonga, army chief of staff; and Jacques Musemakweli, head of military intelligence. By rights, since Patrick was now an ordinary civilian, these figures should have had no say over his future. But that was not how things worked in Rwanda.

"They tried to intimidate me by warning me that although I was out I had to be careful with what I said or did," Patrick later wrote. "I asked why I had been brought to the headquarters since I was dismissed from the army, and they insisted they had come as 'friends' to discuss a few issues."[3] Although Kagame himself was away in Uganda, attending a Commonwealth Summit, the source of this advice was clear.

"In actuality I knew the president had put this together as some kind of warning and threat regarding how I should behave after my release. They told me to be careful whom I talk to and what I talk about, specifically my views on politics, human rights, press freedom, and foreign policy. Otherwise I would never know what might happen to me."

"We know you are anti-government," one of the generals said, "and that is the reason why you have been in jail all this time."

Patrick's reply was bitter. "I've been there 18 months and none of you came to visit me. I've resigned, I don't belong to you, I am no longer part of you, I don't know why you have even brought me here."

The argument lasted several hours, and neither side backed down. Finally, Patrick was free to go home, where his anxious family was waiting.

There was clearly still some element of residual compassion among his former colleagues, however. One of the generals later telephoned the family home to warn Patrick that Kagame, briefed about the heated exchange over the phone, had said he was returning from Kampala to personally deal with his former intelligence chief "for life."

Still, Patrick hesitated, measuring the consequences of leaving the country into which he had poured his energies, all too aware he might never return.

Three days later, the same general phoned again. "Please leave the country," he told Patrick. "You didn't respond the way you were meant to and they're going to deal with you once and for all. It's over for you."

His informant, Patrick later wrote, "was aware of what they were planning and he could probably never have lived with it." Leah says she doesn't know which general warned him, but it might even have been Kabarebe, the man who crowed so publicly and so crassly when Patrick died. "I think Kabarebe in his heart of hearts knew he was doing wrong, but he was carrying out his boss's orders."

Portia, visiting from college in South Africa, was at home at the time. "I just bawled. I've never cried like that before. I remember him looking at me and looking at my mum and saying 'This is why I can't forgive Him.'" They both knew which "Him" was being referred to.

It is typical of Patrick's brand of hedonistic sangfroid that at a time when anyone else would have been anxiously compiling lists and packing bags, he instead hosted a spontaneous party. As word spread that he was out of prison, friends and relatives gathered at the house without being invited. Someone put some music on, cold beers were cracked open, the surrounding streets filled with parked cars, the chatter swelled.

"We were very, very many, the house was full," remembers a family member who was among the guests. "He was jazzing, so happy, moving from group to group, socializing, mixing drinks, making introductions."[4]

At some point, she recalls noticing Patrick hunched over, talking intently to another relative in Runyankole, not Kinyarwanda—a way of keeping the exchange private.* "I think that's when they were plotting the departure." Always the perfect host, Patrick was not about to allow a mere flight into exile spoil a good bash. Besides, he knew he was effectively saying goodbye: to his social circle, a family home, the city of Kigali, Rwanda itself. An occasion calling to be marked.

---

* cf "Note on Terminology" at the end of this book.

That night, the two men set off, driving northeast. Before reaching the official border checkpoint at Kagitumba, Patrick left the road and plunged on foot into the watery marshland. He was in familiar territory on the other side, the very region of western Uganda where he'd been born and raised. His tension eased. He rested in a village, and the following morning hopped on the back of a *boda boda* motorbike bound for the city of Mbarara, where he arranged a lift to Kampala. His exile had begun.

The timing and route of his departure were sources of grim personal satisfaction. "He told me later," recalls a Western ambassador friend, "that he chose to leave that particular night, going via Uganda, because Kagame was on a state visit to Kampala at the time. It showed Kagame who was the smarter of the two, who was in control of the situation."[5]

He would dearly have liked to stay in Uganda. But he was quickly led to understand that his presence was creating political problems between the neighboring states. Kagame had berated Museveni for allowing him in, and Patrick was aware of being tracked by Rwandan intelligence agents, who operated with impunity across the border.

The Kigali rumor mill briefly had him in Qatar—a fact the US embassy relayed back to Washington. In fact, Patrick's next move was to cross into Kenya, where he scouted out possible jobs only to encounter the same problem. "I had been warned that Kagame knew that I was in Kenya and I was asked for my own safety to leave." He flew to Tanzania, where Leah and the children joined him for Christmas. The family took the ferry to Zanzibar and strolled along the beaches like ordinary tourists.

But once again, proximity proved an issue. At Dar es Salaam's airport, he nearly walked into a disembarking Rwandan general, who, appalled, put one hand over his eyes and said, "I never saw you." He was chatting to US writer Jason Stearns in a hotel in Oyster Bay when a Rwandan military delegation walked in. "Patrick spotted them across the room and his face lit up. With a huge grin on his face, he immediately went to greet one of the Rwandan generals involved, who didn't know where to look."[6]

Patrick was on excellent terms with Tanzanian president Jakaya Kikwete, and during his tenure Tanzanian and Rwandan intelligence officials had established close working ties. Now that proved a problem. A former MI6 officer got a swift phone call from Kigali after meeting up with his old friend one night in Dar. It was from Colonel Emmanuel Ndahiro, the toothy head of Rwanda's National Intelligence and Security Service (NISS), Patrick's longtime rival for the presidential ear. "He made no bones about it, immediately telling me who I'd had dinner with the night before: Patrick. I was very impressed. The message was clear: 'We're onto you.'"[7]

Patrick was clearly still too geographically close to Rwanda. Once again he was warned that Kagame had complained about his presence to the Tanzanian authorities. After two months, he felt obliged to leave.

So on February 12, 2008, Patrick flew to Johannesburg. With its humming freeways and gated communities, its giant advertising billboards and identical shopping malls, the City of Gold can taste disconcertingly bland, peculiarly un-African. But Patrick's children were already enrolled in South African schools and colleges, and several relatives and old friends had also made the country their home. Basing himself here would allow Patrick—crucially—to remain on the African continent, while distant enough from the Great Lakes to feel safe. That, at least, was the idea.

Initially, he moved in with David Batenga in Centurion, a rapidly expanding middle-class suburb on a stretch of dry, rolling veldt where a key battle in the Anglo-Boer War was once fought. In one direction, Centurion is linked by the high-speed Gautrain, one of the ANC's proudest national projects, to Johannesburg's bustling business heart; in the other to the jacaranda-lined avenues of Pretoria, South Africa's government and diplomatic center. Prices are lower than in either of those two longer-established cities, and the achingly new transport infrastructure makes the distance commutable.

It was time to recoup, to reassess. At the age of forty-seven, he was starting again. One of the issues that loomed before him was financial. As his career had foundered, the family had been forced to rely upon Leah's import-export business and rental income from a house the couple had built on Kigali's outskirts. Both were likely to be forfeit now, and as for Patrick's farm in Uganda, a dozen relatives lived on the property, complicating any possible sale.

"He was saying, 'I need a car, I need a house, I need a bank account,'" remembers David. "At first I didn't question—he was an elder—but at a certain point, I asked him, 'Don't you have any insurance policies, any savings?'"

When Patrick said no, the nephew was incredulous. One of Patrick's most controversial jobs had been running Rwanda's Congo Desk, funneling gold, coltan, and diamonds from occupied DRC east through Rwanda. Like many of Patrick's acquaintances, he had assumed his uncle had made the most of his position to sock something away, preparation for a rainy day that had now arrived.

"Didn't you use your opportunities to buy units in London, Kampala?" David asked. Patrick's reply was sardonic: "Did you want me to be corrupt, then?"

The failure to prepare a financial escape route seems extraordinary, given the precariousness of Patrick's job and the temptations that came his way. My suspicion is that as the RPF plunged from military crisis to interventionist adventure to international peace talks, with Patrick ping-ponging from the presidential office to business-class lounge, five-star hotel, and ministry boardroom, self-enrichment seemed the least of his priorities: there was simply no time. David cites a different factor: the arrogance of hubris. "You know, these guys thought they were gods. Nothing would ever touch them. So they had no need to prepare for tomorrow."

Busy studying for his accountancy articles, David was ill placed to deal with his clever uncle's sudden, uncharacteristic dependency. "He was stuck in the house the entire time. He didn't know how to get around, to drive, the location of the various malls." So David suggested recruiting a driver and fixer.

It meant taking a risk, as it involved reaching out to the Rwandan community in South Africa, a group whose undercurrents, rifts, and mutual suspicions were a faithful reflection of the country's recent history.

Exile is a time when a newcomer is simultaneously repelled by, and drawn to, his own kind. When political asylum seekers land in a new country, their heads tell them to steer clear of their own community, which is all too likely to include embassy spies and government informers. For a while they succeed, but as the months pass and the gray sense of alienation bites, they find themselves gravitating toward those who speak their language, eat their food, and understand their jokes.

South Africa's Rwandan diaspora included Hutus who had left in the 1990s and were therefore suspected by Tutsi compatriots of genocidal sympathies, Tutsis who had fled the massacres and were on good terms with the Rwandan embassy in Pretoria, and, increasingly, disillusioned Tutsis like Patrick, who had once belonged to the RPF—individuals often both hated by the Hutu refugees for their role in toppling Habyarimana and avoided by Kagame loyalists who realized it was dangerous to associate with them.

They survived as South Africa's newly arrived migrants do. After apartheid's end, hundreds of thousands of Zimbabweans and Ethiopians, Nigerians, Congolese, and Somalis moved into the shantytowns that black South Africans were abandoning, having been offered places in new estates equipped with running water and electricity. The Rwandans joined part of a hustling urban underclass whose members wait tables, sell newspapers at traffic lights, wave cars into parking lots, and drive Ubers.

David heard about a former member of Rwanda's Directorate of Military Intelligence, a young man who already knew Patrick, now working as a taxi driver. "So I took a gamble and suggested him."

•

Emile Rutagengwa is one of the lost boys of the genocide, part of the human flotsam and jetsam thrown up by that explosion of unparalleled brutality.[8]

Within seconds of our sitting down together, he calls up the WhatsApp feed on his smartphone and starts swiping through a series of photographs of his Tutsi family, who came from Kigali. A long-necked, graceful, elderly lady—"My great aunt. Killed in the genocide"—*swipe*—a dewy-eyed young woman, looking straight at the camera—"My younger sister. Killed in the genocide"—*swipe*—another beautiful girl, a smile hovering on her lips—"My younger sister. Killed in the genocide"—*swipe*—a serene-looking matron—"My mother. Killed in the genocide"—*swipe*. He shrugs and closes the phone, but clearly the swiping could go on and on. His entire family—"My father, my mother, auntie, uncle, brothers, sisters, grandmother, grandfather, grand uncle"—were all wiped out in the genocide. Transcribing my notes after our meeting, I first typed, "34 members of the extended family" onto my laptop, then realized I had missed a very clear zero. The notebook read, in fact, "340 members of the extended family." Some things are so terrible, the mind fails to compute. Since Emile attributes the mass extermination to his decision to join the RPF rebel movement, to the agony of loss is added the torture of personal guilt.

Emile joined the RPF as a teenager and rose to the rank of captain. After the Hutu government had fallen and the RPF taken over, he had joined intelligence, where Patrick was a distant—if respected—superior.

But by 2001 he had lost faith. "I was tired of the system, I didn't like what the RPF was doing." Disgust at the RPF's indiscriminate killings and its neglect of its youngest, most vulnerable soldiers had sent him first to Uganda, then Kenya, and finally South Africa. In two minds about what to do next, he had started calling Patrick in Kigali. "We used to chat. He advised me not to come back, because they'd kill me. Instead, he sent me some money." Typical of Patrick, it was the gesture of a fellow human being, rather than an apparatchik. Its spontaneity sealed Emile's loyalty forever.

Emile's terrible family history ensured he was granted political asylum in South Africa. Now Patrick was also in the country and needing help. The ex–child soldier and former spy chief immediately bonded, and David was grateful for the support. "Emile really became family, more of a bodyguard than just a driver," recalls David.

Emile, who arrives at our appointment driving Patrick's old car, cherishes the intimacy of those early, bachelor days of Patrick's exile. "It was our job to keep him safe. We drove him around, found him somewhere to live, picked him up, took him shopping, me and David. We were his team, with him twenty-four hours a day. Only we knew what he did. It was our secret."

Emile prided himself on the military professionalism he brought to the role. David had no security awareness—"He's just a fucking civilian," Emile says with tolerant affection—"When I was with Patrick, his visitors wouldn't even know I was there. I'd be at a nearby table. Or he'd be in one car, I'd follow behind, one white, one blue."

Then he echoes a phrase I have already heard on David's lips. "He was my father, my friend, my leader, and . . . " the coda catches me by surprise: "my comedian." With Patrick, Emile says, you were always laughing. And then he does what every person I speak to researching this book does at the mention of Patrick's name, even those who barely knew him. His lips curl in a fond, reminiscent smile.

•

Patrick moved first to a Pretoria suburb and then to a house on the Irene View Estate in Centurion. At this stage, Leah was still flying back and forth between Johannesburg and Kigali, trying to keep her business alive, so Patrick played the unfamiliar role of homemaker for their youngest son, Richard, who was enrolled at a Pretoria school. After his high-octane globe-trotting, he reveled for a while in the humdrum. But it couldn't last.

He needed paid work, but while undoubtedly blessed with rare skills and precious experience, it wasn't clear how he could now put it all to good use. South African intelligence was keen to milk him for information about Rwandan-backed militias operating in DRC. American and British intelligence officials pressed him for details on the controversial Congo Desk. But neither role involved a regular salary or an office to go to.

Networking landed him one job that was right up his alley. In Somalia, the Transitional Federal Government was under constant challenge from al-Shabaab suicide bombers. UN Special Representative Ahmedou Ould Abdallah, who had met Patrick in Burundi, decided it needed an intelligence service capable of infiltrating al-Shabaab. In mid-2009 Patrick was offered a consultancy by the Somali Ministry of Internal Security. But it was only a six-month contract, and the persistent tremor Patrick suffered made it hard for him to use a keyboard. It was David who typed up the report.[9]

Patrick had not switched off his capacious brain. He sensed in his bones this was just a lull, that he needed to remain up to date and fully briefed. The chitchat on email, on Skype, and by text never stopped. Working his smartphones, each one a Rolodex of contacts spanning East, Central, and Southern Africa, he soaked up information.

For years, prominent Rwandans and high-ranking foreign officials had gotten into the habit, when negotiations with Kagame stumbled, of consulting Patrick, the laid-back go-between who would sympathize, explain each side's perspective to the other, and do his best to smooth ruffled feathers. That habit was hard to shed, even when they knew they were no longer talking to an insider.

On top of that Patrick possessed another resource: a covert army of informants recruited over the years. During his time as an intelligence chief, he had always kept an eye out for Rwandans who had fallen afoul of the law, who needed money or had long-standing scores to settle: their needs and grievances offered useful points of leverage.

Given the genuine liking they often harbored toward Patrick, the men and women he had once recruited to snitch for the government were easily persuaded to keep reporting to him in exile. It was just another layer of deceit, after all, to be added to the mille-feuille of dissimulation that was Rwandan society.

A key informant was Aimé Ntabana, a Kigali-born Tutsi who, like Emile, had lost virtually his entire family in the genocide. Patrick had met Aimé in the mid-1990s, when the RPF was tightening its grip on Rwanda and he was conscious of how little its largely Ugandan-raised elite actually knew about the country. Strangers in their own land, the rebel leaders needed local guides. Trusting, deeply damaged, Aimé stood in desperate need of a patron and mentor. They could help one another.

Aimé belonged to a group of young Rwandan *rescapés* who frequented Kigali's bars and restaurants. He knew most of the local journalists whose reporting might make a difference to the RPF, and he had friends among the Hutu and Tutsi business families who had fled to Europe, North America, and Africa, potential investors the RPF wanted to lure back to rebuild the nation.

"Aimé knew a lot of people," recalls Leah. "He was the kind of simple boy who people would set out to undermine, but he was brilliant in his own way." A rich source of gossip, Aimé was willing to serve as go-between, relaying reassuring messages from the RPF to families who were unhappy in exile but fearful of prosecution on return. "Patrick returned so many Hutus and Tutsis who had fled. Aimé would carry messages to tell them, 'There is no problem, you will be protected.'"

Patrick came to depend on the young man. He went so far as to assign Aimé responsibility for the Kinyarwanda-language newsline IGIHE, part of a panoply of websites, newspapers, and magazines the RPF subsidized to pump out positive news about Rwanda.[10] Aimé had treated the Karegeya household in Kigali as a second home, popping in and out at will. He dropped into Leah's import-export offices, too, and she took a liking to him.

It was Aimé who made the original fateful introduction to Apollo, another Kigali boy and one of his buddies, a young Muslim in trouble with the law.

From exile, Patrick continued to milk Aimé for insights into goings-on in Kigali. The older man's absence must have proved hard to bear, because after a few months Aimé flew to South Africa, where he spent a full month at Patrick's house. The decision proved a mistake. After Aimé returned to Kigali, the young man was picked up by the intelligence services, thrown into a *cachot*, and tortured. "They tortured him so badly, I heard he was blind when he came out," says Leah. It was the first of many lessons Kagame would deliver to show the cost of his disapproval.

Gathering up information allowed Patrick to gauge how deep discontent with Kagame's style of rule ran, not just in the Hutu community but also among former Tutsi insiders—Anglophone former Ugandans in particular—who felt they had been promised liberation only to be casually cast aside by Rwanda's new regime. He reached out to the discontents, inviting members of various opposition parties in Canada, the United Kingdom, Europe, and the United States to fly to Johannesburg.

"The RNC was really Patrick's idea, but you don't just launch a party," says Emile. "There were talks, contacts, discussions. We were quietly building an international network."

There were plenty of reasons for these constituencies to suspect and hate one another, given the wrongs so many of them had done one another, but they shared a rejection of the status quo. Patrick saw the importance of bringing them together.

And then, in February 2010, everything changed. General Kayumba Nyamwasa, Rwanda's former army chief of staff and the country's great war hero, came to stay.

•

Meeting the General, or "General"—as he is usually referred to, even by his wife—is not something done at short notice. His security team needs time to make the necessary arrangements. You state your case, lodge your request, and then, if approved, you wait. You will only know on the day itself if the meeting is happening.

There's no question of driving to the General's house—after six meetings I still had no idea where he lived. A bodyguard, one of the crème de la crème of South Africa's military police, will come to collect you, rolling into your guesthouse compound exactly on time in a four-wheel-drive so high off the ground you feel, scrambling onto the seat, like a toddler climbing the stairs to bed. The bodyguards adopt a de facto uniform. Their heads are shaved and they boast the dense, tight physiques of men who spend hours in the gym. They favor jeans and long-sleeved cotton shirts, worn loose, not tucked in, the better to conceal their weapons. You are never told where you are headed, and each time the venue is different.

The men are scrupulously polite—"Mem," they call me—but tend to ignore their passenger as they negotiate junctions, roundabouts, and freeways, chatting in Afrikaans. Occasionally, tacking across the veldt, passing rolling meadows, picturesque rural farmhouses, and the vast eyesore that is the Diepsloot slum, you'll realize you have been this way before, fifteen minutes ago. They have been driving you in languid circles, either to confuse you as to the destination, or because arriving too early represents a security faux pas.

Ask them what they think of the man they are guarding, though, and their reply is immediate, apparently heartfelt, and offers an insight into why General Kayumba is so feared by Kagame, his former boss: "Ach, we love him too much. He's like a father to us." The General clicks with ordinary soldiers, who instinctively trust him. He always has.

Eventually you may pull up in the forecourt of a roadside steakhouse, where you'll be led to the darkest cluster of seats, hidden from view by a brick column, your back against a wall. Or you'll bump down a dirt path to a country lodge, where ibis pick at the grass and sprinklers feed a jewel-green lawn, to await the General in an open-air rondavel. The bodyguards carefully place themselves at a table distant enough to prevent eavesdropping, while keeping the two of you in constant sight.

Some find these conditions too unsettling—"Me, get in a car with armed strangers and drive to some undisclosed location? No way!"

exclaimed one South African publisher scheduled to meet him—and the encounter does not take place. It was not always thus, but what happened four months after the General joined Patrick in exile locked him in what is essentially a comfortable cage. His security arrangements, paid for by the South African state, are a reflection of a haunted president's terror. However drippingly contemptuous Kagame may sound in public—and the state-controlled Rwandan media's obsession with the General's activities is in itself a giveaway—he fears no one as he fears General Kayumba.

I heard many descriptions of the General before I met him, and they perfectly captured the polarized nature of Rwandan reality. "I felt I was meeting an African philosopher king," one television director told me. A European ambassador was less complimentary: "That man has a huge amount of blood on his hands." A former Rwandan soldier, a man himself dismissed by the General as a congenital liar—that Epimenides paradox—warned me, "He'll lie to you from A through to Z." "He's a sweetie," said a Western military adviser who had accompanied the General on many an anti-insurgent operation, adding, "He's also a cold-hearted killer." The reaction from a journalist friend was even more startling: "*Soooooo* hot."

The General is certainly aristocratically good-looking, the characteristic Tutsi high forehead combined with a Grecian nose and smooth, dark skin. His physique is thickset and sturdy, though, not the etiolated nomad's build. Stories circulate of him hoisting a wounded comrade onto his shoulders and running to safety under fire. Famously, he saved Kagame's life in the bush more than once. This element plays a part in his popularity with soldiers, for if there is one thing fit young men admire, more ardently than women, it is athletic prowess.

Many of the RPF's core members grew up in refugee camps, an experience that left them constantly aware of their outsider status. *Aigri*—"acidic," "embittered"—are the adjectives Rwandans often use when referring to that group. Not the General and Patrick. They came from families of middle-class, well-educated Tutsis who had for generations effortlessly passed as Ugandan locals. Because that was exactly what they were.

Thanks to their contribution to President Yoweri Museveni's guerrilla struggle, either could have chosen to spend the rest of his life

51

in Uganda. Instead, both made the RPF's fight their own, becoming firm friends in the process. Theirs had been a choice, not a necessity, and with that difference went many deeper ones.

Falling from favor, the General had asked to retire. But Kagame had ruled that option out. Instead, in 2004, the president had appointed him ambassador to India, the kind of posting reserved for someone a suspicious head of state wants well out of the way. The General had accepted his banishment, drawing up plans in New Delhi to study for a PhD. He'd been a star pupil at secondary school: a career in academia was a distant aspiration.

Then the General's mother died, and he flew back to Kigali for the funeral. "That's when I realized how the government had got into witch-hunting," he told me.[11]

When friends and family clad in white, Rwanda's traditional color of mourning, gathered in the small town of Rwamagana to mark the matriarch's passing, only an idiot would have failed to pick up the day's message. Not a single member of the government the General represented, not a single officer of the army he had once commanded, was among the 1,000-strong crowd. The establishment had delivered a devastating snub.

Digesting the calculated insult, the General attended a government retreat in the northwestern town of Gisenyi. He was preparing his return to India when he was summoned to the RPF secretariat. It would be his first attendance at an RPF meeting in five years.

The scene sounds like a replay of Patrick's dressing down. Walking into the room, the General registered just what a heavyweight panel had gathered: an array of top military, police, intelligence, and party officials. Once again, Kagame made himself scarce, but throughout the meeting the General noticed how both the police chief and Jack Nziza, a brigadier with a reputation as a presidential hatchet man, kept slipping in and out of the room. They were clearly relaying updates and returning with instructions from the boss, somewhere nearby, pulling the strings.

The accusations against the General seemed as wispy and tenuous as Rwanda's morning mists. There was something almost childish about the charges, their subtext more reminiscent, in the craving for respect they exposed, of playground than boardroom.

"It appears you no longer subscribe to the ideals of the RPF," said one questioner. "Since you left some people in the armed forces here always remained loyal to you. The newspapers write positive things about you all the time and criticize the government, while you never deny it." Kagame's subtext was clear: *I hate the fact you are popular.*

Then came, "Why do you think government officials didn't come to the funeral? What was the issue, do you think?" *See what it's like out in the cold?*

And finally: "We know you have been constantly talking to Patrick." *I bet you two are saying bad things about me behind my back.*

"My reply was, 'I've never asked anyone to love me,'" the General told me. He said, "I've lived in India for five years and none of the journalists writing these articles is a friend. If they are writing it's nothing to do with me, I never brief journalists." He brushed away the funeral snub: "You guys never came for my mother's burial, but if you had, she would not have resurrected. We had a problem finding enough seats, your presence wasn't missed." As for Patrick, the General made no attempt to deny the accusation: "All of you here know Patrick is my friend. My children and his children are like brothers and sisters. Just because he's left, it won't mean I stop talking to him."

The response was chilling: "You're talking to an enemy."

For a moment the General thought he was about to be arrested on the spot. Instead, he was told to delay his departure while he reconsidered his positon. "What you should do is write an apology to Kagame," one RPF colleague advised him. The meeting broke up at midnight. He was given until 8 p.m. the following evening to present the necessary mea culpa.

"I knew the purpose of the letter," the General told me. Letters of apology had become obligatory rituals of abnegation, Rwandan versions of the humiliating "struggle sessions" staged during Mao's Cultural Revolution. Any such letter would immediately be leaked to the media to discredit him in the Rwandan public's eyes. Kagame would also ensure it was read by Western donors—"I knew he'd give it to the British and American ambassadors"—to justify whatever treatment was subsequently meted out.

It was too much. "I said to myself, 'I won't give him the chance.'"

The General emailed his wife, Rosette, in New Delhi. "I said, 'Don't be surprised if I leave the country. Be prepared for the consequences for you and the children.' That night I didn't sleep at all."

In the morning it was his turn to take the *subway*. It meant calling on the services of a trusted former driver, Richard Bachisa. "I want to go to Uganda, but I don't want to use the official route," the General told him. He knew the small roads, had fought on many of them in the early 1990s. Heading for Kagitumba, just as Patrick had done three years earlier, they drove until they were a few miles from the frontier, where Bachisa stopped the Land Cruiser and the General got out. The guards at the border post might already have received orders from Kigali. While Bachisa drove across the frontier in his empty car, his boss walked to the river dividing the two countries.

It was a departure replete with irony. As an idealistic young soldier, he had led a contingent of fighters who had crossed into Rwanda at Kagitumba in 1990, part of an RPF guerrilla movement bent on claiming by force what Juvénal Habyarimana had for decades denied them: the right to live in Rwanda. Twenty years later, wearier and warier, he was running like a criminal in the opposite direction, fleeing the very government he had helped establish.

It had rained and the swirling river ran deep, heavy with the topsoil leached from Rwanda's furrowed hillsides. The odd crocodile lurked in that soupy, coffee-colored water, he knew, but he had no choice. The General waded in and swam to the other side, then trudged to rejoin the road, waiting in wet clothes until Bachisa picked him up. Another high-profile RPF figure had joined the ranks of aggrieved exiles.

•

The RPF system closed behind him like cytoplasm and immediately began producing the antibodies required not only to ensure that he never returned, but that his legacy was obliterated. Discrediting a lauded hero of the RPF liberation struggle was never going to be easy, but with persistence—and persistence is any government's most formidable weapon—all becomes possible. As the great propagandist of the twentieth century, Adolf Hitler, knew, "If you tell a big enough lie and tell it frequently enough, it will be believed."

In the days that followed the General's departure, a grenade went off near the Kigali Genocide Memorial site. Fred Muvunyi, a journalist working for Contact Radio, was one of the first people on the ground, taking notes as the injured were taken away.[12]

It was not the first such grenade attack and it would not be the last. Old grenades were being sporadically thrown in the capital, in the southwest border town of Cyangugu, and in Rwanda's Western Province, part of what was assumed to be a not-particularly-effective destabilization campaign by the Forces Démocratiques de Libération du Rwanda (FDLR), an extremist Hutu movement set up in DRC by Habyarimana's former army soldiers and militiamen.

"The day after the explosion," Fred remembers, "the police came to the radio station wanting to tell the public who was responsible. An inspector told me on air—it was big, breaking news at the time—that it was the FDLR." Interview complete, Fred offered the inspector a lift.

"We were near the sports stadium when I got a call from police headquarters saying that actually, it was Kayumba who was behind the grenade explosion and I was to tell our listeners so. I laughed and said, 'I can't say that because I don't believe it. How can you change your mind in just a few minutes?'" When the caller insisted, Fred said, "If you want to say that on air you can, but I won't."

They drove back to Contact Radio's studio, where the police inspector, Fred remembers, couldn't quite bring himself to make the necessary U-turn on air, instead of saying "Kayumba Nyamwasa," blaming "elements from our enemies." From then on, he recalls, the government would recite the mantra "It's Kayumba" incessantly and the attacks became "Kayumba's crime." "But we journalists knew the grenade attacks were part of an FDLR campaign.

"I don't hold any brief for the guy, but why on earth would Kayumba, a Tutsi, throw a grenade at the Genocide Memorial site, of all places? Tell me why anyone would do that, even if they had a political statement to make?"

Fred can be free with these opinions because he, too, is now an exile. He did well enough professionally to become the director of the Rwanda Media Commission, set up in 2013 to protect journalists and campaign for media freedom. There he inevitably clashed with the authorities. So he fled to Germany, where he has been granted political asylum.

"When that topic of the grenade attacks comes up, I always say to people, 'I know for a fact it's bullshit.'"

•

At the ambassador's residence in New Delhi, Rosette and the children were briefly locked in a standoff with Rwandan embassy officials, who demanded they quit the premises while simultaneously sabotaging any travel plans by canceling their diplomatic passports.[13] While the General waited for his wife and children to arrive, he stayed with his old friend Patrick, whose fate increasingly seemed linked to his own.

Sharing breakfasts and cracking open beers, the two men could finally talk freely, without fear of being bugged or monitored, snooped on and betrayed. Perhaps the reverberations reached Kigali, for two weeks after the General's arrival, the first call came.

Patrick was traveling in Kenya, and Emile and the General were together at his house in Centurion watching television, when the younger man's cell phone rang. It was a cousin of Kagame's, advising Emile that someone important wanted to speak to him. It was Brigadier General Jack Nziza, the bug-eyed, bucktoothed permanent secretary at the Ministry of Defence, a man who had acquired the unenviable nickname of "the Terminator."

"Immediately I told General," Emile recalls. When Nziza rang fifteen minutes later, he put the phone on speakerphone and pressed "record." Nziza had an assignment for the former army captain, he told Emile. "You're there with those guys, what can we do to persuade you, to make it worth your while?"

Make what worthwhile? Why, killing either one or the other, preferably both.

CHAPTER THREE

IF AT FIRST YOU DON'T SUCCEED

His craving for revenge on me is completely unsatisfied: there have been, so to speak, physical blows, but morally nothing has been achieved. At the same time he is clever enough to realise that even today I would not change places with him: hence the psychology of a man stung.

—**Leon Trotsky**, five years before one of Stalin's
agents killed him with an ice axe

F rom the day he took the *subway*, Patrick never seems to have entertained much doubt that his former friend wanted him dead. But there's a difference between hoping for an outcome and exploring every conceivable practical means to bring it about. What explained the grim determination with which Kagame suddenly set about the task?

Patrick certainly knew where all the skeletons were buried. The years he'd spent working in both Uganda and Rwanda's intelligence services meant he was on top of the region's every secret. Now all that knowledge could be turned against Kagame. But solo, there had been only so much damage Patrick could do.

Kagame's hounding had, counterintuitively, brought about exactly the scenario the president feared most. The canny spy boss with the international network—regarded by his African and Western counterparts as Kagame's *éminence grise*—had joined forces with the former army chief of staff adored by Rwanda's restive troops. By thrusting together two marginalized exiles, united in their shock and anger, Kagame had effectively weaponized them, creating a credible challenge to his rule. And who knew better than he of what the two men were capable?

"Kayumba was head of intelligence in the bush, army chief commander, and now he is in the same house as the chief of intelligence," says Emile. "You have to be worried, you have to act before they do. The combination was lethal."

For three years, Patrick had worked behind the scenes, and there had never been any violence, Emile recalled. "Before Kayumba's arrival, it was all peaceful for us. The violence began when the General came. Things changed then. The war started."

In the RPF's inner circle, the fact that this kind of existential challenge merited a terminal response—liquidation—was taken for granted. The standard liberal criticism voiced of rebel movements who take power is to say they "fail to make the transition to civilian government." The truth is usually simpler: no transition is attempted at all; the habits, mindset, and structures of a military guerrilla movement simply shift wholesale from the forest dugouts to the capital city.

Back in the bush, when iron discipline held the key to success or failure, the leaders of the RPF always dealt with perceived challengers swiftly and summarily—no one took a vote. Kagame's strategic vision had not altered one whit since then. Survival—whether his own or the country's, the two were increasingly fused in his own mind—justified all methods.

Once in power, Rwanda's military elite so readily embraced the notion of targeted assassination as an effective solution to a problem that it developed its own vocabulary. Theogene Rudasingwa, who spent four years as Kagame's chief of staff, learned the terminology even as he felt increasingly repelled by the assumptions behind it.

"There's a word in Kinyarwanda: *kumunywa*. It literally means 'to drink someone.' What it meant in RPF language was 'to eliminate someone.' In their own circles they talked about killing people like flies. 'Why don't we drink him?' you'd hear them say."[1]

The casualness of these discussions, recalls Theogene, reflected the boss's matter-of-fact approach to both death itself and to possible repercussions. "Kagame would always say, 'When someone dies, it's over. You deal with the consequences, but the problem is of a different nature. Those *wazungus* [white people] make noise but over time, they forget it.'"

•

"People say, 'How did you know it was Nziza?'" says Emile, remembering the fateful phone call. "But of course I knew him. He was my former boss, so I knew his voice very well, from the days of the Struggle. And he knew me very well, too—and would like to kill me right now!" he says with a laugh.

The General had attended Uganda's Makerere University with Nziza in the 1980s, and the brigadier had served directly under him for twelve years at Rwanda's Ministry of Defence. Listening in, the General, too, effortlessly identified the caller.

And so the courtship began. On his return, Patrick—who, after all, knew all there was to know about the business of "turning" a reluctant source into a double agent—oversaw a drawn-out process of seduction in which Nziza unwittingly played the role of both prey and would-be predator. Like fly fishermen teasing a trout, the three men set about luring Nziza into both revealing his hand and incriminating himself.

With Patrick and the General seated on either side, Emile would press "Record" and the trio would listen as their former colleague in Kigali discussed arrangements for the hit. "It was totally surreal, like a scene from a movie," remembers nephew David Batenga.

"We spoke many, many times," says Emile. "I didn't refuse [the job] immediately. We had to record them, play them psychologically, so we would say, 'What do you want me to do?,' or, 'We can organize this. . . . ' They were offering me all kinds of things in return."

Patrick seemed to relish the grotesqueness of the experience. On one occasion, he actually picked up the call and briefly spoke directly to Nziza, who assumed he was still talking to Emile. The intended victim, discussing the practicalities of his own execution with his would-be murderer: it's hard to imagine a stranger, darker experience. "They're crazy, those guys," Patrick would say afterward, shaking his head.

There were various reasons for recording the conversations. One was a simple matter of self-protection. "The first thing was to know exactly what their intentions were, what they were planning," explains the General. "Then you know how to guard yourself. And for some time that worked: we knew what they were doing, and that helped us."

The second motive, the General said, was political and strategic. The men who would go on to found the Rwanda National Congress were well aware of the generous "pass" that much of the international community routinely granted Kagame. They would only win support if they made some dents in Kagame's image. The higher up the chain they could attribute responsibility, the better.

"We really wanted to expose them," said the General. "What Kagame does is kill people and then he blames the victim. So the idea was that if anything happens, there should be evidence to know who is behind the killing."

For any recording to have that effect, though, it needed to be both detailed and specific, to allay suspicions that words had been taken out of context or misinterpreted. Nziza had shown either breathtaking chutzpah or extraordinary carelessness in ordering a hit over an easily monitored cell phone. But he took some rudimentary steps to protect himself.

Patrick and the General were never referred to by name: instead it was "Muzungu" (white man) for light-skinned Patrick and "Number One" for the General. The challenge, for Emile, was to draw the conversations out in the hope that Nziza would eventually grow impatient and forget the customary euphemisms, spelling out in ever more explicit detail what precise action was required and whence his orders originated.

But Emile, it emerged, was not the only pawn in this chess game. Patrick was still in steady contact with Aimé Ntabana. Suddenly all concern, the head of Rwandan military intelligence, Dan Munyuza, flew the young man to Nairobi for medical treatment to help him recover from the period of solitary detention.

Then Aimé was allowed to move to Kampala, where, with government funding, he rented an apartment in Namungoona, a modern housing estate, and tried to set himself up as a farmer and businessman.

All this support, it was made clear, came at a price. Aimé's tasks would include putting Munyuza in touch with Rwandans living in South Africa who would be willing to get close to the General and Patrick and monitor their movements, with a view to an eventual hit.

Aimé dutifully provided names and numbers. But every Rwandan Aimé hooked Munyuza up with was known to the General and Patrick. Even as Munyuza reached out to them, these would-be assassins were relaying the contents of their conversations to the two exiles, who then persuaded them to start taping the exchanges, just like Emile. Together, Aimé and Emile—Patrick's two orphaned surrogate sons—had become the linchpins of a complex counterespionage operation.

It was a role fraught with risk for Aimé, given his proximity to Kigali and the porous border between Uganda and Rwanda. "I used to tell him, 'Why don't you run away to Europe? These people will find you there and kill you,'" says Leah. But the deaths of his family members had given the traumatized young man the despairing bravado of someone with nothing to lose. "He would say 'Ah, I'm like a dog. Who wants to kill me? What am I living for? All my people have died. If they want they can kill me, but I can't support them.'"

•

In April 2010, General Kayumba's wife, Rosette, and the children arrived in Johannesburg, distressed and overwrought. The family moved into a house in Athol Mews, in Johannesburg's upmarket Melrose district.

The following month they were joined there by Richard Bachisa, the driver who had helped the General flee Kigali. The General had left him with $300 in cash and instructions to sell the getaway Land Cruiser and keep the proceeds. Bachisa had attempted to set himself up in business in Uganda, but had called the General's sister to say Rwandan intelligence operatives had tried to kidnap him. Conscious that he was partly responsible for Bachisa's problems, the General advised the young man to fly to South Africa. Bachisa moved into the basement in Athol Mews and resumed his old duties as family driver and errand boy.

Although Patrick and the General were no longer sharing a home, they remained in constant contact as they drew up plans for an umbrella opposition group embracing all Rwandans, whether former members of Habyarimana's regime, RPF dissidents, or genocide survivors, Anglophone or Francophone.

It was vital to demonstrate ethnic and social evenhandedness, so leading Hutu politicians, such as former prime minister Faustin Twagiramungu, were courted, with mixed success. When he passed through Johannesburg in May, Theogene Rudasingwa met up with the two and joined the conversation, but the former presidential aide was wary of plunging back into politics.

In the meantime, the relentless calls from Kigali, along with the taping, continued. At least three times a week, the General and Patrick would meet to review the recordings. As the weeks passed, and Nziza showed signs of losing patience with his supposed hit man, Emile began to pick up some disturbing hints. Nziza, he felt, knew far more about the General and Patrick's movements than could be explained by the information Emile and Aimé's various contacts were feeding him.

"At a certain point," remembers David, "Emile sat Patrick and the General down and said, 'Guys, be careful. Someone in your inner circle knows where you are and what you're doing.'" Kigali, they realized, must have someone else on the inside, but no one could work out who the mole might be. "They say that the man who kills you is the man you trust," Emile told me. "The General was living with a man who was selling him out."

The answer became clear—although it took a while for the various pennies to drop—when the FIFA Soccer World Cup, hosted by South Africa, ensured the eyes of the world were trained on the country. At that moment of surging national pride, both the South African government and domestic media agreed, nothing could afford to go wrong.

On June 12, 2010, the General and Rosette were returning from a quick shopping trip, with Bachisa at the wheel. While at the nearby mall, they would later tell police, Bachisa had received a phone call he ignored, and the General had commented that he seemed to receive—and ignore—many such calls. The General was sitting in the front passenger seat, Rosette behind. As the electronic gate to their residence opened, a man suddenly materialized on the right-hand side of the car, banging on the side and yelling, "Brother, brother, help me!"

Alarmed, the couple shouted at Bachisa to drive into the compound. But instead of hitting the accelerator, Bachisa slowed. With the stranger hanging onto the side of the vehicle, he entered the compound, then, bafflingly, stopped and opened the window on the driver's side, allowing the stranger, who they could now see was holding a gun, to reach across his chest and take aim at the General. Bachisa seemed frozen, muttering only, "*Afande baraturashe*"—"They are shooting us, boss"—as the man opened fire.

The attacker had been aiming at the General's head, but his unsteady grip and the target's swift reactions—this was not, after all, the first time the General had come under fire—meant he made a hash of it. As the General ducked to the side, opening the car door, he was shot in the hip, semi-paralyzing a leg. The hit man then ran round the front of the car.

"He expected me to be on the floor, and to come round and finish me off," the General told me. Instead, the attacker met the General coming in the opposite direction. The General grabbed the man's gun hand, crunching it in his own so that the spring mechanism jammed. He wrestled the man, calling on Bachisa to hold him. Instead, the driver sat limply watching as the assailant drew a knife, shouting, "I will kill you, I will kill you." Pushing him off, the General bolted for the house, Rosette following him. Once inside, he slammed the security gate behind them as the assailant took to his heels.

The wounded General was taken to the Morningside Clinic in Sandton. A shocked Patrick soon headed to the clinic, rallying any Rwandans he trusted to form a de facto security cordon around the building. But as a court would later hear, the General was not safe there, either. While he was receiving treatment, his enemies attempted to finish him off in his hospital bed.

As police, journalists, and sympathizers milled anxiously outside the clinic, the bandaged General worried about Bachisa, concerned that South African investigators might use him as scapegoat. "They better leave him alone," he told Rosette. It was only when Bachisa was arrested that the driver's puzzling behavior was explained. Emile had been correct: Kigali had had a man on the inside all along.

Acting on the time-honored principle that the one person you don't see coming is the person closest to you, Rwandan intelligence had recruited Bachisa. His call to Kayumba's sister, claiming he'd been the target of a kidnap attempt, had almost certainly been prompted by the calculation that the General would take pity on his former employee, allowing Kigali to slip a collaborator into his household. The young man had been sitting in the General's blind spot ever since.

At the eventual trial, the court would hear that a staggering 447 calls had been made between Bachisa and Vincent Ngendo, part of a two-man Rwandan team sent to Johannesburg to arrange the hit. Ngendo and a businessman called Pascal Kanyandekwe, the director of a Rwandan aviation company, the prosecution claimed, had flown in together to recruit a local hit squad.[2]

The slightly shambolic gang they pulled together, which included three Tanzanians, was originally told that the target was a Nigerian fraudster who had diddled someone out of $150,000. But when press cuttings bearing photos of the General were produced as aides to identification, the gang's members realized the operation's true nature. They were given a spare key to the General's security gate and told that the door to the family home would be left unlocked. The murder was originally meant to take place in the General's bedroom.

The attorney appointed by the Rwandan government with a watching brief must have cringed when one of the numbers cited during the trial was identified as a cell phone belonging to Colonel Emmanuel Ndahiro, Rwanda's head of national intelligence.

After the first bungled attack, Kanyandekwe and Ngendo had flown back to Kigali, the former then returning, the prosecution asserted, to oversee a raid on the clinic. That, in turn, was preempted when the police flagged down a blue Nissan, found to be carrying the hit squad, a rope, and a bottle of chemicals. It seems that both strangulation and poison, probably intended to be injected into the General's intravenous drip, were being considered.[3]

•

Sudden violence has an invigorating, crystallizing impact. Hearing of the botched assassination attempt on the General in the United States, the previously wavering Theogene Rudasingwa shed any doubts.

"Instantly, I decided I was going to fight President Kagame's dictatorship to the end," he later wrote.[4]

Patrick, too, was aware of crossing a Rubicon. In the days that followed the shooting, according to a Ugandan intelligence source, he received a message—the third such—from Kagame. "Come back," it read. "We'll let bygones be bygones."[5] Whatever Patrick might have initially felt, the brutal directness of what had been attempted made reconciliation impossible now. Trust was out of the question.

A side effect of the shooting was that it allowed him to separate genuine from fair-weather friends. When it broke, the news triggered an avalanche of calls and emails from contacts concerned about his safety. But many of those who had once chased him for introductions, people whose school fees he had funded or whom he had extricated from political scrapes, stayed silent. The Rwandan regime, everyone knew, had a long reach. Anyone consorting with Patrick now would be putting their business contracts, diplomatic relations, research access, or media accreditation at risk. Patrick was too smart a student of human nature not to understand their motivations. But it did not make the experience any more pleasant.

Soon after, we met at a Lebanese restaurant on the Edgware Road in London. When we talked about the attack on the General, Patrick rolled his eyes, scoffing at the perpetrators' clumsiness. "To do it at that moment, when the eyes of the world are on South Africa, when everyone is talking about crime, and the one thing that the South Africans really want is to persuade the world they are on top of security . . . what a time to choose!"

Having identified Bachisa as a fifth columnist, he told me, the South African police had allowed him to continue communicating with Ndahiro before picking up the driver. "So, *so* stupid, the trail led immediately right to the top. There should have been no direct communications at all." The way he said this suggested Patrick might be talking from personal experience, I reflected, of previous hits, better executed.

The General spent a month in the hospital as the police pursued their inquiries. The bullet had splintered his hip bone, lodging too close to the spine to risk surgery. "I still have a bullet lodged at the base of my spine," he told me on our first meeting, reaching down to gently probe his back. "I can feel it here."

Once he had checked out of the clinic, the lives of both men and their families clearly had to change. The General had been scheduled to deliver a series of lectures at Pretoria's Institute for Security Studies when he'd been shot, but public appearances were clearly out of the question now.

Each man was given twenty-four-hour-a-day protection, half a dozen military policemen assigned by the South African state to keep them alive. The General, his wife, and their children moved to a new, guarded house in Centurion, and Patrick relocated to a villa in the Pretoria suburbs. "The Willows" was situated next to a military barracks, equipped with CCTV, high metal gates, and permanent guards. The days of freedom were over.

These were expensive arrangements for any foreign government to commit to, but as far as Pretoria was concerned, a point of principle was involved. It wasn't so long ago that ANC leaders had themselves belonged to an organization labeled "terrorist" by the apartheid government, its exiles haunted by the fear of assassination by South African undercover agents. Safe havens were sacrosanct in Pretoria's eyes.

"When the general was shot, the official reaction was one of total shock and outrage," remembers former South African ambassador Thembi Majola. "The response was, 'Really? You want to come and do this rubbish here, when the whole world is watching the World Cup? What does that say about your view of us as a country?'" South Africa's high commissioner to Rwanda was recalled—a sign of deep displeasure—even if both Pretoria and Kigali were at pains to play down the implications of the move.

Rwanda seemed remarkably unembarrassed by the whole incident. At African Union (AU) meetings in Addis Ababa, where South African diplomats labored to establish what they saw as their country's natural place as the continent's post–Cold War dominant power, Rwandan officials would repeatedly bring up the issue of the exiles' presence on South African soil, making clear that supporting votes on important resolutions were conditional on cooperation. Cooperation meant the arrest and deportation of these enemies of the state.

South Africa would not oblige, but while funding these protection arrangements, it warned Patrick and the General to keep their political activities discreet. They could stay, but they would have to behave.

The point was reinforced when Patrick, returning from his London trip, flew back into Oliver Tambo International Airport and straight into a showdown at immigration. Despite his furious protests, a South African official confiscated the UNHCR passport, on which he had relied since Kigali had canceled his Rwandan one. He was to spend the next few years attempting, without success, to get the passport returned, suing the very government upon which he depended for his safety.

By the time of his death, the authorities still hadn't offered an explanation for the passport's confiscation. The truth—which Patrick suspected—was that Kigali had formally complained to Pretoria about his movements, claiming Patrick was buying arms and laundering money on the RNC's behalf during his travels.

Without papers, Patrick was effectively grounded, coralled within South Africa's borders, a fact that severely curtailed his work mustering support for an embryonic political movement.

•

On August 9, 2010, Rwanda staged what was only the country's second presidential election since the genocide.

Few could describe the buildup as conducive to a free vote. In January of that year, Hutu opposition leader Victoire Ingabire had returned to Kigali after sixteen years in exile, intending to run. Instead, she'd been jailed. The grenades the government blamed on the General and Patrick kept exploding sporadically in Kigali, claiming few lives but leaving residents jittery and terrified.

In April, the authorities shut down *Umuseso* and *Umuvugizi,* two independent newspapers, and in June, the latter's acting editor was shot dead outside his house in Kigali.[6] A month later, the body of the vice-chairman of the opposition Democratic Green Party, Andre Kagwa Rwisereka, was found lying in marshland. The dead man, a former senior RPF member, had been partially beheaded.[7]

The manner of his death was not seen as random. Back when the RPF had been an underground movement, members took a bloodcurdling oath on joining. "I solemnly swear, before everyone present, that I will work for the RPF family, that I will always defend its interests, and that, if I divulge its secrets, I will be decapitated like any other traitor," it read. The message was clear: "Betray us and you die."

The week before the vote, a Ugandan newspaper published a long interview with Patrick in which he called on Rwandans to rise up. "A dictator can never step down, they are brought down," he said. "Kagame will have his breaking point and I think it will be very soon." To those unaware of all the brewing plots and phone calls, the interview seemed foolhardy, a de facto declaration of war. In fact, mortal combat had already been engaged.[8]

In the pre-genocide era, the RPF had derided election results showing Habyarimana routinely winning over 99 percent of the vote. Old habits, it seemed, die hard. This time the National Electoral Commission allotted 93.08 percent of the vote to Kagame, on turnout of 97.5 percent. Kagame was matching the kind of eyebrow-lifting tallies once recorded by Saddam Hussein in Iraq.

From the diaspora came the dissidents' scornful response: the publication of a fifty-seven-page "Rwanda Briefing," coauthored by the four pillars of the emerging new movement: Patrick and the General in South Africa, and Theogene and his brother Gerald Gahima, Rwanda's former attorney general, in the United States.[9]

Simultaneously a dissection of national malaise and rallying cry, the essay described Rwanda as "a hardline, one-party, secretive police state with a façade of democracy." Kagame, said the authors, had corrupted the RPF's founding ideals. Rwanda had two parallel governments, with true power held by an informal group recruited exclusively from the Tutsi minority. "The government is not considered legitimate by the majority of the population in general and the Hutu community in particular."

Denouncing "the licence to kill" enjoyed by the security services and their record of arbitrary arrests, torture, killings, and disappearances, the four said modern Rwanda was a more fearful place than Uganda under Idi Amin, far less free, even, than before the genocide.

Kagame's "cult image" in the eyes of the international community was, they suggested, a form of racism: "the result of prejudice on the part of people who do not expect anything in Africa to be done right." The exclusion of Hutus from meaningful power-sharing made a return to violence inevitable. They called for national dialogue to avert this, and the establishment of a new coalition government.

The briefing's publication, recalls Theogene, caused enormous excitement in Rwanda, where the fact that four such high-profile players had joined forces was seen as an indication that Kagame's quick, military removal was "in the making and possible." "Many in Rwanda's military were sending messages to us, saying they were behind us, should a spark be ignited. We were under pressure to 'do something.'"[10]

In early December 2010, the Rwanda National Congress was formally established at a meeting in Bethesda, on Washington's outskirts. Pledging to push for democratic change by peaceful means, the signatories unveiled a ten-point program aimed at stopping human rights abuses, ending impunity, and nurturing the rule of law. Since neither Patrick nor the General could now travel, the final document bears ten names but only seven signatures.[11]

But while members were proud to claim chapters in ten countries, that fact underlined the movement's most obvious weakness: How do you mobilize an organization scattered across three continents? The RPF had done it once: Could the RNC repeat the exercise?

The issue the Kagame regime would seize upon, though, was the links the RNC went on to establish with Hutu groups connected to the genocidal FDLR. It was all very well for Patrick to joke that he'd be happy for anyone—including Kagame himself—to join the RNC as long as they shared its principles. For many Tutsis in Rwanda, any contact with these national bogeymen placed the organization beyond the pale.

Kigali hit back on January 14, 2011, when a Rwandan military court sentenced General Kayumba, Patrick, Theogene, and Gahima to twenty years in prison in absentia for threatening state security, promoting ethnic division, and insulting the president. For good measure, the General and Theogene were also given an extra four years each for deserting the army.[12]

•

By January 2011, just as Nziza was showing signs of tiring of Emile's procrastinating tactics, a new player made his entrance on South Africa's Rwandan exile scene.

There is a Zelig quality to Robert Higiro, a man who seems to slip quietly into the background, taking up position almost unnoticed in a range of starkly contrasting historical snapshots. When we first met in a Washington bar, he seemed, in his dark, turtleneck top, a very

Europeanized African exile, chic and world-weary. A photo taken back when he was a major in the Rwandan army shows a quite different man, pristine in uniform, ceremonial sword aloft, marching ramrod straight alongside Kagame during troop inspection. I have also seen him, bespectacled and professorial, being interviewed on US television about Rwanda's human rights record. When I mentioned this chameleon-like quality, he did not seem displeased. "Well, you have to play the part, right?"[13]

Raised in Kampala, Robert joined the RPF the year it crossed into Rwanda. Today described by Rwanda's state-owned media as a "disgraced ex-soldier," he clearly excelled in his chosen career. Training officers at several Rwandan military academies, he was also selected for the peacekeeping force Rwanda dispatched to Darfur at the UN's request. But he had become angry at the arbitrary arrests of comrades and made the mistake of voicing his views in the bar, only to be given a lesson on Rwandan society's famous duplicity.

"A general summoned me to army headquarters and I was told, 'Every single person you spoke to used to report back on you, while you never did. You never learned the system, did you?'" It could have been a compliment, but was clearly not meant as such.

Decommissioned, Robert found himself virtually unemployable, struggling to support his wife and two children: "When they take you out of the army no one will work with you anymore. They want you on your knees." Looking back, he wonders if being ostracized in this way was part of a longer game. "They know if you're out of a job, you're going to be vulnerable, worried about school fees, and do what they want. So maybe there was a plan."

Hired by a French private security company, he was posted to Senegal. It was then that the Rwandan Directorate of Military Intelligence reached out. "They sent someone to meet me in Dakar, who told me they had a job for me and to expect a call."

When the call came through it was Dan Munyuza, head of military intelligence. He made the same offer Jack Nziza had dangled under Emile's nose. Robert had gotten to know Patrick in 2004, when the latter attended one of his training courses. That provided a way in. If Robert could engineer Patrick's and the General's assassinations in South Africa, Munyuza said, he would not only be generously rewarded, he would be a national hero.

He had sensed what was coming, but Robert was appalled. "It never crossed my mind to do it," he recalls. "Why should I do that? For whom? I was a friend to Patrick, a friend to his family." The suggestion that this amounted to a patriotic duty seemed ludicrous, and as for the promised "reward": "Come on! I've been working for you for twenty years and *now* you're going to make me rich?"

And so he did what so many of the young men approached in this way would: "I called Patrick in South Africa and told him, 'I have a situation: I'm supposed to kill you guys.'

"We laughed about it. 'It's not only you,' Patrick told me. 'They have other guys here who have been paid to do it.'"

But even as the two men joshed with one another, Robert recognized that with that one phone call from Kigali, he, too, had been handed the equivalent of the pirate's Black Spot.

"The thing is, I know how the system works. Whether I kill them—which is not an easy thing to do, by the way—or not, it's over. Your life has been screwed up." In Kagame's Rwanda, neutrality was not an option. If Robert failed to carry out the assignment, he would automatically join the list of enemies of the state, risking the same fate he had refused to mete out to a friend.

When Patrick said, "Why don't you come over here and we'll figure out what to do?" Robert obeyed, taking a looping route via Uganda to Pretoria, where he moved into an apartment. With his rent covered by the government in Kigali, he would spend the next year operating as a double agent, occasionally meeting up with diplomats from the Rwandan embassy.

His task, Patrick and the General explained, would be the same as that asked of Emile and the other Rwandans Aimé had helped recruit: recording as many incriminating conversations with Rwandan intelligence as possible before the realization dawned in Kigali that he was never going to deliver the goods. "Get the evidence and then get out," they advised.

The two men suggested Robert invent a relationship with a South African major with supposed access to their security details. Robert's experience with the UN force in Darfur, which had included South African officers, made this credible. He would tell Kigali that this fictional character could either arrange for the various bodyguards to do the job themselves or drop their guard long enough to let in a

Rwandan hit squad. It was a complex plan with many moving parts, which allowed for long and torturous discussions, all to be taped.

Meeting up with Patrick in restaurants and bars that had first been checked by the latter's bodyguards, Robert would hand over the tapes and receive guidance on what tactics to adopt during the next phone conversation. The longer Robert could spin things out, the better the chances of extracting precious nuggets of damning information.

Robert found his undercover role simultaneously stressful and tedious. "I was supposed to be a busy man, negotiating with a bunch of people. So I had a lot of time on my hands. You go and have a beer, come back, and wait for their calls. The tricky bit was getting Munyuza to spell it out."

Robert, Patrick said, was to demand $1.5 million for the hit. "Are you mad?" expostulated Robert. "That's too much money!" Patrick laughed. "You think you know these guys better than I do? I know them. They are very desperate." Sure enough, when Robert mentioned the sum, Munyuza barely blinked. Like any decent buyer, he bargained the price down a notch and sought to place conditions on disbursement. Explaining that Kigali had already lost a lot of money on agents who hadn't delivered, Munyuza offered $1 million, to be paid in installments.

The two men haggled like a project manager and a builder's foreman on a construction site. The South African military officers, Robert told Munyuza, refused to do anything until they were paid up front, but Munyuza insisted on payment upon completion.

The reward, Munyuza made clear, would be higher if the supposed assassin pulled off a one-two punch, eliminating both Patrick and the General. "If we managed to hit both of them," Munyuza said, "the others would shut up. . . . If he could kill two birds with one stone and eliminate them both at once, he could earn more. Even one alone, the enemy would be weakened. Their supporters will be finished."

All of this was priceless material. But Patrick and the General hoped for even more. "Sometimes I got them to admit to some of the other assassinations," says Robert.

The previous January, Jean-Bosco Rutayisire, an accountant for Bourbon Coffee, a popular fast-food company in Kigali, had been found strangled next to his car.[14] Rutayisire was a distant cousin of

Patrick's, and the latter suspected the murder was part of a campaign of collective punishment leveled at friends and family left behind. "I got Munyuza to admit to that, I had it on the record," says Robert, with quiet satisfaction.

A key aim was to establish a chain of command leading from men like Nziza and Munyuza to the very top of the pyramid, to Kagame himself.

Throughout history, leaders finding themselves publicly vilified for organizing high-profile assassinations have resorted to blaming the subordinates. "Goodness, I never meant *that!*" they exclaim. "Those fools totally misunderstood me." That excuse was always going to be a tough sell in a country whose president was routinely applauded for his micromanaging attention to detail. The multiplicity of top Rwandan officials involved in these assassination plots, the sheer number of hit men approached, the length of time over which the attempts extended, made the interpretation particularly difficult to swallow. While it was theoretically possible one subordinate might have disastrously misinterpreted his master's wishes, the notion that three—Nziza, Munyuza, and Ndahiro—could all make the same mistake, over not just months but years, hardly seemed credible. But the more evidence Patrick and the General's agents collected, the harder it would be for Kagame to try and play that card.

As the months of chitchat passed, Robert began to get a grasp of how Kagame managed relationships within his inner circle. Like many an autocrat before him, he believed in keeping subordinates in a state of constant mutual suspicion, each vying for his approval. No one trusted anyone else; nor were they ever allowed to feel secure.

In this environment, when Kagame made clear he wanted something done, aides tumbled over themselves to prove their loyalty. The ordering of a hit on a perceived enemy of the state resembled a government's competitive tendering process, with rival officials jealously keeping their assets to their chests, refusing to compare notes as they raced to be the first to nail the contract and win the boss's praise.

So Ndahiro primed Bachisa, Nziza spoke to Emile, and Munyuza talked to both Robert and Aimé, along with Aimé's contacts. "All of them have their own agents in the field. If you talk to Nziza, Nziza will tell you not to talk to Munyuza, and Munyuza will tell you not to talk to Nziza. That's how it works," Robert said.

Kagame's classic divide-and-rule policy was aimed at both improving performance and preventing possible challengers from emerging. But it resulted in a careless plethora of foolhardy approaches, and a multiplicity of phone calls and recruitment "interviews" in which public exposure became not just likely, but inevitable.

•

I n July 2011, Patrick and the General publicly released the first in a batch of tape recordings.[15] With the number of plots being hatched in Kigali outstripping even their expectations, transparency seemed the most effective response.

"We realized we were not in control of our agents," says the General. "So we released the tapes as a form of deterrence. The Rwandan government should know that we know. And they should not lie, because after I was shot, immediately the propaganda machinery in Kigali said I'd been shot by criminals operating in South Africa. We wanted the Kinyarwanda community to be aware of exactly what was going on."

The General and Patrick approached Rwandan journalists who had fled abroad after their newspapers had been closed down by the government. Granted asylum in Scandinavia, the journalists were still trying to keep working, shifting their operations online. Here was a chance for these unhappy reporters to strike back.

A batch of key recordings—those that stood out from the rest for their cringe-inducing explicitness—were selected, transcribed, and put out by the likes of *Umuseso* and *Umuvugizi*. The identities of the men receiving the calls—Patrick and the General's double agents— were kept anonymous, but the callers were exposed in full.

And so, in the age of the Internet, it is possible for any ordinary member of the public to enjoy the surreal experience of eavesdropping on an African intelligence officer ordering a political hit. Google "YouTube," "Assassination," "General," and "Kayumba," and you can listen to Kagame's henchmen at their sinister work, with subtitles in English and French helpfully provided.

It's a strange sensation, rendered even more disconcerting by the smidgeon of sympathy one ends up feeling for some of these killers, who sound both lugubrious and chronically put-upon as they struggle to bring a dragging operation to what must have felt like an increasingly unlikely climax. As payment and access are discussed, one catches a whiff of the tearing anxiety of life in Kigali's kill-or-be-killed inner circle, with Nziza, in particular, complaining about the conditions under which he is expected to perform.

In one conversation, taped after the first botched attack outside the General's compound, Nziza sounds both hungover and mournful as he goes about trying to arrange the hit on the Morningside Clinic, asking all the while how many times and where exactly the General was shot and how "Mzungu"—Patrick—is reacting. The exchange is punctuated by weary sighs and the "eehhhh" typical of Kinyarwanda conversation—the equivalent of a Western "mmmm."

"I'm in deep trouble, listen . . . " Nziza tells his agent. "The man I talked to you about before thought I was lying, that I was the one who'd ordered it." "Who?" asks his interlocutor, trying to draw him out. "The top guy . . . at the top level. . . . He thinks yours sincerely is responsible for this. No matter what you say, I'm in trouble." "Are you talking about the president?" nudges the agent. At which point Nziza senses a land mine and warns him not to say anything incriminating over the phone: "This could also cause problems."

In another conversation, with a different intermediary, Nziza becomes comically exasperated at the man's failure to grasp the practical impossibility of locating a $500,000 cash payment—intended for the team that is to infiltrate the clinic—on a Sunday in Kigali.

"It's Sunday today. You cannot mobilize," he tells the agent, who then suggests putting someone on a plane with the necessary cash. "But that's not the problem! That's not the problem! I just told you it's Sunday today! We have to follow the procedure to gather all those things you need, it's almost impossible." Banks are banks, and official paperwork is paperwork, even when it comes to paying for an extrajudicial execution.

The impact of the tapes' release on the Rwandan public and the community of analysts and academic researchers who follow Rwanda was electric.

For many in the Hutu community, the recordings merely confirmed the view they had always held of a ruthless regime with a knee-jerk capacity for violence. But for Tutsis who had joined the RPF in the 1990s for high-minded, altruistic reasons, the effect was shattering. The officials exposed were not distant strangers—Kigali is a city of just 1 million, and these were men they had worked along-side, bumped into at parties, or were distantly related to. Many Tutsis had felt growing unease at the signs of increasing authoritarianism coming from Kigali: here was devastating evidence of a movement that had lost its moral compass.

A Rwandan doctor, now living quietly in Europe, puts his hand over his face when he recalls hearing the recordings. "I knew all those guys," he told me. "I dealt with them, their wives and their fam-ilies, so I really knew them, and I immediately recognized the voices. I just stopped listening. I couldn't bear it.[16]

"Kagame used to sit Karegeya's son on his knee. Me, when I have to carry out the most minor treatment, I lie awake at night worry-ing whether I'll do it correctly. And this man who used to have his friend's son sitting on his lap . . . " he simulates a man taking two guns out of hip holsters, methodically firing each—"bang, bang"—coolly blowing the smoke away and reholstering. He grimaces. "And that's it, no remorse. It just stuns me."

Belgian academic Filip Reyntjens happened to be teaching a Rift Valley Institute field course in Bujumbura when the recordings surfaced on YouTube. He immediately put the obvious question to Rwandan presidential policy adviser and author Jean-Paul Kimonyo, who was lecturing at the same event.

"I said, 'Listen, either Munyuza and Nziza do things behind Ka-game's back, and then they should be sanctioned because it's very serious. Or, second possibility, the tapes are fake. Third possibility, Kagame knows it, agreed it, and ordered it. There are only those three possibilities.' I broached it with him on several occasions: 'Jean-Paul, which of the three?'" By the time the conference ended, Reyntjens still didn't have an answer.[17]

"There was uproar in the system, with people saying, 'How could they be so amateurish? How they could expose themselves in this way?'" recalls the General. "But for Kagame, the end justifies the means. If people are ready to kill for him, he will not mind how many times they get exposed. His response is, 'I'll do anything and deal with the consequences later.'

"So there was huge, huge embarrassment, but he still continued using the same system—and he is still using it now."

The media leak formed only one part of the exiles' strategy. It followed months of briefings with the intelligence services of Rwanda's key donor governments. In Pretoria, Patrick gave copies of the tapes to the intelligence operatives from the United States and to the Dutch, French, and other embassies—easy enough meetings to arrange, given the friendships he had forged with Western and African intelligence services during his career. His trip to London, during which the two of us met, was also an opportunity to hand the recordings over to MI6, which circulated them around the Foreign Office and Department for International Development (DFID). In Washington, Theogene did likewise, handing the tapes to the FBI. Whatever these Western government ministers might say publicly, they could not claim to be unaware of Kagame's tactics.

In the months that followed, Rwanda's globe-trotting president and his closest aides—many of whose voices were on the tapes—were sternly warned when they visited donor countries that such behavior would not be tolerated on foreign soil.

Linda Thomas-Greenfield, the US assistant secretary of state for African affairs, would later tell a House of Representatives subcommittee that the US government repeatedly raised concerns—in "all our engagements"—about "human rights violations, about reports and allegations of extra-judicial killings, about disappearances" with Rwandan government officials, including Kagame himself.[18]

"They have denied their involvement in all of these cases, but we have been clear in our messaging that this will have a real deep impact on our future engagement with the Rwandans," she assured the subcommittee.

Yet no major donor moved to sever aid or impose sanctions, or considered exposing Kigali's plots to public view. It was a decidedly limp response, given that Western allies were being presented with evidence of an African government—one they had generously subsidized for years—blithely exporting an ambitious political assassination program.

The closing of minds was a tribute to the RPF's success in shaping the narrative and was perhaps tinged, too, with a sense of just deserts. The RNC's founding fathers—Patrick, Theogene, Gahima, the General—were, after all, the very men who had created that narrative. Now here they stood, claiming that everything they had argued so convincingly had been a lie. "Fool me once, shame on you; fool me twice, shame on me," goes the saying. Why risk being burnt a second time?

And although Patrick and the General successfully broadcast their message to the Kinyarwanda-speaking community, they failed to get the tapes aired by the likes of the BBC, CNN, or Al Jazeera. On the surface, at least, it was a puzzling miss by a spy chief who counted scores of foreign correspondents among his friends.

When I ask the General what explained it, he cites a practical issue. While many Rwandans instantly knew who was speaking on the tapes, foreign news outlets would have wanted to verify the voices—a technically complex process—before broadcast. But something else—the quiet expectation of not being believed—also seems to have played a role.

"The press was not very willing," he acknowledges. "Remember, in 2010/2011, that's when Tony Blair and Bill Clinton were working very vigorously for Kagame, and the Western media had been duped into believing in this 'economic miracle,' and a lot weren't interested in listening to us. We had tried very many times and we were hitting a brick wall.

"We'd have wanted more," the General admits. "But the way it came out was the way it normally comes out with killings in Rwanda. We were not surprised. These things happen when you are the underdog."

There's an element of the domestic abuse victim's muteness about his response. It's a reticence I've noticed before when talking to Rwandans. The events in this tiny African country have been so extreme, the choices Rwandans were forced to make so grotesque, that outsiders tend to react with open-mouthed incredulity. Hearing themselves sounding semi-crazed, seeing the light of belief dying in interviewers' eyes, Rwandans learn to self-censor. They find themselves locked into a relationship of strange complicity with the regime. *We may hate one another, but only we understand ourselves.*

•

Kagame's attention extended far beyond South Africa, Patrick, and the General.

All too aware of the threat diaspora communities could come to represent—the RPF, after all, had been born in exile—Kigali treated geographical distance as irrelevant in its drive to silence criticism and preempt potential challenge. And while disaffected members of the RPF and the Rwandan armed forces were its primary interest, targets would come to include Rwandan journalists, human rights workers, civil society activists, opposition party members, and successful businessmen who dared question Kagame's rule from afar.

The country where Rwandan exiles felt most exposed was Uganda. Despite various bitter fallings-out between the regimes, historical links between the two guerrilla movements that had become neighboring governments meant that citizens of each country could circulate virtually unnoticed on each other's soils. Thousands of Kinyarwanda-speakers lived inside Uganda's borders, which made it particularly tricky for those on the run to distinguish friend from foe.

In Kampala and Mbarara, there was little expectation among newly arrived Rwandans that the Ugandan police might warn them if they were in danger. No, the Ugandan police were the problem, with the inspector general of police, Kale Kayihura, a man on excellent terms with Kagame, seen as turning a blind eye to the Rwandan agents who operated inside his country, left free to intimidate, threaten, kidnap, and kill.[19]

In November 2011, Charles Ingabire, a former Rwandan child soldier turned journalist, was shot as he left a bar in Kampala where he had been drinking with a friend.[20] Ingabire, who had had a request for resettlement turned down by the UNHCR, worked for the Inyenyeri website, which was critical of the government in Kigali, and had joined the RNC. He had already survived one attack in which he'd been hit over the head with a hammer and lost his laptop. This time he died.

The murder raised questions over the safety of Joel Mutabazi, a former Rwandan army lieutenant and presidential bodyguard who had fled to Uganda one month earlier. Unlike Ingabire, Mutabazi had been granted refugee status by the UNHCR and placed in a UN safe house outside Kampala. But how safe was that likely to be?

Most Rwandans in flight tried to spend as little time as possible in Uganda, logging their requests for political asylum in Kampala but then pushing for safe haven much farther afield. But wherever they went, the regime quickly followed, with Rwanda's embassies serving as the various intelligence agencies' hubs and points of entry into unfamiliar foreign societies.

In Sweden, police had become concerned about the unhealthy level of interest the Rwandan embassy in Stockholm was showing in Rwandans who had applied for political asylum in the Scandinavian country. Jean Bosco Gasasira, who edited *Umuvugizi*, was a particular concern.

After surviving a beating by three men with iron bars in Rwanda, Gasasira had sought asylum in Sweden in 2010, the year *Umuvugizi* had been suspended by the authorities, and its acting editor, Jean-Léonard Rugambage, shot dead as he drove through the gates of his Kigali home. He had continued publishing feisty anti-government coverage from exile, and had poked his head farther above the parapet by helping the RNC transcribe and broadcast its assassination tapes.

Acting on a tip-off, Swedish police began monitoring the phone owned by a forty-four-year-old Burundian calling himself Emmanuel Habiyambere, who lived in the central lakeside city of Orebro. Habiyambere, it turned out, was actually Rwandan, and his real name was Aimable Rubagenga. His communications with Kigali—later revealed at trial—cast inadvertently hilarious light on a plot by military intelligence to build detailed profiles of the Rwandan dissidents on Swedish territory.[21]

This time, the callers were generals Jack Nziza and Charles Kayonga, hungry for addresses, telephone numbers, and other background information on the Rwandan refugees in Sweden. Their conversations were just as strangely maladroit as those Nziza and Munyuza had conducted with their would-be hit men in South Africa. Once again, the spy chiefs paid only lip service to the need for discretion, relying heavily on the Kinyarwanda language to prevent eavesdropping and using only the crudest of euphemisms. "Bananas" was code for the dissidents—Rubagenga would claim at trial that he had been planning to import the fruit, but no one believed him—and "cooking oil" was almost certainly a euphemism for "cash."

"The man who eats bananas will guide you," Rubagenga is told in one conversation. "Go to the place to meet the man who will eat a lot of bananas. Focus on the bananas."

The hookup appears to have failed. "He who would eat the bananas has moved north to another city that starts at T," Rubagenga explains. "We are looking for that city in the computer to get the address." Later on he raises the issue of funding: "Tomorrow I'm going to look for the banana market, but I don't have enough cooking oil." He is told not to worry, that he will be sent "cooking oil."

As Swedish investigators probed the story, the police became concerned enough about Gasasira's personal safety to advise him to go to ground. The journalist cut off his cell phone and disappeared and in February 2012, Evode Mudaheranwa, the second-highest-ranking official at the Rwandan embassy in Stockholm, was expelled "for activities incompatible with his diplomatic status"—the recognized euphemism for "spying."

In October the following year, the district court in Orebro sentenced Rubagenga to eight months in prison, making Sweden the first country to prosecute a suspected member of a Rwandan hit squad.[22] Gasasira immediately reappeared, telling the media that once Rwandan military intelligence had collected his particulars, the aim had been to poison him.[23]

Britain's police force was simultaneously becoming concerned about certain members of the Rwandan community in the United Kingdom. In the run-up to an RNC conference scheduled to take place in London in May 2011, three Rwandan exiles were astonished to receive separate visits from the Metropolitan Police warning them their lives were in danger.

René Mugenzi, a tall Hutu with an open, wide-jawed face, left Rwanda at seventeen and eventually landed in the United Kingdom, where he became a social worker. He had attracted Kigali's attention by repeatedly raising the RPF's record on human rights during talks delivered at British universities and before a committee of British members of parliament (MPs).

He viewed this as constructive criticism, he told me when we met at a London bookshop—"I'd say, 'I'm not against you, I'm not an enemy, I'm trying to help you because you're not on the right path'"—but it led to him being labeled a troublemaker in Kigali. "They offered me £10,000 to stop. We'd be sitting like this, in a café, and they would have a bag of money [with them] to buy me off. They couldn't believe I was acting independently. They thought the old regime was using me."

After he'd criticized one of Kagame's speeches, he said, presidential confidant Colonel Emmanuel Ndahiro met up with him in London and uttered one of the oldest threats in the book. "He told me, 'If you don't stop, we know where your parents live.' So I joked back, 'They live in Holland. I know where your family lives, too, they live in Rwanda.'"[24]

Such levity was clearly misplaced. As the RNC get-together loomed, Mugenzi's wife received a call from Scotland Yard's anti-terrorist unit, asking if he was anywhere near his home in Thamesmead, a suburb in southeast London. "Ten minutes later the cars were there with plainclothes police, some of them armed. Some came inside the house, others stayed outside," Mugenzi said.

Western intelligence and security services are legally obliged to pass on assassination threats to potential targets. In Britain these are called "Osman warnings," after a landmark case brought by the family of Ali Osman, a businessman murdered by one of his son's teachers, who argued that the police knew what was pending and could have intervened.

Mugenzi showed me his copy of the warning he received, headlined, "Threats to Life Warning Notice." It reads, "Reliable intelligence states that the Rwandan government poses an imminent threat to your life.

"The threat could come in any form," the statement goes on, adding that in other high-profile cases of this kind, "conventional and unconventional means have been used." While promising to "take what steps it can to minimise the risk," the letter specifies that day-by-day or hour-by-hour protection by the British police is not on offer. Mugenzi was urged not to go to work for a few days, to avoid Rwandan public gatherings and going out alone, and to install CCTV outside his home.[25]

The same Osman warning was delivered to Noble Marara, a former Kagame bodyguard working in the Thames area who had begun publishing scabrous articles about Kagame, and Jonathan Musonera, a Rwandan army defector and one of the founding members of the RNC. "My wife, she is scared," Musonera told the BBC. "We have cut off the home phone. The children now they stay at home, they can't go out. I take this problem very seriously."[26]

One of those due to attend the RNC conference, a former RPF intelligence officer based in Brussels, was removed from his Eurolines coach on arrival at Folkestone's Eurotunnel terminal, questioned for six hours, and sent back to Belgium by British counterterrorist officers who suspected him of being part of a Kigali-instigated assassination plot.

The story was splashed across the British media. The Kigali government did what it always does in such awkward circumstances: it denied everything. "The government of Rwanda does not threaten the lives of its citizens wherever they live," declared High Commissioner Ernest Rwamucyo. But whatever protestations were made in public, the British authorities were clearly under no illusions as to what the Rwandans were up to. *The Independent* revealed that even before this latest incident, MI5 had felt impelled to warn Rwamucyo to halt the systematic harassment of Rwanda's critics in Britain.

Once again, Rwanda had shown a staggering indifference to a host government's domestic sensitivities and, ironically, its own interests. Britain, which had given Kagame's Rwanda £400 million in aid by that point, was the country's biggest bilateral donor, handing over an annual £55 million in the form of annual direct budgetary support, a highly desirable form of funding, as it allows a government to spend the money as it sees fit.

If South Africa's government was hypersensitive at the time of Kayumba's shooting to any incident likely to reinforce negative tourist preconceptions of the country, the Rwanda High Commission's behavior came at a time when a nervy British government was braced for both Islamic terrorist attack and covert activity by Russian agents. Four years earlier, the poisoning in a London sushi restaurant of former Russian agent Alexander Litvinenko, using the radioactive substance polonium, had caused a near breakdown in relations between London and Moscow.

The British government did not appreciate its police force being distracted by the settling of internal scores by a supposed friendly African state. "It was a spectacular own goal," a former British intelligence official told me.[27]

"Here was an ally showing no compunction about making these plans on the soil of its closest international ally just as it had shown no qualms doing the same thing on the soil of its closest African ally. It was a major blow to the Kagame administration's reputation. There was a feeling a line had been crossed; it furthered the sense this was a thuggish regime that didn't deserve to be supported."

Yet if that was the sentiment in the ranks, the reaction at the top was more indulgent. When Paul Kagame visited the DFID, the overseas aid department, in London later that year, its head, Andrew Mitchell, raised the subject of the Metropolitan Police's Osman warnings. The situation, the Conservative Party secretary of state told the president, looked bad either way. If Kagame had known about it, then he was a would-be murderer, and if he hadn't, he wasn't in control of his own country, which seemed hard to credit.

But Mitchell was not disposed to judge harshly. Like his Labour predecessor, Clare Short, he was a fervent, long-standing supporter of Rwanda. While still only shadow development minister, he had set up Project Umubano, a social action group that flew Conservative MPs to Rwanda to build schools, train teachers, and pass on business expertise. They always returned smitten.

Kagame denied any involvement. "I didn't know, Andrew." It appeared to suffice. "I'm inclined to believe him," remembers Mitchell, citing a famous episode in English history in which four knights, supposedly overinterpreting King Henry II's wishes, slaughtered Archbishop Thomas Becket in Canterbury Cathedral. "I tend to favor the 'turbulent priest' scenario."[28]

Mitchell's wife is a doctor, and the couple count Colonel Emmanuel Ndahiro, who once served as Kagame's personal physician, as a friend. When Mitchell raised the issue of the recordings made by Patrick and the General with Ndahiro, he also got—to his relief—a blank denial. "I swear to you, Andrew, that is not my voice on the tapes," he told the British politician. Unfamiliar with the concept of *ubwenge,* the upper-class Mitchell may have struggled to grasp the fact that "a gentleman's word is his bond" might not hold true in this instance.

Aid continued, and the British authorities had every intention of showing Kigali the diplomatic courtesy of keeping quiet about the Osman letters. It took the rebellious act of a British civil servant, astonished to discover that his employers intended to keep the matter under wraps, for the story to reach the media.

"I was so pissed off at the thought that the Foreign Office knew Rwanda was quite ready to take out exiles living in London, but was planning to keep that information to itself, that I let the press know," he told me.[29]

CHAPTER FOUR

PLOTS THICKEN

The exile is a ball hurled high into the air.
—Salman Rushdie

The RNC ringleaders had played their most potent weapon—public exposure—and the harvest had been distinctly modest.

In the process they had burnt some of their boats, revealing to Kigali which of its operators in South Africa could and couldn't be trusted. Emile's role as a double agent was over. Aimé was likely to come under suspicion, and a concerned Patrick started working on securing the travel papers that would allow him to move to South Africa. Robert had already left, rebasing in Belgium, although he was determined to put the material on the tapes to further use.

For Patrick, life under twenty-four-hour surveillance swiftly began to chafe. He found the constant scrutiny unbearable, he told me when we met in one of South Africa's anonymous malls. Oh, he liked the men well enough, he said, with a nod to his two shadows, sitting at a nearby table. "But their bosses don't want me doing this or that. Everything you do, anyone you meet, has to be prepared and agreed beforehand. It's impossible to be spontaneous."

Portia had adjusted best, but Elvis and Richard, he said, jibbed at the lack of freedom. "They are younger. No cinema. No sleepovers. They cannot bear to live like this."

Not only had foreign travel become impossible, but meetings had to be vetted beforehand, and he wasn't allowed to host friends at The Willows. As the months passed, Patrick came to feel the men protecting him were deliberately sabotaging his activist work. "Of course he couldn't stand it," recalls one South African judicial official. "He'd been the most powerful intelligence man in Central Africa and he was just trying to do his job."[1]

It was against this backdrop that Leah flew with Elvis to Knoxville, Tennessee, in January 2011, where she launched the laborious process of applying for political asylum in the United States. Located smack in the US Bible Belt, a city famous only for its association with the Everly Brothers, Knoxville seems at first glance a strange choice for a sophisticated African émigré carrying so much political baggage. The family's only connection was a distant cousin who had once worked there as a nurse.

But for Leah, the city's very parochialism was part of its appeal. Cities like New York or Washington host large African diaspora communities whose friendliness could not be taken for granted. The years of plots and pursuit had left her feeling hounded and distrustful.

"Here I feel safe," she told me when I interviewed her at her Knoxville home. "People here don't know anything about Rwanda or who I am. So I feel free." She joined a local Pentecostal church and signed up with a private company providing carers to the elderly. Richard joined the two at the end of the year.

"Patrick was happy for us to leave," says Leah. He had been haunted by the idea that he might be attacked while driving with the family and they could become collateral damage. At one stage, following a tip-off, South African intelligence briefly assigned a security detail to monitor Portia while she attended college in Cape Town. Patrick, back in bachelor mode, may have felt lonely at times in his overly large villa, but he felt less anxious, too. "It's better for me to fight these fights on my own," he told his wife.

But in late 2011, even as the trial of the men arrested for General Kayumba's attempted manslaughter was underway, relations between the South African authorities and the Rwandan dissidents took a nosedive.

"There was a strong altercation between Uncle and National Intelligence," recalls David Batenga. President Zuma was coming under relentless pressure from Kagame to extradite the two. South African companies were heavily invested in Rwanda, from Costco supermarkets to MTN cell phone networks. South Africa's mining companies worked the rich mineral seams of eastern DRC, and its weapons firms sold armored cars to Rwanda's army. Not to be on speaking terms with Kigali was immensely awkward.

Mo Shaik, South Africa's head of foreign intelligence, was asked to find a solution. What he came up with was suitably radical: "They wanted to relocate Uncle and the General to Haiti, to the Caribbean," recalls David.

The move would cut their geographical links with Africa, something they needed if the RNC was ever to amount to anything. And there was the small matter of their survival. The UN peacekeepers stationed in Haiti in the wake of the 2010 earthquake included a contingent of Rwandan police officers. Kigali had already demonstrated its readiness to dispatch agents across the African continent to liquidate them. The extra distance wasn't going to make a difference. "Uncle could have been extradited or finished off there," says David.

The General saw the Caribbean destination as no more than a way station. "We were to be renditioned through there. The final destination was Kigali, and the South Africans knew it."

The response was blunt. "Over my dead body," Patrick told South Africa's National Intelligence. The two men reminded their hosts that they not only held South African resident status but were logged with the UN as political refugees. David recalls, "Only UNHCR had the power to move him, Uncle pointed out."

Over the next few years the South Africans would keep pushing the Caribbean option, sending teams of intelligence officials to reconnoiter possible venues and work out the costs of round-the-clock private security there. The General and Patrick were even offered a generous financial package to move. They refused to budge. Understandably suspicious now, the two men both wondered if Zuma would eventually give way. "Uncle started being wary of their intentions," says David.

Then a small incident triggered an irrevocable decision. One evening, Patrick discovered that the South African bodyguards assigned to his protection had quietly clocked off, locking him inside The Willows and disappearing with the keys. "I ran away from a prison only to be in a prison again here," he complained to Leah over the phone.

It was different for the General, he told a Ugandan friend. In contrast with Patrick, General Kayumba had never spent time in detention, and he didn't balk at the relentless surveillance. "But I do," Patrick said. Given the choice between safety without freedom or freedom without safety, Patrick opted for the latter. "No more security guards," he announced.

Never lacking in self-confidence, he believed he would always be one step ahead of his enemy. "He was overconfident, I think," recalls Theogene. "He knew the way Kagame worked and he felt he could outsmart them. The tapings would have emboldened Patrick, encouraged him to let down his guard. 'I know the plot, I'm on top of it,' he'd have thought. But he was taking a calculated risk."

Informing South African intelligence that he would be taking responsibility for his own safety in the future, Patrick moved into a small villa in Krugersdorp, a brand-new housing estate, but a robbery one night swiftly exposed the weakness of its security system. David was the one who suggested trying the Featherbrooke Estate in Ruimsig. With a permanently manned barrier and gate, the estate boasted South Africa's latest in security technology. It was not 100 percent foolproof, but nothing ever could be. "He was a fatalist," says David. He would say, "If you're meant to die like this, you'll die. You can't run."

It was a brave—perhaps foolhardy—decision, given that he had just learned of a new plot to end his life.

•

In February 2012, Jennifer Rwamugira, an oncological nurse working at the Rwandan Military Hospital in Kigali, was called in for questioning by the then head of the NISS, General Karenzi Karake, usually known as "KK."

Jennifer tells me the story sitting on the deserted terrace of a funereally quiet hotel in Centurion overlooking a yellowing, fetid stretch of water, a venue of her choosing. The meeting has involved the customary wary email jousting and she has brought along a de facto bodyguard, a former Rwandan army officer. But she has the confidence of a career woman who has reached the point in life where she knows exactly what she wants to say.[2]

At NISS headquarters, Jennifer was kept waiting for five or six hours—a simple but effective technique for demonstrating who is in control. The general never did make an appearance, but Jennifer could guess why she was there. It was because of her connection to Kennedy Gihana, RNC secretary-general.

Jennifer had met Kennedy while she was studying nursing at Tshwane University of Technology in Pretoria—two Rwandans drawn together by their unfamiliarity with a foreign culture. The two had become close friends, and since Kennedy's role in the RNC brought him into close contact with Patrick and the General, she, too, had ended up socializing with the two prominent dissidents. "Karegeya and Kayumba were like parents to me. We were like family."

When Kennedy mentioned that he felt ready to marry, she had written a letter of introduction to her younger sister back in Rwanda, who she thought might make a good match. Once the two were married in a traditional ceremony, her sister had flown to South Africa to live with Kennedy there. As for Jennifer, she had returned to Kigali—a decision she came to regret.

As she sat waiting for "KK," her husband, who also worked in intelligence, grew so alarmed that he called Lieutenant Colonel Franco Rutagengwa, one of KK's subordinates. "They're going to kill my wife," he said, begging for help. Jennifer was moved to Franco's office, and the serious questioning began. "Look here, Jennifer . . . " began the colonel. What Rwandan intelligence wanted, he explained, was her help in compiling a dossier on the RNC.

It was the first of many interrogations, staged three times a week. "They wanted me to say that the RNC was planning to bring down the government, setting off bombs." When Jennifer showed reluctance, Franco threatened her. "She thinks she's being clever but anything could happen to her," he warned her husband, who begged her to play ball. Franco outlined the unappetizing fates that had befallen various members of Patrick's and the General's families. "They gave me a lot of examples of what had happened to them," she says.

Then her PhD supervisor at Wits University sent her an invitation to defend her doctorate in South Africa.

"Franco knew about the invitation before I did. He came to my home the night before I left. He was there till 2 a.m., trying to tell me what to do. He said they would help accommodate me in South Africa, to get close to the General, Patrick, Kennedy, and Frank [Ntwali] and update them on their thinking. They wanted me to report back on all the RNC meetings and what was being said."

When Jennifer asked how she was supposed to communicate with her handlers, Franco gave her a cell phone with $150 in credit. Whenever she socialized with the RNC leadership, she was to buzz him—call his phone just once—then go to her room and wait for him to call back.

Instead, on her arrival in South Africa, Jennifer threw away the phone, briefed Kennedy on what had happened, and told her boss at the Rwandan Military Hospital she would not be returning. Franco switched to relaying messages via her husband. She was sent $500 in cash to be spent on phone credit and four new SIM cards. She was to alternate these in her handset on a weekly basis, the better to escape detection.

The envisaged scenario was the one Dan Munyuza had already sketched out for other exiles. "They said they could give me a poison to give [RNC members]. They told me, 'It can't be diagnosed if you get sick, you can put it in their drink when they go to the bathroom,'" says Jennifer.

Franco was none too fussy as to the victim. "He said if I could poison all of the inner circle—Kennedy, Frank, Emile, Karegeya, the General—it would be great, but the most important were Karegeya and the General. They knew I had a lot of access. They thought it would be easy for me." Once again, the hit-and-miss nature of the approach is one of the most disturbing things about it.

Bizarrely, Jennifer's willingness to include her own brother-in-law among her targets was taken for granted. The psychopath struggles to recognize that not all human beings feel as little as he does. Rwandan intelligence was showing similar tunnel vision, struggling to grasp such basic concepts as family affection, the ties of friendship, or even a principled rejection of violence. When Jennifer pointed out that she would be violating her nurse's professional code of conduct, Franco was reassuring: "Don't worry, you can do this." She could become a government minister, he suggested, at the very least she would be given a medal.

As the realization that she would not play ball slowly set in, her handlers went one grotesque step further, revealing the stunted extent of their moral universe. Finally accepting that Jennifer was of no use to them, they asked her to speak to her sister. "They wanted me to talk to my sister and get her to do the job and poison Kennedy." *Do us a favor, will you, love, and kill your husband and the father of your children?*

"They're sick," she comments. "They really need help."

Instructions about discreet "buzzing" had now been abandoned. She was given a new handler, who kept calling, sometimes twice a day. Instead of cooperating, she told Patrick—"such a sweet, funny man!"—everything, becoming yet another stool pigeon turning double agent. The topic became a joke between the two. If she was with Patrick when her phone rang, he would laugh and say, "You should answer that!"[3]

•

There were plenty of other indications of just how closely the RNC's founding members and those close to them were being tracked by Kigali, and how willing sovereign African countries were to pander to the Rwandan president's well-known touchiness in order to keep the peace.

In June 2012, Portia was returning from a visit to her grandmother in Mbarara when, in the early hours of the morning, she was pulled off a flight she had just boarded at Entebbe, bound for South Africa.[4]

Ugandan immigration officials told her that her Rwandan passport had been canceled, and she would be unable to fly on. Baffled by the instructions he was receiving from on high, the head of immigration took the tear-streaked student to see General Kale Kayihura, Uganda's head of police, a man who knew her father. To her amazement, he said, "We hear that you like to abuse the president on Facebook." He meant Kagame.

"I remember I actually laughed, from shock. 'Are you, the Ugandan police chief, sitting in front of someone with zero power and influence, a twenty-two-year-old student, and telling me that the reason

I can't fly to school is because the president is on Facebook?' *What*???
I Skyped my dad and said, 'Why wouldn't anyone in authority say
"this is nonsense"?'"

She would spend the next few months in self-imposed house arrest
at her aunt's house in Kampala—"The police told me, 'This could escalate, so don't go out on the streets,'"—as Patrick pulled strings to
get her the alternative passport she needed in order to leave.

The image of Kagame poring over the Facebook entries of his
former colleagues' children, choking back his anger as he registers
the jibes among the emojis, LOLs, and exclamation marks, is almost
as comic as it is sinister.

In August 2012, another, far more serious, incident illustrated the
risks the dissidents were running.[5] Driving to a meeting near Oliver Tambo International, RNC regional chairman Frank Ntwali was
pulled over on the freeway by what appeared to be a police car, lights
flashing. Having verified Ntwali's identity, the two supposed officers
pulled out knives and attacked from both sides, stabbing him repeatedly in the shoulders and back. During the assault, which left Ntwali
hospitalized, his wallet went ignored. The police car later turned out
to have been stolen.

A disturbingly similar event occurred after Gervais Condo, one
of the signatories of the RNC's founding proclamation, flew in from
the United States for his first face-to-face meeting with Patrick and
the General.

The recruitment of Condo, a tall, burly, Francophone Hutu who
had served as a parliamentary deputy and diplomat under Habyarimana, represented a major coup for the movement, but the three
men had communicated until then via Skype. The visit gave Condo
a chance to meet his new collaborators, but also a taste of the hair-
raising risks RNC membership brought with it.

With Patrick, now without South African minders, at the wheel,
Condo had gone to pick up a third RNC member at the airport.
As they drove back across the veldt, a car attempted to flag them
down. "I was in the passenger seat, they were in the other lane, and
I could see three men, showing us their police badges," Condo told
me. "They did it once, twice, three times—the guy we'd got in the
back began shaking, he was so frightened—but Patrick refused to
stop, making a gesture of 'off with you.'"[6]

There was nothing discreet about the approach, which was staged in the middle of the day. "We'll never know if they were just bandits, or had been following us from the airport," said Condo. "But Patrick said, 'You never know what happens if you stop.'"

Condo remembers registering the stark contrast between the General's and Patrick's respective security arrangements—one under constant surveillance, the other roaming at will, often alone—and raising the issue with the latter. Patrick shrugged off his concerns. "He said, 'It can happen, it might not happen. I felt I was in prison.'"

Rwandan intelligence, with him gone, was nothing like as impressive as they believed, Patrick assured the others. "The trouble with you guys is you think Rwanda's intelligence is James Bond. But I was James Bond, and I left."

But friends noted that a certain resigned fatalism had crept into Patrick's behavior. "One time, we were at a friend's house, looking across at some trees, and I made some remark about how that would be a good place for a sniper to be positioned," remembers Frank Ntwali. "Patrick laughed dismissively and said, 'That's the trouble with Rwandans, they always see murder everywhere.'"

Trying to keep his spirits up, Patrick focused on the task in hand, which included the creation of a short-wave radio station to complement Radio Itahuka, the RNC's internet-based mouthpiece, already set up by Theogene. He reached out to Rwandan journalists in the diaspora, but most of them proved reluctant to support the project, either too scared or wary of the notion that a former intelligence chief could now turn media boss.

Serge Ndayizeye, half Hutu, half Tutsi, saw things differently. Granted asylum in the United States and based in Louisiana, he had no journalistic training, but with coaching from Patrick, Radio Impala, a platform for the broader opposition, eventually saw the light of day.

"Patrick would call on Skype or WhatsApp to discuss the program's contents each morning, always smartly dressed, shaved, and showered," Serge remembers. "He'd give me advice, comments. It was important to send out a consistent message, he said, not to deviate from the main theme. 'Keep it simple. Never forget that what you are doing is propaganda,' he would always say."[7]

In mid-2012 there was at least some cheering news. The contents of a report drawn up by a UN group of experts investigating militia groups operating in eastern Democratic Republic of Congo were leaked.[8] Rwanda had long denied any involvement with the March 23 Movement (M23), a group of Congolese Tutsis that had established a de facto administration on the border between DRC, Rwanda, and Uganda, levying taxes on the local population, extracting minerals, and recruiting child soldiers.

The report said precisely the opposite, accusing the authorities in Kigali, in keeping with Rwanda's long tradition of muscular intervention in the region, of providing M23's fighters with ammunition, training, and reinforcements. It cited James Kabarebe and Jack Nziza by name.

For once, the donors reacted. The European Union, Netherlands, Germany, France, Sweden, and the United States announced they would be freezing aid to Kigali. The United States' war crimes office went so far as to warn Rwanda's leadership that it might face charges of "aiding and abetting" crimes against humanity in DRC, just as Liberian president Charles Taylor had done for supporting rebels in neighboring Sierra Leone.[9] In Britain, the outgoing Andrew Mitchell authorized one last aid payment, only to see the move overturned by his successor.[10]

Patrick had been one of the many sources consulted by the UN experts. No one knew better than he the makeup of the many rebel groups operating in the Kivus, the various commanders' quirks and histories. Over the following year, he would continue supplying information about Rwanda's covert role in the Kivus to the intelligence services of Tanzania and South Africa, both due to contribute troops to a special UN brigade in DRC. He had opposed Rwanda's meddling in its giant neighbor's affairs since 1998, and now he'd been given an opportunity to jinx it.

•

In May 2013, Patrick's counterespionage operation was dealt an unexpected blow—Aimé Ntabana suddenly disappeared in Kampala. The first domino in a long column of mahogany and ivory that would eventually lead to the intelligence chief's murder had just toppled, but no one in the South African diaspora had heard its quiet click.

"He went to have a coffee with a guy with links to the Rwandan embassy and he never came home," says David Batenga. "We don't know if he's dead or alive, but we assume the worst. He was a resourceful kid, and if he was in jail he'd have contacted us by now."

Fretting, Patrick thought of going to the media with the story. Leah remembers that it was Apollo, Aimé's old friend, who persuaded him not to. "Patrick used to tell him, 'Aimé has disappeared, we need to talk about it,' and that boy would say, 'Let's wait and see.'"

Apollo was another one of the "Kigali boys," useful to military intelligence for his contacts in the old regime and instinctive understanding of pre-genocide Rwanda. Apollo came from a well-to-do Muslim family—his parents had once controlled Rwanda's gasoline distribution. A former classmate remembers him as "a sweet and harmless boy" and adds, "When news broke of Karegeya's assassination, what shocked us all was not that Karegeya had been killed—that was always on the cards—but that Apollo, of all people, had been involved!"11

Apollo owned the $1 million Cine Star cinema complex in Nyamirambo, Kigali's Muslim district, and enjoyed the freewheeling lifestyle of the playboy businessman, traveling widely in the Middle East and Europe, where he was briefly detained on suspicion of drug trafficking. Then in 1994 Rwanda acquired grimly puritanical new masters, and adjustments had to be made.

"Apollo's big mistake was not to realize that he was living in a different Rwanda," says a Western intelligence official who worked in Kigali during that period. "He'd grown up in a country where you could more or less speak your mind. He didn't realize he was now in a Rwanda where you were under constant scrutiny. He was just a soft, spoiled boy who had no idea who he was messing with."12

The blunder that brought Apollo to the RPF's attention was the purchase of a Porsche Cayenne, complete with a personalized number plate. "No one in Rwanda at the time had a Porsche Cayenne," said my intelligence source. "If anyone was going to buy one, it should have been someone in the RPF. So they jailed him, to show him what was what." Apollo was sentenced for "human trafficking"—helping fellow nationals flee the country.

Head of external intelligence at the time, Patrick helped spring Apollo from prison, but like so many before him, the young man discovered that freedom came with strings attached. "Patrick told him,

'Now you know who runs the show. And in return for your freedom, you'll work for us,'" said my source. He had joined Patrick's secret army.

Apollo's business interests often took him to the Congolese lakeside town of Goma, which sits smack on the border with Rwanda, a natural gathering point for Tutsi traders, militia leaders, Congolese politicians, diamond dealers, arms traffickers, and soldiers-for-hire. There Patrick used him as bait, encouraging Apollo to shoot his mouth off about his problems with Kigali and see who pricked up their ears and echoed his complaints, coaxing dissent to show its face. The supreme irony is that Apollo's side job was always entrapment, his specialty luring regime opponents to dodgy rendezvous. Yet when the very technique Patrick had coached him in was turned upon himself, Patrick would fail to spot the glint of the trap's steel jaws opening.

Apollo's position in Patrick's affections had in part been cemented by the latter's time in prison. Apollo had been one of the few Rwandans outside Patrick's immediate family brave enough to visit him when he'd been serving jail time in Kigali. It was the kind of gesture Patrick was not likely to forget.

The playboy's friendship with Aimé was another factor in winning Patrick's trust. Once Patrick went into exile, Apollo, like Aimé, continued feeding him information. But clearly, at some stage, Rwandan intelligence spotted what both young men were doing. The two friends went on to make very different choices—perhaps it boiled down to the presence, or absence, of an instinct of self-preservation.

With his cover blown on the release of the tapes, Aimé had every reason to keep a low profile. Instead, his lack of discrimination when it came to socializing with Rwandan visitors in the bars and nightspots of Kampala and Entebbe raised eyebrows among contemporaries. "Aimé was reckless somehow," recalls Robert Higiro, who met up with him passing through Uganda. "If someone called him up, he'd just go and meet them."

Subsequent events have convinced many in the RNC that Apollo was intimately involved in Aimé's disappearance, which coincided with an interlude in which Apollo went mysteriously off radar. "I think Apollo may have been the one to make Aimé die," says Leah Karegeya. But in this murky world of informants, agents, double agents, treason, and lies, it's hard to know who betrayed whom to Rwandan intelligence.

What is clear is that while Apollo is alive and well, Aimé has not been seen since, and his name, often misspelled, is included in the lists drawn up by Rwanda human rights groups of Kagame's victims. His last entries on his Facebook page date back to April 2013. After that there are only worried comments from family and friends, clearly prompted by the automatic birthday reminder Facebook sends out each October. "If you are alive happy birthday and if you are gone rest in peace," reads one poignant entry from Leah. "Je te souhaite d'être encore en vie pour nous," reads another—"I hope you are still alive for us."

Aimé's disappearance not only removed from the scene a key agent who could have alerted Patrick to the fact that Apollo had been "turned" by Rwandan intelligence, but left Patrick more dependent than ever on the news Apollo brought from Kigali.

Patrick's entourage was surprised—and uneasy—at the intimate contact the former spy chief now granted the young man, who was occasionally to be found tucking into breakfast at Patrick's kitchen table in Ruimsig. "I started suspecting Apollo after we lost Aimé," remembers Emile. "Patrick should have paid more attention."

If Emile was distrustful of Apollo on knee-jerk grounds—"It's hard to trust a Muslim," he grunts—he also had more considered reasons. "Apollo's profile was not clear. He was someone who was very interested in money. He came to Patrick from Rwanda and went back to Rwanda—in intelligence you deal with that sort of person from a distance, because he has 100 percent access. I told Patrick, 'Be careful, this is the one who can kill you'—I told him straight."

But Apollo kept shuttling in and out of South Africa. He now dangled as bait the supposed defection of a top Rwandan general said to be on increasingly strained terms with Kagame. Just like Aimé, Apollo also professed to be anxious about his own safety, and raised the possibility of a permanent move with a sympathetic Patrick, who promised to do what he could to help.

Apollo, Patrick's friends realize now, was probably casing the joint. To access Patrick's gated Featherbrooke Estate, tenants used fingerprint identification. When visitors were arriving or leaving, the security men at the gate would call the tenant's personal cell number for permission. So while Apollo could access Featherbrooke when he was by Patrick's side, if anything happened to his host, he'd be unable to get out. He must have advised his handlers that a hit there would be unwise—hence the charade at the Michelangelo.

The last time Emile met Apollo was in early 2013. When he dropped in at the Featherbrooke estate, Patrick mentioned he had a visitor sleeping upstairs. "Do you have a new wife?" joked Emile. "No, this Swahili guy"—"Swahili" being lazy shorthand for "Muslim"—"is staying here." Emile was taken aback. "One day I'm going to come over and Kagame himself will open the door," he quipped, but he was genuinely alarmed. "I told Patrick, 'Someone coming from Rwanda, even if he's your friend, your brother, you don't put them up in your house. He could poison your coffee.'"

"You're right," acknowledged Patrick. But then he quoted an old Kinyarwanda saying: "You never know who will kill you."

Later, Emile noticed an unfamiliar silver phone, Apollo's, charging on the kitchen counter. This was no ordinary model. "It was a huge phone, a BlackBerry model I've never seen before, really heavy. I asked Apollo, 'Where did you buy that?' He told me he got it in Qatar, that it cost him $10,000 and that it was a model you could only buy in Arab countries, a model no one could ever trace you on.

"Patrick picked it up and he said, 'You were robbed.' We made it like a joke. But now I wonder what that phone was doing. The guy was already on mission by then, and he was on the inside." Maybe, muses Emile, James Kabarebe was listening in on the device.

That afternoon, Emile and Patrick agreed to ferry Apollo, who said he was in town to buy a consignment of spare tires, to the American Express office in Sandton to change money. Emile was driving, Apollo sitting directly behind him. As they headed for the highway, Emile felt the hairs rising on the back of his neck: his military instincts kicking in. He was responsible for Patrick's security, but the seating arrangement meant his head was an easy target for a point-blank shot from behind, his hands were busy, and the concealed weapon he was authorized to carry hard to reach.

"A really strange feeling came over me, so I stopped the car and told Patrick, 'Come and drive,' and told Apollo to sit in front, so

Patrick could show him the sights." As the three men changed positions, Emile muttered to Patrick, "This is not security, I'm the one with the gun and I'm the one who is driving." To Apollo, he cracked another one of those not-really-funny jokes at which Rwandans excel. "Go tell Kigali that Emile doesn't trust you," he said.

It was the last time the playboy businessman and the self-assigned bodyguard would meet. Emile is convinced his overly revealing words were faithfully relayed to Apollo's minders in Rwanda, and the necessary adjustments made. "I'm sure he went to Kigali and said, 'Emile doesn't trust me and he's always carrying a gun.' So they made sure to separate us."

The next time Apollo came over, Emile reckons, he told Patrick, "I don't want Emile to know." Emile adds: "If you said to Patrick, 'Come alone,' he was the kind of guy who'd respect that. So the next time they met, I was not around. Kigali knew very well that without me, Patrick would have no security."

After losing a loved one, the mental torture of "what if" and "if only" is hard to resist. Particularly in a situation in which a man was hired expressly to prevent what happened from happening. "I can promise you," says Emile. "If I'd been there, I would never have allowed Patrick to go to that room alone."

•

Ennui, that gray sense of hopelessness so often coupled with an acid awareness of personal failure, is the exile's curse. By 2013, the journalists, former spies, and diplomats who called on Patrick when they passed through Johannesburg, arranging meetings scrupulously staged in public places, registered a steady leaching away of the ebullience that had been his hallmark.

A business analyst friend who had moved to Oslo urged Patrick to relocate in Norway, but the thought of those long winter nights and all that Scandinavian earnestness, so at odds with his impish personality, did not appeal.

He had already formally applied for political asylum in the United States, a move that would have allowed him to join Leah and the kids. But both parents struggled to imagine Patrick in Tennessee. "When I got to Knoxville I looked around me and I thought, ah-ah. This is not for Patrick," says Leah. Since the Department of Homeland Security showed no sign of being swayed by the case he'd made, the decision was, in any case, out of their hands.

The excitement of the taping project was over, and Kigali's relentless global campaign continued notwithstanding. In one shocking demonstration of its reach, former presidential bodyguard Lieutenant Joel Mutabazi, supposedly under twenty-four-hour protection in Kampala, had been snatched by six Ugandan police officers and handed over to the Rwandan authorities, along with Innocent Kalisa, another army officer who had jumped ship.[13] The RNC believed the operation had been coordinated by René Rutagungira, a former Rwandan soldier who had reinvented himself as a Kampala-based businessman, but was suspected of serving as Kagame's eyes and ears in Uganda.

Ahead of Patrick lay decades of campaigning and politicking, trying to turn the RNC into a viable entity. The man who had helped overturn first a Ugandan and then a Rwandan regime knew exactly how much hard grind that would involve. Driving along Gauteng's buzzing freeways, shuttling from one antiseptic mall to another, Patrick registered the thoroughness of his alienation. It had been three years since he'd spent any quality time with the kids. He had lost his home, his livelihood, and his family and was now trapped in a country preoccupied with its own apartheid story, where Rwanda's tragedy held no resonance at all.

Worse than all of this, for a man now in his fifties, must have been his horror at the belated realization of the huge part he'd played in creating the regime he was now fighting, installing a fresh dictatorship to replace the one blithely toppled by his younger self—a young man whose driving impulses he struggled to understand.

He was ready now to admit to things he had once vehemently denied. He could no longer see the rationale of crimes he—like all the RPF elite—had once told himself were necessary sacrifices. At our last meeting, he told me he'd been reading Alexis de Tocqueville on democracy, biographies of Napoleon Bonaparte and Abraham Lincoln, trying to work out the riddles of despotism and hierarchy, revolution and power.

"I feel I was brainwashed, and I am only now waking up," he confessed. "It's taken that long. The thing is that if you keep being told something is right, over and over again, if everyone says the same thing, you do end up believing it. Looking back, I feel I am not the same person I was before. I don't recognize him."

Patrick Smith, veteran editor of the authoritative *Africa Confidential* newsletter, noticed that the man who had once held court in the Umubano Hotel's gardens in Kigali, uncrowned prince of the Kagame regime, looked pale and unhealthy. "He was in bad shape," Smith told me. "God knows Patrick always used to drink a lot, but now it was truly gargantuan amounts."

Hrvoje Hranjski, the Associated Press's former correspondent in Kigali, rang regularly from Manila, where he'd been posted as bureau chief, and the two men hatched wistful, never-never plans for Patrick to visit the Philippines. Patrick was anxious to reach out to Samantha Power, who had been nominated US ambassador to the United Nations. Patrick had met her in the mid-1990s, while she was in Kigali researching her seminal book on genocide, a time when Patrick was at the height of his powers. She was exactly the kind of influential player whose views on Rwanda Patrick hoped to sway.[14] "Our last phone call was in November or December 2013," Hranjski recalls. "Patrick said, 'They're after us. But we're taking precautions.' I wish I'd recorded that conversation now."

The *London Times* correspondent in South Africa, Jonathan Clayton, who had gotten to know Patrick as Reuters bureau chief in Nairobi during the same period, also registered the toll the years had taken when he met Patrick in a mall halfway between Pretoria and Johannesburg, six weeks before his death.

"He wasn't in any way boastful or backslapping," remembers Clayton. "Just rueful, modest, quiet and reflective. Definitely looking back and wondering—as we all do—where it had all gone wrong. And you could tell that he was struggling to make ends meet."[15]

Poverty reveals itself in myriad small ways: scuffed shoes, a fraying shirt collar, a jacket baggy from overuse. Another former journalist friend was startled to be asked for a short-term loan. Patrick, who had always played the role of generous family provider, was struggling to cover his children's school and university fees.

Sometimes Patrick would pick up his smartphone and randomly call one of the high-ranking Rwandan officials who had shucked off their friendship as neatly as a snake shedding its skin. All their

phones, he knew, were being monitored. What more exquisite scenario could there be than a former colleague having to laboriously
explain to the ever-suspicious Kagame just why he was chatting to an
enemy of the people?

But such moments of mischief were increasingly rare. When an
American photographer friend passed through Johannesburg, he
stayed the night at Patrick's place. Spooked by the thought of being
raided by a hit squad, the guest was unable to sleep. The two ended
up talking till 3 a.m. about Patrick's worries for his children, his fears
for the future, the years he had spent as a half-naked herdboy following his father's cattle as they meandered across the hills: a past
that now seemed one of idyllic innocence.

"He'd become—how can I put it—less of an asshole," the photographer told me. "The Patrick who'd come to meet you at Kigali
airport in a brand-new sports sedan and drive you through town with
one hand on the wheel, so arrogant and full of himself, was gone.
He'd suffered, and this time he showed the vulnerable side of himself, soft, human, and fragile. He was full of regrets."[16]

The habitual bravado was now underscored by bone-deep despair.
He was conscious of living in borrowed time. "He knew the rules.
He'd written the rule book, after all," said a friend from the Uganda
days. "He must have realized what he'd created was too good for them
to allow it to be destroyed."[17]

Meeting him at the Michelangelo, Patrick's ex-MI6 buddy was dis-
mayed by his mood of heedless nihilism: "He was the most depressed
I've seen him, strolling casually from garage to foyer without a sideways glance, taking no notice of possible surveillance. He referred to
himself as 'a dead man walking.'"

Veteran human rights investigator Carina Tertsakian, whose reports on Rwanda for Amnesty International and Human Rights Watch
had been a thorn in the regime's side over the years, saw the same
weary flippancy when she met Patrick on the fringes of a conference
in Johannesburg.[18]

"He drove up on his own to the hotel as you and I would, parked,
and walked over to where I was sitting. When I said, 'Are you crazy?
How can you drive around like that?' he just gave that big Patrick
laugh and said, 'Don't worry about me, my dear, I'm already dead.'"

The run-up to Christmas 2013 provided yet another warning—if any were needed—of what dangers lay in wait for RNC members. Zigzagging across the road, a BMW crashed straight into Kennedy Gihana's car when he was driving through Pretoria. "He hit the car on the side, exactly where I was sitting," says Kennedy. His femur was broken in two places.[19] Although it was yet another one of those incidents that could be passed off as the result of South Africa's famously dangerous roads, Kennedy is in no doubt it was another hit ordered by Kigali.

The scream from Patrick's mental siren should have been deafening. But there are few things more exhausting than maintaining a state of constant alertness. And in Patrick's mood of grim personal reckoning, what could have been more welcome than a visit from his friend Apollo? That mindset must explain behavior many have found baffling in a hardened former intelligence chief.

An old intelligence friend in Kampala ruefully ponders Patrick's final recklessness: "What's shocking is that all Patrick's meetings were in bars and restaurants, out in open spaces. How he got into that hotel room, I just don't know." And then he echoed the fatalistic credo Patrick himself so often expressed: "I guess it was just his time."[20]

THE HOE

Rwanda's Mwami,
Rudahigwa Mutara III,
visits Brussels in April 1949.

*Photo Inforcongo,
Collection RMCA Tervuren.*

Fred Rwigyema.
New Vision.

Young rebel leader
Yoweri Museveni
is sworn in as
Ugandan president
in Kampala in 1986.

*William Campbell,
Getty Images.*

CHAPTER FIVE

MY ROOTS ARE BURIED HERE

The ache for home lives in all of us. The safe place
where we can go as we are and not be questioned.

—Maya Angelou

Few capitals come greener than Kampala.

Sprawling, like Rome, across seven hills, Uganda's largest city nudges the equator, and at this latitude vegetation runs riot. Flapping fronds of *matooke* and banana fringe the toffee-colored slopes, gardens sprout papaya and avocado trees, avenues are lined with jacaranda and flame trees, and hedges of hibiscus and bougainvillea serve as road divides. The city where the RPF's key figures spent their formative adult years looks, from a distance, like a giant bowl of salad, ripe for munching.

Such lushness drew admiring sighs from white explorers who stumbled upon the kingdom of Buganda in the 1850s. "I felt inclined to stop here a month, everything was so very pleasant," wrote John Hanning Speke. "Wherever I strolled I saw nothing but richness and what ought to be wealth. The whole land was a picture of Quiescent beauty, with a boundless sea in the background."[1]

Nestling in the hills north of what the locals called Nnalubale, but Speke baptized Lake Victoria, Buganda was a sophisticated, centuries-old kingdom that had thrown sturdy roads and aqueducts across surrounding territory. Ruled over by a feared *kabaka*, it boasted a fleet of 230 war canoes and a 125,000-strong army, which was regularly dispatched to fight its great main rival, the Bunyoro kingdom to the northwest.

Like the Swahili traders who had preceded them, offering guns in exchange for ivory, the new arrivals left convinced this was a land ripe for the plucking, and they took that message back to their European capitals. As the partitioning of the continent, dubbed the Scramble for Africa, got underway, Catholic White Fathers from France—supported by Germany—vied with Protestant missionaries from Britain and Muslim traders from Zanzibar for the souls of the Kabaka and his subjects. A series of religious civil wars broke out between their converts.

The British eventually won the contest and a pact was signed with the Baganda, whose forces were then deployed to subdue Bunyoro and Acholiland to the north, while treaties were agreed with the neighboring kingdoms of Ankole and Busoga to the west and east.

The Imperial British East Africa Company was granted the right to run Uganda and given the task of building a 660-mile railway from Mombasa to Lake Victoria's eastern shores, the better to tap the interior's wealth. But the task proved too much for the company. In 1894 London took over, and the protectorate of Uganda was declared.

In contrast to Kenya, a settler colony, Uganda was administered under a system of indirect rule, with the British delegating authority to Baganda officials who fanned out from the capital. But they could be just as high-handed and contemptuous of local ways as any white outsider, insisting on their *matooke* food staple, way of dressing, and Luganda language being adopted.

As it edged toward independence, Uganda was a highly polarized territory, divided by language, religion, and ethnicity. The main fracture line ran between the neglected north and the cotton-producing, prosperous south. But the south had its tensions, too: between Baganda royalists bent on independence and non-Baganda; Democratic Party (DP) members aggrieved at their Catholic community's second-class status and the dominant Protestant Uganda People's Congress (UPC). When the Union Flag was lowered in October 1962, independent Uganda's course looked decidedly wobbly.

In most African countries, a portrait of the president hangs in every office and over every shop counter, more quiet recognition of who is boss than gesture of affection. The lobby of the *Monitor* newspaper office in Kampala boasts not one, but nine such portraits, marking Uganda's ten presidencies: Edward Mutesa (the Kabaka), Milton Obote, General Idi Amin, Yusuf Lule, Godfrey Binaisa, Paulo Muwanga, Obote (again, only worse this time), General Bazilio Olara-Okello (just two days), General Tito Okello, and Yoweri Museveni.

Perhaps the gallery is management's way of tactfully embracing a range of political opinion, or perhaps it's a discreet warning of just how easily things can and have gone wrong, for at least two of those faces come with associations of pure horror.

Modern Uganda, historians always remind their readers, has never experienced a peaceful transfer of power. Kampala's most striking feature—the marabou storks that hypnotically ride its warm eddies, wheeling like vampires over slums and prosperous neighborhoods alike—were once attributed to the human carrion left littering the streets by rival militias vying for control of the seven hills. Those kinds of memories have a long reach.

Taking the oath of office on January 29, 1986, Bible in hand and a bewigged white chief justice at his side, Yoweri Museveni promised an end to all that: "Nobody is to think that what is happening to-day, what has been happening in the last few days is a mere change of guard. . . . [T]his is a fundamental change in the politics of our government."[2]

Young and trim, dressed in green fatigues and flanked by fighters of his National Resistance Army (NRA), Museveni still spoke with the western Ugandan accent that labeled him a Munyankole "country bumpkin" in the eyes of the Baganda aristocracy. "The problem of Africa in general and Uganda in particular is not the people but leaders who want to overstay in power," he wrote in a book published that year.

Museveni, or "M7," as he is known, is thicker-set and better-spoken these days, and his presidency, in its sixth term and third decade at time of writing, drips irony. There's no talk of quitting now. "I am the one who hunted and killed the animal. Now they want me to go, where should I go?" he tells voters.[3] After violent brawls in the Ugandan parliament, the age limit preventing him from running for yet another election was scrapped in 2017, paving the way for his own presidency for life.[4]

109

Impatience among Uganda's millennials and members of Generation Z—who have never known any other president—is rising, as the violence in the runup to the 2021 elections demonstrated. At home, Museveni is the man who knows every backstory and who can call in a million favors. "It's like France under Louis XIV, 'L'État c'est moi,'" a Ugandan businessman tells me, half admiringly, half in exasperation. Abroad, Museveni has become the Grand Old Man of East Africa, a spider sitting at the heart of a regional web of interference and influence.

The former schoolteacher always knew his rebel group was destined to be more than a forgettable garble of initials. An ideologically driven pan-African liberation crusade, the National Resistance Movement (NRM) saw its mandate as exporting change across the continent, and it has certainly done that, if rarely in the purely altruistic way originally envisaged. Museveni achieved that ambition thanks to the special bond he forged with one beleaguered ethnic community in particular, the one into which Patrick, General Kayumba, and Paul Kagame were all born.

•

Their story starts in the subregion of Ankole, 170 miles west of Kampala, a four-hour drive along one of East Africa's key arteries, the Kampala-Masaka-Mbarara highway, which tracks the northern shores of Lake Victoria before plunging into the Central African hinterland. It's a road used by every truck, bus, and pickup from Uganda, South Sudan, or Kenya heading toward Rwanda, Tanzania, and the Democratic Republic of Congo's landlocked east.

Once you leave the capital, you are soon in classic Buganda countryside. Majestic mango trees line the road and in their shade women preside over kiosks, selling phone scratch cards, cupcakes, and cartons of milk, keeping an eye on children playing on the orange earth. *Boda boda* motorbike drivers sit astride their steeds, waiting for business.

Even before you cross the equator the landscape begins to change. The *matooke* plantations and plots of cassava and maize give way to undulating wetlands, papyrus seas rustling with snakes, insects, and birdlife.

The villages are simple affairs, rows of single-story *amadukas* clustered along one main drag. Brilliantly painted, these stores double as de facto advertisements for popular local products: "Sadolin: Colour your World," "My Paka Paka. Uganda's No One network," "Mo Kash. My Savings, My Loans," and the ubiquitous Coca-Cola, red as arterial blood, with its instantly recognizable swirl of a logo. Stop for gas, and youngsters in white, red, or blue overalls—each village boasts a different color—rush the car, thrusting cool sodas and beef skewers through any open window.

Gradually, the landscape becomes barer and drier. The vast trees and palms give way to scraggy thorn bushes. The livestock shifts, too. Friesians imported from Europe produce more milk than indigenous breeds, but they struggle with the heat. The farther west you go, the more often you spot herds of long-horned Ankole, the giant cattle cherished by African presidents, wending their way through the anthills and euphorbia cactus like modern-day mammoths.

One of Museveni's tricks is to invite dignitaries to visit him at his ranch in Rwakitura, where he chats about affairs of state while watching his herd file past: he knows the name of each bull, cow, and calf. It drives home the message that the president remains a man of the people, a simple African herdsman at heart.

The turnoff from the highway to Rwakitura, about forty miles east of Mbarara, is impossible to miss. Yellow election campaign posters are usually plastered to its signpost and the tarmac is as smooth as dark glass. The avenues and driveways leading to presidents' homes are always the best in Africa.

No mango trees now: the bones of the hills protrude through the black cotton soil; the grass looks like a dry, browning pelt; and the occasional scarlet flash of a flame tree provides the only moments of color. This land is officially gazetted as Lake Mburo National Park, and the number of cattle strictly controlled, but it still looks old and exhausted.

This is Ankole, modern-day successor to one of the traditional kingdoms abolished in the postindependence years. The city of Mbarara, its de facto capital, has prospered mightily under Museveni's presidency, which transformed it from a dusty fueling stop to what a guidebook hails as the "most rapidly expanding town in Uganda."

The soundtrack of progress—the scream of timber mills and the clink of hammers against brick—seems to last all day in Mbarara, which has its own rush hour, its own bustling markets, conference hotels, and tourist trade—white visitors heading for the Queen Elizabeth National Park and Bwindi Impenetrable National Park, home to half of the world's endangered mountain gorillas.

Patrick's farm, an hour and a half's drive from Museveni's, lies in Biharwe, a spot made famous by a total eclipse of the sun that took the King of Nkore by surprise in 1520, just after he had beaten the kings of Buganda and Bunyoro in battle. Aghast at the sudden darkness, his army fled, abandoning the cattle they had taken from their enemies.

Here you leave the tarmac and head down a meandering dirt track, rolling up the windows to avoid a mouthful of grit. Bounce along for a few miles, slowing occasionally to allow a flock of goats to pass, hang a left along an aromatic alley of cactus, and you emerge on Patrick's land.

Patrick moved his relatives to this hillside dotted with thorn trees in 1991, using his government salary to buy a 385-hectare estate. He was playing the role of rescuer, for by the time they settled here, the family had endured intimidation and eviction, bitterly registering as they moved through a series of displaced people's camps that while they had always considered themselves Ugandan, their neighbors saw things rather differently.

Outside the oldest bungalow, there's a plot in which one of Patrick's brothers and his father, John Kanimba, who died aged 105, lie buried. When Patrick was murdered, visitors began arriving, paying their respects, waiting for what they knew would be a big event: his interment on the same patch of land. Four cows were slaughtered to feed them: the compound was full of people for a month, reminiscing and mourning. But the body never arrived, and eventually everyone took their leave.

Patrick adored Biharwe, sneaking away whenever he could find the time from his stressful job in Kigali, a four-hour drive across the border with Rwanda. He'd wake at dawn and watch the pink light creep across the valley, picking out the graying anthills, warming the chill slopes. "You wouldn't even know he'd arrived. He'd put on his Wellington boots and go and milk the cows. He loved that," remembers his younger brother Ernest Mugabo.[5]

Then he'd spend the rest of the day playing the gentleman farmer, overseeing the digging of a dam by local laborers, discussing the best species of *matooke* to plant with a cousin, drawing up plans for staff living quarters. Sometimes he brought the kids, taking Richard and Elvis to meet the herd, passing on a skill as natural to a Tutsi as horse-riding is to a cowboy: how to milk.

Patrick grew up in a traditional Tutsi household. Despite his Catholic religion, John Kanimba was a polygamist, and as a child, Patrick was never too sure which of the two women he ran to for comfort when he scabbed a knee was his birth mother. There were twelve children; he was the fourth boy.

Pastoralists par excellence, a Tutsi family might appear virtually destitute to outsiders when in fact they were often rich in their own eyes, their savings embodied in mooing, chewing, jostling, form: constantly expanding Ankole herds that required them to move every couple of years in search of fresh pasture.

"Cattle are *everything* to the Banyarwanda," explains Ernest. "You'll find someone with a thousand cattle living in a tiny hut.

"As kids, we never ate. We just drank milk for breakfast, yogurt for lunch, and milk for dinner." Many Banyarwanda spent their entire lives without ever tasting eggs, fish, or chicken. On special occasions, an arrow would be shot into a cow's artery, the blood baked until it hardened to form a kind of bread, dipped in ghee.

Modern medical treatments and vaccinations were unknown. A sick Tutsi child was treated with herbs, pre-chewed tobacco, or a gulp of colostrum, the antibody-rich milk from a cow that had just calved. Cuts were sterilized in cattle urine. Elders regarded Western-style clothing as bad for children; youngsters often wore nothing at all as they roamed with the herds.

Jane Keshoro, Patrick's mother, lives in the most spartan of the estate's three bungalows. The living room is dominated by a tatty sofa set, foam bursting from its holes. The cement walls, painted turquoise, are pocked, and torn curtains flap in the breeze. What beauty there is lies outside, through the window: a long view of rolling, tawny hills.

Around the room, in glaring contrast to such simplicity, hang the giant family portraits Patrick moved with him from house to house. Leah, Portia, Elvis, and Richard: their beaming faces look out, aglow with expectation.

Jane Keshoro knows they are there, but she can no longer see those faces. Now in her midnineties, she suffers from glaucoma.

Patrick used to fly her to South Africa for treatment, but now she is almost completely blind. She has developed a technique for finding her way in and out of the bungalow, feeling with her feet for the cement lip that skirts the building. She greets those who knew her son with disconcertingly intimate kisses on the lips, then captures and keeps hold of a hand as her helpers serve smoked milk, an Ankole specialty, in beautiful grooved black pots.

Jane's grandfather—Patrick's great-grandfather—moved from southeastern Ruanda-Urundi to Rubaare, a settlement southwest of Mbarara, in 1926. The grandfather had allowed his cattle to stray into a reserve owned by a German settler, who promptly confiscated them. Patrick's feisty ancestor did not take this lying down.

"He got his bow and arrows and went to find the *muzungu*," says Jane. "The *muzungu* said, 'If I give you back the cows, where will you graze them?' My grandfather said, 'You're going to give me the area to graze them in.'"[6] The German—perhaps surprisingly—obliged, directing Jane's grandfather to better pasture to the northeast, across the border in what was then Britain's Ugandan protectorate.

So the light-skinned, six-fingered baby born to Jane Keshoro in February 1960 was a third-generation Ugandan who was fluent first in Runyankole, western Uganda's main language, and only then in Kinyarwanda, whose questing gaze, as the boy grew, would naturally direct itself northeast toward Uganda's capital, Kampala, rather than southwest toward Rwanda's Kigali.

"I'm a Ugandan, both my father and mother were Ugandan," says Jane. "I was very surprised Patrick got so involved in Rwanda." She shakes her head. "It was a mistake."

•

By the time Patrick was born, the Banyarwanda—the Kinyarwanda-speaking community to which he belonged—constituted one of Central Africa's biggest ethnic groups, its footprint stretching from eastern Zaire to western Tanzania and up to western Uganda. At its core sat the tiny, mountainous former kingdom of Rwanda. The community's geographical overflow was explained by a series of migrations prompted by acute land hunger, popular resentment at high taxes, a series of bitter royal wars of succession, and ethnic tensions that seemed to deepen with every decade.

Modern history is so exercised by the injustices inherent in Western colonialism's greedy nineteenth-century land grab that it sometimes makes the mistake of assuming Africa's mini-states and kingdoms lived in something approaching harmony until that point. But the Scramble for Africa was not a uniquely European phenomenon. Study the legendary Shaka Zulu's subjugation of a swath of southern Africa, Abyssinian emperor Menelik II's military expeditions across the Horn, or the various wars waged by Buganda's *kabakas* on their neighbors, and the picture that emerges is one of competing expansionist drives rubbing up against one another. The European powers eventually beat a range of African would-be Alexander the Greats at their own game thanks, in large part, to ownership of the Maxim gun and the Enfield rifle.

When Germany's envoys established a relationship at the turn of the nineteenth century with the Mwami, the Kingdom of Rwanda was one of Africa's most centralized states, highly organized, rigidly disciplined, and deeply suspicious of visitors and the potential for change they represented. The royal court had achieved that status after centuries of conquest and subjugation, with rival princes and warlords either killed or co-opted—a record of violence discreetly played down by local historians today.

The Mwami Yuhi Musinga cannily used German firepower to further extend his rule. When defeat in World War I spelled the end of German East Africa, with Ruanda-Urundi transferred to Belgian control, he played the same game with Brussels as long as he could, before the tiger inevitably turned upon its rider and he was banished into exile.

Growing up, Patrick fell asleep listening to tales of legendary battles, clan alliances and fallings-out, dastardly poisonings, and noble conquests recounted around the fire by elders who effortlessly carried generations of Rwandan dynasties in their heads.

There was more than a touch of *Game of Thrones* about the royal court they described, with its sunken-eyed, treacherous teenage king, its Machiavellian Queen Mother, its pygmy executioners, and its symbolic royal drum, decorated with the severed testicles of the Mwami's enemies and imbued with awesome spiritual power.

The palace compound was a vipers' nest of scheming gossip, two-faced informers, incestuous couplings, and deadly familial plots—

Musinga's father, Rwabugiri, a leader of Napoleonic grandeur, had executed his own mother, his biological father, and one of his most important wives, while Musinga, egged on by the Queen Mother Kanjogera, deposed his own stepbrother and executed two stepbrother princes suspected of coveting the throne.[7]

Battalions dispatched to eliminate challengers wiped out every man, woman, and child in their compounds in order to extinguish rival bloodlines. That pattern would have been familiar to an Egyptian pharaoh, Roman emperor, or medieval English king. The retribution Kagame wreaks on his enemies' relatives suggests that concept of collective punishment still holds resonance in Rwanda today.

The most striking thing, to outsiders' eyes, was the rigid stratification of Rwanda's feudal society. The Tutsi aristocracy accounted for only 14 percent of Rwanda's population but owned most of the country's cattle and dominated the standing army. The Hutus, accounting for 85 percent, did the farming and were locked into a client-patron relationship with their Tutsi rulers, trading labor and a share of each year's harvest for protection and an occasional gift of cattle. Twa pygmies made up the remainder of the population.

Relations between Tutsis and Hutus were already tense and unhappy when European explorers first encountered them. "In the presence of their lords, they were sober and reserved and tried to avoid our questions," Richard Kandt wrote. "But as soon as the Tutsi turned their backs . . . they were willing to tell us everything that we wanted to hear and much that we did not, because I could do nothing about the numerous grievances about which they complained, their lack of rights, their oppression."[8]

The difference between the communities seemed so stark that white visitors decided only migration could explain it, and so Rwanda was presented as an example of the Hamitic Hypothesis, which suggested that Tutsis were originally "Hamites"—Caucasian descendants of the biblical Ham—who had migrated to the Great Lakes from Egypt and Ethiopia, conquering the indigenous Bantu and introducing their more sophisticated, civilized ways. It was obvious which of the ethnic groups—"European under a black skin" versus "the backward Negro"—the colonial powers would regard as natural allies.

The Hamitic Hypothesis is derided today as racist wishful thinking, but its tenacity is perhaps a little more understandable when you look at photographs taken in the 1910s and 1920s in Nyanza, where the royal court was once based. A protein-rich diet of blood and milk, along with decades of inbreeding, meant "Africa's Aristocrats"—as *Life* magazine dubbed the Tutsis—towered over ordinary mortals, reaching down from lofty heights to shake the hands of visiting European dignitaries, who look stunted and dwarfish in comparison.

There's a disconcertingly otherworldly appearance to these etiolated, Giacometti-slim monarchs, with their high foreheads, protruding teeth, and endless legs—an effect exacerbated by colobus-monkey-tail headdresses and sculptured hairstyles known as *amasunzu*. Tutsi royals were built on such different physical lines from the hoi polloi that once they embraced Western modernity, cars had to be adjusted, baths specially designed, bespoke suits ordered. Mutara III Rudahigwa, who took over when Musinga was banished and was the first Rwandan monarch to convert to Christianity, was six foot eight, and his successor, Kigeli V, who died in exile in 2016, seven foot two. No wonder that, comparing these men to the stubby Hutu peasants working the fields, visitors assumed they must be separate races. And so the basis of a system of Central African apartheid was laid.

The Rwandan Patriotic Front blames the Hamitic Hypothesis for the violence that has blighted Rwandan society. "Same culture, same religion, same language," was the mantra of the movement, which argued that Hutu and Tutsi were not racial categories but socio-economic classifications—and fluid ones, at that. Just as in precolonial days, a rich Hutu who acquired cattle could become a Tutsi through *kwihutura*—shedding "Hutu-ness," which was said to require as little as ten cows—Tutsis who fell on hard times and turned to farming could eventually become Hutu. As for the physical differences, while Hutu and Tutsi archetypes certainly existed, frequent intermarriage ensured that a chunk of the population was impossible to instantly categorize.

The Hutu-Tutsi distinction has certainly never been the only one that matters in Rwanda. As US author Jason Stearns writes, "Each of the twenty major clans in Rwanda includes both Hutu and Tutsi, and among each ethnic group one can find poor, landless peasants as well as wealthier princes. To label someone a Hutu and leave it at that neglects that she may, depending on the social context, see herself more as a southerner, a member of the Abega clan, or a follower of the Pentecostal church."[9]

If the divide was not the invention of the colonial authorities, they sharpened and entrenched the difference. ID cards identifying Rwandans as "Hutu," "Tutsi," or "Twa" made the schism official. While the Belgians put Hutus to work terracing hills, building roads, and digging dams under an oppressive system of forced labor, Tutsis were given the majority of administrative positions and privileged access to education. Tutsis were taught in French, Hutus in Kinyarwanda.

Such favoritism might have had less impact in a country offering its citizens room to breathe. But while Rwanda is one of Africa's most beautiful countries—so beautiful, they say, it is where God retires to sleep at night—it is also its most overpopulated. When Patrick was one year old, the country his great-grandfather left behind boasted an average of 121 inhabitants per square kilometer. Today the number is 483. In an industrialized economy, population pressure can be allayed. But Rwanda was an isolated, feudal society dependent on subsistence farming, and access to land meant the difference between life and death.

In 1959, the Belgian colonial authorities dramatically, disastrously, swapped sides. Tutsi intellectuals had been reading the anti-imperial radical writers of the day and started campaigning for the white man's departure. Suspecting the Tutsis of Marxist sympathies, egged on by firebrand young Flemish priests who saw firsthand the grimness of daily life for the Hutu peasant, Brussels abandoned the Tutsi elite, siding instead with emerging Hutu political parties.

The U-turn, which upended existing power relations, could not have been better calculated to foment community hatred. On the ground, activists loyal to an all-Hutu Parmehutu political party founded by Grégoire Kayibanda, and members of a pro-Tutsi monarchist party attacked one another, killing local officials and setting fire to huts. Rwanda's first local elections delivered most administrative posts into Hutu hands, and in January 1961, with Belgium's approval, Parmehutu abolished the Tutsi monarchy and declared Rwanda a republic, with Kayibanda, a Hutu, as the country's first elected president.

Dubbed "*Muyaga*"—the "wind of destruction"—the Hutu Revolution turned Tutsis into fair game. The next few decades saw a steady ratcheting up of violence, each wave readying Rwandan society for the next, bigger wave. Horrors that would have once seemed unthinkable became frequent, then widespread, and finally banal.

In 1959, several provinces saw minor pogroms of Tutsis, and some fled Rwanda. After elections in 1961, more Tutsis departed, some joining guerrilla groups in Burundi and Uganda that dubbed themselves the *inyenzi*—"cockroaches"—in tribute to the insects' indestructibility and persistence. They launched attacks on Rwanda, triggering revenge massacres of Tutsi civilians back home.

A pattern of persecution and exodus had been set that would win the Tutsis an unenviable "Jews of Africa" label. Escalation was built into the process: seeing your homestead burned down and your parents killed makes it likely you will return the favor decades down the line. Each atrocity ratchets up community tensions, raising the odds on a new outrage being committed.

Events in Rwanda's southern neighbor Burundi played a part in this upping-of-the-ante. In 1972, in one of the least-reported genocides of modern history, the Tutsi army there slaughtered hundreds of thousands of Burundian Hutus, targeting any man or boy with education in a cynical drive to eliminate future political challenges. The massacres confirmed Rwandan Hutus in their suspicion that if given a chance, their own aggrieved, ousted former Tutsi rulers would do exactly the same.

By 1990—a year whose significance will become clear—Uganda, then a country of 18 million, was estimated to hold 1.3 million Banyarwanda. According to British journalist Cathy Watson, who wrote one of the best reports on the topic, the group fell into three distinct categories.[10]

Around a third were the descendants of Kinyarwanda-speaking people who just happened to be living inside what became Uganda when its boundaries were finalized in the early twentieth century: a classic example of clumsy colonial map-drawing ignoring realities on the ground. Most of this group of "true Ugandans," as they were labeled, were Hutus who started out as farmers but moved to Kampala when land became scarce, working in Mulago Hospital or for the city council. The Tutsis among them, in contrast, tended to remain in Ankole, employed as cattle keepers.[11]

Half—the category into which Patrick and the General fell—were economic migrants, descendants of Rwandans who had moved across the border between 1920 and 1960 in search of a better life. During those decades, sleeping sickness and warfare caused a drop in Uganda's population, and Baganda landowners struggled to find workers for their plantations. The pay and conditions they offered were far preferable to draconian forced labor in Ruanda-Urundi under the Belgians, and Hutus and Tutsis flooded into central Uganda to pick cotton, cut sugar cane, and graze cattle. There many assimilated, taking on local names and customs to the point where they could barely be distinguished from the Baganda.

The remaining 15 percent of Uganda's Banyarwanda were refugees fleeing Muyaga, and this group came from only one community: the Tutsis. From 1959 to 1964, the UNHCR estimated, 40 to 70 percent of Rwanda's Tutsis walked out of a country where they were no longer welcome. Between 50,000 and 70,000 of them crossed into Uganda.

It was a march seared into the memory of both those who took part in it and those who watched in bemusement. There was a sexual ingredient to the humiliation. Tutsi women are famous for their beauty, and as the human caravan crossed the border, Ugandan men lined the road to weigh up which women they would claim. Many of the women had once belonged to the royal household, but now they were in no position to negotiate terms, so dowries were low. Some Tutsi wives, deciding that sex was now their only survival strategy, camouflaged their husbands as "brothers" and "cousins," becoming suddenly single and available again.

Some of the refugees were prosperous enough to buy land and resettle, blurring into the local population—a process made easier by local Banyankole families who opened their homes to the despairing new arrivals. But the majority poured into refugee camps and settlements in western Uganda: there would be eight in all.

It was this community of "fifty-niners" that would play a small but key role when Museveni came to challenge the Ugandan government of the day. For the toddlers carried into Uganda on their grim-faced, exhausted mothers' backs included the two-year-old Paul Kagame and three-year-old Fred Rwigyema, who would both be taken under Museveni's wing. And it was to this driven minority that Patrick would eventually hitch his own destiny.

CHAPTER SIX

HIDING IN PLAIN SIGHT

We had a friendly conversation, the man shook my hand, told me to keep my spirits up. We know from before that he is certainly no Nazi, that his sister is in difficulties, because her husband, a gardener, has a grandmother who is no Aryan. But then the next day, when I was up there, he happened to come through the room; he stared ahead as he went past, as much a stranger as possible.

—Victor Klemperer,
I Will Bear Witness: A Diary of the Nazi Years, 1933–41

Assimilated in Uganda, yet distinct, the Banyarwanda were in part defined by their language: parents were always careful to keep speaking the throaty Kinyarwanda at home. The second glue was marriage. Banyarwanda might well date outside the community, but they usually married *in*, the matches as carefully planned as those of an Indian prince, arranged by elders taking into account lineage, clan, property, and prospects, with would-be grooms often sent to Rwanda to meet their designated brides and bring them back.

Diasporas tend to become distorted echoes of the communities from whence they came, and Uganda's Banyarwanda were no exception, importing their society's ethnic prejudices wholesale. When a Tutsi grandmother needed a bogeyman to quiet naughty children, it would be a Hutu. "There was this idea of Hutus being dirty, dark, small, and a bit slow," remembers David Batenga. "You grew up with a condescending mindset, of being better."

The typical Banyarwanda family moved at regular intervals, and that presented a problem when it came to formal education. Like many of their generation, Patrick's parents initially regarded it as largely irrelevant, to be endured as briefly as possible to keep the colonial authorities sweet. Instead of sending her children off to school with a packed lunch, a Tutsi mother preferred to dispatch them with a jug to mind the cattle—lunch came straight from the teat.

But for Patrick, fate intervened. The headmaster of one of his many primary schools took his parents to one side and said, "This boy is very bright. He must continue with his education. Let him come and stay with us." Traditionalist families would often take a tentative punt on the future by agreeing to sacrifice one son, who would be dispatched to learn a changing society's newfangled ways. Patrick was a natural for the role.

"He never forgot what that headmaster had done," says Portia. "I remember when I was fourteen my dad drove us with a pile of presents in the car to find the headmaster, to thank him for changing his life."

The two cultures—traditional and modern—clashed head-on right away. John Kanimba, trying to do the right thing, sent a cow with Patrick to his new home and school: a pastoralist's way of ensuring his son got plenty of nourishment. The tethered animal was swiftly butchered and eaten, and Patrick spent months trying to avoid admitting to his father what had become of the precious gift.

When he was thirteen, a visiting uncle had a similar reaction to the headmaster's. "Eeeh, this boy is bright," exclaimed Eliphaz Rwivanga, a former army commander. He and his wife, Mabel, offered to put Patrick up in the family home in Kampala, where Rwivanga worked as a manager for Pepsi.

Patrick moved to the Ugandan capital, acquiring a patina of urban sophistication that set him apart from the other Banyarwanda boys, who regularly met up with one another at weddings, funerals, and festivals. When he returned during holidays to help with the herd, they would dart sideways glances at him, taking in his clothes, his shoes, his new, street-smart way of talking. The General was a couple of years older than Patrick, but felt overawed. "Our family's places were adjacent so we'd meet taking cows to market. But we weren't friends then. He was almost a city fellow, while I was just a boy from the village, herding cattle."

But if life in Kampala meant Patrick caught a glimpse of Uganda beyond Ankole's boundaries, it also allowed him to rub shoulders with a group of Banyarwanda who had experienced a very different upbringing from his own, and who had far less reason to share his sunny disposition.

•

R wengoro Primary School, which sits at the end of a dirt track on the outskirts of the village of Kahunge, forty miles north of Mbarara, looks much like any other school in Uganda, so blankly functional it could be a military barracks.

On either side lie well-hoed plantations of *matooke* and maize fringed with yellow-flowering cassia bushes. Children in neat uniforms shout to each other as they play in the shade of a giant mango tree, but once indoors they turn silent and observe strict etiquette, a girl respectfully kneeling, as Ugandan tradition dictates, on entering the staff room to request a stick of chalk. The school is a modest, single-story structure, and the pristine blue of its new *mabati* roof is distinctly at odds with the rest of the building.

There's a reason for that mismatch. A few years ago, a teacher discovered a Primary Leaving Examination Certificate made out to Paul Kagame, Rwengoro's most famous alumnus, abandoned in a school cupboard. He took it to Rwanda's high commissioner in Kampala, who exclaimed, "This is a big document!" The school sent a delegation to Kigali bearing the precious piece of paper, along with a request for funds to mend the leaking roof.[1] The relationship that OBs—"Old Boys"—maintain with their alma maters is hugely important in Uganda, and Kagame did not disappoint: hence the top-quality *mabati*, along with a brand-new wing.

Former fellow pupils remember a watchful, hardworking boy who excelled at math and enjoyed table tennis. Even then, it seems, Kagame showed signs of a disciplinarian streak. Appointed class monitor, he relished the opportunity to curb his peers' behavior. "When we were shouting in class he'd take down our names and give them to the teacher to make sure we were punished," comments a former classmate. "He hasn't changed."

In the village of Kahunge itself there's a sense of bemused wonder at the fact that quite so many of the key figures in Rwanda's contemporary story spent their formative years here. For Kagame is not the only local hero.

Fred Rwigyema, who took the less popular boy under his wing, attended a school in Mpanga, four miles from Rwengoro, before being admitted to Mbarara High School. Then he suddenly disappeared. Fourteen-year-old Emmanuel Gisa—"Fred Rwigyema" was a nom de guerre adopted to protect his family—had been talent-spotted by Kahinda Otafiire, one of Museveni's right-hand men, on the lookout for adventurous youngsters to join their guerrilla organization.

Rwigyema returned to Kahunge in the mid-1980s, when he was in the National Resistance Movement, and again when he was Ugandan army deputy commander in chief, flamboyantly landing a helicopter on Mpanga's playground. While his titles changed over the years, Fred—everyone referred to him simply as "Fred"—was always in search of the same thing: Banyarwanda youngsters willing to train and fight.

Across the road from Rwengoro's school lived Peter Bayingana, who grew up to become a doctor, one of the Rwandan Patriotic Front's leading intellectuals, and the man who, above all others, was to play a contested role in Fred's future. Another local boy was Frank Mugambage, who became an RPF major general and Rwanda's long-serving high commissioner in Kampala.

They had all flooded into Kamwenge district during Muyaga, part of a human tide decanted from the overcrowded refugee camps nearer the Ugandan border. Up till then, the land had served as a natural corridor for wildlife moving between the national parks. Grazed by antelope, zebra, and buffalo, dotted with thorn trees, it was plagued by tsetse flies and sparsely inhabited, diminishing the likelihood of tensions between new arrivals and local residents.

Many of the refugees who moved in had depended on the Mwami for their livelihoods; some were militant members of Rwanda's monarchist party. But alongside the aristocrats, with their sense of bruised entitlement, there were also poor Tutsis, peasants whose lives in Rwanda had been just as tough as those of their Hutu neighbors.

Each refugee family was given a ten-acre plot. Wattle houses were built, gardens planted, and the end result, to the uninitiated, was indistinguishable from the local Ugandan villages. "They came with virtually nothing, but once they were here they acquired small businesses and cows and began to trade and work as herdsmen," says Sylvester Singila, a former village elder.[2]

The new arrivals kept their heads down, Ugandan officials noticed, while maintaining a distance from their host community. "The Rwandans were afraid, very nervous. So they would keep things secret," says Singila. "You would hear of fights in the community but they would never report them to the authorities. They were very good at obeying orders."

The community was, after all, in a state of shock. The peculiar horror of so much of Rwanda's violence lies in its intimacy: during Muyaga, killings were carried out not by an invading army, but by neighbors and local officials, villagers their victims had for years passed on the road, bought vegetables from at market, and nodded politely to at church.

A biographer once asked Kagame whether his family knew the people who attacked them in 1959, sending them into flight. "Yes, we knew them," he replied.[3]

"That day they were burning homes, killing cattle and people and the plan apparently was to do away with the rest of the people in the area and lastly come to our house. . . . My mother was preparing us for the worst. After a while she told us to go out to the compound and wait there for whatever would happen. She didn't want us to be trapped and killed in the house."

They were saved by their lineage. A member of the Bega clan, Kagame was of royal blood, his mother, Asteria, a cousin to Queen Rosalie Gicanda. Suspecting the family might be in danger, the Queen sent a chauffeur-driven car to their compound in the nick of time. They were driven to the royal palace in Nyanza. When the family tried moving back, they found the house full of refugees. Eventually they crossed the border to Uganda carrying only a few bags of children's clothes.

The privations of refugee life are often cited as an explanation for the RPF's eventual ruthlessness, the hardship—so the theory goes—giving birth to something grim and implacable, just as the humiliations of life in Lebanon's Sabra and Chatila refugee camps in the 1970s gave rise to Palestinian extremism. A visit to Kahunge nuances that interpretation.

Many of the communities that produced the RPF's future ringleaders were settlements, not refugee camps—Ugandan officials insist on the difference—and as far as indigenous locals were concerned, the newcomers actually fared better than they.

The refugees received food handouts from the World Food Programme (WFP), after all, and as the years passed special schools and clinics were built for them. UN scholarships earmarked for refugees allowed the brighter ones to attend secondary school, one reason why Banyarwanda refugees tended to be better educated than the average Ugandan. Schools like Rwengoro regularly scored higher in national rankings than those taking only indigenous pupils.

"They were seen as privileged," says James Bigirimana, who was headmaster at Rwengoro in the 1980s. "When they came, the refugees found the local people were poor. The refugees were supported by the UN, so they became better off than the natives."[4]

But as Bigirimana also acknowledges, the experience of exile cannot be reduced to a tick list of physical needs and WFP deliveries. The cost of leaving Rwanda was as much psychological as physical. "Can you imagine being forced to flee, to lose your property, your wealth, walking long distances on empty stomachs with children? Ach. . . . They were denied their rights, so yes, they were bitter."

Many of the Tutsi refugees, Ugandan officials noticed, initially regarded their stay as strictly temporary, telling their hosts they were praying for the day of their return. Some refused to build with anything more substantial than wattle or straw—they would be leaving soon anyway—while others refused to plant permanent crops.

One of the most contentious issues in Kahunge was the shortage of grassland. Not every Tutsi family could be allowed to maintain a herd, so the refugees were expected to turn their hands to farming, a role normally reserved in Rwanda for Hutus. As often happens, the women adapted better to the wrenching change than their menfolk.

Paul Kagame's father was one of the many Tutsi patriarchs who could not swallow their fall from grace. He had made his living in Rwanda as a coffee broker and refused to demean himself by sowing vegetables. "If I dig, I will die," he said. "If I don't dig, I will also die. So let me die." Thereafter, he retreated into a fug of alcohol and depression.

There was some logic to this state of denial. The monarchist party's pacifist wing hoped to persuade the UN to force the Belgian authorities and Parmehutu party in Rwanda to accept the Tutsis back under an interim trusteeship to be established before independence in July 1962. Its militants, in contrast, believed that once Belgium had withdrawn from Africa, they could fight their way home. Either way, there was little point putting down roots elsewhere.

Inyenzi militants moved between refugee settlements in Uganda, Burundi, Tanzania, and Zaire, picking up what weapons and training they could. But raids on the homeland came at a ghastly price, creating a sense of siege in Rwanda that allowed President Kayibanda and Parmehutu to justify the worst atrocities. In December 1963, following an *inyenzi* raid from Burundi, Rwanda's Hutu population massacred 10,000 to 14,000 Tutsis, prompting appalled reactions in Europe from the likes of philosophers Jean-Paul Sartre and Bertrand Russell.[5]

The savagery of the retribution cut the ground from under the *inyenzis'* feet. Global events were not moving in their favor, either. The establishment of the Organization of African Unity (OAU) in Addis Ababa, which barred signatories from interfering in members' internal affairs, coincided with a shriveling of regional sympathy for the Tutsi refugees. Progressive governments across the continent had mixed feelings about supporting a monarchist movement bent on reinstalling a king.

Balked at every level, Tutsi refugees who were scattered across the African Great Lakes gradually, reluctantly, registered that they were in it for the long haul. The exile of the "fifty-niners" was destined to last thirty years.

•

One Sunday afternoon, I arrange to meet a couple of Ugandans in the Victoria Mall, a small shopping plaza in Entebbe overlooking

Lake Victoria's vast blue expanse. The mall is still so new, only half of its shop spaces have been rented out, but there's a café that serves juice and burgers, and it is already drawing a steady stream of families.

Both my companions belong to a WhatsApp group whose members enjoy thrashing out political questions of the day. One is a Muganda entrepreneur, the other a middle-aged dentist. As we chat, the conversation turns to relations between Uganda and Rwanda, which are so frosty, war seems a real possibility. At one point the dentist blurts out, "Actually, I'm originally a Rwandan myself. Both my parents were born in Rwanda."

Across the table, his friend does a double take: "Really? I had no idea." The dentist's name, they agree, provides no clue. But looking at him now, the businessman registers his ranginess, his height, the proportions of his face. How could he have missed it? He nods, meditatively: "There are so many secret Rwandans in Uganda."

I've sat in on conversations of this sort more than once, and each time I've been as surprised as the Ugandan making the discovery. How could he not already know? They were friends, weren't they? But in the wake of the mass Tutsi exodus of the 1950s and 1960s, hiding in plain sight became something of a Banyarwanda specialty.

Assimilation came easily, as the social and economic distinctions between Rwanda's ethnic communities were mirrored in Ankole: Uganda's Banyankole were split between the Bairu, who settled in the valleys and grew millet and other grains, and the Bahima, a group that included Museveni's ancestors, who wandered in search of pasture for their cattle. Physically, Tutsis could easily "pass" as Bahima, willowy, toothy, high-foreheaded, and dark-skinned cattlekeepers.

Names were malleable. Just as Jews fleeing anti-Semitic pogroms in Eastern Europe lopped off the "bergs," "steins," and "vitches" from their surnames upon starting new lives in the United States, Canada, and the United Kingdom, many Banyarwanda tweaked their names to sound Ugandan. The process of stealthy camouflage was facilitated by sympathetic Banyarwanda officials in Kampala ready to invent fake backstories and issue counterfeit IDs.

But the practice did not pass unnoticed by the authorities, and it fed concerns among politicians that refugees were spilling beyond the confines of the camps and settlements, gobbling up land hungered after by indigenous Ugandans. Worse, the fake IDs meant the refugees could vote, and Milton Obote, Uganda's first executive prime minister, knew who the Banyarwanda would support if they got the chance: his enemies.

Idi Amin was such a flamboyant character that non-Ugandans automatically attribute the country's worst excesses to this comic-opera buffoon. But it was the intelligent, articulate Obote—the man with an instantly recognizable shock of side-parted, grizzled hair—whose administrations actually claimed far more lives. And, tragically, Obote enjoyed not one, but two terms in office.

Obote spent the postindependence years centralizing power in his hands. In 1966, he turned on his previous royal ally, the Kabaka, suspending the constitution and ordering army chief of staff Amin to attack the palace on Mengo Hill. Declaring himself president, Obote banned opposition parties and abolished all Uganda's kingdoms. As a northerner, he relied on his Langi people and the neighboring Acholi for support, handing out government and army jobs to secure loyalty.

Thanks to the evangelizing role the Belgian White Fathers had played in Rwanda, the Tutsis who flooded across the border were predominantly Catholics. While Uganda's Protestants supported Obote, Catholics traditionally supported his rivals. With so many of the refugees known to be ardent monarchists, the republican Obote automatically assumed the new Rwandan arrivals to be hostile.

The refugees weren't helped by the fact that much of Ugandan society was already casually prejudiced against the Banyarwanda. Associated with the lowliest of jobs—herding livestock, working in kitchens, doing laundry—they were seen, when noticed at all, as naturally subservient.

The rivalry between pastoralist and farming communities is as ancient as civilization, and Uganda is no exception. In the eyes of the Baganda, Bairu, and Banyoro, whose ancestors had cleared forest, staked out plots, harvested crops, and clustered in villages and towns, these semi-naked Tutsi wanderers were uncouth hicks unsuited to respectable society.

In the same way that a British comedian will make fun of a Liverpudlian or a Yorkshireman, Ugandan comedians delight in mimicking Banyarwanda accents. Driving in Kampala, you will often hear "*Kanyarwanda ggwe!*" (You Kanyarwanda!) shouted in rush-hour traffic, irrespective of the ethnicity of those involved. It's the equivalent, a Ugandan friend explains, of shouting "You fool!"

"Growing up in Luwero, I came to warm to the Banyarwanda I met, but generally they were despised, seen as the lowest of the low," a former NRM fighter tells me. "I never understood it, but there was a real stigma. It was very like the attitude in Europe to Jews.[6]

"Buganda society is very formal—they are a bit like Englishmen, courtesies matter a lot—but the Banyarwanda didn't have any manners. The men never seemed to know when to wear what. They would button their shirts right up to their necks or put formal jackets over T-shirts and end up looking really silly.

"Our women wore the *gomesi* or *busuti,*" he says, referring to traditional Baganda attire, which leaves very little skin exposed. "Tutsi women were beautiful but they wore dresses that showed their calves—that was unacceptable. A Muganda girl would ride modestly side saddle on the back of a bike; they just sat anyhow." The distaste extended to diet: "We only drank sterilized milk; they drank it fresh from the cow—that's *horrible.*"[7]

As for the languorous *umushagiriro* dance Rwandan maidens performed on special occasions, hands and wrists gracefully mimicking the curved horns and movements of Ankole cattle, Ugandans would snort, roll their eyes, and silently mouth at one another, *"Call that an African dance?"*

In 1970, President Obote began cracking down on the new arrivals. Refugees were forbidden from leaving the camps, growing cash crops, or sending their children to Uganda's secondary schools. Businesses were ordered to dismiss unskilled non-Ugandans, a measure seen as specifically aimed at two communities: the Asians and the Banyarwanda. In the run-up to 1971 elections, Obote further set alarm bells ringing by ordering an ethnic census in Ankole: Was he planning, the Banyarwanda wondered, to first deprive them of the vote, then expel them?

The official antagonism ensured the refugee community became an easy recruiting ground for those setting out to challenge the Big Man of the day. And in Uganda, there has never been a shortage of candidates for that role.

Obote depended upon Idi Amin, his beefy army chief of staff, to enforce his policies, but knew he could not trust his capricious protégé. The suspicion was mutual. Hearing that he was about to be arrested, Amin struck while Obote was attending a Commonwealth meeting in Singapore in 1971, and seized control in a coup carried out with Israeli help. The British government was taken by surprise, but welcomed the development. The Foreign Office had started worrying about Obote's socialist leanings, and Amin, who had trained in the King's African Rifles, was seen as an amiable buffoon.

But "Dada" (Big Daddy), as he was affectionately known, wasted no time in showing his ruthless side. Acholi and Langi members of the armed forces, assumed to be loyal to Obote, were massacred in their barracks, to be replaced by Nubians, former rebels from south Sudan, and members of Amin's own Kakwa community. In Uganda, to know someone's ethnic identity was to know their politics.

For a brief moment, Uganda's Banyarwanda found themselves on the winning side of history. "Amin required legitimacy; and as a strategy he encouraged various minorities to join him in order to expand his political base," writes Ugandan historian Elijah Mushemeza.[8] An invitation to King Kigeli V, Rwanda's exiled Mwami, to rebase himself in Uganda was part of Amin's courtship.

Hungry for protection, and blessed with impressive educational qualifications, the Banyarwanda swelled the ranks of Amin's State Research Bureau, the military intelligence agency which became synonymous with torture and indiscriminate murder. The association did them few favors. As Amin euphoria peaked and waned, the community acquired a reputation for being secretive and aloof, prone to Iago-like deceit.

By the second anniversary of Amin's coup, the US ambassador in Kampala succinctly characterized the regime in a telegram back to Washington as "racist, erratic and unpredictable, brutal, inept, bellicose, irrational, ridiculous, and militaristic."[9]

With his ludicrous titles ("Lord of All the Beasts of the Earth and Fishes of the Sea," "King Termite," "Last King of Scotland," "Conqueror of the British Empire," "Ruler of the Universe," "Uganda's Sportsman No. One"), "Dada" soon became the stereotype of an African military psychopath, his uniform sagging under the weight of self-awarded medals. A tabloid journalist's dream, Amin was said to keep severed human heads in his freezer and joked cheerfully about dabbling in cannibalism.

Amin passed a decree giving his soldiers the power to arrest anyone suspected of sedition, and they applied it with enthusiasm, behaving as though occupying a foreign country, which was no doubt how many of them viewed the situation. A former prime minister was disemboweled and castrated in prison; other high-profile victims included the former central bank governor, a university vice-chancellor, and the Anglican archbishop.

Amin also presided over a full-blown economic catastrophe. In 1972, he gave Uganda's 80,000 Asians ninety days to leave the country. It was a hugely popular move, but it had the same impact as Mobutu Sese Seko's "Zairianization" program a year later, and Robert Mugabe's confiscation of white-run farms in Zimbabwe in 2000. The inexperienced army officers to whom Asian stores, businesses, and properties were given ran them into the ground, and basic commodities ran out. As Uganda's factories slowed to a halt and weeds sprouted on its coffee farms and cotton and tea plantations, exports collapsed.

Talk to any of the men and women who eventually joined a succession of rebel movements and they will recall a moment when a quiet voice inside said, "No, this, I cannot accept."

For Kizza Besigye, who went on to serve as Museveni's personal doctor in the bush, it was the day he went to the Copper Bar, one of the few places in a shortage-hit Kampala where you could still buy a beer. He was a student studying at Makerere University at the time. A young woman, a former fellow alumnus, called out his name, infuriating her date.

"Some huge fellow grabbed me, lifted me off my feet, and he and his friend began beating me, so hard I couldn't see. They threw me into someone's food on a table, and the table collapsed." The humiliated young man picked himself out of the debris, staggered out of the bar, and ran bleeding to a taxi stand. "These were Amin's men, and this was in a public place. It was that impunity, enjoyed by people holding state power, which eventually drove me into the bush."[10]

For Pecos Kutesa, who ended up penning a vivid account of guerrilla life, the turning point was the day Amin's soldiers flagged down the taxi he was taking to town. It had drizzled, and the soldiers at the checkpoint were covered in sticky red mud.

Separating him from the other passengers, the soldiers asked why he was wearing a tie, which he had put on because he was going to a new job in a bank. Pecos made the mistake of explaining in English.

"It was a cardinal sin in those days to answer in English, which, to the soldiers of the time, signified contempt for them, owing to their lack of formal education."[11]

"Today"—replied one soldier in Swahili—"you are going to wear a uniform similar to mine. Lie down. Start rolling." Pecos wrote: "I was rolled in the mud until I was an ochre colour from head to foot. After some time, the soldier told me sarcastically that I was now smart enough to go to work in the bank."

Back in the taxi, there was silence from the passengers, who were glumly aware that the incident could have ended far more unpleasantly. But the iron had entered Pecos's soul: "I had made up my mind to find a way of learning to handle a gun."[12]

•

But every crisis is also an opportunity, and while the iron was entering into the soul of many young Ugandans, there were some who benefited from Dada's quixotic rule. Amin's disastrous "Africanization" program meant boys like Patrick Karegeya and Paul Kagame got places in a decent secondary school.

The two boys' paths crossed well before they hit puberty. Although one was a Ugandan Munyarwanda and the other an impoverished refugee, they were connected by ties of clan, language, and culture. The families socialized at Banyarwanda weddings and funerals, on market days, and at festivals. But Rwanda's future spy chief and his boss only started properly registering one another's existence when they both enrolled at Old Kampala Senior Secondary School sitting snug in the heart of the capital.

One of the oldest secondary schools in Uganda, Old Kampala had been built to serve the offspring of Indians whom the British had originally brought to East Africa to build the railway—the "Lunatic Express" linking Mombasa to the interior—and to work in business and administration. The expulsion of the Asians meant schools that had previously passed over bright African boys suddenly had places to spare.

Life had presented Patrick, the son of a well-integrated Munyarwanda cattle herder, with a series of generous opportunities. Gregarious, self-confident, and easygoing, he had effortlessly capitalized upon his chances. A couple of years ahead of him, Kagame was having a harder time of it.

Kagame had done so well at Rwengoro Primary School that he had won a place at Ntare School, one of the best in the country and Museveni's alma mater. But there his grades had begun to slide, as his status as a refugee, one of the great unwanted, began to register.

"You're a child when these things happen, but you grow up in an environment that affects you in such a fundamental way. . . . Later you come to comprehend that with the terrible life you're living, you are actually somebody with very little, if anything," Kagame told his US biographer. "You hear this history, you see that the life you are living is so terrible, and you ask: Why did this happen to us?"[13]

No longer the dutiful class monitor who got a kick out of enforcing school rules, he ended up being suspended for fighting with pupils he accused of picking on refugees. He had already acquired a reputation as a troublemaker, a boy with "problems," when his bitter, disappointed father, Deogratias, died. Age fifteen, Kagame plunged into a classic adolescent crisis, his natural dourness exacerbated by the awareness of anti-immigrant prejudice.

"I started feeling, in my thinking and whole being, very rebellious. I wanted to rebel against everything in life," Kagame said. He seemed almost crippled by fury. "You were always reminded, in one way or another, that you didn't belong here, that you were not supposed to be here. You have no place that you can call yours."

His suppressed rage left an impression even on those who were disposed to be kind. "What do I remember about Kagame?" asks Jane Keshoro, Patrick's mother. "That when he came to see my son, he would never say 'hello.' He'd go straight through to talk directly to Patrick without a word of greeting."

Weighed down by none of Kagame's issues, Patrick did so well he won a place at the Makerere University School of Law, a distinction also accorded Kayumba Nyamwasa, another Munyarwanda who did brilliantly at school. It was a course earmarked for Uganda's intellectual crème de la crème, since the law was seen as the ultimate in respectable, lucrative white-collar professions.

Kagame, in contrast, left Old Kampala with poor grades. He tried to retake his final year, but an aunt he approached refused to pony up the necessary funds. Meanwhile, his refugee status stymied his dreams of studying in Switzerland or training to become a pilot.

Chippy and frustrated, he joined the thousands of underemployed youngsters hungrily patrolling the streets of Kampala, selling goods bought upcountry to city dwellers for a tiny markup; trading in gold, foreign exchange, and traveler's checks; hovering on the margins of criminality, a fact his colleagues turned opponents have not forgotten. "He was one of those street boys, wasn't he?" sniffs the General when I ask him about the young Kagame.

Occasionally Kagame slipped across the border into Rwanda, walking Kigali's streets and soaking up gossip in bars, taking off before the Rwandan authorities registered his presence. Frustrated and furious, he was a perfect recruit for any political movement promising to change the world.

Then Kagame's boyhood friend, Fred Rwigyema, surfaced in Fort Portal, western Uganda, offering him just that. Fred had undergone a transformation. He had joined the Front for National Salvation (FRONASA), a group set up by a Marxist political activist called Yoweri Museveni. While Kagame had languished in Kampala, Fred had become a self-confident young man, training in Mozambique and Tanzania, where he had learned how to handle a gun. And FRONASA had just taken part in the kind of operation certain to thrill any youngster hungry for purpose. Kagame lapped the details up.

•

For the young Museveni, neither Obote nor Amin was Uganda's real problem. The entire system established by the colonial powers, with its ethnic factionalism and religious sectarianism, needed to be swept away.

Museveni's personal itinerary highlights how, well before the Internet and social media, when televisions and telephones were still unaffordable luxuries in much of Africa, radical ideas nonetheless ping-ponged effortlessly from continent to continent and generation to generation, seeding and feeding young minds.

A Muhima from Ankole, Museveni was born to a family of what he described as "rich peasants," whose lives circulated around milk yields and the health of their herds. Having shown an early interest in politics, he attended the University of Dar es Salaam, where

Tanzanian president Julius Nyerere's socialist ideas held sway, and the likes of Guyanan political activist Walter Rodney, author of *How Europe Underdeveloped Africa*, and Stokely Carmichael, leader of the Black Panthers, were invited to give inspirational lectures.

The young firebrand looked at his own country with jaundiced eyes. The independence generation of African leaders, he concluded, was politically bankrupt, exploiting sectarian differences for personal gain, incapable of building national unity. Armed revolution, not the democratic process, was the only answer. "We knew that dictators had to be actively opposed and that they would not just fall off by themselves like ripe mangoes," he later wrote.[14]

By his early twenties, he had already visited North Korea, learned to handle a gun, set up a revolutionary student group in Tanzania, and arranged for a group of fellow cadres to receive military training from the Mozambique Liberation Front (FRELIMO), which taught him, among other things, the importance of small guerrilla movements avoiding head-on military confrontation and the merits of a "protracted war."

His FRONASA group wanted to get rid of Amin and saw Obote as no improvement, but it faced a problem. Museveni depended on Nyerere for support, guidance, and connections with FRELIMO, and Nyerere wanted Obote, to whom he had granted sanctuary, returned to power. So Museveni bit his tongue, focusing on getting his fighters properly trained, buying weapons, and establishing a network of secret cells across Uganda.

Museveni got a first, painful lesson in how *not* to topple a dictator when FRONASA joined an abortive invasion by Obote's forces in September 1972. Only 46 of the 330 men who set off across the Tanzanian border made it safely back from Uganda.

The Organization of African Unity condemned the botched attempt, and Nyerere was obliged to sign a peace agreement with Amin recognizing his regime, which meant Museveni could no longer count on the indulgence of the Tanzanian authorities. Confidence waning, he got married and took a teaching job in Moshi, northern Tanzania.

But by 1976 he was ready to reenter the fray, setting off for Mozambique—seen as the place to learn how to wage Marxist revolution—with a group of fighters whose training he intended to personally oversee. The unit, which included Fred and Museveni's own, much younger brother Salim Saleh, would eventually form the core of what became the National Resistance Army (NRA).

Museveni had originally been deeply suspicious of the Banyarwanda. The community's willingness to be recruited by Amin's loathed intelligence service had left a scar. So why, on his second attempt, did Museveni look to it for recruits? Obote's supporters regarded the explanation as blindingly obvious, pointing to what they claimed was a convenient mystery over Museveni's birthplace and his father's place of burial. Museveni was not Ugandan at all, they claimed, but Rwandan: he was merely looking to his own.

Whatever his origins, Museveni had certainly grown up around the Banyarwanda, and he understood what made the community tick. One thing he knew was that they saw themselves as perennial outcasts: this was a community whose youngsters felt they had little to lose in joining any rebellion promising to overturn the existing order. He knew how to put that sense of alienation to good use.

"I'd go to secondary schools and start talking about love of one's country and see who showed interest," remembers Kahinda Otafiire, who later rose to become Uganda's justice minister. "Then we'd take them to the Mbarara area for a one-month study group, and during that time I'd identify the ones who were brave and motivated. Fred was one of those. He was either fourteen or fifteen. We took him to train as a fighter in south Mozambique and when he came back he helped us recruit some of the Banyarwanda boys in the camps."[15]

In October 1978, the increasingly paranoid Amin fell into a trap of his own devising. He sent troops to seize Tanzanian land running along the Kagera River, which he claimed belonged to Uganda. He had just provided Tanzanian president Julius Nyerere with the excuse he needed to rid himself of an increasingly erratic neighbor. "I knew Amin was finished," Museveni later wrote. "He played right into our hands."[16]

Pumped up by recent acquisitions of Soviet missiles, jets, and artillery, Tanzania's army counterattacked, its men going into action alongside Ugandan anti-Amin groups that had united under the banner of the Uganda National Liberation Army (UNLA). A contingent of Libyan troops sent by Gaddafi to Amin's rescue soon found themselves on the front line, as the retreating Ugandan army focused on the more interesting job of looting.

By April 11, 1979, the Uganda-Tanzania War was over, and Amin had fled, eventually finding safe haven in Saudi Arabia. Museveni, whose FRONASA force had swelled to 9,000 men, was named minister of state for defence in the new government, and a military commission set about returning Uganda to civilian rule. The young radical played along, but his skepticism ran deep. As far as he was concerned, the job of transforming Ugandan politics was only half done.

Within months, ethnic rivalry and mutual suspicion ensured the constituent parts of Uganda's anti-Amin coalition were at each other's throats. Demoted to minister of regional cooperation, Museveni jibbed at the discovery that young Banyarwanda he had recruited to FRONASA, including Fred—one of his best fighters—were being systematically disqualified from joining UNLA on the grounds of nationality. Aware that the ground was being cut from under his feet, he quietly prepared to return to the bush. With him would go both Fred and Kagame, who, inspired by his friend's example, had by then completed a seven-month Tanzanian course in espionage and information-gathering.

•

This was a period of immense political volatility, but even in the most restive times, pupils go to school, couples get married, and universities run courses. As Uganda boiled, Patrick enrolled at law school in Kampala.

One of Africa's oldest, most revered universities, Makerere's campus sprawls across a hillside studded with ancient mvule trees, perches for the ubiquitous marabou storks. They swoop aloft with alarming suddenness, the whoosh of their wings sounding like Armageddon's arrival, as students loll in the emerald shade below, debating the state of the world.

Nyerere strolled across Makerere's lawns in the 1940s; Kenyan novelist Ngũgĩ wa Thiongo found his antiestablishment voice here in the 1960s; and political scientist Ali Mazrui, future Kenyan president Mwai Kibaki, and writers V. S. Naipaul and Paul Theroux all taught classes here. The list of alumni, which includes the likes of John Sentamu, archbishop of York, and British journalist Yasmin Alibhai-Brown, is a roll call of the men—and some women—who have shaped postindependence East Africa.

Patrick was there to study, but given the pace of events in Uganda, political engagement felt like a duty, not an option.

"It was four months after the fall of Idi Amin," remembers Kenneth Kakuru, a contemporary who became a lifelong friend. "Zimbabwe had not yet been liberated, a Portuguese administration was still in place in Mozambique, Cuban troops were fighting alongside the MPLA [Popular Movement for the Liberation of Angola] in Angola, and the Sandinistas were in Nicaragua."[17]

The world's political tectonic plates were shifting, and Utopia shimmered on the horizon. Most of Makerere's young professors—men like lawyers Dani Wadada Nabudere and Frederick Jjuuko—had attended the University of Dar es Salaam, another bastion of radical socialism, and they were brimming with pan-African idealism and postimperial rhetoric.

"They definitely had an impact on all of us," says Kakuru. "You're young, you think you can change the world." Embracing anything other than socialism would have felt bizarre, in light of the African continent's colonial experiences and its gritty reality. "It was romantic in those days to be leftist."

Patrick plunged into student activism. In May 1980, Obote returned to Uganda, and elections—the first in eighteen years—were set for December. As a Catholic, Patrick's choice would traditionally have been the Democratic Party. But the DP felt like yesterday's movement. Museveni had set up an umbrella group offering voters an alternative, and Patrick became chairman of its very active student branch.

Museveni was one of many Ugandans to regard the polls that followed, in which Obote's youth squads toured the country telling voters they would win "whether or not you vote for us," as a nasty, pointless farce. Sure enough, the UPC claimed victory, and Uganda embarked on what is dubbed "Obote 2," a chapter far more violent than "Obote 1."

Tanzanian troops still occupied the country, and with every day that passed, Nyerere's principled army of liberation came to resemble more closely its thuggish, dysfunctional predecessor.

"Tanzanian soldiers who had come as humane, soft spoken liberators, suddenly turned into smiling but sadistic killers," remembers Pecos Kutesa. "Owning sunglasses, watches, television sets, radios and other gadgets became death sentences."[18] Prominent Ugandans were gunned down on the streets. The city's discos and nightclubs closed at noon, since the shootings would inevitably start around 3 p.m. and go on until the next morning. Amin had gone, but the capital felt, if anything, less secure.

The main problem the disaffected Museveni faced, thanks to UNLA's demobilization program, was an acute shortage of weapons. If the initial number of his would-be guerrillas was tiny—it ranges from twenty-eight to thirty-four and forty-two, depending who tells the story—weapons were in even shorter supply: "Thirty-four men, *but only twenty-seven guns*," a veteran will correct you, with a wag of the finger. "Just twenty-seven guns."

So the operation that thrust Museveni's new guerrilla movement into the public limelight on February 6, 1981—an attack on Kabamba, a military barracks three and a half hours' drive west of the Ugandan capital—had a simple aim: get some guns.

•

Whenever Museveni had studied a map of Uganda, working out where his various guerrilla movements needed secret cells, certain locations always came up. Not surprisingly, given its role as a cradle of youthful idealism, "Makerere University" was always one of the names.

Patrick was a trusted pair of hands as far as the NRA, operating out of a safe house in the Kenyan capital, was concerned. As he entered his third year at law school, he was busy connecting would-be recruits to its organizers. Wannabe guerrillas would sneak across the frontier, gather at the collection point in Nairobi, and, if judged suitable, be smuggled back into guerrilla strongholds inside Uganda to learn how to fight.

This was a dangerous game to play, and one that inevitably drew the authorities' attention. It was the era of *panda gari*—"Get into the car"—when Obote's security services toured the streets, loaded suspected rebel sympathizers into pickups, and drove them off to interrogation centers from which they never emerged. "Computermen"—undercover agents—would hang around campus gates, whipping away students whose battered bodies would later be found decomposing in the forest. As his finals approached, Patrick realized he risked joining them.

Determined to secure his degree, he placed himself under a form of protective house arrest by not straying outside Makerere's protective gates. "He stayed inside the university, never going out, until exam time," says a family member. "When he had put the last full stop on the last page of the last paper, he put his pen down and left."[19]

The following day, Patrick boarded a bus bound for Nairobi and the NRA's collection point. He got as far as the bustling border crossing at Busia before being hauled off the bus, arrested, and bundled into the trunk of a security officer's car. He was driven back to Kampala that way, a demeaning, terrifying drive. At the other end, he was hauled out and accused of being an enemy of the state.

Patrick spent the next three years as a guest of Luzira Maximum Security Prison. Situated to the south of Kampala and originally intended for hardened criminals, the British-built penitentiary held murderers, rapists, pimps, burglars, and car thieves alongside its political activists. Professor Yoweri Kyesimira, a prominent political dissident and fellow inmate, took one look at the baby-faced, vulnerable-looking young man and arranged for the two to share a cell.

The prison, like all public buildings in the Kampala area, had been completely looted. "There were no blankets, eating bowls, chamber pots and electrical light bulbs or anything else that provided minimum comfort," recalled Bob Astles, Amin's white former factotum, whose six-and-a-half-year sentence there overlapped with Patrick's.[20]

Hot water was forbidden—the inmates used what few chamber pots remained to surreptitiously heat drinking water for tea and coffee. Sugar and matches were banned, and Luzira's staff sold the soap bars and blankets the Red Cross donated on the open market. Inmates used one hand to wipe their behinds; the other did service as a plate. The prison's meager water supply was infested with leeches.

In a memoir published after his death, Astles described the frequent use of the "triangle," a wooden easel to which blindfolded prisoners were tied naked by the wrists and ankles, then whipped until they screamed. The Tanzanian soldiers who guarded the prison made sure the Ugandan warders showed no leniency, and when a prisoner escaped, those remaining would be lined up to have their heads systematically bashed with rifle butts.

The judicial process itself was a charade. Never brought to court, like most of that era's political detainees, Patrick received an occasional visit from his university friend Kakuru. But the only member of the family brave enough to make the long trip from western Uganda was Jane Keshoro, his mother.

"No one else dared go, it was *so* risky," says the family member. "So here was this illiterate woman, coming from the village on her own. God knows how she got around town. Her husband was afraid she would be killed. But each time she came back saying, 'I saw him. He's alive.'"

CHAPTER SEVEN

THE BUSH WAR

They are more to me than life, these voices, they are more
than motherliness and more than fear; they are the strongest,
most comforting thing there is anywhere: they are the voices
of my comrades.

—**Erich Maria Remarque,**
All Quiet on the Western Front

S amuel Sawaye unlocks the gate of a little caged compound,
leans over the heavy lid sealing the stone-lined vault, and
yanks at its metal handle. A proud "Historical"—the honorific applied to veterans of Museveni's guerrilla movement—he is
wearing a neon yellow shirt with the motto "NRM is my party" em-
broidered above the breast pocket. I wonder if this is a standard part
of his wardrobe, or he has put it on in my honor. Pulling the cover to
one side, he looks at me expectantly.

Standing at the foot of one of the biggest mango trees I've ever
seen, in whose branches a large hornbill flaps and occasionally
screams, I pause, in the grip of a sudden torpor. I feel a deep urge to
stay where I am, relishing the shade a little longer.

"Don't you want to see the bones, then?" asks my Ugandan driver,
puzzled. "No, yes, I do. Of course I do." I walk over obediently and

peer into the darkness, thinking, but not saying, that I have seen enough bodies in my lifetime, perhaps, and I am not sure how much they teach anyone but the forensic examiner.

The vault is not full. It's been more than three decades, after all, and the bones have been steadily crumbling and settling as insects, fungi, small burrowing animals, and the relentless onslaught of the rich Ugandan heat do their work. Bones are also quietly filched from time to time—to be used by witch doctors, it is assumed—hence the padlocks and the wire mesh fence.

They do not smell, they are not grotesque. Just a bit . . . untidy. What I assume to be clavicles, tibias, ribs, and vertebrae have turned feather-light and wispy with the years. Gently subsiding into a powdery brown loam, they look more like bleached roots, dried branches, natural growths than mortal remains. It is only the skulls that retain the power to shock, because they are so unmistakably human.

Some 4,000 lie buried in Kikyusa, just one of the 33 such memorials scattered across the Luwero Triangle, a 2,800-square-mile cheese slice of land radiating north-northwest of Kampala. They bear witness to the huge price locals paid for Yoweri Museveni's decision to use the area as the operational base for his campaign to unseat Obote's administration.

A plaque declares that the monument is in memory "of freedom fighters who died during the protracted war of NRM/NRA 1981–1986." It's a conveniently ambiguous formulation. The vast majority of those killed in Luwero, everyone acknowledges, were civilians. By mere dint of dying, it seems, they picked a side.

The natural tendency for any guerrilla movement "going into the bush"—almost a rite of passage for a generation of African would-be politicians—is to head for the most geographically remote, least-populated area. Mountain ridges pitted with caves are good places to hide from aerial surveillance, deserts destroy armies who don't know where the oases lie, foot soldiers panic in dense jungle. So why did Museveni, on his second attempt at overturning a government, choose to base himself in the Luwero Triangle, rather than his home territory of Ankole?

Proximity to Kampala held the key. For much of the campaign, the NRA's frontline camp, dubbed "Black Bomber Command," lay fifteen to twenty miles north of the capital. Parliament, the ministries, and several military barracks were all tantalizingly close, as were the studios of Radio Uganda, obligatory port of call for any would-be coup leader. Wounded guerrillas could even be smuggled into Mulago Hospital for treatment by sympathetic nurses and doctors. Nerve center of every Ugandan regime, ten times bigger than any other Ugandan city, and a hub for regional trade, Kampala was where the country's key highways converged and its railway culminated.

Luwero's thick tree cover and meandering papyrus swamps meant the area could effortlessly swallow up men, vehicles, and arms, while the soil's fertility—guerrillas returning to previously occupied areas would find that discarded cassava stems had spontaneously put down roots—ensured that for the first part of the war, at least, there was food aplenty.

The local Baganda, whose revered Kabaka had been sent packing by Obote and Amin, had no reason to love the regime. In addition, the area contained a large community of Banyarwanda and Bahima, who had moved there to tend cattle and pick coffee, tea, and bananas. They were naturally sympathetic to the NRA, with its Banyankole and Banyarwanda recruits.

Museveni's admirers hail the move, today, as a strategic masterstroke. Tactically, perhaps. What dulls the choice's brilliance, though, is the death toll. A sense of tamped-down reproach seeps into conversations with residents of Luwero. "The local people feel that given the suffering they endured, they ended up being rewarded with very little," a local journalist told me. "They feel forgotten."

This quiet glade on the outskirts of Kikyusa market town was where villagers were brought by government forces for "screening," to weed out rebel collaborators from loyal citizens, Sawaye says. How does any army establish loyalty in the space of a few minutes? "Government forces couldn't distinguish between the two—there were no uniforms, after all. So they would just kill whoever they suspected."[1]

After the war, villagers returning to the eerily quiet region began gathering up the bones that lined the roads, filled the pit latrines, and lay scattered across the fields and marshes. Normally, a Muganda is buried on the family plot with elaborate ceremony. But entire clans had been wiped out, making identification often impossible and leaving no one to claim the dead. Surreal ossuaries—mute expressions of collective trauma—took impromptu shape. In open fields, on the concrete ruins of houses, along wooden trestle tables, hundreds of skulls, thousands of femurs and tibias, were laid in neat rows. "The display of bones has become an art form," noted the British journalist William Pike.[2]

The trestle tables, with their disconcerting displays, played a helpful political role when Museveni began facing calls for multiparty elections. "Remember, this is what multiparty democracy got you," they warned onlookers. The new president got into the habit of bringing ambassadors and journalists to the memorials to underline the merits of his sui generis "no-party" system. But the locals found the constant reminder of atrocity upsetting, and elders complained that the souls of the dead would never be at peace. "In the Baganda culture, you have to bury the dead," explains Sawaye. Residents were glad, he says, when in the 1990s ceremonies were staged across Luwero, and the bones finally interred. "We were a bit relieved."[3]

He points over the hill, to where what started out as a force of 6,000 local men, armed with just one British-made rifle and a few bows and arrows, took a vote on which of the various militias fighting Obote to support. The choice, between a plethora of acronyms, highlighted how faction-ridden Uganda had become. They opted for the NRA and were sent in return commanders to teach tactics and instill discipline.

The government's key advantage was its command of the air. "We used to teach villagers to hide their fingernails, as they would catch the light and give away their presence to the helicopters and planes," says Sawaye. Another guerrilla trick was to position jerricans—so garish they were bound to catch a pilot's eye—in places where a bombing raid could do no harm.

Back in the mid-1980s, the hardwood forest was even thicker than it is today, and villagers easily dodged army checkpoints as they took hidden fighters cassava, jackfruit, and bananas. Later, when those supplies dried up, everyone was reduced to eating shrubs, animal hides, green leaves, anything they could lay their hands on.

The villagers also ferried another commodity of huge importance to any rebel movement: information. In Kikyusa it was gratefully received by a bespectacled, earnest young man with a distinctive, reedy voice whose angular, bird-like features radiated intensity. While Patrick was doing time in Luzira prison, his future boss, Paul Kagame, was learning the basics of undercover work.

Locals remember a skinny youngster so neatly dressed he was initially assumed to be a government spy—"No, he's one of us," they were told. He learned Luganda impressively quickly in order to communicate with the villagers, and he carried not a gun, but a stick. The NRA knew better than to put its brains at risk, and fighting was never one of Kagame's prime duties. Kagame spent three years in the area, serving as an intelligence officer for the NRA.

"His job was spying on where government forces were stationed, what kind of weapons they had and what tactics they were using. Local villagers would give him information and he'd relay it to High Command," says Sawaye.

Distinctive rocks—he points to one still nestling under a mango tree—served as "dead letter" boxes, where scraps of paper detailing army movements and troop strength would be cached by villagers to be picked up later by the NRA—a classic piece of intelligence tradecraft. "Kagame came in with those ideas."

•

The NRA's first attack on Kabamba barracks on February 6, 1981— the raid involving the legendary twenty-seven guns—featured a tarpaulin-covered truck, crammed with hidden guerrillas, being driven into the barracks. As a guard questioned its driver, a Peugeot 304 with Museveni aboard zipped out from behind the lorry, and the shooting began.

The operation, in which Fred Rwigyema, Paul Kagame, and Museveni's brother Salim Saleh all took part, proved a disappointment, as a Tanzanian soldier hunkered down in an underground armory proved impossible to dislodge. It yielded only sixteen rifles, a single rocket-propelled grenade launcher, and eight vehicles. But the first step had been taken, a precedent set: government barracks and training centers would be the NRA's main source of supply.

Museveni had by 1981 learned the painful lesson of previous botched guerrilla operations. With 11,000 Tanzanian troops still stationed in Uganda and his former fighters scattered across the country, he could not afford head-on confrontation. A "quick war" would only play to the enemy's strengths. "We advocated instead a guerrilla war of pinpricks against the enemy, tiring him and only going on to the conventional stage when we had marshalled enough forces in material, men and experience to overwhelm them," he later wrote.

If the result looked scrappy and often felt humiliating, so be it. "Freedom fighters must sometimes spend a great deal of time running away, which may look cowardly to a general in an air-conditioned room but for the fighter on the ground represents survival," he recalled. "In revolutionary warfare, the mere fact of an insurgent surviving and not being eliminated is in itself a success."[4]

Museveni's group was overwhelmingly a movement of southerners and westerners, the majority of the fighters—setting aside the Banyarwanda—from regions that hated Obote for his dismantlement of the kingdoms and the brutality shown by his soldiers, almost exclusively from the north.

Fighters noticed how the CHC (Chairman of the High Command), or the *Mzee* (old man), as they called Museveni, made a personal effort to connect with each new arrival, teasing out family connections and painstakingly explaining the movement's aims and modus operandi. In Tanzania and Mozambique, it had been drummed into Museveni that a good soldier is always more than a man with a gun; he must grasp the struggle's revolutionary purpose. And so a political commissar was appointed to each NRA unit, and classes in politics, economics, and history held in the bush.

NRA commanders saw themselves as representatives of a people's liberation army, not mere grunts, a fact that may explain the extraordinary number of memoirs that today crowd the shelves of Kampala's bookshops. Self-conscious philosopher-warriors, their authors quote Sun Tzu's *Art of War* with confidence and can distinguish their von Clausewitz from their General Giap.[5]

On the surface, this was an army of peers. Traditional military ranks, considered a hangover from colonial-era armies, had been done away with, with the exception of the High Command. "The ranks were simply Junior Officer 1 or 2 and Senior Officer 1 or 2," recalls Pike. "It was, however, difficult to find out if an officer was JO2 or SO1 as they all called themselves 'commander.' This was one of the simple pragmatic decisions that led to the NRA victory. It bred an egalitarian atmosphere and a spirit of self-sacrifice."[6]

In reality, decision-making rested with a clique of Banyankole and Banyarwanda fighters who either were related to Museveni, had grown up with him, or had been part of the original group that accompanied him to Mozambique and Tanzania. Salim Saleh was part of that trusted inner core, and so was Fred Rwigyema.

Virtually a child soldier, Fred was of an age to need a father figure when he first went into the bush, and that role was provided by Museveni, who appointed Fred to his team of personal bodyguards. "It was a mentor/mentee relationship," remembers Otafiire. Others said Fred was more like a surrogate son. A bitter rivalry with Museveni's brother could easily have developed; instead the two became best buddies, with Fred playing the role of charming Patroclus to Salim Saleh's gruff Achilles.

The two men were so close, they were known as "the Siamese twins." "Pinch one and the other cries out," comrades would joke. When Salim Saleh, a spare giant of a man, was wounded in battle early on in the Luwero campaign, a bullet passing through both forearms, Fred burst into tears, assuming his friend was dying. Saleh survived, and having demonstrated that they kept their nerve in the heat of battle, the two were assigned individual commands.

The guerrillas learned some basic rules. Sleep in the day, move at night. At base camp, hygiene matters. Dig latrines and don't pee at random in the bush, or you'll end up living in your own filth. When on patrol, stay off the main roads and take dirt tracks, trekking cross-country in single file. Use runners to pass messages between units, never a radio—too easily monitored. Never camp in the open or on low ground. Before you sleep, always dig yourself even the shallowest of trenches, or a sudden artillery attack will blow you to smithereens.

But if his own account—and those of many of his lieutenants—are to be believed, Museveni's main lesson was: never alienate the population on whose support you depend. "The population was the water and a guerrilla is a mere fish . . . so he should never antagonise the water," as Pecos Kutesa put it, borrowing from Mao.[7]

So: no raping, looting, drunkenness, or requisitioning. Pay for your food with cash—breaking into banks to acquire it if necessary—and if your men do misbehave, come down on them like a ton of bricks. Guerrillas deemed to have crossed the line were executed, in public, to show villagers how seriously the NRA took the issue of discipline. It's in this context that Paul Kagame's name crops up once again.

Kagame's disruptive phase was behind him now: the military had given him structure and focus, while his friendship with Fred ensured he was treated seriously by his new comrades. Every school playground, sports team, or work crew boasts a dominant alpha male around whom hovers a tremulous shadow, egret to his buffalo. Kagame and Fred fitted into that familiar pattern of male bonding.

Spotting the same aloof, censorious qualities that had surfaced at Rwengoro Primary School, Museveni assigned Kagame to work under Jim Muhwezi, a Makerere law graduate famous for a rocambolesque escapade in which he had disguised himself as a woman to escape into the bush. Muhwezi drew on his experience working for Uganda's police force in his new role running the NRA's military intelligence.

As the NRA's territorial footprint expanded, so did the area over which Kagame roamed. "I used to walk long distances," he later told a biographer. "Sometimes I was sent up to two hundred kilometres away, either in search of contacts or places the guerrilla group could move to in the bush. I would study the territory, see if there was enough water, if there was terrain to hide, if it was likely that people would support us."[8]

To keep abreast of government movements, NRA High Command relied on monitoring the army's uncoded radio messages, a vital source of information. Kagame, it turned out, had the right kind of mindset when it came to dreaming up Machiavellian schemes to outwit the enemy.

The plan he dreamt up to eliminate a sub-county chief in Kalungi who had been tracking down youngsters likely to join the NRA was one example. Kagame persuaded his fellow fighters to draft a letter thanking the sub-county chief for his help, saying that without him the rebels' efforts would not have been successful, and saying they hoped such cooperation would continue. The young men put on school uniforms—shorts and shirts—got on bikes, and dropped the letter near an army road block. A few days later they heard that the sub-county chief had been arrested and executed.

"It was very clever," one of them told me. "We had never thought of that—how you can use the enemy to destroy itself."[9]

But enemy activities were not the main focus for the NRA's military intelligence. The department's primary task, Jim Muhwezi told me, was counterintelligence. "Their job was checking for subversion and infiltration *within* the movement."[10]

In the early days, when the movement was small and desperately underequipped, it was achingly vulnerable to fifth columnists and informants. The other danger was sheer carelessness. A bored comrade's decision to sneak off to town to visit a relative might betray a unit's position. A guerrilla who acquired a regular girlfriend in the village, or who was a little too fond of his beer, was likely to blab.

Kagame's job—monitoring his fellow fighters—would not have been to everyone's liking. But it perfectly suited his watchful personality. A puritanical teetotaler, he never seemed to let his guard down, keeping himself at arm's length from the men, who came to feel he was constantly totting up their failings in some personal Book of Judgment.

Guerrilla fighters swiftly get to know who can run the fastest, carry the heaviest equipment, march without complaining. Kagame possessed none of these attributes: his wiliness was what won him respect. But that admiration was laced with trepidation.

"He was a strict disciplinarian," is the mantra NRA fighters nowadays use to describe the young Kagame, and when you ask them to expand—something they will only do off the record—it's clear this is the gentlest of euphemisms. "There was a perception that he was the enforcer, the punisher," says General Kayumba. "It was common knowledge."

When a disobedient guerrilla came up for court-martial, it was often Kagame's job to make the case for the prosecution, revealing what he had discovered during the course of investigations to a disciplinary committee. Kagame requested the death sentence with such alacrity that he acquired a nickname that dogs him to this day: "Pilato," they called him, in tribute to Pontius Pilate, the man who ordered Jesus's crucifixion while washing his hands of moral responsibility.

Contemporaries marveled at the triviality of the infractions deemed to merit capital punishment. If two fighters were talking, a third joined them, and the first two fell silent, that alone was considered reason enough to assume a plot was being hatched, and the two might end up being sentenced to death.

"What crimes were considered serious enough to merit execution?" I asked an NRM Historical who served in Luwero at the same time as Kagame, a man who has gone on to become a successful politician.

"Internal rivalry, indiscipline, fighting, sneaking off to get a beer, making noise or dropping something when we were moving, leaving your comrades during an ambush—those were all reasons. He wouldn't hesitate to send them to their graves."[11]

"Did Kagame personally administer the death penalty?"

"No. But I was at meetings where he would read out the names of those who were to die, and then he'd send parties on missions to their units to carry the sentence out."

My next question was instinctive, I blurted it out. "Did Kagame enjoy it?"

"Very much so." He sucked in his breath. "He enjoyed it too much."

Bitterness over how and why certain NRA fighters, often regarded by their comrades as inspirational figures, were singled out for the death penalty still surfaces today among former fighters. But Muhwezi defends the need for harsh action. "Counterintelligence is very important for a guerrilla movement. There was a lot of suspicion that we could be infiltrated."

And the young men—and some women—who joined the movement had already witnessed enough brutality, administered by Amin and Obote's troops, to understand the need for discipline. It's a mindset civilians struggle to grasp, the Historical admits, and which it can take decades to shed. "In the military you don't question orders, you have that drummed into you. '*Order ni moja*,' people would say: 'There's only one order.' We were young, we didn't question it at the time. I only questioned it later."

•

As news of the first, flamboyant Kabamba raid spread, recruits materialized. The following months were spent consolidating a clandestine movement that now boasted 200 men. Museveni split the force into six units deployed across the Luwero Triangle's five districts, with a mission to lay ambushes and attack police posts and administrative centers.[12]

An April attack on a government detachment based in Kakiri, seventeen miles northwest of Kampala, in which Pecos spotted Fred "calm, composed, smart as usual and firing like a drill instructor," resulted in such a generous haul of guns, mortars, and bombs that the guerrillas could barely haul their loot away. Belatedly realizing that carriers mattered just as much as fighters, Museveni appointed a special company of commandos whose responsibility was removing uniforms, shoes, ammunition, and guns from the enemy. Slain soldiers were stripped to their underpants, not out of disrespect, but practical necessity.

Museveni was still hungry for weapons, so along with six companions he crossed the front line, boarded a boat, chugged in darkness across Lake Victoria to the Kenyan port of Kisumu, then drove to Nairobi. Having signed a deal there with the head of a Baganda militia, he set off for Libya, where he persuaded General Muammar Gaddafi to make good on a promised arms airdrop.

Over the following months, the NRA targeted river crossings and bridges allowing access in and out of the Luwero Triangle, using antipersonnel and anti-vehicle mines provided by the Libyans to carve out an operational zone with the town of Semuto as its de facto capital. Inside that zone, the movement set up Resistance Councils staffed by peasants, precursors of the local councils on which Museveni would eventually base Uganda's national administration. A state-within-a-state was being created, and "cadres" were appointed to teach the masses the meaning of their ideological struggle.

The NRA seemed to have the wind in its sails. But in June 1982, the Ugandan army's chief of staff, Major General David Oyite-Ojok, launched the first major government offensive against the rebels, "Operation Bonanza." His artillerymen systematically shelled Luwero's forests, while wave after wave of troops fanned out from the army's base in Bombo.

It was at this point that Obote set his sights on the Banyarwanda community, which was supplying Museveni with so many of his fighters. The ethnic cleansing program he set in motion eliminated any distinction between Ugandan Banyarwanda and refugees. Whether they had crossed over in the 1920s, 1960s, or their presence predated colonial map-drawing, anyone speaking Kinyarwanda was suddenly designated "foreign," other.

"If a dog gives birth in a cowshed, it does not turn into a cow," Chris Rwakasisi, Obote's minister of security, famously declared as he ushered in a program of collective punishment that would ensure that Patrick's and Kayumba's families, among many others, lost everything for which they had worked.

•

I t began with a series of inflammatory speeches gleefully reported by the government-owned *Uganda Times*. The Banyarwanda had illegally voted in the elections, Obote claimed: they flirted with terrorists, they had been responsible for most of the atrocities committed by Amin's State Research Bureau, and now they were supporting "bandits."

In September 1982, egged on by Rwakasisi and Patrick Rubaihayo, the agriculture minister and local MP, Mbarara's district council ruled that all members of the Banyarwanda community were to be moved to the existing refugee camps. Like a flu bug, the virus of ethnic hatred had successfully jumped across Rwanda's border and found a new host.[13]

Patrick's brother Ernest recalls that their father was one of the local Banyarwanda who protested. At a public meeting in Mbarara, John Kanimba upbraided Rwakasisi. "Our father said, 'We have never been refugees. I was born here, my grandparents came here a long time ago.'" The minister was unabashed. "Those who came early from Rwanda should go early," he told the meeting. Houses of the Banyarwanda started going up in flames.

The systematic killings, rapes, and pillaging, targeting both citizens and refugees in western Uganda, began a month later. While the UPC's youth wing, paramilitary special forces, and the police were usually in charge of operations, neighbors and former friends gleefully joined the fun. "A conservative estimate is that 45,000 head of cattle and 16,000 homes were destroyed," reported Cathy Watson.[14] Nearly 80,000 Banyarwanda either fled into the camps, crossed the border into Rwanda, or sat trapped at the border after Rwanda closed its frontiers.

There can be few experiences more traumatizing than becoming, overnight, an alien in your own land. The primal fear of the hate-fueled mob coming to get you, burning torches in hand, runs through our human DNA.

In the 1970s, the quest for fresh grazing had brought Patrick's family to a hillside east of the town of Isingiro, looking down on the plains of Tanzania, where they had built a little brick house. Almost overnight, all that was taken.

Jane Keshoro remembers the steady ratcheting up of intimidation. "We'd never seen guns before. The first time they took cows and money. The second time they were raping and they carried jerricans, which they'd set fire to." The molten plastic, dripped on victims, was used as a method of torture. "So we left."

She remembers the raids being conducted by "northerners," soldiers in uniform. But for Ernest, who was just fourteen at the time, it's the role played by those he had regarded as neighbors and friends that sticks in the mind.

"It was horrible. There were meetings where people would even make bookings: 'Me, I'll take Ernest's place, you take so-and-so's place.' So you see your friend, your neighbor, coming to burn you out. Among ourselves, there had been no problems up till then."

The episode triggered the equivalent of a cognitive thunderclap. "It was the first step to knowing we were not local. We had always insisted we were Ugandans, yet by their acts they showed we were not."

Owners of 150 head of cattle, Patrick's family had been seen as prosperous. The mob left them with only livestock so old and sick it was not worth stealing. John Kanimba and his two wives and nine children drove it across the hills and down into Nakivale, Uganda's oldest refugee settlement. There, in a long, dun-colored valley, biscuit-dry and swept by hot, gusty winds, they joined tens of thousands of Tutsi refugees who had already spent nearly two decades there.

For the new arrivals, the adjustment required was immense.

Once proudly self-reliant, the family had only the clothes they were wearing, and now depended on WFP handouts, just like everyone else. Raised exclusively on milk and yogurt, they were suddenly presented with a diet of beans and *posho* (maize meal). Many fell sick on the unfamiliar food. And there was never enough. "What do I remember?" Ernest puts one hand to his stomach, remembering its constant growl. "Hunger, hunger, hunger."

Hearts hardened quickly in Nakivale: survival required it. "Sometimes you'd go to queue in the morning and return in the evening without any food," recalls Jane. "Sometimes people were so weak, they'd faint, and be pushed out of the queue. If you loved someone, you would not send them to the camps. The camps were like prisons."

The next years saw a series of relocations from one refugee settlement to another, the family each time attempting to build up their depleted herd only to see the best livestock stolen time and again.

Old friends could do little to help. If the worst of the violence swept through Uganda's west, Banyarwanda in the capital did not escape, either, their social status providing no protection. Eliphaz Rwivanga, the Pepsi manager who had generously taken Patrick under his wing in Kampala, lost his job and was chased back to Rwanda, where he died.

General Kayumba's family was being brought similarly low. Born in Rukingiri, seventy miles west of Mbarara, he had enjoyed a thoroughly middle-class Ugandan upbringing. His father had served in the King's African Rifles, the regiment trained up by British colonial authorities, later joining the Ugandan civil service, acquiring a herd of cattle and becoming a health inspector.

"We weren't rich, but we owned land, and a hundred head of cattle," recalls General Kayumba. "I grew up never lacking for anything, my sister and all my brothers went to school, so you could say we were privileged." His father had expected to spend his old age tending his herd.

All that was ripped away. "In 1982 Obote's men came and swept away everything he had worked for, taking all his cattle," the General says. "He only escaped ending up in one of the refugee camps because Mbarara's district administrator gave him protection."

If Obote's campaign was intended to deter members of the community from joining Museveni, it dramatically backfired. The impact on the Banyarwanda community was electric: rather than smothering resistance, the authorities whipped it up. Now allotted "pariah" status in Ugandan society, Tutsi youngsters knew that for them a quiet life was ruled out. Enlistment to the NRA soared.

"Museveni was welcoming anyone who was willing to fight and he saw in the Banyarwanda that spirit of resoluteness," my Historical source explains. "When you had a Munyarwanda you'd send him to recruit other Banyarwanda, in the schools, at university, in the camps. People like [Fred] Rwigyema, they convinced many others."[15]

Once the Ugandan administrators and UNHCR and WFP workers had left the refugee camps for the night, the clandestine meetings began. Impassioned, fiery speeches in Kinyarwanda were made to murmurs of disquiet and mounting applause. In the following days, teenage boys and young men quietly slipped away to join the NRA.

In Kampala, one of those who signed up was the twenty-four-year-old Kayumba Nyamwasa. Seminary-educated, he had never dreamt of going into soldiering, a career choice regarded as thoroughly disreputable by middle-class Ugandans. "When I was young I wanted to be a veterinarian," he told me. "The vet was the man you called when a cow was dying, so he was the man I used to admire."

Now he was haunted by his father's humiliation. "That stigma remained with me. It dawned on me that while I was a Ugandan on paper in fact I was not a citizen, and that the citizenship issue was key. It drew me closer to other Rwandans." Fresh out of college, he felt no qualms about shelving his personal ambitions and heading into the bush. "I wanted to fight discrimination, to be part and parcel of a project of asserting a Rwandan identity, so I became a soldier by default."

To many fellow recruits, these were just NRA fighters like any others. But those who got a little closer remarked on the single-minded ferocity with which the Banyarwanda guerrillas fought, their almost suicidal readiness to take risks. "If you were facing an enemy that was hard to overrun you'd form a crack unit. That meant choosing exactly the right selection of arms and the very best fighters," my Historical source explains. "And they would often be Banyarwanda." The first to volunteer for operations, the Banyarwanda would be the last to give up in the face of lacerating enemy fire.

For the "fifty-niner" refugees, that prowess could perhaps be traced to fireside tales they had heard of proud *intore*, the Mwami's warriors, going into battle, and the assurances Tutsi elders had given them that they were destined to return to the beautiful country their forefathers had ruled for 800 years.

But with the Ugandan Banyarwanda, the explanation was simpler. Many had thought themselves an integral part of a society that, it now turned out, no longer wanted them. As motivations go, the knowledge that you have nothing to lose probably trumps loyalty to your friends, or even belief in a higher purpose. "They didn't have much to go back to," recalls my Historical contact. "So they would be very daring."

•

In late 1982, the Ugandan government's Operation Bonanza began to bite and the NRA's stocks of land mines and ammunition ran low. Outnumbered and outgunned, it was forced out of the counties where the guerrillas had enjoyed food, cover, and local support and driven northwest into drier, more sparsely cultivated land.

Salim Saleh led a disastrous attack on a military base at Bukalabi in which ten NRA fighters were killed and he was seriously wounded, a raid triggered by both territorial ambition and hunger for weaponry. While an estimated 1 million civilians were now inside NRA-controlled territory, after two years of insurgency, the 1,500-strong guerrilla movement still owned only 400 guns.

May 1983 saw a mass exodus of civilians. "It was a pathetic sight," wrote Pecos Kutesa. "Old women and men, toddlers and babies strapped to their mothers' backs, with each person carrying the few valuables that the enemy had not looted." Government forces shelled the bedraggled columns of villagers all the way. In the hemmed-in Luwero Triangle, famine began to set in. Out in government-held territory, civilians were "screened" by the army—a death sentence for many—and penned into internment camps, the aim being to drain the NRA of its civilian support.

The situation got so serious that Museveni considered relocating to the border with Zaire, but a few successful attacks lifted morale. Setting up camp in Ngoma, a wild stretch of shrub and grassland fringed by protective hills, the rebels struck a deal with local Bahima cattle herders, who agreed to supply the fighters with a steady diet of fresh beef.

NRA numbers kept expanding, but the government's counterinsurgency campaign was gaining traction, too. Under the guidance of North Korean artillery instructors, Obote's army learned to lower the sights on their antiaircraft guns and "Stalin's Organ" rocket launchers. Aimed at ground level, the missiles beheaded fighters and amputated limbs.

Just as the NRA was forced onto the back foot, its luck changed. Major General Oyite-Ojok, always a hands-on commander, had been making active use of an aging fleet of helicopters, which clattered above the trees to pinpoint rebel bases. In the evening of December 2, 1983, shortly after takeoff, the helicopter in which he was traveling exploded, killing all aboard. As a battle for succession immediately began—a contest that took predictably ethnic form—the army canceled its ground offensive.

In February 1984, confidence was high enough for the NRA to reach out of its comfort zone and attack a barracks in Masindi, on the road to Murchison Falls, a blitzkrieg of an operation commanded by Salim Saleh in which 700 men covered eighty miles in two days, hitting the base when soldiers were hungover from a party. The NRA's tally this time was fourteen trucks' worth of arms, including a thousand submachine guns.

It was the biggest operation the guerrilla army had attempted and marked a turning point in the Bush War. When William Pike became the first Western reporter to visit the NRA in the field later that year, he registered that the Luwero Triangle was firmly under rebel control. He also absorbed the zone's strange, haunting silence: the vast majority of its inhabitants were dead or gone.

•

Throughout this period, civilians were being killed, in numbers that stand in bleak counterpoint to the fierce romanticism with which so many of the NRM's gray-templed veterans view the episode.

The debate over exactly how many, in what circumstances, and who was responsible simmers on, as complex as the society that gave rise to such violence. Pick up a few histories of Uganda in a Western university library, and you catch a taste of the various accounts' irreconcilability and the blazing fury they still evoke. Not just in the texts themselves, but the outraged comments readers have scrawled on their pages.

Skepticism is not confined to critics of the late Obote. When I told a former NRA guerrilla turned scholar I met on Makerere's campus that I planned to visit some of Luwero's memorial sites, he shook his head. "I refuse to go to Luwero," he said. "I don't want to be part of all the lies being told."[16]

The absence of clarity in part reflects the fact that Uganda in the mid-1980s had become a very frightening place for human rights organizations and journalists to operate. In the day, officials from the International Committee of the Red Cross (ICRC)—not usually easy to rattle—would drive into Luwero to visit the thirty-six internment camps set up by the government. But at night, when so much of the killing took place, these potential witnesses were careful to be back in Kampala, itself a grim city wracked by sporadic gunfire and prowled by the dreaded "computermen."

Reports from Luwero filtered out notwithstanding—of rapes, burning villages, and massacres, of camps turned into places of torture, deliberate starvation, and extrajudicial executions.

Obote countered by claiming that yes, villagers were being slaughtered, but not by his men. The perpetrators were NRA "bandits" who had either donned government forces' uniforms or were wearing them already, since so many rebels were army deserters. Their brutality was part of a cynical "false flag" operation, he claimed. The worse these rebels-disguised-as-soldiers behaved, the more likely it became that terrified villagers would rally to the NRA's side.

It was an explanation foreign embassies and the World Bank, whose aid was propping up Obote's government, were initially all too ready to accept. Since Obote, the British in particular felt, had brought to an end the rule of a psychotic buffoon—Amin—his administration deserved support, rather than criticism.

One Western human rights worker who spent six months slipping in and out of the Luwero Triangle—who still prefers to remain anonymous—fumes at that self-deception. He became convinced that a razed-earth policy was at work. One particular evening, when he bumped into an army unit mustering on the outskirts of a village, sticks in his mind. "I don't know who he thought I was, but the commander saluted when he saw me. I asked what he was up to and he replied, 'We're going into that village to kill every man, woman, and child. No dog will be left alive.' And that was what the unit proceeded to do."[17]

In August 1984, the complicit silence was finally shattered. In congressional hearings in Washington and interviews with US newspapers,

Elliott Abrams, the US assistant secretary of state for human rights, claimed that 100,000 to 200,000 civilians had died in the previous three years in the Luwero Triangle, either shot, starved in the camps, or tortured in illegal detention centers.[18]

The British government, leaping to Obote's defense, countered with an estimate of 15,000 dead, which Obote would later blame on ill-disciplined troops, accidental deaths in "cross-fire," and "bandits" posing as soldiers.[19]

But days later, Britain's *Observer* splashed journalist William Pike's account of his trip into the bush across its front page, an article that forever changed the way the international community viewed the Obote regime. He had seen firsthand the bodies dumped in shallow trenches inside abandoned ICRC camps, sprawled across the front rooms of looted houses, or simply left to rot in the open.[20]

Could the NRA have been responsible? For Pike, who would later go on to edit the Museveni government's newspaper, that scenario makes little sense. "When you asked villagers what had happened, the refrain you kept hearing was 'the army did this, the Acholi did that,'" he told me. The peasants he met were friendly toward his NRA escorts, not demonstrating the fear you would expect locals to show toward men seen as predators.

The same human rights worker who spent six months visiting the Luwero told me he never personally stumbled across an example of an NRA atrocity, and that if they had occurred, "they wouldn't have amounted to one percent of the abuses committed by Obote's army." He found it hard to believe villagers would have been unable to distinguish NRA fighters from southern and western Uganda, who spoke Luganda and Swahili, from Acholi and Langi government soldiers. "It's just not credible."

After the Bush War, Dr. Patrick Bracken and Dr. Joan Giller, an Irish psychiatrist and an English gynecologist, respectively, worked with Luwero's traumatized victims for the Medical Foundation for the Care of the Victims of Torture, a British NGO. "We were there for three years and interviewed hundreds of people. The villagers we spoke to were quite clear that the people who committed the atrocities were UNLA, not NRA," says Dr. Bracken.

When I ask them what testimonies lingered, there is a short pause. "There was one incident in a village in which two boys were ordered to bite each other's ears off," Dr. Giller recollects. "They were friends, you see. And I also remember a mother describing how a soldier raped her daughter in front of her, pushing the girl's legs above her head so violently, both legs were broken. Those are the kind of stories you remember."[21]

How can any human being commit such horrors? Revenge is one explanation. The Acholi and Langi had themselves been brutally purged from Amin's army in 1971, summoned to barracks and shot in the thousands by supposed comrades-in-arms. As Rwanda's own experience would prove, victims turned killers are capable of extraordinary viciousness.

But most analysts point to the schism between Uganda's southern "Bantu"-speakers and northern "Nilotics," a historical rift entrenched by British policies of divide-and-rule. To empathize with a peasant grandmother begging for mercy, you must first accept she is a member of the same species. For Obote's soldiers, Luwero's inhabitants were "other," and killing them—after playing various cruelly amusing games—came easily.

Yet allegations of NRA atrocities linger, and the reason is their source. They are repeated—off the record, of course—not just by former members of Obote's government with an interest in rehabilitating stained reputations, but also by some of the men who once fought on Museveni's winning side.

One former NRA fighter I interviewed acknowledged being present at more than one "false flag" attack. "There were situations I witnessed where members of the public were killed just to give the impression that the government army was responsible," he said. "I saw that. We wanted the villagers not to be government supporters. But these were uncommon incidents, only used in dire circumstances."

The motive for extreme cruelty, in this scenario, is different. Coldheartedness is excused by the deterministic Marxist theory, which dictates that the worse conditions become for the proletariat, the better it is for the revolution, so sacrifices must be made. But it requires a certain kind of mentality to be able to coolly turn such implacable theory into practice.

There's another allegation that stubbornly surfaces in discussions of the Bush War, and this one involves the *kafuni*, a short-handled hoe used to dig holes and loosen soil. Part of any Ugandan farmer's standard tool kit, it became associated during the Bush War with something grimly specific: a method of execution used by the NRA to dispatch suspected informants.

In theory, accountability was one of the NRA's central tenets, and when justice was dispensed in rebel-held territory, the process was open—hence the testimony collected by intelligence officers like Paul Kagame—and the sentence carried out in public.

In reality, former NRM rebels will tell you, *kafuni* was often used not so much with fighters who had become a problem—although that did happen—but with members of Obote's youth squads, villagers suspected of collaboration, or those who simply happened to be in the wrong place at the wrong time, the bodies quickly buried in shallow graves in the dark of the forest.

A hole would be dug and the suspect made to kneel before it, elbows strapped together behind his back in a technique known as *kandoya*. A sharp blow to the back of the head with the *kafuni*, if correctly administered, killed instantaneously, and the body would tumble into the ready grave. *Kafuni* not only had the advantage of being silent, but it saved on ammunition, a key consideration for a group that had to steal every bullet. "That's how you kill pigs," my Historical contact explained. "It's a Communist method, very harsh. With *kafuni*, those deaths were not made public, and the bodies were never seen again."

When I asked Winnie Byanyima, a former NRA guerrilla who went on to lead Oxfam and the Joint United Nations Program on HIV/AIDS (UNAIDS), about the use of *kafuni,* she just grimaced: "You know, war is ugly."[22] Kizza Besigye, Museveni's doctor in the bush and Winnie's husband, was a little more forthcoming, specifying that *kafuni* had only been used in the movement's early stages. "It has to be understood within the context of the time. The NRA was in total concealment. They could not cook, or light any fires, they had to maintain total silence during the day, and managing people also had to be done in total silence."

The problem is that the term "suspected informant" covers a multitude of sins. It can apply to a village sneak who relays information about NRA patrols to a UNLA army base for ready cash, food, or protection. But it could also apply to villagers who had the misfortune to bump into a guerrilla unit, for example, just as it was preparing an ambush or stealthily advancing on a government position.

The former NRA fighter who told me he steered clear of Luwero because of "all the lies" explained—in a voice suffused with pity and regret—the precise circumstances in which *kafuni* might be used.

"Say you were going on patrol at night. There are seventeen of you, twelve of you go ahead and five hang back. You come across a villager, someone who is very humble, a simple person, friendly, drunk, willing to please. You say to him, 'Come along with me,' and he follows without questioning, you pass him back down the line. And that happens once, twice, three times. . . . You keep passing those people back down the line. Later, when you return to the unit, all those people are gone.

"There were holes in the ground that we'd dig to defecate in and then cover up, because you couldn't leave any trace of your passing. Those people would be killed and put in those holes."

And he adds, "Those are the kind of operations Kagame was associated with." For Kagame's reputation as a "rigid disciplinarian," his "Pilato" nickname, was not solely rooted in the role he played collecting evidence against court-martialed NRA fighters. It extended to what any human rights organization would regard as extrajudicial execution.

Still clearly deeply troubled by his past, this former fighter raises two questions to which he would like answers: What happened to NRA recruits who became too ill to fight, and checked into sick bay, and what happened to those who decided, on principle, that the rebel's life was not for them? In theory, he recalls, the latter were escorted to the front line and waved on their way. "But after liberation, we did not see those men again," he says. In both cases, he suspects *kafuni* was used to eliminate a conundrum no guerrilla movement is equipped to handle. "Once you were in, you were in, you could not go back."

One of the NRA's first acts after rolling into Kampala was to set up a Truth Commission, chaired by a venerable Supreme Court judge, to establish a historical record of human rights abuses in Uganda. Justice Arthur Oder toured the country holding public meetings at which traumatized witnesses gave evidence, with the *New Vision* newspaper running graphic daily accounts of the sessions on its back page.

In theory, the inquiry should have settled the question of who did what to whom in the Luwero Triangle. But Museveni's pragmatic need to reconcile with Amin and Obote's supporters swiftly leached away support for the process. By year two, the inquiry was running out of money. When the final report was published, eight years after the commission's creation, only a thousand copies were printed, and they were not widely distributed. "I never met a Ugandan who had read Justice Oder's report, and most were unaware that it even existed," an American author later wrote.[23]

Luwero's skulls retain their secrets. For the moment, the NRM's version of events drowns out alternative accounts and skeptical voices, but one suspects they will bubble up like some irrepressible volcanic spring when Museveni quits the scene.

It's probably naive to expect a definitive account of *any* historical episode, let alone one so drenched in pain and loss. But the disagreement over what happened in Luwero carries a lesson. In war, even a war widely deemed to have been won by the more virtuous party, no side can credibly claim to have emerged with clean consciences and spotless hands. The inability to establish an agreed narrative for the Bush War was a harbinger of the deafening clash of story lines later seen in Rwanda.

CHAPTER EIGHT

ON TO KAMPALA

The revolution is not an apple that falls when
it is ripe. You have to make it fall.
—Che Guevara

In the cool of a moonless night, Ali Porteous is setting up
an impromptu film viewing on a beach on Bulago Island. A
spinach-green knob breaking Lake Victoria's choppy surface,
Bulago gazes across the waters to Entebbe's twinkling lights. It is inhabited by a community of fishermen, a score of expatriates, and
a strumming, preening, flapping population of cormorants, storks,
and kingfishers.

Ali, a British former documentary maker who owns the hotel, has
been persuaded to show some of the material shot when she and
her partner became the first television crew to visit Museveni in the
bush nearly four decades ago. It's a good evening for a screening.
The previous night, lightning cracked apart a tar-black sky. No moon
means no lake flies, which can swarm in such abundance their dry
corpses have to be swept like sawdust from the hotel stairs come the
morning.

As the footage runs there are murmurs from the Ugandan guests as they spot the familiar faces: Museveni, Salim Saleh, Kahinda

Otafiire, Jim Muhwezi. How young they look! Check out those side-burns, those flares, all that hair . . . they could be going to a Jackson 5 concert! And how skinny! No politician's paunches here. All elbows, shoulders, and hips, these young men possess the stern physical elegance of chronic malnutrition.

For a few seconds, a jeep appears, bearing a tall, slim warrior. He's wearing a dark beret, but you can just see his hair beneath, with a distinctive streak of white. His complexion is flawless, his gaze clear, his expression serene. "And there he is," breathes Ali. "The most beautiful man in the world." She does not bother to identify him.

Back in the 1980s, Ali and Tim Cooper were the kind of bucca-neering filmmakers ready to take extraordinary risks to secure material no one else could offer. Fresh from filming the Tamil Tigers in Sri Lanka, they heard about a suspected genocide taking place in central Uganda and hooked up with an NRA liaison cell in London, determined to see for themselves.

The two arrived in Uganda and crossed government lines one evening in early 1985. On contact with the NRA, they were rigorously grilled to ensure they were not government spies, but then made welcome, and the NRA commanders and the filmmakers soon became genuine friends. None more so than Fred Rwigyema, and Ali quietly fell for him.

You get a whiff of the mutual attraction in a black-and-white photograph taken at the time. Ali, Tim, and their new mates are sitting cross-legged inside a banana-fronded shelter, gazing at the camera. Tim's elbow is hooked proprietorially over Ali's, but she is turned ever so slightly toward Fred, who is hunching his wide shoulders to squeeze into the space. For a battle-hardened guerrilla, he looks surprisingly bashful.

Ali and Tim spent six weeks in Luwero, constantly on the move. Like Pike before them, both were impressed with the movement's discipline. "There were very few camp followers, very few women. What there were, instead, were lots of children, who had run to join the NRA when their villages had been attacked. It was the funniest thing to see, children commanding the men, whacking them over the head during operations to go in to fight."[1]

They were hungry all the time. "They came from an area where there had been a lot of cattle and so they were quite fat, but where we were there was bugger all to eat, just jackfruit and *posho*. We spent a lot of time foraging. And we never had enough water."

Getting the images out to the world became the challenge. Afraid of being caught with incriminating material, Ali and Tim entrusted the footage to the NRA and crossed back into government territory, masquerading as missionaries. They had to wait three nail-biting weeks before the film canisters, smuggled by boat across Lake Victoria, arrived in Nairobi.

They were editing the footage at Channel Four's headquarters in London when a Ugandan government minister turned up unexpectedly, bearing a suitcase full of cash and a simple request: "Don't show the film."

The bribe was declined, but the official's instincts were sound. Coming on top of Pike's account in the *Observer*, their coverage provided Western governments with their first sustained glimpse of the Marxist "bandit" Yoweri Museveni and his movement. He came across well: serious, impassioned, articulate. It was enough to convince many Western policymakers that a transfer of allegiance might finally be in order.

The NRA was on the cusp of a major deployment. Still hungry for weapons, Museveni decided to travel abroad once more to muster diplomatic support, making another clandestine trip across the lake. Before he left, the NRA divided into two. Taking with him a contingent of sick and elderly civilian stragglers, Fred trekked west, heading toward the Rwenzori Mountains. The rump NRA remained in Luwero.

Obote's army interpreted the maneuver as a sign the guerrilla movement was close to collapse. What followed instead was a two-pronged assault by both NRA forces—operating 250 miles apart—that stretched government forces well beyond their operational limits.

The mood in Ugandan army ranks was becoming mutinous. As the campaign had turned against them, Acholi soldiers had become convinced they were taking all the casualties, while their Langi colleagues sat safely in their offices. In July 1985, three days after the western town of Fort Portal fell to Fred's forces, Uganda woke to yet another military coup, this one staged by Tito Okello and Bazilio Olara-Okello, two Acholi generals.

"Obote 2" was over. The man himself fled to Kenya and then on to Zambia as looting broke out in central Kampala. The new president, Tito Okello, made the customary gesture and released the political prisoners his predecessor had jailed. Patrick Karegeya was among a truckload of inmates driven from prison to Kampala's City Square, where they were unceremoniously dumped.

•

P atrick's university friend Kenneth Kakuru went to pick him up, negotiating his way warily through a city being steadily trashed by its residents. Taking one look at Patrick, prison-pale and reeking of stale sweat, he took him to buy a new outfit. Then the two went back to the lodgings Kakuru shared with Joseph Tinka, another Makerere contemporary.

Briefing Patrick on what had taken place in his absence, Kakuru begged him to learn the lesson of the past three years. "For God's sake, Patrick, get out of politics! You're a lawyer. Finish your bar exam so you can practice. God has spared you this time. Make the most of it. It's time to settle down." Patrick meekly agreed. He told his on-off girlfriend Leah, who was also putting pressure on him to sort himself out, that he would travel upcountry to see his parents and discuss marriage.

Instead, Patrick went to town and never came back. The next time his friends saw him, it was the fall of Kampala, and Patrick, reborn as an NRA guerrilla, was wearing camouflage and toting a pistol. When it came to things he cared most about, it turned out, Patrick knew how to keep a secret.

He joined the NRA's Seventh Battalion, nicknamed "Black Bomber Command," stationed in Luwero. The years of sustained Banyarwanda recruitment meant this was a group peppered with familiar faces. Kayumba was one of them. For six months, they shared a three-man tent, an experience calculated to build mutual trust.

Patrick was joining the revolution late, but still in time to experience the guerrillas' rough-and-ready existence. If food was in short supply, so was clean water, and the fighters were infested with lice. The moist equatorial climate encouraged trench foot, and when they removed their cheap rubber boots, they often peeled away layers of dead white skin. "It was a very tough life," recalls the General.

Patrick joined military intelligence under Jim Muhwezi's command. "These young boys who joined later from the schools and universities, they weren't trained militarily, they were educated, so we didn't use them in battle," says the latter.[2]

There he met fellow "Old Boy" Kagame. The two young men's outlooks could not have been more different. In contrast with the judgmental Kagame, the easygoing Patrick had no problem understanding why an officer might slip off for a beer. And Muhwezi noticed that Patrick possessed an almost Tourette's-like compulsion to deliver razor-sharp insights, rendered palatable by humor. "Patrick was a big mouth. People used to say, 'He says aloud what other people don't dare think.'" An impish sense of humor, his boss noticed— tellingly, in light of future events—often pushed Patrick to the very limit of what was acceptable in a military setup.

Perhaps Patrick got away with it because he was joining the NRA when the war's outcome looked increasingly assured. Or perhaps it was simply because he was Patrick, and people always cut him more slack than others. "I think he never went through the degrees of soldiering and part of him remained civilian, in some way. But it could verge on indiscipline. You can't remain a rebel in a security organization," reflects Muhwezi.

•

In the coup's wake, Tito Okello, who had formed a marriage of convenience with the Democratic Party, set up a Military Council and offered Museveni a seat at the table if the NRA suspended its campaign. Kenyan president Daniel arap Moi offered to host peace talks in Nairobi. But sensing that victory was now within reach, Museveni was in no hurry to negotiate, making one demand after another while his two fronts gobbled up territory in western and central Uganda.

With the NRA controlling two-thirds of Uganda, including its most fertile and heavily populated areas, Resistance Councils were once again being established in guerrilla-held territory. Young recruits streamed in in the thousands to join the movement.

By August 1985, Kampala had become a divided city, with the five separate militias that made up UNLA's fractious military junta controlling different hills, from which they gazed at one another with almost as much suspicion as they nursed toward the NRA.

The Bush War's penultimate chapter consisted of the sieges of army barracks at Masaka and Mbarara—operations commanded by Salim Saleh—where hundreds of famished soldiers resorted to eating rats as they waited for reinforcements that never came. In December 1985, Masaka's barracks surrendered to the NRA; one month later, Mbarara's barracks did likewise.

All that remained was for the NRA to make a multipronged assault on the capital, leaving the roads east and north toward Kenya and Sudan open as escape routes for deserting government troops. Patrick's battalion played the dominant role in the fall of Kampala. As the NRA advanced, with ammunition dumps exploding one after another, Obote's North Korean advisers finally took to their heels.

A euphoric Pecos Kutesa was struck by the watching public's almost casual curiosity. "They had been accustomed to coups and to them ours was no exception. The only divergence was that these new coup-makers were talking the local language and their physical features resembled those of local people."

"What new rules have you got for us?" onlookers asked his fighters. "Should we show you good shops to loot?"[3]

Some of the last fighting took place on the fairways of the Kampala Golf Club, where the bodies of eighty retreating government soldiers were left scattered. The departure of the Okellos, boarding helicopters bound for the northern town of Gulu, signaled the end. As panicking troops drove looted vehicles out of the city or surrendered, the NRA leadership met in the Kabaka's former palace in Lubiri on January 27, 1986, to discuss the way ahead.

Agreeing that a National Resistance Council (NRC) would act in the absence of an elected parliament, they appointed Museveni president. "In the previous two decades, many of the governance problems in Uganda had arisen out of the failure by politicians to control the military. The new government now sought to put the military, if not in control of the politicians, then at least in a central role," writes Daniel Kalinaki.[4] Forty percent of NRC seats would go to NRA fighters.

It seems supremely ironic now that the men gathered in Lubiri also debated how long the movement should stay in power, and that when various NRA members suggested five, seven, or ten years, it was Museveni who berated them for losing their moral compass. He wanted two. Eventually he was persuaded this wasn't long enough to effect root-and-branch change. A compromise was agreed: the NRM would quit the scene after four years.

A ragged victory parade drove through the center of town, with Commander Fred Rwigyema, spurned Rwandan refugee turned Ugandan liberator, standing proudly at the helm of the leading jeep as the crowds rang alongside, chanting "*Museveni oyee, Obote chini*" (Up with Museveni, down with Obote). Kagame missed the big day. Plagued by eye problems, he was in Nairobi getting treatment.

Museveni always played down his military dependence on the Banyarwanda, his "boys," as he liked to refer to them. "They were not a very big number," he assured a British filmmaker decades later. "They were a tiny proportion of our forces, but they were there." Contemporary historians tell a different story. Mahmood Mamdani estimates that the NRA was 16,000-strong at the fall of Kampala and that roughly 4,000 were Banyarwanda, while Prunier puts the total slightly lower, at 14,000, with 3,000 probably Banyarwanda.[5]

For Museveni's supporters, Rwigyema's pole position in the convoy reflected the pan-African nature of a liberation movement that placed ideology before ethnicity: even a noncitizen, it showed, could reach the zenith. For his enemies, the message was cruder: "westerners" had taken over Uganda, and that was only thanks to the prowess of their Rwandan cousins, little more than mercenaries for hire.

The parade was filmed by Ali Porteous, back in Kampala for the big day. Despite being three months pregnant, she had walked with the NRA forces into the city, catching glimpses of old NRA friends, quietly hoping to bump into Fred, exhilarated to be witnessing one of those tectonic historical shifts that transform continents.

The two crossed paths at the Grand Imperial, one of several central hotels the NRA commandeered as it worked out what to do next. With their emergency generators, satellite dishes, wine cellars, and stocks of tinned food, big hotels are natural magnets for invading guerrilla forces, offering services that have collapsed in looted government offices and private residences.

Ali was filthy and desperate for a wash, and the ever-gallant Fred came up with what seemed like a brain wave: the hotel swimming pool. It must have seemed a great idea . . . blue reflections bouncing off the water . . . the cleansing tang of chlorine. Fred found the keys, the two climbed over a gate, and in the penumbra—the power was off—Ali got in the water.

What followed was the stuff of screaming nightmares, the kind of B-movie horror that can keep a therapist busy for decades. As her eyes adjusted to the dark, Ali realized there were dark objects in the water, softly bobbing alongside her. Not life buoys, she slowly registered, not random flotsam and jetsam. "The pool was full of bodies." Slowly, carefully, trying not to touch, not to look, she picked her way back to the pool's edge, shuddering as the corpses brushed against her.

•

A nother westerner who watched Fred drive past was William Pike, standing on the balcony of the central Speke Hotel. He, too, knew he was witnessing history in the making. A twenty-seven-gun attack on Kabamba barracks had culminated in Kampala's fall. It was effectively the first time a guerrilla army in Africa had seized control of the state, he reflected—the MPLA's and FRELIMO's victories in Angola and Mozambique in the 1970s had only been made possible by Portugal's revolution. "Uganda now seemed like the Nicaragua of Africa," Pike wrote.[6]

His glowing assessment is, perhaps surprisingly, echoed by Kizza Besigye, a man who became disillusioned enough with Museveni's style of rule to challenge him for the presidency in the 2000s. "By any standards," Besigye told me, "it was an incredible achievement. The fact that a totally internal struggle, not touching any borders, conducted by local people, with hardly any support from anywhere, succeeded within five years. For those of us who lived it, we have incidents that will be forever etched in our minds."

Perhaps, with the benefit of hindsight, the Bush War was *too* successful for the good of modern Uganda or the Great Lakes region. For Museveni and his cadres emerged convinced they could both wage and win a virtuous war—a heady, dangerous belief for any armed force to hold. The impact victory had on Museveni's young Banyarwanda acolytes, whose ambitions extended beyond Uganda's borders, was perhaps even more profound. Warrior princes at the peak of their physical powers, they emerged believing they could achieve the near-impossible, convinced they were immune to the banal limitations that overwhelmed lesser mortals.

The problem with history is not that people fail to learn its lessons, but that they learn the wrong ones. There were glaring differences between Luwero and northern Rwanda that meant policies that had worked in the former in the 1980s would fail in the latter in the 1990s. But flush with confidence, only some of Museveni's "boys" were disposed to notice.

One precedent set in Uganda was certainly faithfully echoed in Rwanda. The RPF would take up and make its own the NRA notion that in the right cause—and who but a visionary commander could fully glimpse that higher purpose?—massive civilian sacrifice was a price worth paying. The trestle tables of Luwero would find their echo in the red-brick churches and sports stadiums of Rwanda, strewn with the corpses of *petits Tutsis*, who, like their Ugandan predecessors, had never been consulted on the revolution's desirability.

•

Patrick's family were camping in Kanyaryeru, part of the former Lake Mburo National Park, on a stretch of land Museveni had allocated for displaced victims of the NRA campaign, when he finally came for them after liberation, the gangly student transformed into a salaried government official flanked by obedient escorts.

Over the years I occasionally sent Patrick books I thought would interest him, nonfiction works examining the zeitgeist or recent history. One I regret never sending him was *Memoirs of a Fortunate Jew*, whose Italian author, Dan Vittorio Segre, belonged to a family of Jewish landowners so well assimilated in Piedmontese society in the 1930s that they barely bothered observing Jewish rites.[7]

A family of ardent nationalists, Segre's mother actually became patroness of her local Fascist Party's women's organization, while he unthinkingly joined its youth wing. It took Mussolini's announcement of a raft of anti-Semitic legislation to wake them from their complacency. Had Segre not fled to Palestine, where he joined the Israeli army, he could easily have joined the 8,000 Italian Jews killed in the Holocaust.

Patrick had undergone a similar awakening. The young political activist had matured into a man who understood from personal experience the price people like him paid for a leadership's cynical manipulation of Ugandan society's latent tribalism.

175

In a 2010 interview with a Ugandan newspaper, granted from exile, Patrick would describe himself as having been born "to a refugee family." It wasn't true—not a single member of his family had been expelled from Rwanda—but what had happened to Uganda's Banyarwanda in the 1980s meant the distinction seemed largely irrelevant.[8]

While Patrick's parents and his other siblings moved into the Biharwe estate, his brother George returned to the old farm in Isingiro, where I drove one evening with Ernest to talk about the past. The *matooke* plantation we drove through, fronds flapping in the breeze, was sown with seeds paid for by Patrick. As we talked, a favorite piebald cow called Chiremba strolled up to nuzzle George, who patted her head affectionately.

The people who had taken over the plot during Obote's ethnic cleansing campaign vacated the premises without a fight when he returned, George told me, knowing they were trespassing. He is still baffled by what happened, he says, unconsciously echoing his mother: "I was born here, I had children here, my father and mother came from here, and I feel completely Ugandan."

The memory of what passed between this family and the locals who set upon them remains, but life must continue. Rural life is communal: tools must be borrowed, livestock goes wandering onto nearby land, bottles of lethal *waragi* end up being shared at the local bar. "Now, those people, if you meet them, they say, 'I was forced to do that by the government,'" chimes in Ernest, voicing history's hoariest excuse for injustice. Then he shrugs.

CHAPTER NINE

BAND OF BROTHERS

Il était mince, il était beau,
Il sentait bon le sable chaud.
—**Edith Piaf,** *"Mon légionnaire"*

You need to shift into first gear and press the accelerator to the floor to reach the top of Muyenga, or "Tank Hill," as it is known. It is Kampala's highest and steepest hill, hence the town planners' decision to install the city's giant water tanks at its summit. If you don't commit yourself wholeheartedly to the slope, you risk finding yourself yanking on the hand brake in sudden panic as your engine stalls.

Once dubbed "the rich man's slum," Muyenga's rents these days are too high for ordinary Ugandans, so the district has become popular with ambassadors and aid workers. But back in the mid-1980s, when the NRM was just getting its feet under the table, this was where a generation of new appointees bought plots of land, blithely ignoring planning regulations.

At the very top, clinging to Muyenga's side, is the Hotel Diplomate, a gloomy, wood-lined establishment. The Diplomate's bar was once *the* place to be seen, but near-permanent gridlock means the in-crowd does its after-work drinking down in the valley these days.

A stuffed she-lion in a glass case on the landing surveys the scene, her fur mostly gone despite a "DO NOT TOUCH" sign. Confident no one important is listening, a diplomat sits on the terrace, cell phone to ear, loudly discussing his email inbox with a secretary back at the office.

One thing hasn't changed: the Diplomate's terrace still boasts "the best view in Kampala," as the billboards promise, a more than 180-degree panoramic view across the slums of flood-prone Katwe and Kibuye to three overlapping rucks of hills—Nsambya and Buziga are the closest; beyond them surge Kololo and Kibuli; Lubaga, Namirembe, and Mbuya form the outer ring.

Up here, at demigod height, you're looking down, for once, on the wheeling marabou storks and circling kites. It's cool and quiet, the city center traffic gives off no more than a hum, and the new banks, ministries, and hotels where business is done these days are a distant cluster of glistening glass fronts catching the setting sun. A good spot to take a meditative breath and ponder.

Lean over the verandah and you can spot the high-walled plot of land that once held the Karegeya home, tucked just below the Diplomate. The modest bungalow Patrick rented here, since replaced by a more impressive two-story villa, became a favorite gathering place for Museveni's "boys," the Banyarwanda kernel at the heart of the NRA.

Military men to the core, they appreciated the fact that anyone making their way to the house would be visible a good half hour before arrival, granting visitors plenty of time to disperse if they preferred not to be seen together. It was the equivalent of sitting with one's back to the wall. Patrick, who relished the murmur of voices and clink of glasses, was always the warmest of hosts, and if the beer ran out, the Diplomate's bar was just a short stroll away.

These were good years for "the boys." The NRA, in the process of transforming itself into the 100,000-strong Uganda People's Defence Force (UPDF), had started throwing its recruiting net far beyond its base in western and central Uganda. But a grateful president, mindful of what he owed them, had rewarded their loyalty with a spray of titles and positions in Uganda's new, third republic.

Some saw the appointments as evidence of ethnic favoritism toward western Ugandans, mirroring Obote's Acholi bias and Amin's generosity toward men from West Nile in the past. But to some extent, they were the natural consequence of the early involvement of the Banyarwanda in the movement. "Because they were good fighters, they got good positions of command in the NRA," recalls a retired general. "And when we took over government they were in almost every department, not just defense: in the police force, the civil service, the foreign service, everywhere."[1]

Fred, now a major general, had been named deputy commander in chief of the armed forces, second only to the president when it came to military decision-making. Kagame, appointed major, was director of finance and administration in the new military intelligence department set up by General Mugisha Muntu.

The two were as close as ever, with Fred playing the part of gentle restrainer when Kagame, giving in to the temptation that presents itself to the newly powerful, had those of whom he morally disapproved arrested.

"You saw Kagame's true character coming out, even then," says Leah Karegeya. "I used to wonder what was bugging him. He would order these Ugandan businessmen arrested just because they had made money, calling them 'thieves,' and when a beautiful woman walked by, he'd call her 'a whore.' 'What's his problem?' I'd ask myself. 'Why call them that?' But Fred would persuade him it wasn't the right way. And Fred was so charismatic everyone listened."

Dr. Peter Bayingana, who had abandoned a medical practice in Nairobi to join the NRA, had been appointed director of the Ugandan army's medical services. Lieutenant Kayumba Nyamwasa—as he was then—became assistant district administrator in the northern town of Gulu. The chief of military police, Kaka Kanyemera, was another Munyarwanda, as were several army brigade commanders, including Major Chris Bunyenyezi, commander of the 306th Brigade, head of the NRA's training service. Frank Rusagara, who became a key RPF intellectual, was in charge of the Ministry of Defence budget.

As for Patrick, after a short stint with the army in Lira, northern Uganda, he'd been recalled to Kampala to fill an assistant director's job at military intelligence, focusing on counterintelligence. He was now a lieutenant. "We used to hate soldiers when we were young," marvels Leah, "and he had promised me not to become one." That meant regular meetings with intelligence officials at the Western embassies, whose governments had transferred their support from

Obote to Museveni with the smoothness of long experience. It also meant schmoozing with members of the ANC, such as Jacob Zuma, whose offices were located in Muyenga.

Pursed-mouth censoriousness does not make for the most convivial of atmospheres, so Kagame was not always the most popular of drinking buddies at the get-togethers up on the hill. "Don't bring him tonight," members of the group would sometimes urge Patrick. "We don't need that stress. He spoils the atmosphere."

But Kagame was Patrick's direct boss now, so that wasn't always possible. And the former was often at a loose end. The "Pilato" nickname had stuck, and Kagame's Ugandan colleagues tended to avoid him. "No one would speak to him in the barracks," remembers an intelligence official. "The soldiers talked about 'the long arm of Pilato.'"[2]

Compared to many of his contemporaries, Patrick had seen little active combat, but it was already enough, as far as he was concerned. "He'd changed," remembers a cousin. "For some reason, he never wanted to appear a military man. He didn't use military escorts, he would drive himself around town in a white Datsun pickup, and he wore T-shirts and jeans, not a uniform. Yet he was a Big Man—a director of counterintelligence!"[3]

They were all frantically busy. Uganda's entire administrative system was being restructured, using Resistance Councils as building blocks. Uganda's war-shattered economy needed a massive electroshock, and Museveni turned for help to the International Monetary Fund (IMF) and the Paris Club of donors, while urging Uganda's Asians to return and claim their weed-infested plantations and bankrupt businesses. The erstwhile socialist had quickly been forced to recognize the merits of capitalism.

In ministries and departments, no one counted the hours as they attempted to get the machinery of state cranking back into action. The new appointees worked hard, but they played hard, too. Most of the former guerrillas were receiving regular salaries for the first time in their lives, and a government scheme made them eligible for generous bank loans. All the things that had been placed on hold during the puritanical Bush War years were suddenly possible: buying houses, acquiring land, dating, proposing marriage, and starting families. They were young men in a hurry.

Fred, his platonic flirtation with Ali Porteous behind him, married Jeannette Urujeni. A young Burundian Tutsi of royal stock, she had met him when he'd been injured in the Luwero Triangle and smuggled into an NRM supporter's home in Kampala for treatment. Kayumba Nyamwasa began courting Rosette Bajeneza, the daughter of Rwandan cattle herders who had crossed into Uganda in the 1940s. Fred was originally scheduled to give the speech at their wedding, but Kagame ended up filling in when proceedings were delayed.

Patrick had initially been based in Kololo military barracks, where he'd acquired a reputation as something of a ladies' man. Gap-toothed and medium in height, he could never be described as handsome. But his face was alive with a questing intelligence. His heavy-lidded eyes were disconcertingly light, the amber irises flecked with brown, while his skin was a smooth honey.

No woman, in any case, ever spent time with Patrick because of his looks. "He was *savagely* funny," recalls a former date. "He was always talking—Patrick couldn't stand a second's silence—and he loved laughing. He would laugh until the tears ran down his face."[4] Even more alluring, perhaps, was his insatiable curiosity and his readiness to actually listen to the answers.

When Leah got pregnant with Portia, he signed for the house in Muyenga and the couple moved in. They never held a formal church wedding. It was a detail the busy Patrick never quite got around to, although the couple's parents staged the traditional ceremonies, including handing over Leah's dowry—three cows—in their absence. But his bachelor days were at an end.

Kagame would be the last of the group to get hitched. Tutsi matches are rarely spontaneous affairs, and his was no exception. Relatives he approached recommended Jeannette Nyiramongi, daughter of a Rwandan subchief who had fled to Burundi.

The Bush War was over, but the fighting was not: it never, in fact, entirely died away. The NRA's enemies had fled north, crossing the Ugandan border, only to regroup and counterattack.

One insurgency, in particular, proved unnervingly formidable: the Holy Spirit Movement led by Alice Lakwena, a spirit medium from Gulu who heard voices telling her to liberate the country. A Ugandan Joan of Arc, she led her men into battle carrying a lamb in her arms, and her Acholi followers, many of them former UNLA soldiers, were told that if they smeared themselves in shea butter, they would become bulletproof. They advanced singing hymns, making no attempt to take the enemy by surprise.

In charge of the campaign, Fred waited for the Holy Spirit Movement to get as far as Magamaga, a barracks east of Kampala, then his troops simply mowed the fighters down. Her force crushed, Alice fled to a refugee camp in Kenya, but the rebellion sputtered on in the north, reborn as the Lord's Resistance Army and led by Joseph Kony, a former choirboy and Alice's cousin, who was also prone to visions.

Museveni's new army would remain preoccupied with insurgencies in its borderlands for the foreseeable future, alternating between full-throttle attacks, drawn-out negotiations, and generous offers of amnesty to neutralize its myriad enemies.

But the Banyarwanda boys' commitment to Uganda was not what it had been. "Our struggle was not their struggle," remembers Kizza Besigye. The rolling military campaigns had begun to feel like someone else's fight. What had been left unsaid among them during the bush years now needed to be explored, and that was why they began meeting in secret at Patrick's home, looking across Kampala as the sun went down and the lights of the city came on.

Ambitious dreams were bubbling up in the group. But they would only take concrete form if someone took the lead and provided the community with a focus, voice, and destination. The man in question, as it happens, was not Paul Kagame.

•

Men of whom one can honestly say "I never heard a bad word said about him" are rare, but Fred Rwigyema appears to have been one of them.

The first time I saw his photograph—he is usually shown looking wryly amused, sporting a rakish beret that partially hides the distinctive white streak in his hair—it graced a commemorative calendar on sale at a kiosk in Kigali's bullet-pocked airport a few months after Rwanda's genocide. I knew some of the names and faces of the top RPF cadres, but not this one. There was something about the image that made me cock my head and wonder: Who was he? Why did he merit this tribute?

He was young, he was beautiful: even at the front, unwashed and unshaven, Fred somehow always managed to look impeccably groomed, parade-ground-ready. Contemporaries recall that no man looked better in uniform. A slim, smooth-skinned, self-deprecating Hector, he was admired by men for his almost suicidal courage in combat and adored by women for his compassion.

Faces soften when his name comes up. In the bush, when supplies were scarce, back when the NRA guerrillas were all cheekbones and jutting angles, Fred would refuse to eat until his men were fed, and he slept next to them on the ground. When they were wounded, he went to their hospital bedsides, and if fighters broke the rules and harder-hearted colleagues—friends like Kagame—called for their disciplining, he'd plead unashamedly for a second chance.

I've met a former child soldier who adopted Fred's name in the hope of acquiring some of his valor, a journalist who baptized a first son after him. News that the legendary Fred was on his way could itself tilt a battle in the government's favor, with rebels scattering when they saw ropes being thrown from a helicopter clattering overhead. "They knew it was Fred coming, so they just ran," a former RPF fighter recalled. "And his feet hadn't even touched the ground."

"He *saw* people, he noticed them," said the same man. Fred had the ability—shared by the likes of Nelson Mandela and Bill Clinton—to persuade even those crossing his path for the briefest of moments that some intimate connection had been made, their loyalty requested and instantly granted. And then this man, who met Fred on less than a handful of occasions, surprises me with an extraordinary remark: "He was the most important part of my life."[5]

The Luganda language has a term: *muyaaye.* It can be used in a pejorative sense—"a layabout, a bum"—but in a political context, the emphasis is on accessibility, the absence of pretension: "a regular guy," "one of us," "a mensch." "Fred was a *muyaaye,*" a Kampala journalist told me. "And so is Salim Saleh. But Kagame most definitely isn't, and never could be."

Fred's impact on crowds has remained with Charles Onyango-Obbo, former editor of Uganda's *Monitor* newspaper. "People talk about charisma. I don't know if it's real, but Fred had that quality. He was a great soccer supporter"—Villa, Uganda's preeminent club, was Fred's team—"and I remember there was a match being played at Kampala's main stadium. He walked in, not in uniform, just wearing slacks and a green polo shirt.[6]

"It was incredible. The stadium just erupted. People were standing in the aisles, shouting his name. He was our guy, our hero. The reaction was so overwhelming, kickoff had to be delayed for five minutes. That was the effect Fred had."

As is the way with celebrities, everyone who lived through those years and mixed in NRM circles has their own Fred story. Reporting on the campaign against the Holy Spirit Movement for the BBC, journalist Cathy Watson described how 400 soldiers who had mustered in a playground, hepped up for a planned operation, were shushed by Fred, who had noticed that children inside the classrooms were sitting their primary school certificate exam.

"This is a potential turning point in their lives," said the young commander who had never completed his own education, putting a finger to his lips. "It was a magical moment, somehow," Cathy told the *Focus on Africa* program, "all of these armed men sitting obediently in total silence for hours."

Noble Marara, who went on to join the RPF, remembers standing as a boy by the bedside of his older soldier brother, who had been terribly wounded during the Alice Lakwena attack. "Fred was touring the hospital with his bodyguards, wearing a Thomas Sankara T-shirt. He came up to my brother and said, 'Franco, are you going to die?'" His brother tried to rally for his commander's sake, pooh-poohing his injuries. "I can't die for no reason," he said.

"Fred looked in his face and he could see my brother was going. 'We will meet in Kigali,' he said. Then he went to visit the other patients, most of who[m] were Banyarwanda, and when he returned, Franco had died. So Fred flew us all back to the village in his helicopter to bury Franco, and the soldiers spent a week shooting in the air to mark my brother's passing." Such gestures were remembered.

But my favorite anecdote comes from one of Patrick's relatives. Fred dropped in at her sister's house one evening, when she was still at the age when a child passes unnoticed in adult company. "He always arrived in a casual way, not making a fuss, wanting everyone to be happy." A Western rock-and-roll hit came on the radio and Fred walked to where her sister's baby lay gurgling in its cot, picked up the child, and started dancing to the music, serenading the baby. Her face lights up at the memory. "Ah, Fred, he was always so full of life."[7]

He must have known he was loved, because what comes across in all the stories is a marked absence of the need to score points or dominate his fellows. It was a quiet self-confidence that inspired one generation and has reached out posthumously to a second. It's as though Fred has become the receptacle into which the RPF's hypermasculine warriors, men stretched taut as violins, poured the softer sides of their personalities.

"Fred is the reason I joined the RPF," Robert Higiro, one of the men hired to kill Patrick, once told me. "If I'm talking to you now, it's because of Fred. And you know, I never even met the guy."

He belongs to a group of inspirational Africans—Patrice Lumumba, Steve Biko, and Thomas Sankara also feature there—who will be forever bathed in a James Dean glow of What Might Have Been. Some believe he should by rights be the president of Rwanda today. Others dismiss that notion as fanciful, pointing out that he was a military man with no political experience, so who can say what kind of leader he would have made? "Fred would not have run a country," says John Nagenda, Museveni's former official spokesman. "He simply wouldn't have. He was just too gentle."[8]

I'm not sure Patrick agreed. Once, when he was still based in Kigali—but already no longer enjoying presidential favor—I asked him if he thought Rwanda would have been different had Fred survived. He looked at me as if I were an idiot.

"Of course. *Everything* would be different."

"Why?" I asked, surprised by this sudden vehemence from someone whose views were usually so quicksilver.

"Because Fred had a totally different personality." He didn't need to spell out with whom comparison was being made. "He was *inclusive*. He embraced everyone, he didn't push them away. This problem we have with the Hutus. . . . He would have included them."

But it's possible for an adored national icon to privately see themselves as an outsider. Kagame's sense of rejection by Ugandan society set in at adolescence; with Fred, always more inclined to grant his fellow man the benefit of the doubt, the process seems to have taken longer.

Many originally saw Fred as an "integrationist," the term used for refugees bent on melding seamlessly into Ugandan society. "We had no idea he was Rwandese when Otafiire recruited him from school!" insists former Ugandan prime minister Amama Mbabazi. "Many young men angry with what was going on here in Uganda were joining to fight at that time—the Banyarwanda were just part of them."[9]

That view clashes with the memories of Kenneth Kakuru, Patrick's friend from law school, who crossed paths during childhood with many Banyarwanda. "Fred absolutely had the refugee mentality," he insists. "He had grown up in a refugee camp, had gone to school as a refugee, and I don't think he ever felt he really belonged. Fred," he says with a laugh, "was probably planning his return at primary school, back when I knew him."

Both men may well be right. National identity is never fixed in concrete. Under the heat of political circumstance, it turns waxy, changing shape and consistency. Fred certainly made a transition from cheerful, would-be Ugandan citizen to wary outsider, and that moment of crystallization probably came a good seven years before Kampala's fall.

In 1979, when the various armed factions that had fought Amin formed a new government, the faction leaders—hugely suspicious of one another—agreed to disband their forces to create a new Ugandan army. Museveni, appointed minister for defence, watched in alarm as his FRONASA movement was split up and its fighters told they would have to be formally vetted before they could reenlist. "They said our men had no training," recalls Mbabazi. "So we offered to send them on a short course at the military barracks in Jinja and sent off a list of prominent fighters, people like Fred and Salim Saleh, to take the course. Fred was rejected.

"Fred's name was resisted by Obote's forces because he was seen as Rwandese. In our society," Mbabazi says regretfully, "there are people who look at you and all they see is your group identity."

Decommissioned, Fred was reduced to playing the role of Museveni's bodyguard and driving aides like Mbabazi from place to place. "It was terrible, it hurt Fred deeply. So we fought. We talked about it with [President] Binaisa and we reached a compromise and said Fred and people like him should be granted citizenship without delay to solve this matter once and for all. But when I told Fred, he rejected it, he was furious.

"He felt he had given his life to defending the country and then this enlistment issue came up and he was treated like a foreigner. It was probably a turning point for Fred. He must have concluded then that we in the NRM were just the same as Obote's forces. He came to feel he had to have his own homeland."

By the time Fred returned to Kampala as a conquering hero, he had changed. The man being cheered to the rafters one moment knew he could be sneered at a split second later. "We inherited the cars that had been left behind by Amin's politicians," Mbabazi recalls. "Fred used to drive a big Mercedes Benz, and you know, he was a tall man, extremely handsome, so he got a lot of attention. And he told me that the street boys would watch him go by and he'd hear them saying 'Ah, these Rwandese. . . . ' It offended him."

A line under the matter should have been drawn in July 1986, six months after Museveni seized power, when the president ended requirements that anyone seeking citizenship provide proof their great-grandfathers had been born in Uganda. Any Munyarwanda who had been resident for more than ten years could become a citizen, he ruled, a category that would embrace all the refugees who had fled the Hutu revolution.

Instead, the rug was yet again whipped from under Banyarwanda feet—or that was how it felt. Calls by politicians for a census of the armed forces, requiring "noncitizens" to be discharged, raised fears that a new witch hunt of Banyarwanda was pending. As president, Museveni now had a new range of constituencies to court, lobbies to cajole, and the jibe that he was not actually a Ugandan at all had left its mark.

Banyarwanda alarm seemed justified when in 1989 Museveni removed Fred as deputy army chief, appointing him deputy minister of defence, a shift from active service to administration. Appointments to the armed forces were being made and swiftly reversed as Museveni tried out different arrangements, but suspicion comes easily to the outsider. The NRA had used them to get what it needed, many Banyarwanda concluded, and now they were being dumped. If this could happen to Fred, of all people, what prospects awaited less well connected members of the community?

Then, in August 1990, a dispute over land blew up in Uganda's west, where Banyarwanda pastoralists who had supported the NRA during the Bush War had been grazing cattle on state-owned ranch land. Taken aback by the level of public fury at the perception that "foreigners" were being granted special favors, Museveni performed a characteristic about-face, ruling in favor of "Ugandan citizens" and against "squatters."

During a parliamentary debate that followed, Museveni allowed members to conclude that Banyarwanda would henceforth be barred from owning land or holding government office. "For the Banyarwanda refugees," comments historian Mahmood Mamdani, "the die had been cast." The "fifty-niner" refugees and Ugandan Banyarwanda formed a far from homogeneous community, but the forces of history were pushing them closer together.[10]

•

By this stage, the Tutsi diaspora stretched from Quebec to New York, Nairobi to Bujumbura, Lomé to Dakar, Brussels to Paris. Its members worked tirelessly, via social clubs and cultural associations, to keep community identity alive.

In Kampala, a refugee welfare foundation had initially been set up to help Banyarwanda who fell afoul of Amin's regime. It morphed into the more militant Rwanda Alliance for National Unity (RANU), a discussion group of intellectuals and former Makerere students interested in exploring how to build the yellow brick road that would lead the Tutsis all the way home. Obote's hostility toward the Banyarwanda forced RANU to move to Nairobi, in Kenya, where it operated underground.

An early RANU member was Gerald Gahima, Rwanda's former attorney general. One of the four founding members of the Rwanda National Congress alongside Patrick, the General, and Gahima's brother Theogene, he now lives in Washington's forested outskirts, where he shuns conferences and skirts shy of most media interviews.

"It was a clandestine organization. We didn't have a house. We set up cells in Kenya first, and then in Rwanda, and the authorities got to hear about us and would sometimes raid the cells. We had a newspaper, which was cyclostated [duplicated], called *The Alliancer.* At the start it was just a few hundred people, then it ballooned."[11]

RANU was portrayed by the Rwandan President Habyarimana's regime as a group dedicated to the restoration of the Tutsi monarchy. "Nothing could have been further from the truth," says Gahima. "We did not get on with the king at all. RANU was quite leftist, Marxist, it believed in equality for all. The main influence on RANU was Museveni, and his inspirations were Che Guevara and Samora Machel."

In RANU's view, members of King Kigeli's coterie were stuck in the past, brooding pointlessly over the role Belgium had played in the monarchy's downfall. RANU's focus was the here and now, and its ire was directed at the Hutu regime. One of its driving forces was Dr. Peter Bayingana, whom Gahima considered a friend. Intelligent, handsome, and extremely ambitious, "Peter had vision, he had passion," he recalls.

Originally, the movement was purely civilian. But Amin's ousting in 1979 had a galvanizing impact. With plenty of time on his hands after failing to reenlist, Fred began reaching out to RANU, to the exiled King Kigeli—now based in Kenya—and to ordinary Banyarwanda, staging meetings aimed at ironing out community differences.

During the campaign for Uganda's 1980 elections, high-profile Banyarwanda campaigned for Museveni's political party. And when Museveni rejected the election results and launched his armed struggle, it felt like a signal. Banyarwanda began signing up for the NRA in droves. "We were young and young people are idealistic," remembers Gahima, who watched friends succumb to the siren call, while resisting himself. "Museveni was seen as our passport home. The feeling was, 'If Museveni can do this, we can, too.'"

Obote's ethnic cleansing campaign turned that flow into a torrent as refugee school-leavers who had once hoped to integrate into Ugandan society found their way barred. "Many of the young men," writes Gérard Prunier, "had felt that Rwanda was an old story, their parents' story, and they were now Ugandans. And then they suddenly discovered that people among whom they had lived for thirty years were treating them as hated and despised foreigners. The shock was tremendous."[12]

RANU stalwarts like Peter Bayingana abandoned civilian life to join their fellow Banyarwanda in the bush. Knowing how to handle a gun, how to give and take orders, was clearly going to be useful if they were ever to return to their land of origin. "Capacity building," they called it. "We increasingly saw the need to master military science if we were ever to overthrow the Rwanda dictatorship," Bayingana later told journalists.[13]

When the NRA split into two in 1985 and Fred led his contingent toward the Rwenzori Mountains, the course he plotted conveniently took the NRA fighters past many of the old refugee camps in western Uganda—familiar personal territory—allowing him to recruit yet more Banyarwanda as he passed.

Many Ugandan and Rwandan civilians blithely assume that during the years in the Luwero Triangle, a covert deal was hatched between the Banyarwanda "boys" and their Ugandan comrades, amounting to, "We'll fight for you now, if you help us later." Gahima slaps down the notion. "There was no deal. I would not have discussed this with anyone as it would have been treasonable."

Infiltration, after all, was exactly what the NRA had trained intelligence operators such as Kagame and Patrick to spot and quash during the years in the bush, with those caught often paying with their lives. No Munyarwanda was going to fall into that trap. "You cannot set up a liberation movement within another liberation movement," insists Gahima. "It would be a very serious crime, with serious consequences if discovered. They had to hide that they were members of another organization."

It's a tribute to the Tutsi knack for secrecy that even men the Banyarwanda fought, slept, and ate alongside often had little grasp of their comrades' identity or thinking. Accustomed to operating below the radar, shielding behind adopted names, and often "passing" as Banyankole, the Banyarwanda were careful not to speak Kinyarwanda around other fighters. As far as fellow fighters were concerned, they shared the values and agendas of any other NRA guerrilla.

Personal security was not the only explanation for such discretion. Museveni's "boys" knew that the entire dynamic on which Rwanda's postindependence politics operated jarred with the NRA's ideological vision, heavily influenced by Julius Nyerere. "Hutu" and "Tutsi" were seen as colonial concepts, and pining for an ancient homeland meant giving in to reactionary instincts when the liberation of the entire African continent should be the true revolutionary's aim.

"We were pan-Africanists," growls Salim Saleh. "The number one priority as an NRA cadre was to get that 'tribe' thing out of your head."[14]

The community's careful self-policing continued after Museveni liberated Kampala. But with a grateful president in charge and Banyarwanda holding key posts in the new administration, there was more room to stretch. Hungry for advice on how to turn the varied aspirations of the diaspora into a dynamic mass movement and effective political force, RANU turned to Tito Rutaremara, a Communist philosopher based in Paris.

Rutaremara moved to Kampala to set up a task force. The result was a secret "school for cadres," which flew Tutsis from across the world to Uganda to receive an education in political philosophy and the history of Rwanda. RANU was effectively mimicking the consciousness-raising techniques Museveni had adopted when he had dispatched fighters to train in Mozambique and Tanzania.

"We would bring in university kids, train them, and send them out to mobilise," Rutaremara told a US biographer. "We told them, 'We have to liberate our country, but we have no means. The means is ourselves.'"[15] Freshly indoctrinated cadres set off to mobilize refugee communities in Uganda, Zaire, Tanzania, Burundi, and Kenya. They even reached into Rwanda, establishing cells that hurriedly spread the word before President Habyarimana's intelligence services arrived to make arrests.

It was a time of heady, bubbling excitement. Utopianism is the man-trap of diasporas. Cut off from the gritty reality of daily contact, exiles' understanding of the society they left behind becomes blurry. Prunier was struck by the dewy-eyed romanticism of the discussions staged by Tutsi cadres he met in Kampala during this period. "They were like the White Russian community in Paris after the Bolshevik revolution, dreaming of their homeland, trapped in a fantasy world. The Rwanda they pined for wasn't a country which actually existed."

For any resistance movement, funding is a key weak point. So mobilization involved persuading the diaspora to contribute generously enough to deliver self-sufficiency: 10 percent of salary for those in formal employment, with comparatively well-off Tutsis in Western Europe expected to provide more than their cash-strapped African brothers. Fred approached Tribert Rujugiro, a Rwandan who had fled to Burundi and established what would become Africa's biggest tobacco company, who agreed to back the organization.

Many members were conscious of another RANU weakness. If the movement was ever to acquire a sizable following, its message needed to reach far beyond a Tutsi minority that counted for only 14 percent of Rwanda's population. The hundreds of thousands of Hutus who had crossed into Uganda, DRC, Tanzania, Burundi, and Kenya over the decades, taking up work in the plantations and copper mines, along with the royal court's many Hutu retainers, needed to be persuaded that Habyarimana's regime deserved opposing because it was corrupt, predatory, and nepotistic: issues that had nothing to do with ethnicity.

If it was to prove its good faith, and signal it represented more than one narrow interest group, RANU needed to showcase Hutus in high-profile positions. Fred and his comrades put out feelers to Alexis Kanyarengwe. A former Rwandan army colonel who had played a key role in the coup that had toppled President Grégoire Kayibanda, Kanyarengwe had fallen out with Habyarimana and was living in Tanzania.

A slow courtship of Hutu activists and politicians in Rwanda who had been marginalized by Habyarimana's clique began. The policy ruffled feathers among those whose loathing of Rwanda's Hutus had been hard baked into them in the refugee camps, but seemed self-evident to former NRA cadres. "Let those guys have the government ministries and parliament, let them have the surface appearance of power," Fred would reassure his Tutsi comrades. "As long as we have the army, then we can defend our people."

In December 1987, in a sign of its gathering confidence, RANU moved its annual congress from Nairobi to Kampala. During that semi-clandestine meeting, which Kagame missed as he was attending a training course in Cuba, the movement rebaptized itself the Rwandan Patriotic Front (RPF). Joining, for civilians, involved *ibanga,* an oath intended to drive home the seriousness of their commitment. It was not deemed necessary for serving members of the military.

The congress adopted an eight-point manifesto. Suspiciously similar to the NRM's, it still differed in small yet significant ways. Whereas the NRM had placed democracy at the top of its list of priorities, this one put national reconciliation—code for "repairing relations between Hutus and Tutsis"—first.

For many exiles, the document felt like a revelation, saying all the right things. "Its talk of ethnic reconciliation, equality, of fighting against prejudice, of respect for the law, of the need to set up institutions, the fight against corruption . . . it was inspirational," recalls a Tutsi who was studying in Belgium.[16]

But the RPF was far from a smoothly blended organization. The Mwami's descendants, in fact, seemed to have inherited the royal court's capacity for whispered intrigue and faction-fighting.

Fred Rwigyema and Paul Kagame, the two men with whom the RPF would become most closely associated, were only formally invited to join in 1988. The reason, Gahima explains, was the simmering rivalry between two young and charismatic potential leaders. Not Kagame and Fred—there was no question at that point of Kagame assuming prominent status—but Peter Bayingana and Fred. "Peter and Fred did not get along, and that's why Fred wasn't asked to join until then. There was an unresolved leadership question there."

The tension between the two young men was partly premised on intellectual snobbery. Bayingana had gone to college and qualified as a doctor, whereas Fred had left school at just fourteen. "Peter did not regard Fred, because of his lack of education, as an appropriate leader," says Gahima.

If Peter patronizingly looked down on Fred, he actively disliked his sidekick. "Bayingana despised Kagame's violence and his divisive methods," says General Kayumba. "He hated his killing." The feeling was entirely reciprocal, and so was the suspicion many Fred loyalists nursed toward Peter.

In the eyes of Banyarwanda fighters who had been at Museveni's side since the early days, Peter's brilliance failed to compensate for the fact that he had never been one of "the twenty-seven guns" and, crucially, had no direct experience of combat. But that affiliation gave Peter's supporters another stick with which to beat Fred. Fred's closeness to Salim Saleh and filial relationship with Museveni were well known. Was he actually capable, they wondered aloud, of putting the RPF's interests before the NRM's? Or would a man sometimes seen as too emollient, too empathetic, simply serve as a conduit for his Ugandan patron's wishes? "Why does Rwigyema always tell Museveni everything?" Chris Bunyenyezi, a Bayingana ally, once asked a Ugandan intelligence official. "What's wrong with him?"[17]

The power struggle finally exploded into the open at a meeting of the RPF leadership, where Tito Rutaremara and several of the longest-standing NRA members accused Peter of using his regular visits to the refugee camps in Burundi, Zaire, and Tanzania to mobilize support not for the movement as a whole, but for Peter's own leadership bid.

When the torrent of complaints had ended, Fred spoke. "Have you all finished? Has no one here got anything good to say about Peter?" There was a slightly shamefaced silence. He stood and addressed the room.

"This Peter you are talking about, he was a practicing doctor in Nairobi. He could have stayed there. Instead he came to the bush, bringing lots of medical supplies, to join the NRA. He is someone I am very, very proud of. As for his education, it's great that he is an educated man. This movement needs winners." The move was typical of Fred: embracing, humane, de-escalating. It was also smart. By endorsing Peter so unreservedly—Peter was regarded from then on as his de facto deputy—Fred had underlined who really was boss.

The RPF, in any case, did not have the time for a drawn-out leadership contest. Pumped up and ready for action, Tutsi youngsters were so desperate to *do* something that they could barely be controlled. "They were becoming unruly, a problem," recalls one of Patrick's Ugandan former colleagues.[18]

In 1989, Charles Kabanda, head of the RPF's civilian wing, threw down the gauntlet by leading thirty would-be fighters into Rwanda's borderlands; from there they challenged Fred to follow suit.

Fred gave chase and persuaded them to return, and Kabanda was arrested. But it was a warning shot to both him and the RPF's executive committee: delay would no longer be tolerated, the political squabbles must end. And to be effective, members registered, the organization was going to need military experience, hierarchical discipline, and Museveni's tacit support. "There was no way we could start a war with a general who would be unsellable to his juniors in the military," recalls Gahima. Fred was accordingly voted RPF chairman.

The journey from refugee welfare organization to guerrilla movement was complete. In General Kayumba's eyes, there had never really been a contest. "There was no rivalry between Fred and Peter. There was no rivalry between Fred and *anyone,* because Fred was incomparable in the eyes of Rwandans. His credentials were too extreme, too accepted, by both military and civilian. There was simply no comparison."

A steady process of militarization got underway as Fred and his colleagues, making the most of the access and resources their positions granted them, set about systematically sucking Banyarwanda into the Ugandan armed forces, the better to poach them for the RPF. Fred, helicoptering into refugee camps and settlements in the west, had played this role before, but then he'd been recruiting fighters for Museveni's NRA. This time he was recruiting for his own, clandestine force. Teachers in local schools would later notice that pupil numbers were down, and occasionally a boy, turned away by the RPF because he was deemed too young, would reappear at an empty desk looking sheepish, head shaved military-style.

The Tutsi diaspora, in a nod to precolonial history, labeled them *inkotanyi* (indefatigable warriors), the nickname given Rwabugiri, Rwanda's legendary nineteenth-century monarch. An army within an army, the RPF resembled an overweight cuckoo chick in a borrowed nest, fussed over by parents blissfully unaware they were fattening up a member of a different species.

Astonishingly, the secret still held—just about—in part because the RPF's leadership decided it wasn't necessary for these latest recruits to have a precise grasp of what exactly was being planned. Their existence, Fred and his comrades agreed, was enough, an investment to be tapped when the time was right. "In that situation you don't need to tell every young person you recruited, 'You know, we need you for the Struggle,'" says Gahima. "All you need is to have this resource, which you have got at someone else's expense, when and where you need it."

•

It's hard to believe, given the intimacy of the relationships between the NRM's top cadres, that Museveni did not know exactly what was going on. Presidential denials would later come thick and fast, but sincerity on this issue was not exactly in Museveni's interest. Reliant on IMF and World Bank aid to get Uganda's shattered economy up and running, he had only just persuaded Western diplomats to place their faith in a former guerrilla chief. He was anxious not to antagonize donors by being caught endorsing the invasion of a peaceful neighboring state.

Many nonetheless insist that while Museveni was certainly aware *something* was brewing, the degree to which vague pining had crystallized genuinely eluded him. Embedded in the state's intelligence network as they were, the "boys" were perfectly placed to ensure that Museveni heard only what they wanted him to hear, and that the get-togethers on Muyenga Hill and at Fred's mother's house were presented in the most anodyne of lights.

"They knew the Rwandese were preparing something, I am sure," Rutaremara later told a British researcher. "Museveni knew that the Rwandese were organizing themselves, but he did not know how."[19]

Winnie Byanyima, UNAIDS's executive director, has known the president for most of her life. Museveni spent part of his childhood growing up in the Byanyima household. Fiercely intelligent, she trained as an aeronautical engineer and worked as a covert agent for the NRM—a job at Entebbe's airport gave her information about diplomatic and military movements she could helpfully relay—before joining the movement in the bush, where she and Museveni became romantically involved.

Today Winnie is married to Kizza Besigye, whose treatment by Museveni's security forces for the crime of daring to run in Uganda's presidential elections would be reason enough to hate Museveni. But when Winnie talks about her ex-boyfriend there is no trace of anger or vindictiveness in her voice.

"Museveni knew Fred would go back, it was inevitable, but I don't think he knew the timing. [Fred] Rwigyema was listening to Museveni. My reading is that they must have discussed it and Museveni must have advised Rwigyema to hold on a bit."

"Hold on a bit," because Museveni had been discussing the fate of the Banyarwanda with President Habyarimana since the mid-1980s, well before Kampala fell to the NRA. The bilateral meetings continued after the NRA's accession to power, as they gave an increasingly worried Habyarimana a precious opportunity to raise the troubling issue of the growing number of Tutsis in Ugandan army ranks. However Museveni might attempt to gloss them over, the extent of the "capacity-building" among the Banyarwanda was certainly not lost on Habyarimana.

"He told Museveni, 'You people are training the Tutsis to come and invade us,'" said a Ugandan official present at these talks. "And we were categorical. 'No, we admit we have them in our army, because they were refugees, victims, like all the others—most of our combatants came because they were victimized—so they have come, they have trained, we don't deny it, but we are not organizing them, we are fighting our war, we are not going to fight yours.'"[20]

Habyarimana's worst fears seemed confirmed when he attended the 1988 ceremony at which formal ranks in the Ugandan army were handed out to the onetime NRA guerrillas. "Habyarimana was invited to the ceremony in Lubiri barracks as a guest of the government," remembers Besigye. "I'll never forget how he looked that day. I remember his bewilderment at seeing Fred Rwigyema there being decorated."

Standing ramrod straight, Fred made deliberate eye contact with the flustered older man as he accepted his decoration as major general. *See what the refugee children of yesteryear have become*, read the message in his eyes. *We are coming to get you.* "Habyarimana," says Besigye, "looked really, really fearful."

As the bilateral meetings continued, Museveni nagged Habyarimana to defuse the issue by accepting the principle of a Tutsi "right of return." "He kept telling Habyarimana, 'You really need to find a solution,'" recalls the Ugandan official. "If you have problems with the refugees, you really need to start looking at how to settle them back home."

But Habyarimana was adamant. "Rwanda," he would say, "is like a glass of water filled to the brim—it cannot take a drop more. There is no room to put them, there is no land." That position only made sense, his Ugandan counterpart countered, if one assumed the Rwandan population would remain indefinitely dependent on subsistence farming. "But, President," Museveni told him, "why do you think they all need to be farmers? Some could go back and become shoemakers. There are other jobs they could do."

Museveni's blithe assumption that he would be the ultimate arbiter of the Banyarwanda "problem" grated with plenty of the RPF's secret members, who registered both the absence of any sense of haste and the fact that they were never invited to take part in these presidential tête-à-têtes. It left them fearful and suspicious of the likely outcome.

There was a very African element to Museveni's inability to grasp the seriousness of their concerns. Even in modern African society, "elders" expect levels of obedience and respect from youngsters that seem bizarre to Western eyes. The fifteen- to twenty-year age gap between the NRA's founding fathers and their Banyarwanda acolytes fostered an attitude of avuncular concern that blurred into condescension. "We used to look at the RPF as young sons, not even brothers," a retired Ugandan commander told me. "Those boys"— he cites the biggest names in the RPF at the time—"those boys were my escorts."[21]

Museveni was not the only head of state pressing unwelcome changes on Habyarimana. In June 1990, French president François Mitterrand gave what was hailed as a landmark speech at the seaside resort of La Baule indicating that future aid to Francophone countries would be conditional upon democratic reform.

Initially, it would have required an electron microscope to detect a significant shift in French policy on Africa, but Francophone leaders in the Great Lakes, who had always relied on Paris's uncritical support, correctly sensed a watershed moment. In July 1990, taking his cue from President Mobutu, his friend in Zaire, Habyarimana agreed to end his political monopoly on power in Rwanda and allow multiparty politics. He also agreed to welcome back the refugees.

It was a canny move, whipping away the key grounds for the RPF's principled rejection of the Kigali government. Sweeping progressive change seemed unlikely in Rwanda, but Habyarimana's suddenly conciliatory tone was likely to dry up any sympathy the international community might have been considering extending the RPF.

The preparations in Patrick's home on Muyenga Hill were quietly stepped up. Fred, Kagame, Stephen Ndugute, Kayumba Nyamwasa, Colonel Sam Kaka—the military men who would deal with the operational side of things—gathered to discuss the practical implications of an eventual attack on Rwanda. In July 1990, Fred went on an international mission, visiting Tutsi groups in Europe, Canada, and the United States to raise funds and scout for weapons.

When asked how such preparations passed him by, Jim Muhwezi, by then director general of the Internal Security Organisation (ISO), waxes defensive: "No one suspected they could do such a thing. We did not regard them as foreigners, they were part and parcel of our movement. So it was not our preoccupation to keep monitoring them. If I have people round to my house, how do you know if it's a meeting or just socializing?"

It was obvious where military supplies would initially be sourced: the positions of the RPF men inside the army and police guaranteed access to Ministry of Defence armories and barracks. Frequent trips between the active combat zone of northern Uganda and Kampala served as ideal opportunities for munitions and equipment to be moved to the capital, where they were stored in private homes. "Do you remember, Rosette," the General asks his wife at one point with a smile, "how we hid all those mortars on the balcony of our house in Kampala?"

At the same time as the stockpiling was taking place, Patrick cautiously reached out to a few Kampala-based reporters who the RPF sensed might be willing to relay the story the movement wanted told to both a local and international audience. "Patrick would invite you for a beer, charm you and pull you in," remembers one. "They were always very smart at setting up links, identifying people who could be useful to them, drawing them into their ambit, and then you'd find yourself so deep in with them you could never crawl out again."[22]

Fred did not expect the man who hated wearing camouflage to go into combat; instead he picked a role for Patrick that would play to his strengths. As someone with friends scattered throughout Museveni's administration, Patrick would be the RPF's man on the inside, its voice in Kampala, after the force left. "Patrick was someone they could not ignore because they knew he was very close to the Ugandans," says Leah. "They needed him as a go-between. He was key because he was trusted by both sides."

The night before the big push, Pecos Kutesa recalls bumping into Fred at Bimbo, a popular ice-cream parlor in central Kampala. Fred, he knew, had been provisionally booked on a yearlong course at the US Army Command and Staff College in Fort Leavenworth, Kansas.

Museveni had assigned a few of the high-profile Banyarwanda to these kinds of training courses abroad, fueling suspicions he wanted them out of sight and out of mind.

"I asked him about the course in America and Fred laughed and said, 'Oh, I'd love to go but I think I have HIV,'" says Pecos. A negative HIV test result was a condition of attendance, a hurdle that halted some NRM officers in their tracks, as many had picked up HIV during their years in the bush. "He was joking," Pecos adds. "Because everyone knew that he was happily married and a disciplined man." Pecos understood he was being fobbed off, but didn't know why.

Fred's secret army had been on standby since July. On the verge of ordering his covert force-within-a-force into action, he was not about to go abroad. He had persuaded Museveni to send Paul Kagame to Fort Leavenworth in his place.

Kagame's detractors claim Fred was all too happy to see his friend, a divisive figure who had never exactly endeared himself to his RPF comrades, removed from the scene at a tense time. That seems unlikely, but Fred's readiness to dispatch Kagame halfway around the world at that juncture certainly indicates he didn't regard him as an indispensable player in what was going to be the most challenging military operation of his life.

The last photo taken of Fred was snapped at a soccer match for his beloved Villa. Fred, beret-less, the white stripe in his hair showing, is sitting on a folding stool. Friends loll on the grass by his side. It should be a relaxed, bucolic scene, but Fred looks preoccupied. There are other things on his mind. The look he darts at the cameraman is wary, slightly suspicious.

He was being pulled in opposite directions. On one side chafed the RPF's hard-liners, impatient to be off. On the other stood the president, benefactor, and guide, a surrogate father who kept assuring his mentee that he had the Banyarwanda community's well-being at heart, and appealing to him not to rush into anything.

Fred had always taken direction from Museveni. This time ultimate responsibility fell on his own slim shoulders, and he must have wondered if he was up to the task. His wife had just given birth to a baby daughter, his second child: it was a time when many young husbands would have felt impelled to remain at home.

A sense of foreboding certainly surfaced at a tense final pre-operation meeting held at Fred's house in Kololo, attended by members of the RPF's inner circle. The hardest point in any military operation comes in the hours just before boots hit the ground, when the adrenaline is surging but there is no way of expending the surplus energy.

All those present knew they were taking a massive step into the void, putting the hard-won achievements of the past four years at risk. As Fred accompanied his colleagues to the door, General Kayumba recalls, he stopped in front of a large framed photograph hanging in the entrance, showing him with his closest friend, Museveni's brother Salim Saleh. "If anything happens to me," he told his colleagues, "count on this man."

CHAPTER TEN

EXODUS

We know where we're going, we know where we're from.
We're leaving Babylon, we're going to our Father's land.

—Bob Marley

A t the end of September 1990, Museveni boarded a flight to New York, where he was due to attend the United Nations General Assembly, annual jamboree for world heads of state. Fred escorted the president and his delegation to the airport in Entebbe. It was the last time they would see one another, for the departure effectively marked the signal for the RPF's plans to go into action.

Fred had given Museveni some form of warning, without going into detail, before his departure. "There was A plus B but he only told me of A," Museveni told William Pike in an interview after the event. "Yet I could have helped him."[1]

Major troop movements would normally set alarm bells ringing in any country scarred by a succession of civil wars and coups, but those giving the orders had until recently been at the top of the military echelon, men the president trusted with his life, so no warning signals rang.

What's more, the Banyarwanda boys had the perfect cover: October 9 is Uganda's Independence Day, a state holiday traditionally marked with a massive military parade. This year, they told anyone querying why quite so many army trucks laden with young men had materialized on the roads, heading west, that the parade was being staged in Mbarara.

The planning even extended to basic press coverage. "Rwigyema called to invite me to a football match in Mbarara," says one of the journalists who had been befriended by the RPF. "I was flown out in a Ugandan military helicopter, and in the middle of the night there was the sound of gunfire: the invasion had started. That was their 'football match.'"[2] On the night of October 1, Kagitumba, the main border post between Uganda and Rwanda, witnessed a mass crossing by Banyarwanda army deserters.

Back in Kampala, there was a touch of comedy about what ensued. "Someone called me from Mbarara and said, 'The Banyarwanda are going,'" remembers retired major John Kazoora, then a director at the ISO. "I was shocked." Jim Muhwezi wasn't answering the phone, so Kazoora drove at high speed to his house. "I found him in the bathroom, he came out wrapped in his towel. When I told him I had got this, he said, 'No!'" The two men drove to tell Mugisha Muntu, army commander, at the Army Club. "He was equally in shock and he immediately raised the president, who was in New York."[3]

He answers an obvious question before I put it. "From how Mugisha Muntu was answering, the president was at least pretending he didn't know."

Initial reports, he recalls, suggested no more than a dozen soldiers had defected. "It was just a few, maybe ten people, had deserted, including two or so of the presidential guard. It was much later in the day when stories started coming in that, actually, it was an exodus."

William Pike, then the editor of Uganda's government-owned newspaper, managed to get through to Museveni after an eight-hour communications outage. He has no doubts about the nature of the president's reaction. "I had never heard him, before or since, seem so shaken. He sounded very jittery. I interpreted that to mean he had genuinely been caught by surprise, and that maybe the RPF had taken advantage of his absence to launch the invasion."[4]

The invasion represented a massive international embarrassment. Given his record, Museveni was constantly suspected by the likes of Kenya's Moi and Zaire's Mobutu of wanting to export revolution to the rest of the Great Lakes. He had assumed the rotating chairmanship of the Organization of African Unity (OAU) only three months earlier—a body that stipulated noninterference in members' internal affairs as a principle—and here he was, looking like some expansionist renegade.

Winnie Byanyima, serving as Uganda's ambassador to France at the time, was woken up in Paris by a call from her president. "It must have been one or two in the morning. He said, 'Have you had any news from Mbarara?' 'No, nothing,' I said. Then he swore in my language. 'These stupid bastards. These bastards have taken off,' he said.

"He asked me if I had numbers for people in Mbarara, and I said that I did. 'Call them and let me know what they are seeing.' I had the phone numbers of some military commanders in Mbarara, old comrades from the struggle, and some relatives, so I made the calls and phoned him back half an hour later. He was still seething, absolutely livid. Museveni can pretend, but I know when he's lying, and he was really taken by surprise that night. He kept asking me to repeat things: 'They did *what?* Went across with *what? Heavy weapons,* you say?'"

Fred's timing offered Museveni a fig leaf of deniability, and the Ugandan president made of it what he could. Hoping to partially defuse what was clearly going to be a diplomatic explosion, he sought to alert President Habyarimana, also in New York attending the UN General Assembly. But he had not provided for the quaking obsequiousness that develops around a despot.

"Museveni tried to call Habyarimana, who was staying in the same hotel as us, in order to warn him," says Amama Mbabazi, part of the Ugandan delegation. "The operator refused to put the call through, saying Habyarimana was not to be disturbed. So Museveni rang the Rwandan foreign minister and asked him to wake up Habyarimana and tell him. And the foreign minister said there was no way he was going to do that."

In Paris, Winnie continued to work the phones. "Museveni asked me to keep calling him until he arrived home, so every hour I was picking up more information and calling. That whole night and the next day I followed the movements." As she relayed the information to Museveni, they both began to get a grasp of just how ambitious—and effective—Fred and his colleagues' preparations had been.

"When they signaled for everyone to go, there were defections from nearly every brigade we had, right up in the north," says Winnie. Guards obligingly unlocked armory stores. Section commanders ordered men who weren't taking part to hand their guns to those leaving. Army trucks, fueled in preparation, revved their engines on parade grounds. Streaming out from barracks and border posts, army training schools, factories and farms, even from State House itself, the Banyarwanda headed toward the border.

"It was a thorough operation, everyone knew what their role was."

Everyone within the RPF magic circle, that is. NRA stalwarts felt a confusing mixture of relief, abandonment, and betrayal. Retired captain David Bashaija dates the moment he registered a secret army's existence to the morning he woke in Bombo barracks in Luwero, where he'd been on an officers' training course, sharing a room with Peter Bayingana and another Munyarwanda officer, and found himself alone.[5]

"They left at night, without informing me," he says, his tone still plaintive. "I was their friend, we were together in the bush, but they never said anything. If they'd told me, I'd have gone with them. I'd have wanted to support Fred."

The excitement was, indeed, infectious. Soldiers who had never been in the loop, or who had perhaps known only part of the story but hesitated, scrambled after their comrades. The momentum spread beyond the armed forces. As school buses and pickups were commandeered, even civilians joined the high-spirited exodus.

Winnie remembers the hilarity of those conversations. "My army friends in Mbarara were laughing and saying, 'Winnie, you have never seen anything like this. . . . ' Every Munyarwanda was saying, 'I'm not staying here.' There were places where you could go and hide and wait for the next car coming, and they were just jumping into the convoys. So there was a highly organized group that set off and others who picked up the message and spontaneously joined them."

It was a tribute to Fred's extraordinary pulling power that many of the soldiers who went across that day had no Rwanda connection of any kind. "Many of the boys who went with Fred were Baganda, or

Acholi," recalls Pecos Kutesa. "He was that charismatic." This was not their fight, but Fred was their invincible commander, and where he led, they would follow.

A glorious adventure that, this time, boasted some decent gear. "What did you take?" I ask the General. "Everything!" he says with a sudden burst of energy. "We took everything! Everything that Uganda possessed in terms of military equipment, we got a share of that. RPGs, grenades, SMGs, machine guns, trucks, bullets, boots, uniforms, everything we could carry. Remember that it wasn't an overnight operation, we'd been planning it for years, whatever you could carry, you carried."

By the standards of most modern armies, they were still traveling light: no tanks, no armored personnel carriers, no Stalin's Organs, no heavy artillery. Like many an overconfident military force before them, they believed the war would only take a matter of months— "It'll be over by Christmas" was the refrain—and this was the weaponry deemed most appropriate for an NRA-style guerrilla campaign.

The defections would go on for a month, reaching 4,000 men all told, but 2,500 to 3,000 soldiers crossed over on the first day. Uganda's furious army commander ordered the district officer in Mbarara to follow Fred to the border and give him the message that if things went wrong, he should not bother returning to Uganda. Rwigyema replied—presciently, as it turned out—that he did not need to go back. The story goes that Fred tore the pips from his Ugandan uniform and formally saluted the country where he had been raised before turning his back on it and crossing the border.

Whatever questions he had once posed himself about who he was and where he belonged, everything, now, was clear. The decades in exile were over. He was a Rwandan, and he was going home.

•

In the West, what media coverage there was presented the RPF move as an unprovoked invasion of a peaceful, recently democratized Central African government. Loyal RPF branches across the world took umbrage at the terminology used. "Calling it an 'invasion' was totally inaccurate," says a Brussels-based Tutsi. "This was a *revendication militaire,* the staking of a military claim. There was no way the movement would ever have had any clout in negotiations without seizing and holding a tract of land. It forced the Habyarimana regime to treat us seriously."[6]

But the General snorts at the notion that the RPF crossed the border merely to win a seat at the table. This, he says, is not how military strategy works. "Don't let anyone deceive you. We weren't going to go and stand at Kagitumba and negotiate terms. Every army that attacks intends to win. If we'd gone in and the Habyarimana regime had collapsed in a week, we'd have gone all the way to Kigali. The intention was to *win.*"

In Kampala, the invasion's impact was electrifying. Members of the Banyarwanda community could finally drop the disguise they had assumed, and for many Ugandans, that meant registering their presence for the very first time. When Patrick rang one of his oldest friends to tell him excitedly, "The boys have crossed," the response was one of sheer bemusement. "Which boys?" asked the friend.

Waking up in his compound, Pecos Kutesa registered that something had changed. "The children playing outside were speaking Kinyarwanda for the first time."[7] He had never realized his next-door neighbors were Banyarwanda. Teenage Banyarwanda girls in Kampala suddenly chose to advertise their ethnicity, sporting "I LOVE FRED" T-shirts.

The mass departure was a major humiliation for the Ugandan government—"I was shocked," says Jim Muhwezi. "It was embarrassing for me as head of intelligence." But it came with distinct domestic benefits. From now on, NRM cadres recognized, it would allow Museveni to present himself not as the champion of one particular community, but as a national leader.

"It made things easier for us," acknowledges Pecos Kutesa. "I was very happy they had gone, the whole of Uganda was. We wished them well. They were good people but they had to have a home."

•

The euphoria was short-lived.

Fred's former colleagues waited for him to get in touch, but there was silence. An irritated Museveni entrusted a personal note to a cadre with orders to cross the border and get it to Fred: "Why are you doing this? Have you considered the consequences?" it read. But when the messenger attempted to hand it over in person, he was told

Fred was not available. Picking up a suppressed tension between the RPF commanders, he guessed something had gone seriously wrong and relayed his worries back to Museveni.[8]

In the Karegeya house on Muyenga Hill, Leah remembers the moment when what had seemed like a daring caper turned dark and tragic.

She had become accustomed to the secrecy in which Patrick's work was shrouded, and she knew that her role, as the loyal wife of someone working in intelligence, was to keep quiet and not ask questions. But a few days after the invasion, Patrick's mood changed so dramatically she felt impelled to break the unspoken rules of their marriage.

"What's wrong?"

"Leave me alone," said Patrick. "I don't even want to talk about it."

Later that evening she overheard her husband on the phone, talking quietly to someone she guessed was Kagame in Fort Leavenworth. "I heard him say, 'Things are very bad. You need to come home.' He was sounding so depressed, so distressed. But when I asked him what had happened, he said, 'Mind your own business.'"

Once again, those who might have been expected to be in the loop were not. A Ugandan general attending a cocktail party at the Sheraton Hotel was chatting to military colleagues and government officials when a foreign diplomat came up and whispered, "Sorry about the death." "I didn't know what he was talking about," recalls the general, "And he could see it in my face."[9]

When the news came, it had the lacerating impact of a cluster bomb. Legs buckled, vision swam, the earth tipped on its axis. "Patrick heard the news five days after it happened and broke it to me after eight days. When he told me, I just physically collapsed," remembers a friend in Ugandan intelligence. "There was a couch in my office and I had to walk over to lie down on it. It was just so devastating."[10]

Patrick looked at his friend and nodded. "I had exactly the same reaction when I heard," he told him. "I just collapsed. And then I went and drank *waragi* with the guy who told me for an entire day and night. I couldn't sleep."

Fred Rwigyema was dead. The dancing, smiling, golden warrior had been killed on the invasion's second day. Museveni's surrogate son, Salim Saleh's comrade-in-arms, the RPF's military genius, the Tutsi community's big-hearted hero and hope for a united Rwanda was gone, at the tender age of just thirty-three.

The songs, dances, and dynastic poems that the members of the Tutsi diaspora use to keep their traditions alive—songs the elders recited to the questing refugee boys in exile—make much of the centuries-old concept of *ubucengeri,* divinely ordained self-sacrifice, which dictates that the patriot sheds his blood to save the nation. Fred's position as *umucengeri* (martyr) was now secure.[11] The biblical parallel, for those who knew their scriptures, also held good. Despite leading the enslaved Israelites out of Egypt, despite the trials and tribulations of the long desert crossing, Moses himself never sets foot in the Promised Land.

"The whole of Kampala was mourning," recalls Sheila Kawamara, a young reporter at the government's *New Vision* newspaper, who knew many of the NRM's and RPF's top players. "'Not Fred,' everyone kept saying. 'Not him.'"[12]

It would take a full month for the whispers to be confirmed in the Ugandan media.[13] Before going into print, newspaper editors ordered their journalists to check and double-check the information being relayed by soldiers crossing back into Uganda, many of whom were declaring they no longer saw any reason to keep fighting.

Did something more than shock lie behind that news blackout? "The story of the RPF is built on secrets," a Rwandan journalist in Kigali once told me. "And the first big mystery is: 'How did Fred die?'"

The monthlong delay may well represent the time a traumatized RPF elite and its allies in Uganda needed to digest the news and construct a narrative that provided a publicly acceptable answer to that touchy question. What's certain is that the pause allowed a host of conspiracy theories to proliferate, feeding off one another to create a permanent murk of uncertainty. Former newspaper editor Charles Onyango-Obbo sensed a moment when the narrative shifted and hardened into place: "I remember noticing that about a year later, the story began to change and suddenly we were being presented with this alternative history. But that was necessary if the RPF was going to survive."

It would be inaccurate to say two alternative versions exist. I know of at least four, most of them containing just enough incidental detail to be compelling. Broadly speaking, the rival narratives fall into two distinct groups: the first representing what RPF cadres insist occurred, accounts in which everyone concerned behaved impeccably—perhaps that in itself should arouse suspicion—the second representing what most, but not all, Ugandans I've interviewed think happened, senior and well-connected men and women in the military, government, or media at the time. Tellingly, these pivot around personality clashes and political scissions, presenting senior commanders of the RPF and Uganda's top leadership in a far from salubrious light.

Initially, the RPF let it be known that Fred had stepped on a land mine. But the story was swiftly abandoned, probably because the injuries sustained during an explosion were inconsistent with Fred's wounds. Here is a rough summary of the various accounts given by General Kayumba, James Kabarebe, and by other RPF fighters, some published in newspapers commemorating the events decades later.

On the afternoon of October 1, 1990, around 800 men gathered at the Kagitumba border crossing between Uganda and Rwanda. An advance force had arrived early from the west and captured the border post, taking a Rwandan army unit stationed there by complete surprise. Addressing the troops, Fred told them they were now part of the Rwanda Patriotic Army (RPA), then the men bivouacked, with reinforcements arriving throughout the night. According to the General, Fred divided the invading force into three units. One would advance down the main road to Kigali, the other two would flank it.

The choice of Kagitumba as the main entry point was a first mistake, according to James Kabarebe. In contrast with other border posts, situated in thickly forested terrain, it sat in the open, something likely to work to the advantage of Habyarimana's better-equipped Rwandan army. And Fred, what's more, failed to send fighters to secure nearby vantage points.

According to Kabarebe, Habyarimana's army staged a counterattack the following morning and a shell landed in the camp. "Rwigyema," says Kabarebe, "stood up almost instantaneously, in the heat of the moment, saying we follow him. He led the way. My feeling at the time was, this was a wrong thing for him to do. Why didn't he send his subordinates?[14]

"Rwigyema had always fought from the front. This is how he had commanded in Uganda—with courage and determination. But in Uganda, he was a field commander. Now he was the political and military head of an army." As Kabarebe watched Fred and his commanders disappear along the road, he later said, "I had a sense of foreboding that something could go awfully wrong."

Abandoning the road, Fred climbed a hill to get a view of the enemy's whereabouts, a spot the RPF had failed to secure. A Rwandan army jeep mounted with a machine gun was retreating, firing as it moved. Some RPF sources say the jeep was being driven by French special forces, which were reconnoitering the front line on behalf of the Rwandan army they had been sent by Paris to support.

Fred called for his soldiers to bring a recoilless gun and opened fire at the jeep, which was nearly out of range but fired back. At this juncture, Captain Happy Ruvusha, one of Fred's bodyguards, crops up in many accounts. Ruvusha watched open-mouthed as a lucky shot from the jeep hit his boss—some say it was to the forehead, some the neck. In that split second, the fate of Africa's Great Lakes region changed forever. "*Mujinga amenipiga*"—"The fool has shot me" in Swahili—were Fred's last words. Then he died.

It was not the first time Fred, whose height made him an easy target, had behaved rashly at the front. Colleagues recalled an incident a few years earlier in northern Uganda when, trying to size up the enemy's strength, he had stuck his head above the brow of a hill and would have had it blown off had a colleague not pulled him sharply down.

Kabarebe's contingent met up with the other unit, having fought well and captured a great many guns. "We were excited for the two sides to meet there. We had repulsed the enemy. Then I saw that although the soldiers were happy, the commanders like [Vedaste] Kayitare and [Chris] Bunyenyezi were crying."

So much for the RPF narrative. The rival account, told by Ugandan officials and military personnel, tells of an acrimonious argument over military strategy between Fred, Peter Bayingana, and Chris Bunyenyezi, his long-standing challengers within the movement. Exhilarated by the RPF's swift initial progress, the hyped-up commanders wanted to press on. The Rwandan army had been caught unprepared, they argued; a blitzkrieg could deliver Kigali, and hence control of the entire country, into RPF hands. There was no time to be lost.

But Fred had not sat at Museveni's knee, not imbibed his thoughts on the merits of a protracted "People's War," for nothing. Winning control of Rwanda would have no meaning if the Hutu population regarded the RPF as alien occupiers, he said. The RPF needed to take its time, just as the NRM had done, gradually politicizing and winning over the peasantry. The argument grew heated, tempers erupted. And then one of the two commanders took out his pistol and shot Fred in the head at point-blank range.

In this version, two ambitious commanders, convinced they were destined for greatness, had dispatched a man they regarded as unworthy of supreme office. If Fred succeeded, they knew, his victory would make him a likely eventual presidential contender. "They didn't think that Fred would be an independent leader," explains a Ugandan general. "They were suspicious of Rwigyema for taking orders from Museveni, and that's why they eliminated him."[15]

There are several glaring problems with this account. The most obvious being that those present—and it has to be said that a striking number of this group are no longer alive—insist it never happened. General Kayumba was not on the hilltop where Fred was shot, but says he was part of one of the two flanking units, and heard a detailed account of what had happened from Rwigyema's aide-de-camp, Vedaste Kayitare, in the hours that followed Fred's death.

"Peter Bayingana wasn't in the same group as Fred," the General insists. "He had stayed at the border post to direct arriving troops on into Rwanda." As for a quarrel between commanders, "There was no argument over strategy between Fred and the others. If there had been an argument, I'd have known."

The other problem is that the speed with which the disaster unrolled—Fred was killed on the invasion's second day—barely leaves time for in-depth analysis of military strategy, or for furious arguments to break out.

Finally, it's hard to believe any officer with a smidgeon of intelligence or loyalty would place an entire operation, and the lives of his friends, at risk by killing its inspirational commander at a moment when its outcome still very much hung in the balance.

The fact that both Bayingana and Bunyenyezi were posthumously included, along with Fred, in a group of officers awarded Rwanda's highest honor at a ceremony staged on the thirteenth anniversary of "Liberation Day" in Kigali's Amahoro stadium in 2007 indicates that the RPF view of them has taken firm root, domestically, at the very least.[16]

So why do the conspiracy theories show such tenacity? One reason must surely be that they play perfectly to Ugandan perceptions of typical Rwandan behavior: secretive, treacherous, locked in some twisted love affair with death. "You think it's barely credible a charismatic commander should be killed by his own men on day two of an invasion?" a Ugandan might ask, lifting a sardonic eyebrow. "On the contrary, that's *exactly* the kind of behavior I'd expect. . . . "

If this account is true, Fred's assassination would be the first instance of the RPF ruthlessly executing one of its own, and a sinister harbinger of what was to come. No wonder the likes of James Kabarebe and the General might feel obliged to lie about the incident. Admitting Fred had been murdered would expose the RPF as disastrously faction-ridden, a cannibalistic movement poisoned by treachery at the very top, the last impression any commander wanted to reach a nervous volunteer army. Fragile and exposed, the officers desperately needed to look united and strong. And once the lie had been agreed and articulated, it had to be adhered to, for consistency's sake.

Why would so many refuse to accept the RPF account? Conspiracy theories meet a deep human need, bubbling up at times of screeching confusion. When events feel off-kilter, just plain *wrong*, rational explanations simply won't suffice. We shift to a conspiratorial level, where we find emotional, if not logical, satisfaction. There must be more, we tell ourselves, driving motives hidden below a surface we find abhorrent, unacceptable. And in the RPF's case, surely only a nefarious plot could explain something as profoundly jarring as a universally beloved young man dying with such potential unfulfilled. Fred *must* have been betrayed.

"Anyone who tells you the death of Fred was a normal event is just not right. He doesn't know what he is talking about," muses Noble Marara, former RPF officer. And one senses that his refusal to accept the innocent explanation amounts to a form of respect-paying, of mourning not just an idealized hero but an entire generation's lost innocence.

Suspicions of sleight of hand were exacerbated by the secrecy maintained by Fred's colleagues, desperate to maintain the invasion's impetus. Having buried Fred's body in a shallow grave near the Kagitumba border post, commanders Bayingana and Bunyenyezi nonchalantly granted an open-air interview to a gaggle of journalists just two days later.[17] As they sat explaining the RPF's political vision, there was no hint of anything amiss. When Cathy Watson, one of the journalists, asked for Fred, they were told he was "at the front."

The two pressed on with the offensive, reaching the town of Gabiro, forty miles south of the border, where they became locked into a pattern of attack and counterattack with Habyarimana's army, bolstered by French artillery and air support and a contingent of presidential guards sent by Mobutu from Zaire.

If it was a cover-up, it worked—in part. So great was the confidence vested in this one man, many RPF recruits spent years convinced Fred was still alive. Noble Marara admits to having heard rumors of Fred's death while still at school, but choosing to dismiss them. Later posted to several different zones, he was forced to face the fact that Fred, famous for leading from the front, was nowhere to be seen. Even then, he recalls, he and fellow fighters speculated that Fred had been injured, had gone to recuperate, and would miraculously reappear, hale and hearty, when Kigali fell—anything rather than accept the obvious. "I didn't believe Fred *could* die," Marara said.

But whatever needed to be said in public, an appalled Museveni was not going to meekly accept a whitewash. On his return from New York, he called his generals to an army council in State House at Nakasero, a meeting for which he chose to don army uniform. Beside himself with grief and anger, he paced the room, raging at his subordinates, venting his pain.

"He told us Rwigyema had been a very good cadre, that he was better than all of us," remembers one of those present that day. "He abused Salim Saleh, told him he was nonsense, a drunkard; he abused this and that general, he abused everyone. He said it was only Rwigyema who mattered."[18]

As the generals quailed, Museveni pounded the table and said, "Those who have killed Rwigyema, I will kill them. I will kill them. *I will kill them*": "He said it three times."

Salim Saleh and Pecos Kutesa were dispatched to the border to establish what exactly had happened. And here, once again, the story diverges along two tracks, versions that are irreconcilable yet have both somehow combined, in an episode of classic cognitive dissonance, to leave permanent marks on the narrative of those years.

The RPF version, which General Kayumba endorses, maintains that Bayingana and Bunyenyezi died in an ambush three weeks after Fred's death. Their unit had surrounded a group of Rwandan soldiers on the main road between Kagitumba and Kigali and was negotiating its surrender. Unbeknownst to them, while talking terms, the unit radioed the capital requesting backup. Cannily taking the small "rat roads," the reinforcements snuck up and overran the RPF contingent.

The rival version holds that Salim Saleh, the man whom Fred had designated his avenger, recovered his friend's body from its shallow grave, then ordered Bayingana and Bunyenyezi arrested by Rose Kabuye, the RPF's top female commander. The two were court-martialed in the field on suspicion of Fred's murder, found guilty, and promptly shot by firing squad.

Whether or not Museveni believed Fred had been killed by his own men—the theory goes—Uganda's leader did not want the RPF led by a man who was not "one of us," not part of the NRA's original inner core. "The deaths of these two leaders have been matters of speculation in Ugandan and RPF circles till now," Theogene Rudasingwa writes in his memoir. "Dr Bayingana was smart and independent-minded. With him at the RPF helm, President Museveni could have pondered whether the final outcome, in the best case scenario, would be favourable to Uganda."[19]

Theogene's brother Gahima shares the suspicions about his old friend's fate. "I've always had strong misgivings about the story of the ambush. I don't have any facts, so I won't accuse anyone, but I've always suspected Peter was murdered."

•

Traveling to the front on November 3, Gahima, whose siblings were amid the fighters, was shocked by what he saw. "The second Fred died, there was no leadership. It appeared that Peter was in charge but there were people there who didn't want him, so everything was in a state of complete chaos."

Once Bayingana and Bunyenyezi were also gone—three top commanders in the space of a month—RPF chain of command broke down. Uncertain who would take Fred's place, the force lost the military initiative, and the campaign unraveled.

Strategic errors in planning were swiftly exposed. All those years in the bush had not, apparently, dinned into the RPF leadership some vital principles. In the 1980s, the lush Luwero Triangle had provided the NRM with an excellent base: its heavy tree cover made government surveillance difficult, while the marshland clogged the wheels of army trucks and jeeps in pursuit of the guerrillas. At the start, at least, there were plenty of local food supplies.

The RPF, in contrast, had chosen as its base the Akagera National Park, which runs along Rwanda's border with Tanzania. The area appealed because it was virtually uninhabited: that meant fewer hostile Hutu villagers available to report the guerrillas' every move to the Rwandan authorities. But there the advantages ended.

"This was bad terrain," says Gahima. "There was no cover, not a single tree in sight, and the enemy had helicopters. If the war had started farther west, things would have been very different." Akagera was a government-protected wildlife reserve, so no crops grew on its rolling savannah. Swiftly ravenous, the fighters raided the abandoned tourist lodges, got blind drunk on the bottles in the beer and wine cellars, and shot antelopes and zebras in order to fill their bellies.

Museveni had dreaded exactly a debacle of this sort, which put him in an impossible position. Welcoming the mutineers back into the Ugandan army was clearly out of the question, but whatever he had threatened, the president was not about to punish or prosecute fighters to whom he owed so much. Something had to be done.

Salvation would take the unlikely form of the skinny young man who, by dint of taking Fred's place at the Fort Leavenworth training course, had missed most of the action: Paul Kagame. Explaining his predicament to his US hosts, he took a flight from Washington to

London, where he dropped off his pregnant wife, then flew on to Entebbe.

In a hagiography published by *New York Times* correspondent Stephen Kinzer, Kagame presents himself in savior mode, arriving to comfort his peers when all around him grown men were collapsing. "When I saw the confusion and the disarray, I said, 'My God, what is this thing I have come to inherit and take over? What is it?' There was nothing in its right place, not a single thing. Casualties were lying in the road, so many in such a short time. Even the commanders in charge—one senior one, when he saw me, he just broke down in tears. I asked how he was doing. He was crying like a child, telling me he was glad I was back. I asked him, 'How are things here?' He said, 'There's nothing here! Everyone is dead!'"[20]

For Richard Sezibera, who went on to become Rwandan foreign minister but was an RPF medical officer at the time, Kagame was Fred's obvious replacement. "It was the logical choice because of the force of his personality," he says. "Some people are just natural choices to lead. It wasn't 'Who do we want?' It was 'When is he coming?'"[21]

The fact that on-the-ground leadership of the RPF ended up in the hands of an intelligence officer with little direct combat experience, a disciplinarian feared by the infantry and actively disliked by many of his peers, is formally explained by two overlapping criteria: rank and education.

"Fred's natural successor was Peter Bayingana, but he had died, too," says General Kayumba.

"After him it would have been [Lieutenant Colonel] Adam Wasswa. But Wasswa had never been to university and was not educated. The next in line was Stephen Ndugute. He was a major, like Kagame, but his responsibilities had always been greater, and he was older. But Ndugute had only been to primary school. So Kagame had to take over, it couldn't be otherwise."

Kagame, only thirty-three, would be giving orders to older fighters with far more military experience. "That was a predicament for him," recalls the General. If Kagame had been liked, that transition would have been easier. "But there was the issue of his unpopularity with the officers, which was premised on his profile during the NRA years in the bush. His leadership was questioned from the get-go."

But there were other factors at play. Counting its losses, the RPF knew its future survival depended entirely on Museveni's benevolence. Without access to Uganda's markets and hospitals, there would be neither food nor medical supplies for the troops, and without access to Entebbe's airport, the movement would be internationally marooned.

"At that particular moment," adds the General, "it was clear that we were going to do whatever the Ugandans wanted us to do." And Museveni was only going to extend his shield to cover this battered organization if someone deemed "one of our own" was at the commands.

Gerald Gahima, recounting the same episode, uses the word "imposed": "Kagame was imposed by the Ugandans. There were people who were senior to him in the military, colonels and such-like, but in the Ugandan hierarchy, regardless of your rank, the historical twenty-seven who started the war with Museveni have a special status. Because of that Kagame enjoyed the trust of Salim Saleh and Museveni. He had access to them no one else could rival."

The emphasis on membership of "the twenty-seven guns," Gahima acknowledges, makes emotional rather than logical sense. "But that's the reality of the political situation in Uganda. Kagame was the most senior, because he was one of the original twenty-seven."

In making that choice, Museveni was guilty of a fundamental misjudgment of character, one he would have plenty of time to ruefully savor. Fred's star had shone so brightly it had blinded those around him to the nature of his gray, unprepossessing shadow. Kagame only seemed biddable because he tended to go quiet in the presence of the NRA stalwarts, listening and learning. "Museveni mistakenly thought Kagame to be 'a good boy,'" says historian Prunier: "disciplined, without charisma, a good organizer, and the best choice to lead the RPF." The historian suggests, ironically, that the misconception should be logged in "The Famous Mistakes Club."

On Fred's death, formal chairmanship of the RPF had automatically passed to Alexis Kanyarengwe, in Tanzania, so Kagame became vice-chairman, although—this was to be a recurring theme with the RPF—there was no real doubt as to who was in actual command of forces on the ground.

As he ventured into the battle zone, the invasion turned into a humiliating rout. RPF fighters scrambled to avoid being pinned down in the Akagera Park by Habyarimana's army and its allies. Defectors poured back across the Ugandan border, some committing suicide rather than accept it had all been for nothing, shooting themselves or throwing themselves into the Akagera River.

It was during this period that General Kayumba twice rescued the man who would later order him killed.

By late December, the rebel force had been pushed west, out of the Akagera, but was still holding on to a small patch of hilly land at Nkana, just south of the border. On December 22, 1990, the Rwandan army attacked and an overwhelmed RPF contingent retreated to the north. As they reassembled, the officers suddenly realized Kagame had been left behind. Hidden in the depths of a banana plantation, screened by the thick fronds, he and his escorts had failed to notice what was happening.

"Let's leave the fool," suggested one commander with a shrug. But this was the RPF's new leader and the movement could ill afford yet another high-profile death. "We'd lost a lot of commanders and soldiers already by then, morale was really low and there was very little capacity to fight," recalls the General. "So I got some men and went back to extricate him, because I knew exactly where that banana plantation was."

The unit pulled back to a place called Kanyantanga, and two days later, Habyarimana's soldiers attacked again. General Kayumba had anticipated the onslaught this time and guided Kagame and his escorts to a house across the border, safely inside Uganda. The retreat undermined Kagame's image as a man of action—"He never wants those stories to come out," says the General—and the later course of their relationship makes the episode particularly poignant.

By the end of December, not a single guerrilla remained on Rwandan soil, and Mbarara's main hospital was full of wounded Banyarwanda. Kagame and his officers agreed that the RPF, reduced to 2,000 men, should split. One group would stay on the border to engage with Habyarimana's army. The second would march 100 miles southwest of Kagitumba to the Virunga mountain ranges, where it could lick its wounds after this shambolic, tragic start.

Getting there involved crossing Uganda's Kisoro district, something only possible because Ugandan officials agreed to turn a blind eye to this cross-country trek. Angry talk of court-martials for the mutineers was quietly dropped. "If we hadn't been there to take them back again, they'd have been wiped out," says Winnie Byanyima.

But as academic Mahmood Mamdani writes, the support came with a major precondition: RPF officers were welcome to use southwestern Uganda as a rear base, "but there would be no return to Uganda, no possibility that any of them define Uganda as home. The door had quietly but firmly been shut in their faces."[22]

Just as the RPF had anticipated, the relationships established in the Luwero Triangle made all the difference now. The go-between setting terms was Salim Saleh. "I had a choice—either arrest them all or assist them, helping them to reorganize across the border until they had recovered," he recalls. "I chose the latter. That meant food, assistance with the sick, and logistics. I was dealing with Kagame all that time. It took almost a year for them to recover."

The Virunga Mountains form the border between what was then Zaire, Rwanda, and Uganda. Its volcanoes, active and unpredictable, rise to 14,800 feet, and their cool, forested sides, inhabited by the mountain gorillas once studied by Dian Fossey, are thicketed with nettle beds that deliver thigh-high donkey punches of pain.

Conditions here were grim—food was in short supply, and it was so cold on the slopes that fighters' emaciated bodies were sometimes found rigid, frozen solid, in the morning—but inaccessibility meant safety. The only people who would normally trek up the slopes rather than use the valley floors were poachers, smugglers, or members of small local militias.

Kagame's admirers today present the move as a stroke of genius. "Nobody at that time would have thought of taking the force to Virunga," Sezibera told Kinzer. "[But Kagame] had a plan. . . . This kind of unconventional thinking continued through the war, and it worked."[23] In fact, the idea of moving to Virunga was suggested by Colonel Vedaste Kayitare, who knew the area well.

The RPF was at its lowest ebb, but defeat can rouse a community in ways success does not. Aloisea Inyumba emerged as one of the key women of the campaign. A Ugandan Tutsi appointed RPF commissioner for finance, she set about raising donations for the *inkotanyi*—"our children," she called them—shivering on the mountainside. Tutsis across the world rallied, sending money, clothing, boots, medicines, and food.

Above all, they sent recruits, sons and fathers sometimes joining together. Making up for the many deaths and desertions on the Ugandan side, fresh Tutsi recruits streamed in from Rwanda, Tanzania, Zaire, and Burundi as well as from the diaspora in Belgium, France, Canada, and the United States. All the trips to the refugee camps made by Bayingana and Bunyenyezi were finally paying off.

Just as the NRA had done before it, the RPF now opened its arms to thousands of boy soldiers, who were given only the most cursory of military training before being sent to the front: a fact many of its leaders would nowadays prefer to forget. So confident were they of Ugandan support, those recruiting barely bothered keeping secret the location of the training camps, which usually nestled alongside the government-sanctioned refugee camps and settlements of western Uganda, regularly inspected by the UNHCR and fed by WFP.

"Recruitment and training was very, very open. Not secret at all. Our parents and all our neighbors certainly knew what was happening," says one former boy soldier recruited in Kahunge in 1991, where he was studying at Mpanga Primary, Fred's old school.[24] He recalls how, as a helicopter clattered overhead, RPF recruiters brazenly told their audience not to believe a word of what Radio Rwanda and the Ugandan newspapers had been saying about Fred's death.

"They told us, 'That's Fred up there. The guy is still alive, the struggle continues.' We could see a figure in fatigues waving from the helicopter. It never actually landed, so we didn't get to see his face." He sighs and laughs, asking me not to use his name. "We were such idiots. We believed everything they told us."

This cohort of excited, baby-faced boy soldiers included Emile Rutagengwa, who would go on to become Patrick's right-hand man in Johannesburg. He was just fourteen when he went to a training camp in Nakivale valley. "It was illegal," he says today of the RPF's reliance on underage soldiers. "Kagame really has to answer for that, because there were a lot of us."

But Emile is still in awe of the efficiency of the operation, in which a chain of trusted intermediaries got fired-up volunteers from towns and villages in eastern DRC, Burundi, and Rwanda into

Uganda. "It was incredibly well organized, a whole setup of people taking you in, passing you along, telling you where to go, ready to receive you on arrival."

But there was a dark side to this story, too. In theory, the RPF was not Hutu, Tutsi, or Twa—those labels had been invented by the white man to divide and rule. The movement was one big *umuryango* (lineage group), new arrivals were told, which could never again be divided. To underline the point, party organizers were meant to never be exclusively Tutsi, and new RPF cells were always supposed to include a Hutu.[25]

But when it came to training combatants, the RPF—just like its Ugandan predecessor—was paranoid about infiltration, on the lookout for spies who might relay information back to Habyarimana's intelligence services. Arriving youngsters were rigorously screened, and volunteers deemed to have failed the test were rewarded for their enthusiasm with a shallow grave. *Kafuni,* the farmer's hoe, was once more put to use.

"You'd be asked who your mother was, your father, if you were Hutu or Tutsi. If you're a Hutu you're a suspect, big-time," recalls Emile. "And even if you're a Tutsi they want to know who recruited you, where did you pass, how did you get there? I was young and very innocent, so I tended to be waved through. But some never survived that screening. They were taken away for execution by *kafuni* and we never saw them again. Dan Munyuza"—the man who would later work relentlessly to eliminate government critics abroad—"was responsible for that." Francophone boys from Rwanda and Burundi, viewed with particular suspicion by the Anglophone trainers, often didn't make it through.

The RPF that eventually emerged would, initially at least, be the best-educated guerrilla army in history—a testament to both the educational access the refugees had enjoyed, courtesy of the UN, and the number of volunteers coming from the diaspora. "Almost all its soldiers had gone to primary school, around half had attended secondary school and nearly 20 per cent had reached university," according to Prunier.[26] By the time Cathy Watson visited the rebel force at its base in Rwanda's Northern Province, it was 12,000-strong and included lawyers, engineers, at least one priest, and forty-two doctors.[27]

Integration would prove tricky, given the different upbringings, cultures, education levels, and languages the various recruits brought with them. No divide would cut deeper than that between the English-speaking Tutsis from Uganda, who saw themselves as midwives to the RPF and therefore its natural leaders, and the Francophone Tutsis from Burundi, Rwanda, and Zaire.

This reborn RPF carried the indelible stamp of its new leader, so different from his late friend. "Kagame joined the RPF in the field at a difficult time," recalls Theogene, "and at that critical time his qualities—his discipline, his focus, his control—were very important. But with that comes micromanagement. Kagame is a man who wants absolute control."[28]

Where Fred had effortlessly won his men's respect, Kagame set out to intimidate and overawe. Fighters approaching Kagame were warned to talk in whispers—the jittery, sibilant commander seemed hypersensitive to noise—and not to attempt eye contact.

Top-down discipline—something for which the Rwandan army is still feared and respected today—was rigidly enforced. Doing what he knew best, the man who had once reported schoolmates to their teachers and prosecuted fellow fighters introduced a draconian disciplinary code that listed eleven separate offenses deemed worthy of execution and twenty-four lesser crimes meriting corporal punishment.

It was during this period that RPF fighters revived the nickname coined in the Luwero Triangle—"Pilato," they called him once more, or "Kagome"—"the mean one."

"There were lots of senior army commanders, but only one had a nickname of that sort," a former RPF fighter, one of Patrick's distant relatives, told me. "He used *kafuni* to silence dissent at the top level and right down through the ranks. He made the RPF a perfect army, but by using the wrong methods. If you want to put your house in order, there are limits. You don't kill your own."[29]

Now employed in private security, this former foot soldier puts his finger unerringly on what lay behind Kagame's brutality: gnawing personal insecurity. "He was working out of fear, because he lacked confidence. He knew these senior commanders didn't believe in him. So he used force instead."

•

Rebel movements are only ever as good as their rear bases. In the RPF's case, that base was very good indeed, thanks to Uganda's military and its willingness to collaborate with the man who had stayed behind in Kampala: Patrick Karegeya.

"Once the war starts, you need intelligence, you need contacts, you need help with the passage of supplies," says Gerald Gahima. "If you are buying arms, you need end-user certificates, which are issued by governments. How do you get those? And how do you then transport the weapons? Patrick's presence was totally critical."

In the wake of the invasion debacle Museveni had taken an executive decision. "Uganda decided to help the Rwandese Patriotic Front materially so that they were not defeated," he admitted to African leaders several years later, "because that would have been detrimental to the Tutsi people of Rwanda and would not have been good for Uganda's stability."[30] The understanding between the two movements was so close, Kahinda Otafiire told me, that "it wasn't a relationship, it was a symbiosis."

But Museveni had to tread carefully. France, ready to leap to the defense of the Francophone African states that made up its colonial *chasse gardée* (private hunting ground), saw the invasion by the English-speaking RPF as part of a sinister project by the United States and Britain to shamelessly expand Anglophone influence across Central Africa.[31] And Paris packed a considerable diplomatic punch. Uganda's support needed to be deniable.

RPF finance commissioner Aloisea Inyumba was doing sterling work raising funds, but diaspora cash had to be converted into equipment and supplies, such as a giant batch of summer uniforms a factory in the former East Germany wanted to be rid of, or the black Wellington boots outsiders noticed on the feet of virtually every RPF fighter.[32]

"The Ugandan army had issued us, unstated, with a blank check," says the General. "So if we needed arms or uniforms, Patrick would sort out the paperwork with a woman at the Ugandan Defence Ministry he worked alongside. It was a matter of end-user certificates and tax exemptions. There are a lot of things the Ugandan army gets tax free and Patrick would make sure we benefited."

The fact that Uganda was being forced by its new development partner, the World Bank, to demobilize a sizable number of its armed forces at the time was helpful—it freed up weapons and ordnance for which the RPF was only too grateful.

After work hours, Patrick's house on Muyenga Hill became a very interesting place. "Patrick's telephone was the link between the RPF, the diaspora, and governments abroad," remembers a relative who frequently popped by. "Everyone was coming into that house in Kampala, driving in from all sides, to make phone calls to Brussels, Washington, Paris. Patrick was the lifeline."[33]

Kagame regularly arrived in the early hours, his escorts having driven through the night in order to reach Kampala unobserved. He'd look on disapprovingly as Leah and her female relatives fussed over the exhausted men, slicing up pineapples and preparing glasses of milk, cups of hot tea. "You spoil them," he'd say, before disappearing into Patrick's bedroom to brief his de facto quartermaster and put through a series of calls to backers abroad.

The new leader never bothered trying to charm his colleague's wife, just as he had never attempted to win over Patrick's mother. One evening, she came across Kagame in her bedroom, finishing a call. He looked at her and said, "If people get to know that we are meeting here, we will kill you." The threat's directness took her aback. "I just said, 'Patrick doesn't tell me anything, how would I say anything?'"

The shattered RPF bounced back with extraordinary speed. By January 1991, the force in Virunga was ready to reengage. The Rwandan provincial capital of Ruhengeri lay temptingly just across the frontier. Northern Rwanda was Habyarimana's Hutu stronghold, so a successful strike there would emphasize his vulnerability. Ruhengeri was also the site of Rwanda's largest jail, containing many high-profile Hutu prisoners, including Theoneste Lizinde, Habyarimana's former security chief, who had been convicted of plotting a coup d'état in 1980.[34]

On the 22nd, 700 RPF *inkotanyi* poured down the mountain slopes, broke into Ruhengeri jail, captured hundreds of head of cattle grazing on a government farm, and looted warehouses, the bank, a police station, and a military outpost before returning, laden with food, cash, and military hardware, to their mountain hideaway. The prisoners—whom the warden had been ordered to kill rather than surrender—were freed during the operation, which was overseen by Major Stephen Ndugute, and Lizinde promptly joined the RPF.

Lizinde had copious blood on his hands. Habyarimana's former hatchet man, he had arranged the murders of scores of Hutus opposed to the president before turning on him. But as far as Kagame was concerned, he was both an appealingly prominent Hutu and a likely source of priceless information on the workings of a security system the RPF was determined to destroy.

Under pressure from Rwanda's former colonial master Belgium, the RPF and the Habyarimana government signed a cease-fire in Zaire in March 1991, but it was swiftly broken. Neither side had realistically assessed the enemy's strength, so neither was ready to compromise. As the French boosted its military support, Habyarimana's forces launched a top-speed army recruitment drive and went on a weapons-buying spree. But decades of corruption and mismanagement had taken their toll. In October 1991 the RPF pushed into northern Rwanda again. This time it did not see the need to retreat back to the safety of the Virunga Mountains.

When seeking to identify what triggered Rwanda's genocide, outsiders usually focus on a cataclysmic event—a double presidential assassination—which at this point lay three years into the future. In the process, a far simpler cause-and-effect goes ignored. Enemy invasions, especially when followed by prolonged occupation, change societies.

Coinciding as it did with growing international pressure on the Habyarimana government to open up the political space, the RPF's invasion radicalized a state in which relations between Hutus and Tutsis were already toxic, creating a sense of siege among Hutus who looked at their Tutsi neighbors with ever more suspicious eyes. Even as a new multiparty government was established in Kigali in April 1992, thousands of young Hutus were signing up with militias being established by Habyarimana's most extreme political supporters.

In June, in a major, two-pronged operation planned and led by Kayitare and another seasoned RPF commander, Ludovic "Dodo" Twahirwa, the rebels attacked Byumba in the north and neighboring towns. Habyarimana's troops responded not by fighting, but by mutinying. With the crisis clearly escalating, France, the United States, and Uganda pushed for serious talks between the two sides, and the Arusha peace process began the following month.

A classic donor exercise in knocking heads together, the Arusha Accords—named after the Tanzanian town where negotiations took place—were to prove no more successful than a teacher ordering charges who detest one another to "be nice." Its initial impact was actually to increase the fighting, as both sides attempted to improve their position on the ground before an eventual cease-fire. Crucially, the RPF had been granted a long-standing aspiration: a seat at the negotiating table.

By July 1992, the RPF felt strong enough to move its high command to Mulindi, inside Rwanda, less than 50 miles north of Kigali, taking over what had once been a hilltop tea estate. While the RPF's leadership appropriated the tea factory managers' bungalows, the fighters took shovels to their front lawns, digging deep bunkers. Just large enough to hold a single mattress and a small table for meetings, the trenches felt like dank, dark graves, but the RPF was less than two hours' drive from the Rwandan capital now and needed to be braced for attack, including from the air.

After the rigors of Virunga, Mulindi almost felt like a holiday camp. The hilltop was pleasantly cool when the sun set, but no one here risked dying of exposure. There was a basketball yard, a grass tennis court, and an open-air drill ground. Breezes ruffled the medicinal-scented eucalyptus trees lining the estate, and the bushes rustled with birdlife.

But that wasn't why Mulindi, now designated a National Liberation Museum Park, had been chosen. Its strategic appeal becomes immediately obvious when you stand on the basketball court. Gazing across scooped valleys where pickers stoop over the lime-green tea bushes, the estate boasts views in all directions. Radio masts here could pick up signals from across the border in Uganda, while the passes surreptitiously used by RPF patrols crossing between Mulindi and the main base in the Virunga Mountains were actually in binocular sight.

Military victory was beginning to seem possible, but as the RPF extended its area of control, the Utopian visions mulled over the beers in Patrick's house on the hill fizzled and died. Commanders registered how little they really understood their own country.

For more than three decades Hutu peasants had been fed a diet of anti-Tutsi propaganda, which went down easily after the centuries of resentment Hutu serfs had built up toward their arrogant royal overseers. They were now being told by media outlets like Radio Télévision Libre des Mille Collines that the invaders—portrayed in news sheets as monkey-like creatures with tails—were bent on rein-stating the Mwami and recapturing lands, livestock, and positions. Rwanda would be turned into another Burundi, where the Tutsi army killed Hutus at will, villagers were told. Details of exactly which Hutu opposition politician or human rights activist had joined the RPF largely passed them by.

In the field, RPF fighters were taken aback by the hostility they encountered. "Our soldiers would pass by and the farmers would throw stones at us," one former fighter told me with a rueful laugh. "You'd drive past a local woman, trying to say 'hi,' to make yourself look like a good rebel, and she would tell you the worst words you ever heard." Sometimes villagers even took potshots at the passing fighters.[35]

The problem was exacerbated by the fact that President Habyarimana, anxious to demonstrate that Rwanda was full, had moved peasants from northwestern Rwanda into the border areas, exactly where the rebel group was now digging in.

Attempts to replicate the hearts-and-minds campaign the NRA had successfully waged in Luwero collapsed on contact with the sour, rather frightening reality of operating inside Rwanda, on what should have felt like home turf, but didn't. The RPF's political ambitions shriveled accordingly. "There were in Rwanda no liberated zones where alternate modes of governance were introduced under the benevolent eye of a new administration," writes Mamdani. "There were no Resistance Councils and Committees as in the Luwero Triangle, no effort to reach out to mobilise peasants politically, so as to transform them into a human resource for the struggle."[36]

Where in the Luwero Triangle there had been mutual respect between villagers and rebels, here there was a distrust, which may well explain what came later. When an occupying force registers how thoroughly it is disliked, that its "liberation" is seen by the villagers and farmers as an "occupation," local residents become both a logistical nuisance and a security risk.

And during all this time, the RPF's upper echelons were themselves experiencing some high-profile losses. In a scurrilous self-published book, former Kagame bodyguard Noble Marara lists two dozen commanders—including Wasswa and Kayitare—who were either killed in mysterious road accidents, shot by fellow officers, had IEDs placed under their cars, or were poisoned by lethal injection during the 1990s: not the work of Habyarimana's forces, he claims, but of comrades.[37]

Former RPF fighters regard Marara as an unreliable witness, saying he was too young to have witnessed these episodes firsthand, but they nod in agreement at many of the names he includes in what they believe amounted to a quiet purge. What all these men had in common was loyalty to Fred Rwigyema, the respect of the RPF's foot soldiers, and a thoroughly jaundiced assessment of Kagame.

"When it came to combat, Kagame was never respected by the commanding officers," says Robert Higiro, who got a taste of the tensions between top commanders during the Byumba offensive, when his job was relaying messages between Kayitare, Twahirwa, and Kagame. "These were the guys who actually did the fighting, really ran the war. They were normal guys, and they weren't afraid to stand up to Kagame, to be very vocal when they disagreed with him, which he hated. And if you are afraid of people and you are someone like Kagame, well. . . . "

Ugandan former journalist Sheila Kawamara, a frequent visitor to Mulindi, registered the staff changes taking place. "We heard about a policy of extermination of all the officers who had supported Fred. When you were with them you could sense this climate of fear. Those who were more ruthless rose through the ranks at that stage."

In the business world, it's standard practice for an incoming CEO to wield the axe, briskly sweeping away his predecessor's appointees, who are regarded as innately suspect. The closer you were to the old boss, the more likely you are to be handed your severance package by the new one. In the world of rebel movements, the pink slip takes more permanent form.

This episode is one of the question marks that hover over General Kayumba's career. For it was during this period that he emerged as a rising star in the RPF. A lowly lieutenant at the invasion's start, by

1991 he had been promoted to head of military intelligence. However sour things would later turn, at this stage of his trajectory, the General was a Kagame favorite. In that position he could hardly have been unaware of any plots being hatched against some of the seasoned NRA veterans.

Today, General Kayumba attributes the deaths to grueling conditions at the front, dangerous roads, genuine accidents, and the first inroads of AIDS—a disease that was starting to sweep through the Ugandan army, where most of the RPF commanders had earned their spurs.

If there were grumblings, there was no mutiny. With the RPF badly shaken by the deaths of Fred, Peter Bayingana, and Chris Bunyenyezi, and now in full battle mode, officers told themselves this was not the time for a showdown. As one comrade after another either died or was sidelined, a tactful silence descended. But if these commanders' names were steadily wiped from the record—there is barely a mention of them in the biographies of Kagame—their colleagues took quiet mental note.

•

In February 1993, the RPF resumed its offensive, pushing south into the most fertile part of the country. First thousands, then hundreds of thousands of Hutu peasants were pushed off their land, with numbers ballooning to an estimated 950,000, up to 15 percent of the population.

An army created by refugees had created its own refugee crisis. These internally displaced Hutus gathered in over two dozen squalid camps around Kigali, moving repeatedly. Among them were Burundian Hutus who had already fled vicious pogroms staged by the Tutsi army across the border, determined never to cede power to its Hutu majority.

Bitter, hungry, disease-hit, they were soft targets for the likes of Colonel Theoneste Bagosora. A key member of the *Akazu,* or "Little hut," that had formed around President Habyarimana and his wife, Bagosora was signing up recruits for the *interahamwe* ("those who stand together"), a youth militia fueled by hatred for the *inyenzi,* the Tutsi cockroaches.

In August 1993 the Arusha peace agreement was signed in a ceremony witnessed by the Tanzanian, Ugandan, and Burundian presidents and Zaire's prime minister. It catered for the establishment of a broad-based transitional government including the RPF and five opposition parties, an arrangement to be guaranteed by a small UN force.

While Habyarimana's party held on to the defense portfolio, 40 percent of a new national army, along with half of the officers' posts, would go to the RPF. On paper, Habyarimana had been stripped of most of his powers. But the victory, for the RPF, was to prove Pyrrhic. An increasingly strident Rwandan media campaigned against the return of "feudalists" said to be intent on reimposing oppressive Tutsi rule. The deal struck seemed so outrageous to Habyarimana's side that compliance was never really envisaged. Power shifted from the harried president to the leaders of the *interahamwe* and other militias, who knew no respect for internationally sanctioned deals.

The Arusha Accords ruled out arms imports, undertakings the UN peacekeeping force in Rwanda, along with Western embassies, tried to police. Yet it was puzzlingly clear to diplomats who were sent to patrol the Rwanda-Uganda border that both the Habyarimana government and the RPF were energetically arming themselves.

On the RPF side, that was largely thanks to Patrick. He had been assigned to an anti-smuggling unit set up within the Uganda Revenue Authority. The move to a department created to crack down on illicit exports of coffee beans and imports of bootleg fuel seems at first glance an eccentric career zigzag. But the transfer was no more than convenient camouflage, with Patrick cast in the role of both gamekeeper and poacher. When asked about those supposed "anti-smuggling" duties, Gerald Gahima's response is a quiet smile: "Patrick's role was perfect cover for that job."

Grenades, rocket launchers, and AK-47s are not obliged to travel down signposted highways. Having spent a happy youth herding long-horned cattle across the hillsides of Ankole, Patrick knew the *panya* roads suitable for motorbikes and small pickups and the homesteads owned by the families of RPF commanders where supplies could be quietly stashed.

Unexpected visitors at the Karegeya house occasionally caught a glimpse of something they weren't meant to see: a layer of weapons being laid on a truck's bed, then covered with stacked timber. Sometimes Patrick took the wheel of the leading truck himself; at other times, he would drive ahead in his own car to make sure they weren't stopped at the Ugandan roadblocks. Flashing a grin and his government credentials, he could always talk his way through.

As a first step toward implementing the Arusha Accords, 600 of the RPF's best troops moved under UN escort from Mulindi to Kigali. They had been allocated the former parliament building as a base, and there they stacked sandbags and dug trenches. Nominally, their job was to protect the RPF's designated ministers in the unity government. But in the eyes of Habyarimana's "Little hut," a sinister fifth column had just won access to the capital, any country's beating heart. While both sides publicly declared their commitment to peace, Rwanda was primed for civil war.

THE GUN

Hutus fleeing Rwanda after the genocide walk past machetes and hoes confiscated at the Zaire border, June 1994.

Corinne Dufka.

Rebel leader Laurent Kabila greets newly graduated young fighters in Uvira, February 1997.

Corinne Dufka.

Seth Sendashonga.

Cyrie Sendashonga.

CHAPTER ELEVEN

THE GENOCIDE AND ITS AFTERMATH

The mind blanks at the glare.

—Philip Larkin

In Africa, museums usually come thin on the ground. Under-funded and poorly maintained, they often present a version of history barely refreshed since colonial times. Rwanda is an exception. Today it must boast more museums per square mile than any other African nation-state. In Kigali and Kibuye, Gikongoro and Butare, Nyanza, Mulindi, and Nyamata, distinctive brown signposts point you to venues where the displays are pristine, the labeling precise, and the staff well trained and informative.

This is no accident. After the genocide, Western embassies flew RPF officials to Israel to visit the Yad Vashem World Holocaust Remembrance Center, where they saw how a well-designed museum served to keep the world's collective memory keen, broadcasting a "Never Again" message as nothing else could. The lesson did not go to waste. A trip to the Kigali Genocide Memorial, where 250,000 victims are interred, has become an obligatory part of any VIP visit.

Museums set officially approved narratives in concrete. As the cement solidifies, counternarratives, complexities, and nuances get lost, usually deliberately. Rwanda's heritage sites were always destined to become a vital tool in the armory of a regime bent on determining exactly what is remembered about one of the great traumas of the twentieth century.

For visitors arriving by plane, the most accessible museum site lies just a few miles from Kigali's airport. Back in the mid-1970s, President Juvénal Habyarimana built his villa under the flight path routinely traced by aircraft coming in to land. A military man through and through, he felt most relaxed near his army, and Kanombe barracks lay just up the road.

Officially, the villa serves as the Rwanda Art Museum. Its formal gardens are popular with couples getting married, who hold their receptions under white tents on the lawns. The choice seems slightly surreal, but brutal past and banal present constantly overlap in Rwanda. Unofficially, the villa stands as a testament to presidential paranoia, a reminder of how power tends to change hands in this region: suddenly, and with extreme violence.

If the head that wore the crown lay uneasy, it was with good reason. As a young army chief of staff, Habyarimana had ousted his boss, his soldiers supposedly barricading President Kayibanda and his wife in their own home until they starved to death—the ultimate lockdown. Having shown such implacability himself, Habyarimana spent twenty-one years preparing for the moment when his own turn would come. His men called him "Kinani"—"Invincible": he felt anything but.

Climb the main stairs to the first-floor bedrooms and you find yourself walking on hidden censors, wired up to alarms that were set each night to catch intruders. Outside the first couple's main bedroom sits, incongruously, a large safe, its door propped open. It was kept stacked with bricks of ready cash, the guides tell you. The money needed to be close at hand if Habyarimana and Agathe, his intimidating First Lady, were to buy off their would-be assassins.

From there you can wander into the children's television room, a place, in theory, of laughter and fun. But the wood-paneled walls here also hold grim secrets. One panel opens to reveal a secret gun rack, lined with rifles. Another opens onto a hidden flight of stairs, which lead up into a spacious hidden attic, complete with exercise room, chapel—the Habyarimanas hosted the first papal visit to Rwanda in 1990—and a room where, hedging their bets, the family are said to have indulged in a little sorcery with a favorite witch doctor.

Habyarimana clearly saw this as his last redoubt, the place where the family's menfolk and retainers, armed to the teeth, would hold off the enemy until rescue—in the form of French paratroopers, perhaps?—arrived in the nick of time.

As it turns out, it was all for nothing. He was right to fear for his life, but Habyarimana had only prepared for a ground assault. No home improvement scheme, however cunning, stood a chance against the devastating directness of a surface-to-air missile, launched as he sat next to his Burundian counterpart in a French-crewed Dassault Falcon returning to Kigali from Dar es Salaam on the evening of April 6, 1994.

Hearing the engine of the descending jet, Habyarimana's family knew the president was about to land. Then a missile snaked through the sky, just missing the aircraft. As the French pilot tried desperately to take evasive action, a second missile hit home. The Falcon jet exploded in a ball of flame, showering metal debris and body parts onto the presidential villa's grounds.

The members of a British television crew who drove into the compound after the presidential retinue had fled for Zaire, bearing Habyarimana's corpse, found human brains splattered on the bonnet of a Mercedes Benz parked outside the villa. The president's? One of the flight crew? What's certain is that Habyarimana, along with the eight people aboard, died in full view of his family and retainers, his worst premonition fulfilled. The Falcon's twisted wreckage still lies rusting in a field next to the villa, separated only by a low wall.

The jet's downing and the assassination of not one but two African presidents—Burundi's Cyprien Ntaryamira also died that evening—served as the immediate trigger for the genocide. The Arusha peace talks promoted by the international community—in which neither side had ever truly believed—were over. Rwanda's future would not be decided via diplomacy, now, but by slaughter.

Within hours of Habyarimana's death, Rwanda's presidential guard had erected roadblocks around Kigali and youth militias were fanning out across the capital, on a mission to avenge their slain president and root out the enemy within: not only Tutsis, but Hutu politicians, journalists, or senior officials seen as hostile to the regime. "This is a coup but everything is under control," Colonel Theoneste Bagosora told UN special envoy Jacques-Roger Booh-Booh, signaling a split in the armed forces between a moderate faction and his extremists, bent on extermination.[1]

Up in their headquarters in Mulindi, the RPF scrambled. As a full-throttle military operation got underway, the 600-strong RPF battalion inside Kigali was ordered to move what civilian politicians it could locate to safety.

Prime Minister Agathe Uwilingiyimana was among the first high-profile Hutus to die, killed alongside her husband by Bagosora's presidential guard. Ten Belgian UN peacekeepers who had been guarding her were disarmed and tortured to death, their cries relayed to their commanders on their army radios. It was a canny move, prompting the withdrawal of the UN's Belgian contingent, its largest. French, Belgian, and American nationals were airlifted to safety, while their terrified Rwandan colleagues and friends were abandoned to their fates.

At militia and army checkpoints, Tutsis—their fates sealed by government ID cards pinpointing their ethnicity—were either shot or dispatched like animals at a butchery, Achilles' tendons severed to immobilize them, then hacked to death. Within a week of the plane's downing, the International Committee of the Red Cross estimated that tens of thousands of Rwandans had been murdered.

As in the past, killing was presented to ordinary Rwandans as a patriotic duty. Out in the provinces, local *bourgmestres* and *préfets* called public meetings to pull together lists of victims, while Radio Mille Collines urged its listeners on to greater efforts. Their "work," as the radio announcers termed it, was made easier by the fact that overpopulated, intensely cultivated Rwanda had so little tree cover. On the terraced, denuded hillsides, there was nowhere to hide.

Tutsis huddled in terrified groups in churches, schools, hospitals, and sports stadiums, waiting for grenades to be thrown through windows and roofs pulled down upon them by bulldozers. Once these hiding places had been stormed, their bodies were thrown down latrines, or simply left to rot.

Like other reporters, I learned to spot the telltale signs of a massacre site: handprints stenciled in blood on the walls, fields with mounds of freshly turned earth, Hutu village women on their hands and knees, working away at hard-to-remove stains with bleach and soapy water. The smell of human carrion, I learned then, is like the sound of a bomb exploding: it requires no introduction, you immediately know it for what it is. And it takes a lot of scrubbing to get rid of its stink from the cobbled floor of a church aisle.

·

"**P**erhaps one cannot—what is more, one must not—understand what happened, because to understand is almost to justify," wrote the Italian biochemist Primo Levi after surviving Auschwitz.[2] But it is natural, inevitable, to try, as Levi did his entire life.

No one will ever be able to adequately explain how so many respectable, ordinary members of a community—not the random psychopaths every society throws up—ended up in Rwanda turning on people they had shared drinks with in bars, sat next to in church, jostled up against at the market, and cut them down. Quite apart from the death toll itself, the intimacy of that slaughter, its up-close-and-personal nature, baffles and stupefies.

If we are honest, many of us might admit to being capable of pressing a button consigning a disliked acquaintance to anonymous, distant oblivion. Hence the debate about just how much ordinary Germans really knew about the Holocaust, during which Jewish neighbors simply boarded trains, never to be seen again, and how much guilt those witnesses carry. Rwanda's massacres, in contrast, were pre-agreed, public affairs, conducted using the most democratic of tools. There was no mystery, no ambiguity about what happened. Killing someone with a machete, sickle, or hoe is a messy, exhausting business; the process leaves no room for subsequent sugarcoating.

Xenophobic propaganda, broadcast by Rwandan radio stations, certainly played a role, its impact boosted by a culture of unquestioning obedience toward an all-seeing, all-powerful state that had long peered into every corner of its citizens' lives—characteristics the Mwami's court had bequeathed successive Hutu administrations.

In Africa's most overpopulated country, plain greed—for livestock, for land, for women, for property, for access to water—was also an undeniable factor. In DRC, hundreds of thousands of hectares of equatorial forest serve as an outlet for aching land hunger. In a dirt-poor, landlocked Rwanda, where every plot was already accounted for, self-betterment always seemed like a zero-sum game: for me to prosper, you must fail.

But the key factor was surely fear. "Kill or be killed" is a motivation most of us can grasp. In late 1994, I sat with colleagues next to a gaggle of stocky, bespectacled Hutu nuns being evacuated from southwestern Rwanda aboard a UN military transport plane. We had all heard how Rwanda's priests and nuns had enthusiastically collaborated with the *génocidaires*. "Everyone is talking about the genocide now," one nun piped up defiantly, sensing reproach in our glances. "But the RPF had dug big cement vats, where they were going to throw all of us."

Rwanda's Hutus had watched in horror in the 1960s and 1970s as relatives and friends in neighboring Burundi had been slaughtered by that country's Tutsi army. Only six months earlier, in October 1993, Burundi's Hutu president, an enlightened politician preaching ethnic reconciliation, had been bayoneted to death during a coup staged by Tutsi soldiers, who also murdered parliament's speaker and deputy speaker, the minister for lands, and the director of intelligence. Now another Tutsi force was on the move, and Rwanda's own president—the third Hutu head of state in the region killed by Tutsi assassins, they'd been told—was dead.

Genocides do not take place in a vacuum: there is always a context and a buildup. For decades, in a ghastly mirror-imaging, ethnic pogroms in Burundi and Rwanda had echoed one another, depositing layers of emotional numbing upon each community. Serving to convince both Hutus and Tutsis the other side was morally beyond the pale, they had effectively established mass killing in the collective mind as *the* way in which Tutsi-Hutu tensions were resolved.

•

Anyone who was in Rwanda during that era finds a few choice images clinging to their minds long after the events, sending out tendrils of disquiet. From out of the undifferentiated mass of horror peek grotesque individual anecdotes and the odd story of heroism and self-sacrifice. The Tutsi wife who begged her Hutu husband to kill her before the militias did—and he complied. Was he a hero or a monster? The Catholic priest who ordered the church where 2,000 Tutsi parishioners sheltered to be bulldozed by the militiamen. How could anyone reconcile that with the Christian faith? The trusted Hutu retainer spotted by his Tutsi employer manning an *interahamwe* checkpoint. What was he thinking?

My moment came several months after the genocide, when I was walking up a hilltop on the outskirts of Kibuye, a spot of picture-postcard beauty overlooking the waters of Lake Kivu. Kibuye, I knew, had seen some of the genocide's worst massacres, so I instinctively headed for where experience dictated many must have died: the church on the summit.

It was Sunday, an organ had been playing, the singing had faded, the devout streamed out of the church doors: an idyllic pastoral scene. The parishioners who quietly passed me on the path, which was lined with high banks of exposed earth—a bulldozer had recently been at work, I saw—seemed like model citizens.

They looked neither left nor right, which allowed them to avoid commenting on the sight that suddenly brought me up short. From one of the mounds of earth poked, ludicrously, comically, a brown L-shaped object. A naked adult foot. The piled earth, I realized, was there for a reason. It hid the bodies of Tutsi men, women, and children slaughtered inside the church, whose corpses, after three long months, had probably been starting to smell.

Who can explain how a God-fearing community calmly worships feet away from where the bodies of 11,000 recently slaughtered neighbors and friends—I later discovered—lie buried—buried, what's more, with less care than you would allot an item of roadkill—without experiencing some kind of collective spasm? I couldn't. If instead of a foot—anonymous somehow—a pleading hand, or a recognizable head, had poked out of the soil, would they have felt obliged to do something?

I gazed after the disappearing parishioners. A white soldier was walking down the path, beret on head, high-powered rifle cradled in his arms. He was a Foreign Legionnaire, part of Operation Turquoise, the force President Mitterrand belatedly ordered to southwestern Rwanda. The Foreign Legion is open to all nationalities, and this one happened to be a Brit. He noticed the human foot a split second after I had. "Well, he's got one foot in the grave," he quipped, then carried on past me down the path.

•

Many of the photographs taken of the victims show bodies in the process of deliquescence, melting, waxlike, into the ground, people defined by absence rather than presence: clothes they once bulked out, flip-flops and shoes they once walked in.

That's because most of the press—myself included—came late to the story, and the bodies had slowly liquefied in the African heat. South Africa's April elections—the first since Nelson Mandela had walked free from prison—hogged media attention that year. There is rarely enough room in a news broadcast or Western newspaper for more than one African story at any given moment, and for a long time, Rwanda was simply not that story.

News editors were also, more creditably, concerned for their reporters' safety. The violence seemed both widespread and terrifyingly unpredictable. Much of the UN force had pulled *out*, after all, and it takes a certain foolhardiness to send in an unarmed reporter when men with helmets, guns, and flak jackets are running in the opposite direction.

It wasn't until human rights groups such as African Rights and Human Rights Watch started issuing statements that many outsiders began to grasp that what was happening in Rwanda was not random "ethnic killing" but part of an operation with a deliberate strategy, organizers, and a hierarchy of cooperative agents.

As Habyarimana's forces, weakened by faction-fighting, dissipated their energies slaughtering civilians, the RPF advanced. One force headed east to Gabiro then turned south toward the frontier with Tanzania, aiming to secure provinces where Habyarimana's army was weak. The main force struck straight at Rwanda's core, a column marching at top speed—the RPF was desperately short of vehicles—to join their 600 comrades in Kigali.

Despite RPF's ubiquitous modern-day label as the "former rebel group that stopped the genocide," the movement's priority at this juncture was capturing power, not saving lives.

When, ten days after the presidents' assassinations, the UN discussed reinforcing its demoralized international peacekeeping force in Kigali, the RPF fiercely objected. Afraid such an intervention might save the Habyarimana regime's skin in the nick of time, the rebels said they saw no point. "The genocide is almost completed. Most of the potential victims of the regime have either been killed or have fled," RPF spokesmen Gerald Gahima and Claude Dusaidi airily claimed.[3]

It wasn't true. Human Rights Watch's investigator Alison Des Forges noted that at least 30,000 Tutsis were still holding out in parts of Kigali, while in places like Bisesero in western Rwanda, tens of thousands of Tutsis had formed pockets of resistance. Surrounded by *interahamwe* and army soldiers, they were fighting for their lives, desperately hoping for rescue.

The RPF objected once more in June as President François Mitterrand finalized plans to dispatch Operation Turquoise to Rwanda, claiming, once again, that since all the Tutsis had already died, there was no one left to save. Former RPF general secretary Theogene Rudasingwa looks back on that episode with shame: "Of course not all Tutsis had died," he admits in his memoir. "It would have been worth the effort to save even one Tutsi. Every human being deserves to be saved."[4]

It took months for member nations to contribute troops to the second United Nations Assistance Mission for Rwanda (UNAMIR II), and by the time fresh blue helmets began arriving, the RPF had secured its hold on the east and was turning up the pressure on Rwandan troops that had dug in at strategic sites in Kigali, Ruhengeri, and Bugesera. By July 4, 1994, the RPF had effectively taken the country.

With one exception. Thanks to Operation Turquoise, a chunk of territory in the southwest remained for a while in French control. Paris would only hand it over to UNAMIR after high-profile members of Habyarimana's administration had been ushered to safety— one last act of French loyalty to the late dictator.

Retreating west and southwest, Habyarimana's army and militiamen herded the Hutu population before them like sheep, determined to leave the rebels an empty wasteland over which to rule. In one of the quickest human exoduses in history, 2.1 million refugees crossed into Zaire, Burundi, and Tanzania in the space of three months. In a neatly ironic about-face, Rwanda's Hutus and Tutsi communities had swapped positions.

As the hordes moved, they stripped the countryside with the efficiency of locust swarms. The roads to the border crossings were swiftly lined with stumps that had once been rustling glades of willowy eucalyptus. Refugees are always hungry, and to cook their food, they need fuel. Knowing they would not be allowed to cross into Zaire and Tanzania carrying weapons, the *génocidaires* threw their machetes down by the border posts, and the piles of lethal metal, some still smeared with Tutsi blood, collected in stacks.

On the way out, the fleeing Hutus looted middle-class homes, shops, and factories of anything that might prove sellable. At the bridge dividing Cyangugu in southwestern Rwanda from Bukavu in Zaire, I listed the items abandoned at the frontier: light fittings and metal taps, bookshelves and porcelain toilet bowls, planks of wood and electrical sockets. Everything *including* the kitchen sink. To pillage with such abandon, the perpetrator must assume either that rule of law—the legal system that would ordinarily see them thrown into prison—may never be reestablished, or that they will never walk that route again.

Destiny had the last, bitter laugh. In Zaire, the biblical-scale massacre that was the genocide was followed by a biblical-scale scourge as cholera hit the giant refugee camps thrown up at lightning speed by scores of Western relief organizations. Some 50,000 Hutus died from it and a plethora of other diseases.

That didn't stop the officials who had played such key roles in the genocide from blithely re-creating the dysfunctional society responsible for it. In the camps, little tracks of white stones neatly silhouetted villages and communes, still under tight Hutu *bourgmestre* and *préfet* control, still cowed by the militias and army men. Those who had masterminded the genocide intended to recruit new followers, teach them to fight, and plot their return, just as the Tutsis had done in Uganda's camps. If it had worked for the RPF, it could work for them.

Against all odds, the despised "fifty-niners" had reclaimed their homeland. But at what a cost. A quarter of a million children had lost one or both parents. A generation of traumatized youngsters had either witnessed their parents being hacked to death or watched them wield the machete. The *génocidaires* used rape as a weapon, and almost every Tutsi woman who survived had been repeatedly violated, many catching HIV in the process.

In Kigali, key buildings and institutions had been shredded by shrapnel and mortar fire, while in the countryside tea and coffee estates lay abandoned, terraced fields deserted. Habyarimana's army, and most of Rwanda's civil service and judiciary, had perished or fled, taking with them the country's fleet of buses. Even the central bank's reserves had been removed, making it impossible for the incoming RPF to pay government workers.

"There were dead bodies and mass graves all over the country," recalls Theogene. "There were no functioning schools. Most hospitals and clinics were either teeming with the sick and the wounded, or had closed, staff having fled or died. Economic activity had ground to a halt. There were no telephone links with the outside world. Only through RPF's satellite phone that General Paul Kagame kept could we access the outside world. There was no administration. The Hutu-Tutsi polarization was at its worst in the entire history of the Rwandan state."

•

Despite that grim tally, a rush of adrenaline, of sheer excitement, suffuses the accounts of many of the Tutsis who returned during this period. A testament to mankind's incredible resilience, perhaps, their capacity for emotional compartmentalization conveniently served a steely instinct for survival.

"You have to understand," said Robert Higiro, when I asked him why the memories of many returnees were not as stark as I'd expected. "Yes, hundreds of thousands of people had died. But we'd grown up in the camps. In most cases, these were distant great aunts and uncles, cousins we'd never actually met."

As early as 1991, heeding a dog-whistle call no indigenous locals could hear, Tutsi refugees in the camps of Uganda, Burundi, and Tanzania had started packing up and occupying lands being captured across the frontier by the advancing RPF—in the process helpfully making it impossible for the Hutus who had fled the *inyenzi* to return. Now that trickle became a rush.

Back in the 1960s, the Ugandan government had been obliged to lay on transport, fuel, and personnel to get the exhausted, traumatized Tutsis as far as Kahunge, Fred Rwigyema and Paul Kagame's childhood settlement. The return promised to be a similar logistical nightmare. Instead, the Tutsi herdsmen did what they knew best, cajoling their Ankole cattle the hundreds of miles back to Rwanda, while privately hired trucks were loaded with the elderly and with women and children who could not manage the long walk.

"They left spontaneously, once the RPF captured power," says David Mugenyi, a Ugandan refugee officer. "We didn't have to organize anything; they left of their own accord."[5]

In the diaspora, Tutsi doctors, nurses, lawyers, and engineers—anyone with any skills that might prove useful—packed their bags, applied for unpaid leave, or simply gave up their jobs and booked their flights. Tutsi businessmen drove in from neighboring countries to size up possible markets. War economies are times when long-established monopolies are shattered and entrepreneurialism rewarded: you can taste the opportunity in the air.

One of those hyped-up patriots was Patrick Karegeya. Shortly after Kigali had fallen, in characteristically flamboyant style, he loaded up his car with bottles of Dom Pérignon and drove across the border with two Ugandan friends in tow. Dead bodies still littered the streets of the Rwandan capital, but he was determined to toast the RPF's victory with his comrades.

In late 1994, the RPF's inner circle decided to move Kayumba Nyamwasa from his role as head of military intelligence to commanding the *gendarmerie*—Rwanda's police force. Intelligence would simultaneously be split in two, an internal and external wing. Patrick, it was decided, would make a perfect head of the Rwandan External Security Organisation (ESO).

"I was at the meeting where the decision was taken," says the General. "Since Patrick had been in the intelligence in Uganda, he had built up lots of contacts, and Kagame had already worked with him. Kagame and the rest of us all thought Patrick was brilliant.

"Patrick's job would be to link us with the main intelligence services across the world. He already knew these guys through his role with Uganda's DMI, so his job would be to work out how to get the RPF accepted in countries like Zaire and Burundi."

In a striking illustration of the extraordinary level of cooperation between two former African revolutionary movements at the time, Kagame phoned Museveni and asked him to release Patrick from his duties. And so Patrick relocated to Kigali. The family spent Christmas of 1994 there, and soon after that, Patrick suggested that Leah and the children join him. In May 1995, they moved to Kimihurura district, eventually upgrading to a villa in Kiyovu, a favorite with the incoming RPF elite.

Curious as it might seem, Patrick's decision astonished many of those in Uganda who knew him best. Patrick might have traced his roots back to Rwanda, says Kenneth Kakuru, his university friend, but, like an Austrian or Swiss citizen who happens to speak German, he was Ugandan by nationality, culture, and personality. Kakuru detected no sour sense of alienation, no yawning hollow that had to be filled by a return to a romanticized "home."

"He had no close relatives in Rwanda, he was not a former refugee. When Patrick spoke Runyankole, he spoke it perfectly, without an accent—so did the father—and no Rwandese does that. I never felt Patrick perceived social and political life in Uganda like a Rwandese refugee. He did not have that mentality. He *belonged.*"

The obvious biblical analogy doing the rounds at the time, Kakuru said, ruled out Patrick's participation. "I told him, 'If you're an Egyptian, not a Hebrew, why would you go?' He just laughed it off." Kakuru still ponders the question. "The only answer I can find is that he was acting out of a sense of duty."

I suspect that while Patrick was painfully aware that the land of his ancestors lay in ruins, and that the skills he possessed were in desperately short supply there, he was heeding not so much the call of duty as the summons of adventure. Destiny had dangled before him not just a major promotion but a chance to play a role in an unfolding story of gargantuan proportions. Offered a ringside seat to history, how could someone with Patrick's inquiring mind say no?

Whatever his motives, Patrick kept them to himself, presenting his Ugandan circle with a different avatar from the one adopted with his Rwandan colleagues. "It's just a job," he would reassure family members when he returned to the farm in Biharwe, donning his boots to inspect the herd. "This is where I'll retire."

Leah, more innately Rwandan than Patrick in her values and perspectives, came to see the move as a life-altering blunder. "Patrick should not have gone to Rwanda. It was never his place." The country's riding obsession, she says, never chimed with him. "He never accepted that Hutu, Tutsi, and Twa couldn't live together in one country."

While many of Patrick's younger relatives would eventually follow him to Rwanda in search of jobs or to chase after tempting business deals, his own parents, significantly, stayed put in Uganda. Kakuru remembers that when he helped out by driving John Kanimba across the border to visit the son who had suddenly become a big shot in Kigali, he was surprised to discover the old man had never before set foot there. His views on the country were strong and extremely hostile. When Patrick, in a fit of patriotic enthusiasm, told him he'd bought him some land in Rwanda, his father gave a sardonic laugh and delivered a grim warning. "These are my people and I know them better than you," he said.

•

On the day Kigali fell to the RPF, many of its fighters anticipated an event that never came: for Fred Rwigyema to reemerge like some *deus ex machina*. They knew all the stories, of an argument and betrayal, of a fluke shot or an assassination. But they had still clung to the hope that like some resurrected messiah, he might appear to claim his rightful victory.

"We still had some hope that we would see him sworn in," says Noble Marara, his throat suddenly clogged with emotion. "But it didn't happen, and when they collected his bones I said to myself, 'It is true,' and we had to live with it and finally believe that Fred really had died."

On October 2, 1995, the fifth anniversary of his death, Fred's body was exhumed from a shallow grave on Salim Saleh's farm in western Uganda and flown to Kigali for a hero's funeral. Nothing could have better illustrated Fred's extraordinary hold on the collective imaginations of both the Rwandan and Ugandan military elite than the ceremony that followed.

As regional leaders and a bemused contingent of diplomats looked on, Fred's casket—draped in purple, covered in the Rwandan flag, and crowned with flowers—was carried into the Amahoro stadium on the shoulders of six army officers.

Kagame, allotted the unrewarding role of Joshua to Fred's Moses, said a few respectful words. But it was Salim Saleh, friend, fellow fighter, and surrogate brother, who led the crowd in a chanted "Fred Rwigyema *oyee*"—"Long Live Fred Rwigyema!" "Shout loud, so those in Goma can hear you!" bellowed Saleh, a reference to the remnants of Habyarimana's government and army, camped humiliatingly across the border in Zaire. By his side, bemused by the roars and applause, stood Fred's widow and two small children, a young family Saleh had taken under his protective wing, just as he had promised.

In the stands, RPF commanders rubbed shoulders with the Ugandans with whom they had once shared rations, tents, and duties in the Luwero Triangle: men and women like Jim Muhwezi, Kahinda Otafiire, Mugisha Muntu, Kizza Besigye, and Winnie Byanyima.[6]

But Museveni did not attend. Perhaps he could not bear to, perhaps the thought of playing second fiddle to Kagame, whom he was already beginning to regard as a disrespectful whippersnapper, stuck in his craw. And while the audience included Hutu members of the new government, they felt like strangers intruding on a private, incomprehensible grief. "He's not a hero to *all* Rwandans," Prime Minister Faustin Twagiramungu sourly commented when parliament floated the notion of recognizing Fred as a national hero.

After an all-night candlelit vigil, the coffin was finally lowered into a grave near the stadium as a twenty-one-gun salute was fired. It holds pride of place in "Heroes Corner," set under a white pavilion, in a grave tiled in smooth gray marble.

Fred was finally home. But his Promised Land had turned out not to be a place of milk and honey, but a charnel house. And the methods his men had used to reach it, already coming under growing international scrutiny, were a far cry from what the charismatic warrior had originally envisaged.

CHAPTER TWELVE

THE BEST PRESIDENT RWANDA NEVER HAD

A means can be justified only by its end.
But the end in its turn needs to be justified.
—**Leon Trotsky**

Ask disillusioned former members of the RPF what first alerted them to the fact that the movement they had joined in a rush of youthful idealism had taken a turn down a dark and sinister path, and most will point to the same event: Seth Sendashonga's death in a barrage of AK-47 fire.

A little silvery salamander of shame flips over inside me whenever I hear that. If they are honest, any journalist can list a series of stories they realize, in retrospect, they either missed, played down, or misinterpreted. For me, several are associated with Rwanda's former interior minister.

He personifies the moment I first queasily suspected I had misunderstood what was happening in Rwanda. He is a memory of a job badly done for the simplest of reasons: in the smooth, contoured shape of a widely accepted narrative, his story stood out like a jagged splinter. So the splinter went ignored until it became too painful to bear.

When I tell his widow, Cyriaque Nikuze—"Cyrie" for short—about my guilty twinge, her reaction is gently gracious. "Oh, it wasn't just you," she says with a soft sigh. "So many people had that experience. It was his fault, too, for not being more open. He didn't make it easy for the media, out of loyalty to the party."[1]

My first encounter with Sendashonga came in August 1995, when I was staying at the Hotel Mille Collines. The RPF had just announced a cabinet reshuffle, and the new lineup seemed worrying for a movement that had made so much of ethnic inclusiveness when it captured Kigali. Faustin Twagiramungu, the prime minister, had resigned a few days earlier, complaining that the RPF was behaving like an "army of occupation." Now Sendashonga, Minister of Justice Alphonse-Marie Nkubito, and Information Minister Jean-Baptiste Nkuriyingoma had also gone. All four were Hutus. Had a Tutsi-dominated organization just shown its ethnic teeth?

Bare-faced cheek is the currency of journalism. Kigali is a small city, distances short. I hailed a taxi, asked the driver if he knew where Sendashonga lived, and we headed off, across the valley and up the hill.

It was a whitewashed, modern villa just like every other villa the RPF had commandeered for its dignitaries in the genocide's wake, fringed by a lawn whose grass shoots struggled to establish a hold on the claggy red earth. In a jeep parked outside sat several elegantly long-limbed RPF soldiers. As I rang the doorbell, aware of the jeep on the periphery of my vision, I wondered if they were there to provide security or to prevent Sendashonga from leaving.

Inside, the tiled living room was almost empty. This, too, was typical: all those upper-class homes had been thoroughly looted, leaving them puritanically bare. Unnervingly, it seemed I was the only journalist who had thought of making this short trip. Sendashonga emerged almost immediately, and rather to my surprise—I'd half expected to be turned away—agreed to be interviewed on the spot.

He was a sturdy, well-built man with an impressive mustache. The pajama-like white bou bou he was wearing instead of a suit seemed to underline his sudden joblessness. It said "gardening leave."

He would not go into the reasons for his departure, but dismissed any suggestion that Hutus were being politically sidelined or that the Tutsi-dominated military was making a power grab. "I think the new government will be similar to the old one," he told me, "a mixture of Hutus and Tutsis, civilians and military men. This is not a problem with the army; it is a problem of different perceptions of what is best for Rwanda."[2]

The words were reassuring, but the body language was not. He was not sweating, exactly, but his shiny skin hinted at suppressed tension, strong emotions surging below the surface. Every now and then his dark eyes slipped sideways, glancing beyond the compound wall toward the jeep.

I returned to the hotel, uncertain what I'd just witnessed. *Langue de bois* is the phrase the French use for language so deliberately free of content that it yields as little as a block of wood. I'd been granted an interview, but I'd learned very little.

That evening I met a friend, an intense American diplomat smitten with the RPF. Over dinner, he argued passionately that movements that took power in countries where ethnicity was a touch-paper issue still needed the freedom to reshuffle cabinets to take personality clashes or competence into account. Pointing out that one of those sacked—the transport minister—was a Tutsi, he said he was certain the new cabinet would be just as ethnically balanced as the one it replaced. He was so persuasive that when the BBC World Service rang the following morning for an explanation, I gave a reassuring answer. But remembering Sendashonga's body language, the way his eyes had kept darting to the men outside, I felt a flicker of doubt.

My second—and last—encounter came nearly a year later, on July 10, 1996, when Sendashonga held a press conference in Nairobi's media center in Chester House. I joined the international throng of journalists packed into the dingy restaurant where Sudanese opposition movements and Maasai activists routinely went to deliver their statements.

He had gone into exile in Kenya not long after our interview. There, he'd set up an opposition party with his friend Twagiramungu. Five months before the press conference, someone had called, offering documents exposing dissent in RPF ranks. Sendashonga had driven to meet his informer with a nephew. Both had been shot, but the hit had been bungled.

Sendashonga, who saved himself by opening the car door and rolling under the vehicle—textbook military evasive action taught to him by the RPF—had recognized one of the men who had opened fire. It was his former ministerial bodyguard. The other assailant, arrested attempting to hide his weapon in a gas station toilet, worked at the Rwandan embassy, where he answered to Jack Nziza. Nziza, who would later try to recruit Emile Rutagengwa as Patrick's killer, was third secretary there.

The Rwandan government's involvement could not have been more blatant, but once Kigali had refused an official Kenyan request to lift the suspect's diplomatic immunity, investigations ground to a halt.

I don't remember Sendashonga mentioning the attack that day in Chester House. Instead, with the help of a colleague, he unrolled reams of teleprinter paper, on which were typed not hundreds, not thousands, but hundreds of thousands of names: Hutus he said had been slaughtered by the RPF both before and after the fall of Kigali. Pointing to the tallies for district after district, he estimated that the RPF was responsible for at least half a million deaths.

Many of these killings, he said, had been perpetrated during the rebel movement's advance across the country, when no international human rights observers had been present to bear witness. "The number of casualties on the RPA account is so large that the international community can no longer shield behind the idea this is a disciplined army fighting another army," he said. "We can no longer say this is any army around which the Rwandese can reconcile."

Arguing that both the RPF and Habyarimana's expelled forces were compromised by the amount of blood on their hands, he called for an international mission to be posted to Rwanda and the country run under an international mandate while a new, untainted army was recruited.

As the teleprinter paper covered in names unspooled in the former minister's hands, the atmosphere in the room was a mixture of dismay, impatience, and disbelief.

Most of the journalists present had covered the 1994 genocide. To the French-speakers among them, the notion of a "double genocide"—that killings committed by the RPF counterbalanced those by Habyarimana's forces—was already familiar territory: France's Quai d'Orsay (Foreign Ministry) had been briefing to that effect all along. The English-speakers, briefed by American and British diplomats and officials, had, in contrast, always regarded that as classic, mischievous, disinformation. They almost felt sorry for their French colleagues. Many had struck up close friendships with the new Rwandan elite, considering key members personal friends. Now here was this former Rwandan minister suggesting, it seemed, that the French might have been largely correct all along.

Stumped, I returned to my office and called my boss in London, the Africa editor of the *Financial Times*. Why hadn't Sendashonga said something back in 1995? Why wait till now, when the claim smacked of aggrieved revisionism? Whom was I to believe, the 1995 Sendashonga, or this 1996 version? "I honestly don't know what to think," I told my editor. "But if anyone is in a position to know, it's him."

"Well, there's no point agonizing," he said. "There's no space for Africa in tomorrow's edition in any case." In those days newspaper websites were in their infancy, space finite and fiercely fought over. I'd been let off the hook.

•

Seth Sendashonga was that rare thing: an idealistic, politically savvy Hutu who rejected the single-party dictatorship established by his notional kinsmen and saw power-sharing with the Tutsi diaspora as holding the key to the future. "He was a brilliant gentleman," recalls Twagiramungu ("un gentilhomme brillant"): "an intellectual with no hint of ethnic favoritism about him."[3]

Born in Rwamatamu on the edge of Lake Kivu, Sendashonga became embroiled in politics while studying at the National University of Rwanda in Butare. It was during this period that he started dating Cyrie, a fellow student who was half Hutu, half Tutsi. Publication of an outspoken magazine article criticizing the regime brought Sendashonga to the attention of Habyarimana's intelligence service, and he fled the country in 1975.

He and Cyrie moved to Nairobi in search of work. He found a job with Habitat, a UN agency specializing in urban settlement, and Cyrie, a biologist, eventually joined the UN Environmental Programme (UNEP), part of the same complex in the green suburb of Gigiri. The two formed one of those well-salaried, multilingual, highly skilled African couples driven in and out of the metal-fenced compounds in chauffeured white 4WDs, IDs dangling from lanyards.

They were well matched, intellectually and emotionally. Cyrie's preface to a book of essays dedicated to Sendashonga is almost disconcertingly intimate. "When I was a girl . . . we were told that heaven was full of beautiful rooms and the chosen would be allotted a bedroom," she writes, addressing her late husband. "Ask for one with a double bed and wait for me."[4]

The couple could have worked and lived anywhere. But Sendashonga remained viscerally connected to Rwanda, less than an hour and a half's flight away. As the fall of the Berlin Wall and Mitterrand's La Baule speech sent tremors through Africa's autocratic regimes, he shuttled back and forth between Nairobi and Kigali, meeting Hutu members of civil society and opposition politicians pushing for change.

Sendashonga became one of the signatories of the "Manifesto of the Thirty-Three Intellectuals," which called for an end to Habyarimana's political monopoly on power. When a bevy of brand-new opposition parties sprang up in 1990, they vied for his support. But he found their aspirations disappointingly parochial, dominated either by regional rivalry or by traditional Hutu-Tutsi antagonism. He pined for more than a political game of musical chairs. "These guys don't want to change things at a deep level," he told Cyrie. The following year, when the RPF was still reeling from Fred's loss and its disastrous invasion, he joined it.

Sendashonga, insists Cyrie, was always an independent thinker, who reached decisions at his own pace—"No one could influence Seth, not even me"—but the couple's grasp of the RPF's credo and aspirations had certainly been boosted by a friendship struck with a Rwandan colleague at Habitat. A regular visitor at the Sendashonga home in Nairobi, she was part of the RPF's fundraising and recruitment network.

Sendashonga's value as a recruit was obvious. As a Hutu with a track record of civil society involvement and democratic activism, he would—by mere dint of signing up—send out the message that the RPF represented all of Rwanda's communities, not just aggrieved

Tutsi aristocrats. An educated progressive, a cosmopolitan intellectual, he was also a civilian, who could allay concerns about the RPF's militarism.

But he required wooing, taking exception, for example, to the historical narrative presented in the RPF's written constitution, which depicted Rwanda's precolonial kingdom as something akin to the Garden of Eden, free of ethnic antagonism until the arrival of the dastardly whites with their divide-and-rule policies. The Hutu Revolution that overturned the Tutsi monarchy was presented as a *jacquerie* (peasant's revolt) instigated by the Belgians, rather than as a widely popular response to long-standing inequality and injustice.

"They were glossing over the past," says Cyrie. "Seth told them, 'You have to admit there were genuine grievances before 1959.' He only agreed to join the RPF once those clauses had been rewritten to his liking.

"He was the first Hutu politician from the outside to join. He had nothing to gain. He wasn't a refugee, he wasn't looking for a job, and that's why he was respected. He was trying to show that Rwandans are not condemned to think in terms of Hutus and Tutsis: they should choose their political affiliation based on a shared vision of a more democratic society."

Such was his enthusiasm, Sendashonga tried to persuade his wife to sign up with the RPF. "Come on," Sendashonga would say, "You're so suspicious. You people from Central Rwanda, you never trust anyone." She was half won over, but only half. "I had some kind of instinct. I used to tell him, 'That RPF manifesto, it's too good to be true.' Me, I never joined."

While Cyrie ran the home—their three young children kept her busy—Sendashonga ping-ponged between Nairobi, Kigali, and Kampala. Liaising between the RPF and Rwanda's nascent opposition, he pleaded the RPF's cause, arguing that successive regimes' refusal to address the plight of Tutsi refugees had made armed struggle inevitable. With paper spewing out of the fax machine, the family home felt at times like a newsroom.

When peace talks opened in Arusha, Sendashonga, promoted to the RPF's political inner circle, played the role of behind-the-scenes adviser, as the party's intellectuals—men like Pasteur Bizimungu, Patrick Mazimpaka, and Jacques Bihozagara—pushed for the RPF to not only be included in a government of national unity but to control key portfolios. By 1993, he was spending more and more time at the RPF's base on the requisitioned tea estate in Mulindi.

After the genocide, the RPF was anxious to reassure what remained of a terrified Hutu population that the power-sharing principles of Arusha still held good. While the RPF gave itself the ministries originally earmarked for Habyarimana's party, sixteen of the twenty-two dockets went to the opposition. But all was not quite as it seemed: the RPF vetted candidates put forward by the parties. Its intervention was so blatant that when Jean-Marie Vianney Ndagijimana, former Paris ambassador, was approached and offered the foreign minister's portfolio—a post originally earmarked for another member of his party—a wary Ndagijimana initially refused.

It was Sendashonga, who'd known him since their days as activists, who persuaded him to reconsider. Ndagijimana told me, "I asked him, 'Do you think we're going to see the real democracy we dreamed of under Habyarimana?' Sendashonga said, 'Come anyway, and we will fight *from within*.' It was Seth who really convinced me to take the job."[5]

Everyone assumed that the dynamic Sendashonga would be named president in the first coalition government, in tribute to the work he had put into getting Rwanda's opposition to collaborate with the RPF. Instead, the RPF gave the top job to Bizimungu, a haughty Hutu politician, former director of Rwanda's national electricity company, who had enjoyed close ties with Habyarimana. The appointment was justified on the grounds that Bizimungu also came from Rwanda's northwest, an area needing reassurance.

Unveiling the cabinet list naming Sendashonga as interior minister and Faustin Twagiramungu as prime minister at a meeting with the former opposition parties, Theogene Rudasingwa, Kagame's chief of staff, was clearly surprised by the unenthusiastic response. "He said," recalls Twagiramungu dryly, "'Why aren't you applauding?' and someone replied, 'We're applauding in our hearts.'"

For Sendashonga, it was a massive slap in the face. "Seth was black with rage," recalls Twagiramungu. "He had worked so hard to get the opposition parties to accept the RPF, telling us they weren't supremacists, saying he wanted to make Rwanda the Switzerland of Africa."

However personally galling, there was, in any case, a huge element of symbolism to these appointments. The man who really ran Rwanda now was Kagame—he was appointed both defence minister and vice-president, a post not envisaged by the Arusha Accords and created in the teeth of opposition resistance.

That tokenism extended throughout the administration. "The RPF made sure it was in full control even when it included some Hutu," Theogene later wrote. "Where we had a Minister or any other official who was not RPF or a Tutsi, an assistant (almost in all cases, Tutsi) was deployed. It was another unwritten yet very much known rule about how RPF was to govern. The new administration was Tutsi-based and military-driven."[6]

Diplomats, UN personnel, and journalists all understood and accepted the cosmetic nature of Hutu inclusion. Given what had just happened to Rwanda's Tutsi minority, which had stared annihilation in the face, the new power in the land was obviously not about to meekly hand control back to an ethnic majority it viewed with massive suspicion.

"After the genocide, the people I worked with wanted total power, because of that genocide," recalls Twagiramungu.

Tutsi fear was not the only factor. To the victor go the spoils. The RPF cadres felt they had earned the right to run the country during the grueling years of fighting. Twagiramungu remembers Kagame telling the gathered Hutu politicians, "You must understand the context," before leaving the room. "And everyone agreed and we all took the vows. The 'context,' of course, was: 'We won the war and we could have named me president.'"

If the military men nursed toward civilians the thinly veiled disdain men of action reserve for pen-pushers, there were also pragmatic reasons for the latter's impotence, notes Gérard Prunier. In war-shattered Kigali, the RPF owned all the toys. "Most of the ministers did not even have a proper office, a secretary, stationery or a typewriter, even less a car. So whether it connived at the situation or not, the RPF remained for the time being the only source of real power in the country simply because it had vehicles, fuel, weapons and portable telephones."[7]

Cyrie flew into Kigali for the new government's swearing-in on July 19, 1994. By this stage, she hadn't seen her husband for seven months and had not been privy to the anguished conversations between the civilian politicians. Looking back, she marvels at the gullibility she demonstrated during a conversation with Kagame, over a meal in which he felt obliged to justify Bizimungu's appointment as president.

"Your husband is a good man and we owe him a lot," Kagame told Cyrie. "But it wouldn't be a good idea to make him president. Our biggest problem is Habyarimana's army and we need to appoint someone from Habyarimana's area."

The argument made sense, and she felt at ease enough with Kagame, whose family came from the same village in central Rwanda as her own, to speak openly. Sendashonga's talk of the RPF's ethnic color-blindness had left its mark and—amazingly, in retrospect—she tried to persuade Kagame to scrap figureheads entirely. Rather than go through the charade of appointing Bizimungu head of state, she argued, Kagame should simply declare *himself* president.

"I remember telling Kagame, 'You have to strike while the iron is hot. We need, as a society, to learn that ethnicity doesn't matter.' He told me, 'No, no, no. That would give the impression that was what it was all about. I don't want to be president. I hope in two years' time to get Habyarimana's army under control, then my ambition is to become a gentleman farmer, or to go back to school.'"

Scratch the skin of many a member of that generation of Ugandan or Rwandan military men and you will come across that dream of the gentleman farmer, a reverie rooted in pastoral childhoods spent driving long-horned, moist-eyed cattle across the hills. Patrick nursed it, the General still does, Museveni has seen its ripe fruition. Cyrie was convinced.

She widens her eyes and grimaces delicately, now, at her own credulity. It's the reason why she has little appetite for criticizing westerners who fell for the RPF rhetoric. "And me, I believed him! Whereas in two years' time, of course, he got rid of Bizimungu." Shaking her head in rueful despair, she lapses into French: "*Oh la, la. . . .*"

•

None of the ministerial portfolios in the new coalition government was exactly easy. But Sendashonga's was probably the toughest.

Even a country as small as Rwanda isn't run directly from the president's office. Under the system inherited from the Belgians, effective administration depended on a hierarchy of *préfets, sous-préfets,* and *bourgmestres,* jobs vacated by men who by mid-1994 were living off WFP rations in the tarpaulin *blindés* (shelters) in Tanzania, Burundi, Zaire, and the tranche of southwestern Rwanda controlled by France's Operation Turquoise.

Sendashonga set off for those refugee camps, where he addressed the crowds, urging Hutu officials who had nothing to hide to return to Rwanda, where, he promised, they would not only be safe, but welcome. But like Penelope's shroud, his earnest work was simultaneously unraveled by his colleagues in the new Rwandan security forces.

Thousands of Tutsi refugees were flooding back into the country from Uganda, Zaire, and Burundi, occupying lands and homes abandoned by departing Hutus. Reports streamed in of Tutsi soldiers killing Hutu villagers. These were presented as "reprisal killings" by fighters who, on discovering their extended families had been wiped out by locals, lost control. But often sheer greed lay behind the murders. For Tutsi returnees, whether soldiers or civilians, labeling someone a *génocidaire* was a convenient way of appropriating their assets.

The stolid 1930s brick prisons left behind by the Belgians filled with tens of thousands of Hutus denounced as all-too-willing executioners. There they then stayed, as most of the lawyers, prosecutors, and judges needed to prosecute them either had been killed or had fled. There was a huge incentive for false denunciations.

"When I arrived in Kigali," recalls Ndagijimana, "I found Seth hadn't changed, he was still fighting for what was right. People would come to see me, telling me the RPF wanted to kill them to get their houses, that they were being accused of being killers when in fact they were victims. Each time I would call Seth on the walkie-talkie and each time he would come to our rescue and try and do what he could."

I visited Kigali's main men's prison around this time. There was no room to walk, lie down, or exercise. Men and boys in angelic pink—the incongruous color used in Rwanda for prison uniforms—stood inches away from one another. It was a panic-inducing experience, not because I thought I'd be attacked—the mood was plaintive rather than angry—but because of sheer claustrophobia. While I knew plenty of these men in pink had committed terrible crimes, it was impossible not to feel aghast. If they had sinned, they were paying for it now, with their gangrened, fissured feet, the tuberculosis germs they were coughing into one another's faces, their outbreaks of cholera and typhoid.

Complaints about unjustified arrests and murders all ended up on Sendashonga's desk. General Kayumba, now in command of Rwanda's 2,000-strong gendarmerie, remembers a series of "very, very stormy meetings" with Sendashonga.

"A lot of people were being arrested by RPF cadres. But a lot genuinely *were génocidaires,*" he insists. "Only a few were being arrested because of false allegations." The genocide, he points out, had relied on a host of enthusiastic amateurs. "The prisons were full, crammed, but it takes a lot of people to kill 800,000.

"Sendashonga was very, very adamant about the due process of law," he recalls. "But when you have a chaotic situation you can't have due process. We could mitigate against the reprisal killings but couldn't eliminate them completely. A soldier goes home and finds his whole family gone and the neighbors digging their fields, and he takes action. We couldn't have people in all the villages providing security."

Sendashonga repeatedly brought the subject up in cabinet meetings, which Kagame was in the habit of either boycotting or sitting through in near-total silence. The vice-president may genuinely not have trusted himself to speak, but it was also a classic Kagame technique, a brilliant method of luring others out into the open while keeping his cards close.

"He spoke very rarely," recalls Ndagijimana. "But," he laughs, "You would see his face change. He has a little facial tic." The nervous ministers would become fixated by a vein at one of Kagame's temples, which would start throbbing as soon as RPF atrocities were mentioned. It was the poker player's "tell," a giveaway the vice-president was absolutely furious. "He's a very touchy guy and he would become very het up, very quickly."

For the Hutu politicians who had been persuaded to give the RPF a chance, doubts had begun to set in. Ndagijimana would never forget an off-the-cuff conversation with RPF senior member Patrick Mazimpaka, on a visit to Byumba. Welcomed by local dancing troupes, the foreign minister noted with surprise that, at a time when politicking for any individual party—as opposed to the government of national unity—was officially ruled out, the singers were all explicitly praising the RPF.

"I turned to Mazimpaka and said, 'Isn't this strange? It's just like the days of Habyarimana and the single ruling party.'" The response sent a chill down his spine: "He looked me in the eyes and said, 'So, you believed it, too? My, you're just as naive as the white folk. *Fais gaffe* [watch it]. We told you what we needed to get you on board.'

"I kept asking Seth," recalls Ndagijimana, "'Are you sure we can fight *from within*?' And at the start he would say, 'Yes, yes, yes,' 'We're going to do this,' 'We're going to do that.' He wanted to be patient, and he trusted the RPF. He was a bit naive. We all were, but when you're on the ground and you see certain things, naivete should end."

Sendashonga would later calculate that at least five Rwandan citizens were being killed by the new army each day. During his thirteen months in office, he wrote 760 letters—more than two a day—detailing his concerns about the arbitrary arrests, disappearances, and killings of Hutus, giving precise names, dates, and locations to Kagame and the justice minister. He never received a written reply.

One of those Sendashonga told about the letters was Jan Pronk, Dutch development minister of the day. One of the first European ministers to rush to Rwanda after the genocide and soon a loyal donor, Pronk established a close relationship with Kagame, but not as close as the one he enjoyed with his interior minister. "Sendashonga was one of the men I trusted the most. With Sendashonga it clicked," he told Dutch journalist Koert Lindyer.[8]

Despite his admiration, Pronk felt Sendashonga was being unnecessarily provocative, poking a tiger. "Every incident was a new letter. I thought that was not so wise, because every time he annoyed Kagame."

One gets a sense of a man determined not only to call power to account, but to bear witness to what would otherwise remain the anonymous dead. But each ignored letter underscored the interior minister's powerlessness, which even extended, he discovered, to accessing military camps and prisons where suspected *génocidaires* were held. Here he had a personal interest. His older brother, mayor of the village where they had been born, was arrested while actually staying with Sendashonga in Kigali, accused of organizing the massacre of Rwamatamu's Tutsis. Another brother was accused of cheering at an *interahamwe* roadblock as the militiamen did their work. He, too, was detained.

Sendashonga tried to have both brothers released, to no avail, their guards even refusing to deliver medication he sent to their jail cells, driving home the extent to which the military, not the civilian government, really ruled the roost in Rwanda. "It was done simply to upset and discredit Seth, by showing his brothers were Hutu extremists," reflects Cyrie.

As he attempted to persuade Hutu officials to return, the RPF pressed for its own list of candidates for the posts of *bourgmestres* to be appointed. At the grassroots level, the power-sharing principles of Arusha did not, it seems, apply. "Almost all of the names were refugees recently returned from Burundi, Zaire, Uganda, and Tanzania," recalls Twagiramungu. In other words, Tutsis. The tussle over the *bourgmestres* would be long and heated and would culminate in defeat for Rwanda's Hutu cabinet ministers.

Much of this was barely glimpsed by the diplomats, the UN officials, and the various aid agencies who roared into Kigali in their white, logo-bearing SUVs, overwhelmed by the question of how best to help this devastated society. But then, in September 1994, came an independent survey that made the first serious dent in the RPF's image.

•

The UN High Commissioner for Refugees (UNHCR) had first begun receiving reports of mass killings of refugees by the rebel movement in May 1994. The accusations had been contemptuously rejected by the RPF. The tiny but influential human rights organization African Rights, while acknowledging that the RPF's human rights record left much to be desired, dismissed any suggestion of massacres. "There is absolutely no evidence that the RPF is responsible for large scale indiscriminate killing of civilians," researcher Rakiya Omaar reported, after traveling extensively in RPF-controlled areas. "*The RPF is not implicated in genocide*" (her emphasis).[9]

African Rights' reports carried a great deal of influence because most journalists, wary of venturing into a mine-littered war zone, dutifully observed RPF rules on where they went and how they traveled, relying on human rights groups and NGOs to fill in the gaps.

When UNAMIR commander General Roméo Dallaire met reporters, Ugandan former journalist Sheila Kawamara recalls, "He
told me and my colleagues they couldn't protect us and we were on
our own." So reporters entering Rwanda from the north were effectively embedded within the guerrilla movement. "There was no way I
was going to say to the RPF, 'No, I'm going to sneak over to the other
side and report from there.'"

And the RPF were superb at playing the media. Once the RPF
High Command moved to Mulindi, it set up a directorate of information to vet arriving reporters. "'Approved' journalists were taken
to the massacre sites like tourists and helped to file their stories,"
she recalls. "The RPF were smarter and better resourced than the
journalists they were dealing with. They gave us transport, food, and
protection, they told us the story, and we relayed it. In a way we were
public relations officers, not journalists."

If one issue was the reporters' security, another was language.
Fleeing Hutus often only spoke Kinyarwanda. The better educated
might have basic French but rarely any English, so Anglophone reporters required a translator, who would often end up being the RPF
officer ferrying them around, recalls Kawamara. "I remember interviewing a Hutu who had seen a killing and as soon as he said 'RPF,' I
was told, 'Oh, don't write that down. He's *interahamwe.*'"

Reporters would later recall, with retrospective unease, how eerily
quiet the first areas captured by the RPF had always seemed. When
bodies with their hands tied *kandoya*-style behind their backs surfaced in Lake Victoria, brought by the Kagera and Nyabarongo Rivers, many observers wondered how fresh genocide victims could be
washing down from areas the RPF had long cleared of *interahamwe.*

It didn't make sense, but the tendency was to accept RPF
explanations—in this case that these were old bodies. This wasn't
solely out of intellectual laziness. Covering the genocide had brought
reporters face-to-face with the worst in human behavior. They had
seen the splayed bodies, met the gang-raped women. At the few press
conferences they staged before fleeing, members of Habyarimana's
government, expressing themselves in flowery French, had come
across as thuggish and evasive. No wonder, amid all that horror, the
slim puritans of the RPF, with their direct talk—"Never forget, these

guys spoke *English,*" recalls an aid worker—seemed the incontest-able Good Guys.[10]

Unless you're a pathologist, a corpse cannot tell its story. "It's true I saw bodies, I saw hundreds of bodies," says Kawamara, "in churches, schools, and fields. But who killed those people? You can't tell from just looking at a dead body who killed it.

"I saw fear in the eyes of the people I interviewed, but I didn't know why. We never had the time or opportunity to check what we were told was true. I met those who went into exile later and spoke to them and now they tell a different story to what they said then."

She was so haunted by the sense she had been successfully ma-nipulated, she decided to leave journalism after the genocide. "My stories were instrumental in conveying the RPF's narrative," she says, with impressive honesty. "I returned to Kampala and said to William Pike, 'We're not hearing the other side of the story.'"[11]

Amid the general consensus that the RPF had comparatively clean hands, the UN decided to assess prospects for repatriating the refugees. Now that the war was over and a multiethnic government installed, would it be safe to truck them back? It hired Robert Ger-sony, a US consultant with decades of human rights experience in Latin America, Southeast Asia, and Africa, to carry out a survey.[12]

Gersony, who had worked in Somalia, Uganda, and Mozambique, arrived in August 1994 with a team inclined to be well disposed to the new authorities. He promptly ignored a government directive telling NGOs to stick to the main roads. "The first thing we did was to go down the first dirt track we came to," recalls Tony Jackson, one of the team's members. And what they found down those "rat roads" took them totally by surprise.[13]

In Kibungo, two hours' drive east of the capital, the team came across a red-brick one-story building in the classic Belgian style. "We could see what looked like packages beautifully laid out on the ground in front of it," says Jackson. "They turned out to be bodies. The team counted 150. All fresh, new bodies, fully clothed, in a straight row. There was no one about."

This was an area from which the *interahamwe* and Habyarimana's army had long since been expelled: the killings could only be the work of the RPF. The team drove on, anxious to get moving before they bumped into an RPF patrol. "We were very silent in the car. This wasn't what we'd expected. I was catatonic, in a state of shock," Jackson recalls. Farther down the road, in a church, they found more bodies, one semi-mummified batch clearly dating back to the April genocide, but also another group that had obviously been freshly slaughtered. And so it went on.

Between August and September, Gersony and his researchers conducted 200 one-on-one, extended interviews in 41 of Rwanda's 145 communes and 9 refugee camps, only to be stunned by their own findings, which challenged the unfolding narrative of a disciplined, plucky little rebel movement halting an unfolding obscenity in its tracks.

Far from staging individual, sporadic reprisals, the RPF, Gersony came to conclude, had killed tens of thousands of people in areas falling under its control—he put the number at a likely 30,000—months after the genocide's end. A favorite technique was for RPF soldiers to encourage villagers to attend a "peace and reconciliation meeting" with the new powers-that-be, then open fire on those conveniently assembled in one place. Alongside the gun, hand grenade, and machete, he singled out the hoe—*kafuni*, that old NRA technique—as one of the killing tools used.

"'Revenge killings' was the phrase being used, but this was too systematic to be that," Jackson told me. "This was the best army in Africa. If the same thing is happening all over the place, someone has to have ordered it. In Rwanda, things like this don't happen as a result of local people taking their own decisions."

Gersony was scheduled to brief the Rwandan government and military on his findings.[14] Warned of what was coming, UN secretary-general Boutros Boutros-Ghali ordered Kofi Annan, his number two, and Kamel Morjane, UNHCR director for Africa, to fly to Kigali to sit in on the various meetings.

When Gersony briefed Sendashonga, with only Morjane and a ministerial aide in the room with them, the interior minister leaned forward across the table to unburden himself. "Your account is 100 percent accurate," he told Gersony. "Every single detail of it. I've been receiving reports like this for months and I've sent hundreds of memos to Kagame and have yet to receive a response."

But it was another matter at the meeting at which Gersony's findings of "systematic and sustained killing and persecution" were presented to the Rwanda inner cabinet in Kofi Annan's presence. "Sendashonga didn't want to talk about this matter, and the prime minister felt the same way," recalls Ndagijimana. "Both Sendashonga and Twagiramungu were saying 'This is exaggerated,' and 'You're going to destabilize our country.'"

Ndagijimana puzzles, today, over the personal foible dictating that Sendashonga sprang loyally to the RPF's defense whenever it was publicly assailed by westerners, even as they voiced precisely his own concerns. "He had one way of seeing things with Rwandans, and another with foreigners. With us, he was furious. He would say, '*C'est pas possible!* We didn't wage war to stop the Tutsi killings only to now have troops killing *Hutus!*'

"But when he was face-to-face with a foreign delegation saying they had heard the RPF was killing Hutu civilians, my friend Sendashonga would tell them to mind their own business. At that moment he'd become a little RPF."

Concern that endorsing the revelations might spell the transitional government's collapse, along with a conviction that nothing mattered more at that moment than political stability, must have been a factor in Sendashonga's stance. But African pride, knee-jerk anticolonialism, and the visceral dislike we all feel when being lectured about our own society by outsiders also played unhelpful roles.

On this occasion, Sendashonga could barely conceal his annoyance, Ndagijimana recalls. "'*You guys*,' is how Sendashonga addressed them. It seemed to me you don't say, '*You guys*' when you're addressing Kofi Annan."

UN envoy Shaharyar Khan recorded the outcome in his cable back to headquarters. Unconvinced by Gersony's findings, he repeatedly used a term—genocide—that Gersony himself had been careful to avoid in his report. "The Prime Minister and the two Ministers heard out Mr Gersoni's [*sic*] indictment of mass genocide by the RPA with politeness and equanimity. They expressed shock . . . but made no hint of mala fides," he wrote. Some individual acts of revenge had occurred, Twagiramungu and Sendashonga told the UN, but "it would not be possible for the government to massacre 30,000 people without the world finding out about the genocide."[15]

It was a circular argument—Gersony's report obviously represented "the world finding out." But with UNAMIR's top military brass also expressing skepticism and Sendashonga promising an investigation, the UN—supported by the United States—agreed to sit on the findings and launch its own inquiry, a time-honored method of kicking an issue into the long grass.

Prunier was so close to Sendashonga that he dedicated a book to him. Yet even with him, the interior minister observed the principle of collective responsibility, concealing his dismay. "Both Seth Sendashonga and Prime Minister Twagiramungu . . . lied to me at the time, only to apologise later and explain that they had done so in the hope of helping national unity," Prunier writes.[16]

So convinced were they of the RPF's moral rectitude that both Prunier and Alison Des Forges, Human Rights Watch's veteran investigator, initially dismissed Gersony's findings—the American had been misled and lied to, they speculated, the man had no background on Rwanda—only to later reach many of the same conclusions themselves.

In March 1999, Des Forges would publish *"Leave None to Tell the Story": Genocide in Rwanda.*[17] The main focus of this exhaustive 595-page report on the Rwandan genocide was the role of Habyarimana's government, civil service, army, and militias in the murder of three-quarters of Rwanda's Tutsi population. But the fact that it also contained a twenty-five-page account of RPF atrocities—in which the use of "old hoes" (*kafuni*) made more than one appearance—forever soured the veteran human rights investigator's relationship with the new administration.[18] No tarnishing of the halo would be permitted.

•

How did the RPF, which had emerged from a guerrilla movement largely admired for its discipline by human rights groups in the Luwero Triangle, come to commit atrocities with such enthusiasm less than a decade later? What explained the difference in behavior once these same men found themselves on home soil, where, if anything, they might have been expected to hold themselves to higher standards?

The NRM had always relied upon the Banyarwanda, who were regarded as more ruthless than other recruits in battle, thanks to their history of grievance, to do its most serious fighting. It's possible the absence of other ethnic groups with radically different agendas and perspectives removed a restraining element.

Noble Marara, Kagame's former bodyguard, points to another factor: the loss of the RPF's intellectual crème de la crème. "The commanders who led that war [in Uganda] were trained in Mozambique and Tanzania, their role models were Kwame Nkrumah, Thomas Sankara, Samora Machel, and Nelson Mandela. When we went to Rwanda we were left with recruits who were just finishing cadet course. We lost all the commanders who cared for others and were left with those only interested in power and looting," he said.[19]

"The NRM was genuinely popular, the people of Uganda had had enough of Obote. It came in at a good time. The RPF, in contrast, found itself in a place where we were not liked, at a time when we had lost our role models. We were drained, and then we were attacked."

Then he ticks off a list of purely practical reasons for mass killing in captured territory: "One, we didn't have a place to jail people. Two, we couldn't let people go back to Kigali to expose us, to report back on our movements—'They passed over there, they were on that hill.' Three, there was no procedure for investigations to know whether this person could be part of us, and four, Kagame was just used to solving problems in that way."

And Rwanda's toxic history helped ensure certain solutions appeared not as methodologies of last resort, but mere turns of the country's ghastly ethnic wheel of fortune. As Robert Higiro puts it, "Why would someone like me, who was born and grew up outside the country, want to kill Hutus? The point is that you grow up thinking all Hutus are your enemies, because of what happened to your community in the 1950s and '60s. So when you go back, you'll kill for revenge. But not revenge for the genocide, revenge for things which go far further back, that your parents and grandparents told you about. The troubles between Hutus and Tutsi didn't start in 1994. The genocide was part of a process that began much, much earlier."

Gersony, with whom I've spoken several times, has chosen never to publicly comment on his findings. In any case, his mandate was to record the abuses he uncovered, not to speculate about motives. But human rights workers active in Rwanda at the time note that the geographical locations of the killings identified by Gersony and others formed a spine curving from Byumba in Rwanda's northeast to Butare in the south, suggesting a tactical plan to create a *cordon sanitaire* between RPF-held areas and refugee camps in Burundi and Tanzania brimming with *interahamwe* and Habyarimana's Hutu military.

"The RPF were not in a position to rule without a good degree of intimidation," one told me. "There were still a lot of armed Hutus on the ground and the message to them was, 'We can murder you with impunity and the international community won't do anything about it.' The RPF *did* have good reason to fear the Hutus. The problem was that they targeted the wrong Hutus."[20]

Military tactics elided with Rwanda's age-old anxiety over land availability. Cables sent by the US embassy in Bujumbura back to Washington reveal that in August 1994, shortly before Gersony's team ventured into the field, Ambassador Robert Krueger notified the State Department of what he feared was a deliberate policy by the RPF to terrify Hutus in southeastern Rwanda into exile, turning over farms, homes, and lands to Tutsi refugees who had left in the 1950s and 1960s.

Citing a trusted source with access to missionaries, nuns, doctors, and other expatriates who traveled a cut-off area rarely visited by journalists, Krueger recounted that orders were being sent to Tutsi exiles in Burundi to make themselves available at fixed times and places. Buses were then sent to take them across the border to areas where the Tutsis were told a certain house, hut, or plot—in fact the property of Rwandan Hutus who had fled or been murdered—was "free."

Brutality passes like a virus from one community to another. Eerily reminiscent of what Obote's UPC militias had done to the Banyarwanda in Uganda during the early 1980s, the report horrified the ambassador: "His account is, to me, chilling," Krueger told his bosses.[21]

•

The Gersony "report"—in fact a summary of an oral briefing, as Gersony concluded there was no point typing up an account that most in the UN did not want to hear—acquired mythical status, its contents never made public but familiar to diplomats and UN staff. When a special rapporteur on Rwanda for the UN Commission on

Human Rights asked for a copy in April 1996, he was, infamously, told, "We wish to inform you that the 'Gersony Report' *does not exist"* (emphasis in original).

During my time covering the Great Lakes, I never saw a copy, but everyone knew its rough contents. Nowadays you can find a summary on the Internet. Reading it makes one wonder what must have been going on inside the conflicted Sendashonga's head.

In early October 1994, just as Amnesty International was about to publish a report into RPF mass killings in Rwanda that grimly corroborated both Gersony's findings and Krueger's cables, President Bizimungu left for the United States with his foreign minister.[22] The two men were scheduled to meet government officials in Washington and attend the UN General Assembly in New York. As a Hutu, Bizimungu might have been expected to pursue the issue of Hutu killings as fervently as Sendashonga, but his first loyalty was to the movement that had named him head of state.

"I thought we were going to the US to ask for foreign aid," Ndagijimana recalls. "Then I realized that Bizimungu's only preoccupation was to get the Gersony report classified *sans suite* [no follow-up]. Pursuing the RPF, the argument went, would destabilize Rwanda and the region, the government was young, it needed time, things were going to improve. Whereas in fact the situation was getting worse every day."

While Boutros-Ghali insisted on the UN process running its course, the message from Washington was typically pragmatic: "Help us to help you," they told Bizimungu. In other words: "Stop the massacres and we will help you block the Gersony report."

Disillusioned, fearful, Ndagijimana took the opportunity to abandon ship, the first of the post-genocide Hutu ministers to quit. "When I saw that the president of the republic, a Hutu and a childhood friend, that he too wanted at all costs to stop talking about Hutu massacres, I understood my place was not there."

The Gersony report did, notwithstanding, have a brief beneficial impact. The UNHCR halted any attempts at refugee repatriation, a move that strengthened the position of the Hutu ministers. For the next three months, Human Rights Watch noted, there was a letup in RPF violence on the ground. It was a strong argument for donors such as the United States to maintain pressure on the RPF. Instead, the international community did the opposite.

271

In January 1995 came what Sendashonga dubbed "*la reunion de malheur*" (the unfortunate meeting): a donors' roundtable in Geneva where Rwanda won pledges of $598 million in bilateral aid. Kagame and his colleagues, Sendashonga told Jackson, interpreted the pledge as a clean bill of health. "They had got their knuckles rapped, but they were now forgiven, the international community had gotten over the killings. And it all started again."

By then, Sendashonga was on the verge of despair. Cyrie recalls a poignant moment of unburdening, when her indomitable husband exposed his vulnerability as partner and a man.

Making the most of a UN Nairobi–Kigali air shuttle that allowed her to travel free of charge, Cyrie had gotten into the habit of flying into Rwanda every two weeks carrying soap, oil, and other items that made daily life for a hard-pressed politician a tad more bearable. The shelves of Kigali's looted shops were still empty, basic commodities hard to find.

Since the terminal was only a short drive from the hillside villa he had moved into, Sendashonga usually came in person to meet the flight. But this time Cyrie found herself walking alone through the echoing immigration hall, still pockmarked with bullet holes. No one was waiting, not even a driver. Puzzled, she hailed a taxi.

"When I get home I see that the car is there. I ask the housemaid if Mzee is in. She says yes. I find him in the bedroom, lying on the bed, lost in thought."

She was too alarmed by this strange behavior to berate her husband. "I didn't say, 'Hey, why didn't you come and meet me at the airport?' I just lay down next to him on the bed and said nothing."

Together, the couple stared at the ceiling in silence. Finally, Sendashonga said, "You remember telling me you thought I was making a mistake?"

"Yes," replied Cyrie. "But I respected your choice."

"If I left all this and came to Nairobi, would you still respect me?"

"Of course."

"I needed to hear that," her husband told her. "Because I see you were right. You saw ahead. The government and I are on a collision course and I wanted to know that I would be welcome back."

It pains her now to think of the feisty Sendashonga reduced in that way. "He was so overwhelmed, so depressed. It was so unlike him.

He was so ashamed of the decisions he was making. Things were so bad that he couldn't come to meet his wife at the airport, he couldn't face her." It was about that time, she says, that her husband began talking to colleagues he trusted of quitting.

But worse was to come. "The next time I saw him out of his mind like that," recalls Cyrie, "was over Kibeho."

•

Rwandan history is peppered with tales of female seers, mystics who became channels, in their trances, for disturbing messages from on high. In the early 1980s, a schoolgirl in the village of Kibeho, in southwestern Rwanda, reported seeing a beautiful woman who radiated motherly love. But there was nothing comforting about the visions the Virgin Mary brought first Alphonsine and then two of her fellow pupils: a valley full of rotting corpses, rivers of blood, men chopping off heads and hacking at bodies.

Word spread, and the village of Kibeho became a place of Catholic pilgrimage, the site of the only Marian apparition in Africa to win Vatican recognition. But in 1994 Kibeho became known for something else. The withdrawal of French troops had left 350,000 Hutus in a stretch of southwestern Rwanda known as the Safe Humanitarian Zone, in settlements administered by the UN and the aid organizations. Kibeho became the site of the largest camp for the internally displaced on Rwandan soil.

As the months passed, the new government in Kigali became increasingly irate at the way in which the giant refugee camps in neighboring Zaire were being used as launching pads for cross-border attacks by *interahamwe* and ex-military, recruiting fighters in full view of the aid agencies. It felt even more strongly about the continuing existence inside Rwandan territory of such a camp. Inmates should return to their plots, officials insisted. If they were refusing to budge, it could only be because they had guilty consciences.

Kibeho camp's existence felt like an insult. On April 18, 1995, when the country had just staged a commemorative reburial of 6,000 genocide victims, several battalions of Rwandan soldiers surrounded it, torching shelters and firing warning shots at the 150,000 Hutus inside.[23]

Sendashonga was driving Cyrie to the airport when he got a call from UNAMIR warning him that Kibeho's inmates were being killed.

He drove off to the camp at high speed, then returned to Kigali to brief his Hutu colleagues and win a promise from Kagame that the situation would not be allowed to escalate.

It turned out to be worthless. Over the days that followed, the army fired directly into the pinned-in crowd, first with rifles, then with machine guns and mortars. As Zambian and Australian UN soldiers looked on aghast, Rwanda's new Tutsi army slaughtered indiscriminately, making no distinction between former militiamen, ex-soldiers, simple farmers, or women and children. All were treated as *génocidaires*. When a frantic Sendashonga returned, the army refused him access. The soldiers were busy burying what the Australian Medical Corps estimated to be 4,000 to 8,000 victims.

It might have been possible to conceal events in the remote areas where Gersony and his colleagues had conducted their research, but this mass killing had been staged in full view of the cameras. The photos and ample film footage shot at the scene capture the distinctive, casual mess created by human detritus.

"That was the last time I was in Rwanda," remembers Cyrie. "After that Seth said, 'Don't come back because I'm so angry I don't know what will happen.'"

Over the phone, Sendashonga, the man of peace, told his wife of the homicidal rage he had felt sweep over him as he had watched Kagame later assuring a press conference that a few hundred had died at Kibeho—the official death toll was "only" 338. "I wanted to go for his neck and strangle him," he told her. "For the first time in my life I felt violence overwhelming me." He demanded an international inquiry, but the Western diplomats and lawyers selected to sit on it blandly echoed the official line.

Kibeho marked a turning point in perceptions of the RPF. "For many Rwandans and some diplomats, any notion that the RPF would respect the rule of law, uphold human rights and promote ethnic unity disappeared after the Kibeho massacre," writes US academic Susan Thomson. "Members of Rwanda's political opposition . . . held out Kibeho as the first concrete example of the exact kind of oversight the RPF intended to mete out on majority Hutu."[24]

The scales had certainly fallen from Sendashonga's eyes. He now believed that Kagame and his aides had always intended to establish despotic rule in Rwanda and nursed a deliberate policy of extermination, says Cyrie. Twagiramungu remembers a disillusioned, broken Sendashonga weeping in his office. "We were lied to," Sendashonga told his friend. "People treated us like innocents, like fools."

The two Hutu politicians remained at their posts, but they were only going through the motions now. "Seth and I continued dragging this cross," recalls Twagiramungu. "To be a prime minister without any power is an unbelievable experience. During the thirteen months I held that post, I only managed to chair a cabinet meeting once, when the president was away, and the next meeting, everything that had been agreed was rejected."

Over issue after issue, the RPF hard-liners and their Hutu colleagues—Bizimungu excepted—now disagreed, with the latter increasingly regarded as fifth columnists, to be carefully monitored by military intelligence for signs of potential treachery.

The *bourgmestre* issue resurfaced. "Seth came to show me the list of *bourgmestres*," remembers Twagiramungu. "Out of 150 communes, the RPF had given 120 places to themselves. These were nominated positions, there had been no elections. I hit the table." If the two Hutu politicians were outraged, it was Sendashonga's decision to disband the Local Defence Forces, militias created to fill the void left by the policemen who had fled the country—men responsible for many of the Hutu arrests and disappearances he decried—that triggered a final showdown on August 25, 1995.

At what was to be their last cabinet meeting, Twagiramungu objected to the *bourgmestre* appointments, while Sendashonga refused to rescind the disbanding of the local militias. Kagame's carefully studied patience snapped. Sarcastically suggesting his portfolio be handed to one of the two Hutu ministers, he walked out. "The following day, everyone was trembling," recalls Twagiramungu.

Convinced a united front was vital if the civilian politicians were to stand up to the men with guns, Twagiramungu invited six nervous Hutu cabinet colleagues to his residence. "I said, 'The situation is very serious. Let us all resign,'" he told me. To his relief, all agreed. "The following day, everyone who had left my house went straight to Bizimungu to tell him what had happened." Once again, the tradition of political duplicity surfaced. "Seth and I were the only two who resigned, the rest betrayed us. That night everything was cut: the phones, the lights."

Twagiramungu got his resignation in just before Bizimungu arranged a parliamentary vote sacking him, while Sendashonga resigned the night before his dismissal was announced. The government of national unity was over. The new government certainly included Hutus—the new prime minister was one, from Twagiramungu's own political party—but they could now be in no doubt about the limits of their power. One by one, Twagiramungu, Sendashonga, and Information Minister Jean-Baptiste Nkuriyingoma all went into exile.

After the resignations, the always outspoken Dutch development minister, Jan Pronk, flew to Kigali to try and extend a protective shield over the man he respected. "They have to stay alive," he told the vice-president. "I told Kagame that nothing should happen to Sendashonga," he later said. "How dare you?" responded an outraged Kagame, taking offense.

"He did not like that," recalls Pronk. He did not like that, and he did not pay any attention, either.

•

A few years after the NRA seized power in Kampala, when its hold on Uganda was still tentative and the military elite was chafing at the unfamiliar experience of parliamentary oversight and media criticism, Yoweri Museveni called his army and intelligence chiefs to a meeting. The audience, I was told by a security official present, included both Kagame and Patrick, who were working in Ugandan intelligence at the time.[25]

Someone, the president told them, had floated the idea of picking up some of the opposition leaders giving the new administration a hard time and making them quietly "disappear." He wanted his colleagues to understand his stance on political assassination and relay it through the ranks.

"We will never do this," he said. It wasn't just morally indefensible, it was counterproductive. "Do that and the other side will come back and do worse to you. A white person, you kill him, there are no dependents. Every time you kill an African you leave ten dependents behind who will plot against you. You're recruiting for the enemy."

Museveni's critics claim that over the years the president has disobeyed his own edict, with more than one troublesome politician meeting their ends in suspicious circumstances.[26] Electoral hopefuls Kizza Besigye and Bobi Wine certainly have the physical scars to prove just how tough you need to be to challenge his rule. Disaffected generals, sacked ministers, and opposition leaders have been beaten by police, faced trumped-up charges, and been placed under house arrest. But, crucially, they still choose to stay put in Uganda, an indication that they believe their chances of survival remain middling to high.

The RPF, which modeled itself in so many ways on the NRM, never appears to have aspired to this particular principle. "Those boys, when they were in their own country, they dropped all that," comments the Ugandan official who attended Museveni's meeting. The price of betrayal of the RPF oath was death, after all. No other nation in Central or East Africa has witnessed an exodus of former insiders to rival Rwanda's, and their flight speaks volumes about an entire political class's understanding of the regime's capacity for violence.

Two years after leaving Rwanda, in May 1998, Sendashonga was shot and this time killed, along with his driver, as he was heading home in Cyrie's car. A photograph taken at the scene shows him slumped in his seat, his neck ringed by a bright red bib of blood.

Kigali again denied any role, its officials pointing instead to Nairobi's record of violent crime. "Poor Seti," General Kayumba disingenuously told a Western diplomat at an international conference one week later. "We told him he'd be safer in Kigali, but he didn't listen." Despite the game that would be laboriously played out in the Kenyan courts, I've yet to meet anyone who didn't take government responsibility as a given.

Kenyan police swiftly arrested three men—a former Rwandan soldier called David Kiwanuka and two Ugandans. But the suspects' story of avenging a $54 million debt that Sendashonga supposedly owed Kigali's director of immigration crumbled on examination. Perplexingly, a pistol found on Kiwanuka failed to match the fatal bullets, which were fired by a Kalashnikov.

And this is where Patrick enters the story. In detention, Kiwanuka made a strange request, passing his wife a note on which were written the words, "Call Patrick Karegeya, tell him his brother's son has been arrested." There were no known family links between the two men.

The note sounded like a pre-agreed code. Kiwanuka had worked as an informer for military intelligence, it emerged, with a Rwandan diplomat called Alphonse Mbayire assigned as his controller. Was he sending a message to his boss confirming a job well done?

Patrick had been on good terms with the Dutch embassy in Nairobi, and diplomats there recalled that he was a frequent visitor to Kenya during the run-up to Sendashonga's murder. Western journalists who socialized with the head of external intelligence remembered the same thing. They all wondered if there was a simple explanation, now, for all that traveling.

It wasn't the first time, either.

Speculation had whirled around Patrick's trips to Nairobi following the discovery in October 1996 of the body of Colonel Theoneste Lizinde, Habyarimana's former intelligence chief, dumped in the forest fringing the Kenyan capital. Lizinde had been tied up and shot in the mouth. Hutu gangster turned businessman Augustin Bugirimfura, who had met Lizinde when both men were serving prison time in Rwanda, was later found dying nearby. Lizinde's family believed that the businessman, in a creepy precursor of Apollo's later behavior, had exploited his long friendship with the former intelligence chief to lead the killers—suspected to be Rwandan government agents—straight to their prey.[27]

This time, a precise motive was whispered around. Sendashonga, journalists were told by their Rwandan contacts, had gone a lot further in exile than setting up an opposition party. He had been in contact with the *génocidaires* camped in Zaire. As a Hutu moderate with clean hands, he obviously appealed to an organization with a massive image problem. A guerrilla movement had been in the making, importing weapons and training fighters. Or so they said.

The RPF was hardly in any position to preach, but it had so successfully claimed the moral high ground by this time that Western allies saw its survival as synonymous with Rwanda's stability. From this perspective, Sendashonga's death—the first high-profile slaying since Habyarimana's—seemed less a gratuitous assassination than a case of preventive elimination, rough justice for a rough neighborhood.

The scenario got support from an unexpected quarter in 2009, when historian Prunier claimed his late friend had come to the reluctant conclusion that taking up arms was the only way of remaining relevant. Just before his murder, Sendashonga, he said, had gathered around him 640 former members of Habyarimana's army—screened to exclude men who had taken part in the genocide—arranged training in Tanzania, and reached out to Museveni's brother Salim Saleh to discuss Kagame's ousting. "[He] was fed up of always playing the good guy and always finishing last. . . . [I]t is probably then that some people in Kigali decided he had crossed the danger line."[28]

Suspicion of personal responsibility for Sendashonga's murder was to hover over Patrick for the rest of his life. Like a speck floating across an eyeball, out-of-focus yet definitely *there*, it was one of those unconfirmed suspicions that niggled silently at the back of one's mind. At one of my last encounters with him, the topic cropped up unexpectedly. He mentioned that the opposition movement he'd cofounded had put out feelers to Cyrie and had been pleasantly surprised by her not-entirely-hostile reaction. "I suppose," I said, carefully, unsure of Patrick's position on the issue now that he was out of office, "that she's someone who thinks of you as the enemy."

"Oh, we definitely *were* the enemy!" Patrick expostulated with a laugh. "No doubt about that."

I didn't pursue the matter. I didn't know how to. How does anyone lightly broach the issue of someone's role in a murder over dinner? But when Patrick was still at his peak, someone braver than me did, and the exchange sheds fascinating light on the extent to which he had come to embrace the RPF's exceptionalist rhetoric.

The conversation took place in 2003, in the poolside restaurant of the Serena Hotel in Nairobi. Before any Kagame visit to Kenya—and there were many—a team would prepare the ground, and Patrick often led it. Ever gregarious, Patrick on these trips took to meeting an East African businessman—let's call him Wilfred—an intellectual with a history of political activism under his belt.

The two enjoyed batting ideas around. Wilfred, a particularly avid reader on the Middle East, was hungry for insights into RPF thinking, and Patrick knew he could count on a sympathetic hearing. That day, though, Wilfred challenged Patrick on the movement's history of extraterritorial assassination.[29]

"Why kill Sendashonga?" he asked. "Here was this Hutu leader, a credible moderate, an important symbol of ethnic reconciliation, a man of principle—and you murdered him. Why was that necessary?"

By then, justice had notionally run its course. The three suspects arrested by Kenyan police were acquitted in 2001 after a torturous legal process characterized by repeated adjournments and changes of personnel, the judge declaring he was "persuaded that the murder was political." That same year, Rwandan diplomat Alphonse Mbayire was recalled to Kigali, and a month later a soldier who was supposedly offended by disparaging remarks Mbayire made about his dog shot him twenty times in the head.[30]

Three years after Mbayire's murder, Kiwanuka's body would be found stuffed into the trunk of a car on the outskirts of Nairobi. He, too, had been shot in the head. Gunning down the gunman is the hallmark of the political hit, a giveaway of a covert organization cleaning up after itself.

Patrick did not insult his friend's intelligence by repeating the official Rwandan position. Instead, as restaurant staff discreetly flitted between the tables in the afternoon sun, he unapologetically explained why the RPF had arrogated the right to decide which individuals should live or die beyond its borders.

"You have to understand," Patrick said. "We are a small and densely populated country. We have a higher population density than any other country in Africa. So we have no space for another war. We just don't have the strategic geographical depth."

"Because of that," he continued, "every threat will be dealt with preemptively, and extraterritorially, because we do not have room for it to take place on our sovereign territory. So what you call 'murder' is not a crime, it's an act of war by other means, and if it took place in any other circumstances, we would be congratulated, praised for it."

He went on: "We have chosen to externalize the battlefield and preempt the threat. Externalizing the war zone is part of that policy and so is buffering. So, because of our relative sizes, we will never leave DRC, for example, until there's a government in Kinshasa we can trust. Never Again will we allow a mass killing of our people, Never Again will we allow a war on Rwandan territory, Never Again will we allow anyone to lay a finger on a Tutsi head."

And Patrick spelled out the obvious geographical analogy: "There are two countries in the world that have this doctrine, us and

Israel. This is how Israel sees things, how Mossad acts, and this is how we see it. We will never allow our enemy to land a blow on us and remain standing."[31]

As for Sendashonga, the RPF's fear had been he would team up with the *interahamwe*, rally the Hutu majority behind him, and launch a fresh invasion, Patrick said. "We could not risk a popular civil war. So we had to cut off its head. The idea was a preemptive strike aimed at leadership decapitation, based on the doctrine that the strike must be preemptive and must be external."

Explaining all of this, Patrick sounded neither impassioned nor celebratory, Wilfred recalls. "He was just calm, reflective, and very matter of fact.

"It was not important to him that I be persuaded by his explanation. It was only important that I listened to it and understood it in its fullness. This was a matter of statecraft, of realpolitik, of existential threat and survival."

It's a jaw-dropping conversation. Not only does it give a taste of the rarefied nature of debate within the RPF's intellectual elite—it's hard to imagine Amin or Mobutu discussing an enemy's elimination in such coolly abstract terms—but it exposes how self-conscious the RPF was about the choice of a geopolitical model whose worldview it knew chimed with the West. If Israel could do it, and get away with it, then surely Rwanda could too.

The whole argument, though, begs a question. For Cyrie angrily rejects any notion that Sendashonga was a guerrilla leader in the making, and is furious with Prunier for lending credence to Kigali's justification. "That was one of the stories they spread around. Kagame told Prudence Bushnell, the US ambassador in Nairobi, Seth was training a network in Tanzania to attack Rwanda, and she relayed that to the other Western ambassadors. It was totally false. The Americans fell for it because they wanted to."

Rwandan businessmen had certainly made a pilgrimage to Nairobi to ask Sendashonga to go down this route. Cyrie acknowledges that in Nairobi her husband occasionally met former members of Habyarimana's army—officers who had tried returning to Rwanda after the genocide, only to become disillusioned and go into exile again. Later, she says, he met up with Ugandan and Tanzanian officials worried by the trend in Rwanda toward Tutsi domination. But it never went any further.

"He was always cautious about any armed struggle that would plunge Rwanda into another war. I remember him saying, 'I would only give my okay to a war if I would be given 100 percent assurance that not one single civilian, especially among the Tutsi, would be killed, and this kind of assurance does not exist.'"

The first attempt on Sendashonga's life, she points out, came a good two years before the meetings supposed to have alarmed the regime in Kigali, timing which makes a nonsense of the excuse. Instead, she identifies an alternative trigger. Sendashonga was due to appear in Arusha, where he had been asked to testify before the International Criminal Tribunal for Rwanda (ICTR). "He was killed on Saturday and was meant to go on Tuesday."

Who was Sendashonga being honest with: his wife, or his historian friend? It's yet another episode in Rwandan history in which two stories, both seemingly entirely credible, both from trustworthy sources, undercut one another.

It has been suggested—by French judge Jean-Louis Bruguière, among others—that Sendashonga was ready to give key evidence about RPF responsibility for the downing of the presidential plane. Cyrie dismisses that idea. Her husband's civilian status excluded him from the RPF's military decision-making. No, the insights he was ready to share with the ICTR went to the heart of his decades-long preoccupation: human rights abuses by the organization he had joined with such high hopes. "He would have been asked about the RPF killings of Hutus and the massacres."

From a personal perspective, Patrick's conversation with Wilfred offers a searing insight into how a cerebral, supremely articulate individual could talk himself into finding the morally repugnant not only acceptable but necessary and farsighted. And it comes absolutely dripping with retrospective irony. Four or five years after blithely explaining why Sendashonga's murder was justified, Patrick would find himself doing the very things his 2003 self explicitly told Wilfred merited a death sentence, and paying the same price.

That element of the conversation still baffles Wilfred. "Patrick and General Kayumba were prime architects of that targeted policy, so it's beyond ironic they should have fallen foul of it themselves and become armed enemies of the state," he says. "How, knowing Kagame as they did, having helped build this doctrine, did they think he would react when presented with an existential threat?

"What did they expect would happen?"

CHAPTER THIRTEEN

I WAS JAMES BOND

Diamond life, lover boy,
You move in space with minimum waste and maximum joy,
City light, business nights,
When you require street car desire for higher heights
No place for beginners or sensitive hearts.

—Sade

It's a balmy evening in Kigali in late 1996. As the kites begin to circle above the hills and valleys, the air turns soft and chill. Inside Aux Caprices du Palais, the capital's most sophisticated French restaurant, tables are filling up. The venue benefits from its prime location in Kiyovu, a district favored by International Monetary Fund directors, World Bank officials, and members of Rwanda's new ruling elite. It's a neighborhood where the tops of bougainvillea-draped walls are sprinkled with broken glass, drivers wait in official cars outside high villa gates, and security guards check visitors' IDs as though they really mean it.

A tremor of suppressed excitement radiates through the restaurant as several couples stroll in. Even if you didn't recognize the faces—and everyone does—you would know they are People Who Matter from the assiduousness with which they are ushered to their tables, the way nearby customers pretend not to stare, the alertness of the military bodyguards surveilling the scene.

They look the part. The women, blessed with foreheads that seem to stretch forever, cheekbones any supermodel would envy, are willowy, designer-elegant, and carefully made-up. Their husbands, lean as stripped tendons, come across as quietly formidable, men who have seen action and know it will come their way again. In neighboring Zaire or Uganda, power couples of this standing would bring a concomitant level of noise, the menfolk getting louder with each beer, guffaws carrying as far as the kitchen. But this is Rwanda. And Rwanda specializes in quiet-to-the-point-of-hushed.

After the genocide, there was much discussion of the poisonous role played by the Akazu—"Little hut"—that formed around Habyarimana and his First Lady, a cluster whose anti-Tutsi ideology, it was said, came to outstrip the president's own. But within a few years, a term once associated with Hutu power was back in use, this time applied to the RPF's inner circle.

This Akazu consisted entirely of Tutsis, mostly Anglophone Tutsis who had spent their youths and adult lives in Uganda, at that. "I didn't realize until much later that everyone who was in power and everyone we socialized with was a Ugandan Tutsi," recalls Portia Karegeya. The underdogs of yesteryear were the new Masters of the Universe.

The community had been numbed by the horror of the genocide, its impact would take decades to absorb. But in the meantime there were openings for those of entrepreneurial bent. For those with contacts, seed money, and drive—and that automatically included the RPF elite, spouses, cousins, in-laws, and friends—the opportunities seemed endless.

If, in the Rwandan countryside, Tutsi returnees claimed grazing land, water sources, and farmsteads, in the capital they were establishing companies, going into business, and snapping up government contracts: import-export agencies to bring in desperately needed raw materials, construction companies to repair war damage, a giant new shopping mall to cater to returning consumers, cafés and restaurants to feed workers at reopening government offices.

The Akazu's inner core consisted of six married couples. Kagame, IT expert and telecommunications engineer Sam Nkusi (who had been responsible for RPF communications in the bush), Attorney General Gerald Gahima, Minister for Health Joseph Karemera (one of the RPF's acknowledged "sages"), and their wives, and, of course, Patrick and Leah and the General and Rosette.

Elites rarely come more close-knit than this. It was the most natural of interweavings. Growing up in the introverted Banyarwanda community with every reason to fear strangers, they had been obliged to trust each other with their lives, notwithstanding simmering rivalries and mutual suspicion. A Venn diagram would have shown a series of overlapping, multigenerational circles.

General Kayumba would become godfather to one of Kagame's sons. Jeannette Kagame and Rosette Kayumba set up Green Hills Academy, the first secondary school in Rwanda offering the International Baccalaureate, and would sit together on its board. Sam Nkusi's daughter Jolie would marry Patrick's nephew, David Batenga, while his wife's sister was married to Theogene Rudasingwa, RPF general secretary.

Roughly the same age, the children of the Kagames, Kayumbas, and Karegeyas bounced in and out of each other's houses, ferried by indulgent chauffeurs to the swimming pools of Kigali's few five-star hotels, sharing toys and meals, celebrating one another's birthdays.

Their parents were just as casually intimate.

The men socialized at the American Club or the Cercle Sportif—where Kagame applied himself doggedly to learning tennis—or rough-and-ready bars like the Car Wash for beers and barbecued *nyama choma*. When the women were included, things were raised a notch: dinners at the Kagame or Karegeya places, meals at Aux Caprices du Palais and the Flamingo, the only Chinese restaurant in town.

The socializing did not come without its attendant strains. Africa is a continent where people start early, the equatorial light waking even the most sluggish. But members of the new Akazu were forced to alter their body clocks to suit Kagame's idiosyncratic daily routine. Often waking at 11 a.m., he would routinely work until 9 p.m., then expect colleagues who had been up since dawn to join him for

drinks or a meal. Western officials who popped into reopened ministerial offices in Kigali found their RPF contacts yawning and drained.
"They were all exhausted," laughed one. "They were staying up till
2 a.m. to keep Kagame company, and then having to be in the office
first thing in the morning."[1]

When the Boss called, hungry for entertainment, for distraction,
"Not tonight" was not really an option. "Wherever you were, if he
called you, you'd stand up and go," remembers Leah. She adds, wryly,
"He started dictating a long time ago, now I think about it; we just
never noticed."

Sometimes Patrick did try begging off. "You see me all day, why do
I have to see you in the evening, too?" he once dared ask Kagame.
But things weren't the same without him. If anyone could halt a
slide into sycophancy, some in the Akazu privately felt, it was Patrick,
who had fully signed up to the RPF's founding principle of "constructive criticism."

Constantly skirting danger, sardonic and utterly irreverent, Patrick said the unsayable straight to Kagame's face, getting away with it
because he was so damn funny. "Kagame would be very tough, very
hard in meetings," says Leah. "Then Patrick would crack a joke and
everyone would laugh and relax. In fact, people became worried
about meeting without Patrick there."

And what was true during work hours was even truer once the sun
went down. "Patrick was the only person who could tell dirty jokes in
front of Kagame," recalls Theogene. "He was the only person I saw
Kagame drop his guard with. He would laugh and *laugh*. And while
telling his jokes, Patrick would often say some very blunt things."

His colleagues were grateful, for Kagame's ballooning ego, they
worried, needed reining in. Kagame might be regarded by diplomats
and foreign statesmen as the most powerful man in Rwanda, but he
was still only vice-president. In the eyes of his comrades, who felt not
only that they had all won their spurs on the battlefield but that Kagame had shown no great mettle there, he was only the most prominent of a band of brothers. Not the brightest, not the bravest, and
certainly not the most charismatic.

Roman emperors returning from foreign conquests would ride
their chariots through the cobbled streets, accepting the adulation of

the crowds as they headed toward the Capitoline Hill, and all the while a slave known as an *auriga*, holding a crown of laurel leaves over their heads, would be whispering in their ear, "*Memento homo*"—"Remember you are only a man." Patrick the Jester, Designated Imp of the High Command, the man whose obscene cracks regularly circulated on the RPF's internal computer system, getting everyone quietly chuckling, Patrick was Kagame's *auriga*.

•

Still only in his mid-thirties, Patrick was in his prime. He had been blessed with that rare combination: a job in which personality and professional duties seemed perfectly aligned. "He liked being the spy chief, he loved the mystery and the intrigue of it all," recalls the US author Jason Stearns.

When foreign dignitaries flew to Rwanda, the pretty little girl who ran to greet them on the runway, posy of flowers in her hand, was Portia. When Bill Clinton flew from Kigali to Entebbe in March 1998, fresh from delivering a public apology for failing to prevent the genocide, her father was the man chosen to sit by the US president's side. Patrick was one of The Select now.

His trajectory to the top had been powered by the intimacy of his friendship with Kagame. Wary and distrustful of so many, Kagame let his guard down with his old schoolmate and NRA comrade. "Patrick is the one he talks to in the bedroom," awed RPF colleagues would say, indicating not some homosexual liaison but conversations so vital they could only be conducted in private.

Afflicted with the inferiority complex common to men who never attend college, Kagame nursed a mixture of awe and contempt toward RPF colleagues with degrees. He knew he needed their advice, but hated admitting as much. It was easier when it came from Patrick, somehow. Patrick's earthiness, his man-of-the-people touch, made it easy to forget that he, too, had been a brilliant student.

In Kampala, Kagame had sometimes relied on Patrick, his junior, to write his reports for Uganda's DMI. Now Patrick offered irreverent but insightful advice on how the president should handle himself in VIP encounters, media interviews, and press conferences. He was Alastair Campbell to Kagame's Tony Blair, Dick Cheney to George

W. Bush, Henry Kissinger to Richard Nixon. He even—like some clucking mother—gave tips on how to dress. "Before Kagame gave a speech Patrick would arrive with the suit he was to wear for the event," remembers former bodyguard Noble Marara. "They were selling him to the Rwandans and the international community, after all, so he needed to look right."

The oversight was necessary. Journalists might relish Kagame's military bluntness—it made for great quotes—but there were times when the vice-president's abrasiveness, his obvious impatience with formalities or euphemism, risked creating diplomatic incidents.

"I once asked Patrick, 'Why are you posing with Kagame all the time?'" remembers Abdulkarim Ali, today the RNC's spokesman in the United Kingdom. "Because he was always there, standing next to him in the photographs. Patrick said, 'Posing? Me? I'm just waiting to see what's the next bomb he's going to throw.'" Patrick was the safety catch on Kagame's Kalashnikov.[2]

But "vice-presidential minder" was merely one of Patrick's roles. His brief at "External" was enormous: identifying and assessing the forces bent on the RPF's destruction, working out ways to sabotage and undermine them, and building bridges with foreign governments, which were inclined to be deeply suspicious of a rebel movement that had just toppled an African regime.

It could have been encapsulated in a three-word motto: "Keep us safe." On his desk he kept a heartrending framed photo of a dead Rwandan baby on the ground, encircled by anonymous male boots. It served as both wordless reproach and daily reminder of why he did what he did.

The RPF grasped early the crucial role of public relations. Aid from Kigali's new friends—Habyarimana's Belgian, French, and Swiss donor support made way for US, UK, Dutch, and German funding—regularly contributed as much as 40 percent of the government's operating budget. If the sums were to work, the movement needed to be admired, trusted abroad. How it was depicted in both the local and Western media, therefore, was crucially important.

For these military men, courting the foreign press did not come naturally. A rough army guy, Kabarebe could barely conceal his dislike for journalists. General Kayumba, more sophisticated, was still suspicious: "We used to think you guys were wizards, to be honest, we were afraid of your power," he told me. Smooth, articulate Patrick, in contrast, was in his element.

A born iconoclast himself, Patrick liked journalists' combination of freewheeling lifestyles and moral seriousness, their ingrained irreverence toward the powers-that-be. On arrival in Kigali he had unhesitatingly taken a host of budding young Rwandan reporters under his wing, feeding them stories and contacts. It was Patrick who reached out to Andrew Mwenda, a motormouth Ugandan reporter and radio-show host whose jibes at Museveni kept landing him in jail, and introduced him to Kagame, explaining that a Mwenda-run newspaper could serve as a great medium for getting the RPF's message out across the region. *The Independent*—a publication heavily reliant on Rwandan government advertising—was born.

He also opened his home to the select group of Western reporters permanently stationed in Kigali. Allergic to solitude—"Patrick *hated* being alone," remembers Associated Press staffer Hrvoje Hranjski—he was happy for them to spend hours lolling on his sofa drinking his beer as he worked the two or three phones he had permanently on the go. "He'd always either be on the phone or with his earplugs dangling around his neck," says Hranjski.

The same warm welcome was extended to writers and researchers passing through. These included the *New Yorker* writer Philip Gourevitch and academic Samantha Power, future US ambassador to the United Nations, who both went on to write best-selling nonfiction books on Rwanda in which the RPF is portrayed in an overwhelmingly sympathetic light.[3]

To pick up a foreign magazine or newspaper and know he'd helped bring about the glowing portrayal of Rwanda's new administration printed therein gave him a thrill of quiet satisfaction. He was helping to coax a story of heroic resurrection into being, a saga so poignant and uplifting it would entrance the world.

During these sessions, Patrick never exposed his hand, teasing his new acquaintances instead with what he could tell them but somehow never did. The chat was gossipy and inconsequential—what was going on in the White House, Clinton's sexual misdemeanors—seasoned with the kind of gynecological jokes that are a Ugandan specialty.

Like all the best flacks, Patrick knew there was no point trying to force a chosen narrative into the coverage. "Unlike Ndahiro, the president's special adviser, who you always felt had an agenda, Patrick would never say, 'I want you to write this,'" recalls Hranjski. No, genuine empathy, forged during all those aimless get-togethers, was the best form of persuasion, lubricating a particular version of events into the news so effectively the journalist concerned would be scarcely aware of being manipulated.

An assumption of intellectual affinity was more quietly effective than overt pressure could ever be. "The RPF were likable because they were like us," admits Hranjski. As a young Croat who had witnessed the traumatic breakup of the former Yugoslavia, his identification with the Tutsi story was particularly acute. "It's hard to identify with a Hutu peasant who tills the soil. These guys, you could meet them in bars and discuss films you'd seen, books you'd read. They were in our image—our mirror image—in so many ways."

The challenge was working out where truth ended and spin began, for no one was a more shameless practitioner of Rwanda's national trait—brass-faced dissembling—than Patrick. "Patrick was skilled at telling you things that didn't matter at all," his former MI6 friend told me. "At the beginning you thought to yourself, 'Wow, he's being so open.' Eventually you realized that none of what he was saying mattered."

Fabienne Hara, an analyst for the International Crisis Group, whose authoritative reports were read by diplomats, businessmen, and journalists, learned to weave her way through the Karegeya maze during the chats she had with Patrick whenever she drove over from her base in Bujumbura. "Out of three bits of information, maybe two would be true and one would be outright obvious propaganda.[4]

"But even in the bits that were correct, you could spot a certain line of argument, a narrative being constructed, a certain point of view reinforced. He was very friendly, very open, very charming, and underneath, a killer, of course."

While befriending the journalists and analysts, Patrick was, of course, also reading the reports on them filed by his operatives. Hranjski's closest Rwandan friend was an army officer who hung out with the media pack and whose official duties often involved escorting visiting VIPs. He told Hranjski early on his job also included reporting back on all his meetings with foreign journalists. He also revealed that an operative placed by Patrick's External Security Organisation at Rwandacell, MTN's local subsidiary, was systematically monitoring their phone calls. "Don't be naive, we're listening to everyone," the officer told Hranjski.

"Everyone was spying on everyone else," recalls the journalist. "You were aware of it, but after a bit you learned to ignore it. Rwanda, looking back, was an incredibly paranoid place."

Reporters waiting to interview Kagame would usually find themselves charmingly intercepted by Patrick in the vestibule—that was how he and I first met. Those casual chats, when the nervous reporters were likely to be a little too free with their opinions, gave him a chance to size them up and brief his boss accordingly. And it was positively uncanny how, within twenty minutes of arriving in Kigali, reporters would find themselves sharing a beer with Patrick on a terrace downtown.

With the women, suggestive hints would occasionally be dropped over those beers. Patrick had the keys to a government flat located conveniently nearby. The encounter, already so pleasant, could be taken up a notch. . . . Tutsi culture has always recognized sex as one of the most effective of political tools, cutting usefully across the bureaucratic hierarchy and social barriers.

His strike rate was surprisingly high. Beautiful men are rarely charming: they don't need to be. Men with Patrick's hopelessly goofy looks and modest build, in contrast, learn early how to be liked, a vital survival skill.

"The first time we met, that Sade tune, 'Smooth Operator,' kept running through my head," Associated Press's former Nairobi bureau chief Susan Linnee recalled. "I could see he was immensely charming to women. He was The Great Seducer. If you're a chief of intelligence, if you're a spy, what more important talent could there be than that?"[5]

It was never a question of lechery, one of his old Ugandan friends insists. Patrick knew that whether they worked for news organizations, were employed inside embassies, or represented foreign governments, women could provide him with the swiftest of access routes, their liking for him cutting through hierarchy and across normally closed doors. "People who didn't understand him thought he was a womanizer. They didn't understand. He knew it was easier to get information from a woman than a man, so he set out to get closer to women who were strategically well positioned. It wasn't a sex thing, it was an information thing," he says.[6]

Extramarital liaisons, by this reckoning, were virtually a professional duty. "'A man has to do what a man has to do,' as the saying goes," quips the friend. "Leah knew, but what could she do? He was a loving parent and a loving husband and just doing his job. Patrick was a very good spy."

Gone were the days of the modest white Datsun pickup, the casual T-shirt and jeans. When Patrick wasn't showing off his military credentials, drawing up at the airport in a giant black four-wheel-drive followed by several pickups piled high with soldiers, he would be suave to the point of sleekness.

"It was incongruous to see this ex-rebel arriving to pick me up at the airport in an elegant suit, driving a lovely, closed-top, black sedan," remembers a photographer. "He drove me, one hand on the steering wheel, exceeding the speed limit—or what should have been a speed limit—before dinner and after, when he was decidedly under the influence."[7] When he was ferrying guests to the Cadillac, Kigali's premier nightclub, rules were for the hoi polloi.

Stearns got similar show-off treatment. "He took me out on the town, to clubs and bars. Wherever you went everyone knew him, and everyone recognized he was king of that town." But something about the whole approach jarred. What had happened, Stearns wondered, to the RPF's famous discretion, its below-the-radar reserve? "He was too much the player. It was a very un-RPF way of doing things."

Cultivating the media was only a fraction of the job at "External." Patrick was simultaneously establishing a network of informants to serve as his ears and eyes across the region.

Tiny, inward-looking, and overpopulated, Rwanda was in many ways the perfect environment for a highly effective intelligence service, and it already boasted a solid pedigree. During Habyarimana's single-party rule, a system of community policing had operated at village level, with one official reporting back on each cluster of ten houses (*nyumba kumi*). Reproduced across the country, this cell system perpetrated the notion that snitching on your fellow citizens was not just forgivable, but admirable. After the genocide, the archives of the

Service Central de Renseignements (SCR)—domestic intelligence—revealed Rwanda to have been one of the most intensely monitored societies on earth.

"The files," writes British author Linda Melvern, "revealed twenty-four-hour surveillance reports, and records of intercepted telephone calls and listening devices in hotels and embassies." The archive contained intercepted mail and family photographs, transcribed interrogations, and the updated addresses of Rwandans living abroad.[8]

Impressively, the SCR had compiled the names of every Tutsi teacher, lawyer, clerk, or official in the country. "The names of those judged politically subversive, those who 'distanced themselves from the regime' or those who could not be trusted as unquestioning supporters were listed," writes Melvern.

Now that it was in power the RPF saw no need to eradicate the mindset or habits that had engendered all this paperwork. Kagame, who was known to personally monitor military radio communications in order to keep tabs on his armed forces, had been an intelligence operative during the Bush War in Uganda, after all. No one knew better the value of information.

And so Patrick set about recruiting the Aimés and Apollos of the future, precious assets to be stowed like wine bottles in a cellar.

It did not prove a difficult task. The urge to rat on your fellow man goes deep within the human psyche. After World War II, it was revealed that up to a million citizens in Vichy France had denounced their neighbors to the occupying Nazis. "In a sense, it was the only way people could express themselves in a country where there were no demonstrations, no rights, no vote: it was the voice of the people, although often a mean and petty voice," historian Laurent Joly told a conference on the topic.[9]

The more oppressive the regime, then, the more pronounced the tendency. To inform is to enjoy secret power over another, particularly intoxicating for those who have gone ignored all their lives. Investigating East Germany's Stasi, a surveillance system she found had "metastasized" like a cancer during the Cold War, Australian journalist Anna Funder asked a former recruiter why so many East Germans had ratted on their fellow citizens: "Well, some of them were convinced of the cause," he said. "But I think it was mainly because informers got the feeling that, doing it, they were somebody. You know—someone was listening to them for a couple of hours a week, taking notes. They felt they had it over other people."[10]

Patrick's friendships allowed him to reach deep into the entrails of the Ugandan army—"Patrick heard all the military gossip before Bombo [Ugandan Ministry of Defence headquarters] did," laughs an old friend—and he aimed to reproduce those insights in Zaire, Burundi, Kenya, and Tanzania, inside both those countries' armed forces and their rebel groups.

Stearns would later get a taste of his network's effectiveness at his first meeting with Patrick. Before driving into Rwanda from DRC, he'd spent a few hours batting a tennis ball around with a friend at the run-down sports center in the pretty Congolese lakeside town of Bukavu, looking out across Lake Kivu.

"How did you enjoy your tennis match?" asked Patrick, with a mischievous grin, when they met. It was his way of saying, "We're so far ahead of you. We've been tracking you every step of the way."

•

If "Keep us safe" was the RPF's driving mantra, it was easier said than done. It had taken a generation for the refugee camps in Uganda to produce a rebel group capable of threatening Rwanda's national security. This time around, it would take only a few years.

The status quo, in which a startling proportion of Rwanda's population squatted in forty squalid camps necklacing the frontier, was clearly unsustainable. Journalists and NGO workers based in Kigali, riffing on the annual phenomenon that is the Serengeti's Great Migration, took bets on the date when the "wildebeest"—the hundreds of thousands of Hutu refugees camped in Kivu—would return. It was bound to be either Christmas or New Year's, they joked, ruining their holidays. You could count on it.

Yet the refugees stayed put, refusing to take seats on the UN buses laid on at intervals to ferry them home to their abandoned farms. In the mornings, camp administrators would gather up a sprinkling of dead bodies, which included Hutus who had attempted to board: a clear message from the *génocidaires* to the rest.

The refugees were being used as both shields and hostages by characters like General Augustin Bizimungu, former Rwandan army chief of staff, who was busy buying weapons from Mobutu's corrupt military officers and using Congo's local airports to import ammunition. In camps like Mugunga, thousands of young men were being openly trained in the arts of guerrilla warfare, as the ex-military and *interahamwe* prepared to reinvade.

The camps sat illegally close to the Rwandan border, and the readiness of the likes of Oxfam, GOAL, Concern, Save the Children, and UNICEF to keep providing a rebel-army-in-training with food, water, and medical treatment violated every principle of international law. But aid officials, outnumbered and thoroughly intimidated, turned a blind eye.

In October 1995, Rwanda's new army was coming under attack on the border an average of once a day. By mid-1996, the Army for the Liberation of Rwanda (ALIR) as the Hutu force in exile dubbed itself, had created two large divisions, one focused on attacking Rwanda's northwest, the other on its southwest.

An exasperated Kagame made clear in interviews with journalists like myself that if the international community wouldn't put a stop to the situation, the RPF would. In truth, he and his colleagues had already decided that the only way to neutralize the threat posed by the *génocidaires* involved invading Zaire, breaking up the camps, and forcing the refugees home.

The plan possessed the mixture of ruthless brio and strategic chutzpah the world had learned to associate with the RPF, a movement beginning to feel it possessed a military Midas touch. But if the RPF was going to invade Zaire—its second cross-border operation in only six years—without alarming the African Union, the United Nations, and Kigali's new friends in the West, it needed some kind of camouflage: a frontman who could lend local credibility while doing exactly what he was told. One possible candidate was Laurent Kabila, a Marxist militant from Congo's Katanga Province quietly going to seed in Tanzania, under the protective aegis of a retired Julius Nyerere. Nyerere and Museveni, the two great puppet masters of the Great Lakes, together arranged for Kabila to be driven to Kigali to allow a cautious Kagame to size him up.

Kabila had commanded the Simba rebels who fought Mobutu in the early 1960s, when he had already proved a disappointment. "It is essential to have revolutionary seriousness, an ideology that can guide action, a spirit of sacrifice," wrote a visiting Che Guevara after going into battle alongside Kabila's men. "Up to now, Kabila has not shown that he possesses any of these qualities."[11] Now he was tubby, well past his prime, and militarily irrelevant.

But the man was also genuinely Congolese, "a son of the soil," and in contrast with most of Zaire's opposition leaders, had never been co-opted by "the Leopard," as Mobutu was known. "Kabila might have been old-school, but he had not been bought off. We gave him some credit for that," Patrick told Stearns, adding, with typical frankness, "We weren't looking for a rebel leader. We just needed someone to make the whole operation look Congolese."[12]

Having mulled things over, Kagame gave Kabila the thumbs up. Patrick was dispatched to summon the Mzee—"old man"—from his long political sleep, scattering chickens as he strode across the dusty compound of the grace-and-favor house in Dar Es Salaam Nyerere had gifted Kabila.

Accompanied by his son Joseph and daughter Janet, Kabila moved into a house in central Kigali, where Patrick assigned the then junior intelligence officer Dan Munyuza—the man who would later urge Robert Higiro to poison his former boss—as his main handler.

Three other Congolese hopefuls, with varying levels of experience, mustered there: Andre Kisase Ngandu, aging commander of a rebellion in the Rwenzori Mountains; Deogratias Bugera, a Tutsi architect from North Kivu; and Anselme Masasu. The latter was a serving sergeant in the Rwandan army, but came from South Kivu and was blessed with an instinctive understanding of how to rally Zaire's shiftless, questing youth.

Deeply suspicious of one another, the coalition's members depended on the Rwandans for food, clothing, uniforms, weapons, even travel expenses. The one area where the Congolese could deliver was recruitment and mobilization across the border in Zaire. In South Kivu, in particular, the local Tutsis, known as the Banyamulenge, were increasingly worried by the xenophobic rhetoric being expressed toward their community by Mobutu's officials. They signed up in the thousands.

Patrick traveled the region, shuttling between Kigali and Asmara, Addis Ababa, Lusaka, Luanda, Harare, Bujumbura, and—of course—Kampala, mustering diplomatic support for what would gradually mutate into a covert, nine-nation, pan-African project to topple the aging Mobutu, whom the "Renaissance" generation of presidents regarded as representing everything that was rotten in modern Africa.

The region's future was being shaped by a handful of former African guerrilla movements—not just Uganda's NRM and Rwanda's RPF, but Eritrea's EPLF, Ethiopia's TPLF, Angola's MPLA, and Zimbabwe's ZANU-PF—whose members shared the same heroes, had read the same revolutionary primers, and often knew each other from the bush or the years in exile, men who instinctively bypassed formal governance structures to deal direct. "Patrick was far more than an intelligence chief," recalls Anderbrhan Welde Giorgis, Eritrea's envoy to the Great Lakes in the late 1990s. "People often misunderstand that. The role he played was more like that of a foreign minister."[13]

By late 1996, the rebels, their Rwandan minders, and their backers in the region were ready. On October 18 the coalition published the Lemera Declaration, unveiling the Alliance of Democratic Forces for the Liberation of Congo-Zaire (AFDL). The fact that a small town in South Kivu and the Kigali district where some of the rebels were based had similar names–"Lemera" and "Remera" respectively–conveniently bolstered the fiction that the deal had been signed in Zaire.

A week later, Rwanda's army, commanded by James Kabarebe and Cesar Kayizari, launched a multipronged blitzkrieg on the refugee camps lining Lake Kivu and Lake Tanganyika, encircling the settlements where the *génocidaires* held sway while leaving open a corridor that led all the way back to Rwanda. The vast majority of Hutu refugees obediently plodded home. After two drawn-out, miserable years, the Great Migration took place in just ten days.

I was one of many journalists who stood at Gisenyi's border post watching that biblical human tide. The Tutsi taxi driver who took me there, his car radio blaring disco, drove through the oncoming refugees with a speed bordering on viciousness. From the Hutu refugees, there was no laughter, no chat, no smiles; but there was no wailing, or sobbing, either. The only sound was the strange, feathery whisper produced by thousands of bare feet brushing tarmac.

Somewhere along the border, Patrick was doing the same thing, standing alongside Yemane Kidane, Ethiopian envoy to the AFDL. "I never saw anything like it," remembers Kidane. "I never saw so many people in my life. A sea of people walking, from the morning until the evening time."[14]

Some 800,000 Hutus returned, trudging across the border without screening or checks. But it soon become clear that a large group of refugees, a group including the ex-military, *interahamwe*, and the genocide's masterminds, had peeled off in the opposite direction, plunging into the equatorial rainforest as they headed for Shabunda in the southwest and Kisangani, the trading city built on the Zaire River.

The Rwandan army ruthlessly hunted them down. The RPF wanted the broad mass of the refugees back, but not *these* men. "These are not genuine refugees," Kagame told an interviewer. "They're simply fugitives, people running away from justice after killing people in Rwanda—after killing!"[15] Women, old people, or children who had walked the red jungle roads alongside the fighters were dismissed as so much collateral damage. "Military and civilian were mixed. But everyone had more or less been militarized," was Jack Nziza's careless assessment. "There was no demarcation between them."

So effectively had the RPF seized the moral high ground by then, reporters initially struggled to believe reports of atrocities. When a French diplomat in Kinshasa who was almost shaking with rage assured me and a Dutch colleague that Kabila was the "Pol Pot of Africa," adding, "What is happening in Kisangani will make the killing fields of the Khmer Rouge look like child's play," our response was incredulity. We left the embassy shaking our heads at how an intelligent official could be so blinded by his government's ingrained hostility for the RPF.

I often think of that wasted briefing as an example of how the storyteller's need to identify Good Guys and Bad Guys, culprit and victims, makes fools of us all. If any uncertainty still hovers over what the RPF got up to inside Rwanda itself, there's very little associated with the "excesses"—the preferred RPF euphemism—committed inside eastern Zaire during this episode. This time there were too many witnesses and too many incidents, extended over too many months.

In a 550-page report it finally brought out in 2010, the UN detailed 617 separate incidents in which Hutu refugees were bludgeoned, macheted, bayoneted, shot, or burned to death. Most controversially, it said the "systematic and widespread" nature of the attacks, targeting not only Hutu refugees from Rwanda but also Hutus of Burundian and Zairean nationality, meant they might well merit the term "genocide," this time one directed against the Hutus. No definitive death toll was ever possible, but the UNHCR reckoned that some 200,000 people remained unaccounted for.[16]

Well before that report's publication, human rights investigators registered that the tactics used—UN Special Rapporteur Roberto Garretón detailed how radio appeals were used to summon Hutus to meetings in schools and churches, urging those hiding in the forests to emerge for medical care and food[17]—had a chilling familiarity. The same methods for gathering people in one spot, the better to eliminate them, had been described in the infamous Gersony report. Like a serial killer, the RPF had developed a recognizable modus operandi.

"When reports of the massacres in Kisangani came out, I recognized the NGO workers' descriptions," said one of the field workers who contributed to Gersony's research. "The mobilization techniques, the trucking in of highly motivated troops, the mechanics of how civilians were lured to certain places, the promises made: it was all the same."[18]

By Christmas 1996, the AFDL and its Rwandan backers controlled a sixty-mile buffer zone running along Zaire's border with Uganda, Rwanda, and Burundi. The *génocidaires* faced a stark choice: either to use the refugee return as cover for infiltration of their own country, or to trek toward distant Central African Republic, Congo-Brazzaville, Zambia, and Angola.

The First Congo War, as it would be known, now acquired a momentum of its own. As Mobutu's demoralized army folded like a stack of cards, its retreating soldiers putting more energy into looting than fighting, excitement at the prospect of regime change rippled across the giant country. One by one, Zaire's towns and cities fell, with Angola—which had always resented Mobutu's support for the UNITA rebel movement—now joining the fray. Kisangani was captured in March 1997, after that came Mbandaka, then the mining center of Lubumbashi, then the diamond center of Mbuji Mayi.

If one is to believe the account given by General James Kabarebe, the real fighting was all done by the Rwandans, while the AFDL leadership, which had moved to Goma in "liberated" North Kivu, waited to be briefed on progress, then publicly claimed the credit. Kabila never visited the front, nor did he offer advice, which was fine as far as Kabarebe was concerned, as, he said, "I discovered he did not have any experience in military matters. . . . He only visited captured towns. Whenever we captured a town he would come and talk to the population. By that time of course I would be ahead, heading for another objective."[19]

When Kabila dropped in to receive the misplaced acclamations of a grateful public, Patrick was by his side. "He was the link between Kabila and Kagame, and all the countries in the coalition," says General Kayumba. He hit it off with the Mzee and struck up a particularly close friendship with Bizima Karaha, a South African–trained doctor and Congolese Tutsi who became one of Kabila's most trusted advisers.

Familiarity did not engender respect. A tone of dismissive contempt seeps into every Rwandan assessment of both their Congolese proxies and the enemy, so quick to surrender, so bereft of ideological commitment. "The Rwandans were always very disparaging about the Congolese," recalls reporter Hranjski. "Patrick would make fun of them all the time. 'They're useless, they won't fight,' he'd say. 'We have to tell them what to do all the time.'"

The attitude had an insidious effect on the international press pack covering the story from Kigali. Like reporters "embedded" with the US forces who rolled into Saddam Hussein's Iraq, they persuaded themselves Rwanda's invasion of Zaire somehow represented both just deserts and a promising new start for a country destroyed by poor leadership.

"I totally believed what they were doing in the Congo was right," recalls Hranjski. "I'd swallowed the line that the Congolese were useless, bickering, and that the Rwandans should be given a shot at running the country. They were colonizers, plain and simple, but we were sympathetic. The Congolese raped and looted, with the RPF there were never any reports of raping and looting, so the argument was, 'Look, these guys are not your typical army, they can put your house in order, why don't you let them?' In retrospect, it's amazing what you can rationalize."

In mid-May 1997, the AFDL reached Kinshasa, the ramshackle capital sprawled along the banks of the water-hyacinth-fringed Zaire River. There were brief attempts at peace talks between Kabila and Mobutu, mediated aboard the SAS *Outeniqua*, a South African navy vessel, by Nelson Mandela. But it was all too late. On May 17, Mobutu, in the grips of late-stage prostate cancer, flew with his family to Togo, and Kinshasa fell virtually without a fight, Mobutu's feared presidential guards crossing the river to Brazzaville with their families. The following day the *kadogos,* child soldiers recruited by Anselme Masasu, marched into town.

The First Congo War was over. The revolutionary leaders of the Great Lakes resembled a set of wooden Russian dolls. Inside Julius Nyerere had nestled Yoweri Museveni, inside Museveni lay Paul Kagame, inside Kagame nestled Laurent Kabila. One of the latter's first significant acts was to baptize Zaire the Democratic Republic of Congo (DRC). The other was to nominate James Kabarebe, the Rwandan general who had made it all possible, chief of his new army.

Over the next year, while Kabarebe struggled to shore up his position as the head of one of Africa's least impressive military forces, General Kayumba—first as deputy head of Rwanda's gendarmerie and then as Rwandan army chief of staff—targeted Hutu fighters left behind when the refugee camps emptied, who were attacking in battalion-sized units in Habyarimana's old heartland.

Realizing that the enemy was still adopting the tactics of a regular army, the General made sure his force was the nimbler of the two, using mobile units of 500 men, equipped with armored vehicles, to locate ALIR units, then taking them out with helicopter gunships.[20]

"Kayumba was tactically brilliant," remembers Rick Orth, who as US defense attaché in Kigali witnessed the General in action at close hand. "His great gift was that he understood how insurgents work and that these guys weren't really guerrillas," Orth said. "It's easier to kill insurgents when they're massed. He would create conditions in which they would mass so he could concentrate his helicopters and troops on them. They would scatter, and then he'd do the same thing again."

Victory was by no means inevitable. In February 1998 ALIR reached the outskirts of Gitarama, a town just thirty-four miles west of Kigali. "It was touch-and-go," recalls Orth, "and it was Kayumba's military brilliance that won it. He was out there, he was clearly in control, and that's the reason he was loved by the Rwandan army rank and file."[21]

The campaign was utterly brutal, though, in terms of civilian casualties. Journalists covering what became known as the Northern

Insurgency saw scores of bodies lined up along road verges and were allowed to visit a network of caves at Nyakinama full of rotting corpses—up to 8,000 were said to have been sealed inside, then grenades thrown in. It was the usual problem: Were the dead Hutus really "infiltrators," as the army claimed, or villagers shot as suspected sympathizers? The often-indiscriminate nature of the killings, coming at a time when young Hutu men in the northwest were constantly mysteriously "disappearing," left a permanent stain on General Kayumba's reputation.[22]

By April 1998, Rwanda's security crisis was largely over. Thousands of young Hutus who had been training in Kivu's camps were back in their own country. Reeducated at solidarity camps, they were meekly incorporated into Rwanda's new army. Rwanda's existential fears had been addressed in a manner of the RPF's choosing.

A onetime rebel movement born in the refugee camps of Uganda, whose original raison d'être had been to simply win the right of return, now found itself at the very heart of what, in terms of mineral, oil, timber, and hydroelectric-power potential, at least, was one of Africa's biggest, richest nation-states. The RPF could barely believe its luck.

CHAPTER FOURTEEN

WE HAVE ACCEPTED TO BE DOGS

The fault, dear Brutus, is not in our stars,
But in ourselves, that we are underlings.

—Cassius, *in Julius Caesar,*
William Shakespeare

Patrick Karegeya was not a man who wrote things down. The nature of his job had mitigated against the habit. The only totally secure filing cabinet is the human mind, and a benign tremor, which worsened over the years—sometimes rippling through his body as he tried to sit motionless—meant he found typing laborious. When I once suggested a memoir, he waved the idea away, and Theogene Rudasingwa, who had the same idea, found it impossible to pin his friend down. "Patrick was just too lazy, he loved to talk too much. I'd tell him I'd do it, go round to his place with a notebook, and we'd just end up chatting for hours instead. That's why his death robs us of so much."[1]

The only sustained piece of writing of his I possess is a five-page report he compiled in support of Leah's application for political asylum in the United States. It's not much, but it's precious, as in it Patrick runs through the stages of his falling-out with Kagame as he saw them, charting the disastrous parting of the ways that would culminate in his murder.

What it reveals is slightly unexpected. Many of those who follow Rwandan politics regard 2000 as the moment when a distance developed between the vice-president and many of the RPF stalwarts who facilitated his rise to power. Patrick identifies the schism, instead, as starting earlier, when, as far as the outside world was concerned, he was comfortably ensconced at the system's very zenith.

"My political conflict with President Kagame goes back to 1998," he wrote to the US Department of Homeland Security, "when, in a dubious and manipulative way, President Kagame assumed the chairmanship of the ruling party Rwanda Patriotic Front (RPF) from Colonel Alexis Kanyarengwe."[2]

After protesting army massacres of Hutus in his home province of Ruhengeri, Kanyarengwe was made to resign his honorific position during a March 1997 government reshuffle. As a serving member of the armed forces, Kagame was, in theory, automatically disqualified from taking the RPF's top executive position, a post reserved for civilians. Attempting to do so would mean a Tutsi replaced a Hutu in a high-profile position, a man handpicked by Fred Rwigyema, what was more, in an attempt to reach out to the Hutu majority.

Patrick's view, he tells the Americans, was that the most "administratively correct" way to proceed, if there was to be a change at the top, was for the party chairmanship to go to President Pasteur Bizimungu rather than Kagame.

"I approached him in an advisory manner with my concerns about his taking up the chairmanship," Patrick wrote in the affidavit. "Firstly, that it disregarded the concerns of senior members of the party, and secondly that it was undemocratic. Kagame then stated that it was not a big problem but apparently as I later came to learn through common friends, he took it personally as a sign of my not supporting him politically and doubting his capacity to lead."

The point of friction might almost seem dully procedural. Every Rwandan citizen, every Western diplomat or foreign minister engaging with Kigali, after all, knew who commanded the RPF and that it wasn't either Kanyarengwe or Bizimungu. Why fuss?

The RPF's top cadres did not see things that way. In Kagame, they knew, they were dealing with a master of the sideways maneuver, a tactician whose laser-like vision was all the while fixed on a distant objective. What they glimpsed was the opening gambit in a major power grab. Bizimungu—the man who had helped negotiate the Arusha Accords, and had stuck by the RPF notwithstanding the Gersony report, the firings of less accommodating Hutu colleagues, the Kibeho massacre, and even the murder of Seth Sendashonga—was in Kagame's sights.

Once Kagame, already Rwanda's defence minister and vice-president, had also been elected chairman of the RPF, political stalemate would become inevitable. "The two leaders would be bosses of each other depending on which meeting they were attending. At the Cabinet table, President Bizimungu was the boss but at the Party table vice-president Kagame was the boss," Patrick wrote.

The General was equally skeptical. "In government Kagame would be junior, but in the party he's senior, so where does the power lie?" he told me.

In February 1998 Kagame was made RPF chairman, while Bizimungu was given the vice-chairman's post. "The 'election' of the new RPF leadership happened in a very opaque way," writes historian Filip Reyntjens. "It was unclear which body took the decision and the new composition confirmed the Tutsi nature of the party: among the three members of the executive committee and the eight commissioners, Bizimungu was the only Hutu."[3]

As anticipated, the result was deadlock, recalls the General: "From 1998 until 2000, Rwanda was involved in a political contradiction. The tussle for power between the president and the party vice-chairman came to the fore, and then the conflicts began."

The damage, in his view, was entirely unnecessary. "We were having a transition that would end in 2003 and I couldn't see why Bizimungu wouldn't be allowed to retire honorably. This was a man who had left his Hutu colleagues to join us. I saw no reason to humiliate him. I thought him staying would bring more cohesion."

Museveni and Nyerere, Kagame's closest African allies, shared the General's concerns. So did the United States and the United Kingdom, Rwanda's key donors, and they told Kagame as much, urging him not to alter the status quo. Bizimungu might well be a fig leaf, but in a country in desperate need of ethnic reconciliation, fig leaves matter.

It was a contest General Kayumba came to know intimately as he took on the role of go-between. "I was a very good friend of Kagame, a godfather to his son," he says. "Pasteur Bizimungu and I also had a very good relationship, so I was mediating between the two. There were many angry exchanges, with Bizimungu telling Kagame he had no right to take the lead in cabinet meetings and Kagame telling Bizimungu he had no say over what was decided in RPF get-togethers."

As the two men bickered, the RPF's smear campaign got to work.

Joseph Sebarenzi, a former aid worker and Tutsi genocide survivor who had been named parliamentary speaker in early 1997—theoretically the third most powerful position in government—had started out a Kagame admirer. But he couldn't help noticing how the vice-president would always offer a supportive "Sure! Sure!" whenever he proposed something, only for Sebarenzi to later discover Kagame himself was behind the opposition he was experiencing. For the most part, he didn't get to see Kagame at all, as the vice-president used his secretary to block contact whenever he was displeased. "No one ever really knew what he thought about anything until it was too late."[4]

Now Sebarenzi logged the various phases of the Bizimungu vilification process. "The rumors began mildly at first: 'President Bizimungu rarely goes to his office,' people would whisper to each other over drinks or in meetings. 'He really doesn't do any work.' Then they became weightier: 'He's more concerned with his business ventures than running the country.' Heads would shake piteously. 'It's a shame, really.' Then the attacks became more vicious: 'Bizimungu has psychiatric problems,' people would say. 'He has affairs with other women.' And finally: 'He's become an extremist. He can't be trusted.'"

"When Kagame decided he didn't like someone, they weren't just removed from power, they were ruined," recalled Sebarenzi. "'Everyone ignores a dead dog in the road until it begins to smell—then they want it gone,' Kagame was supposedly fond of saying. And his operatives made sure his opponents smelled like dead dogs."

At the same time as Bizimungu's reputation was being shredded, Kagame brought parliament, which had been showing a disconcerting tendency to flex its muscles, neatly to heel. In March 1999, at the behest of the RPF, Rwanda's four political parties agreed to join a Forum of Political Parties with the power to remove individual MPs—a power till then reserved for the parties themselves. "The forum was sold as a just and fair system of checks and balances on parliament. In reality, it was neither," recalls Sebarenzi.

Once created, the forum immediately began removing MPs seen as troublemakers. "Those who had been active in government oversight or had criticized the government, directly or indirectly, were among those targeted. In the space of about a month, eight lawmakers were gone." What alarmed Sebarenzi was not just their removal, but what happened to each afterward: with one exception, imprisonment or flight into exile. "Few met happy endings," he wrote.

"If there was any doubt who was in control, the forum did not vote out members of parliament who belonged to the RPF or the military—those members were simply told to leave by RPF officials."

Next came the judiciary. The Supreme Court's deputy justice Augustin Cyiza, who had made the mistake of ruling against the government in a dispute with a company, had been removed in 1998, although the constitution did not give the government any such power.[5] Five of the Supreme Court's six judges were now replaced in the space of a year by candidates handpicked by the RPF. "The final nail had been driven into the supreme court's coffin," wrote Sebarenzi.

•

Domestic politics were not the only area of disagreement between Patrick and Kagame. The other thorny area, according to the former's five-page account, was Rwanda's expanding involvement in neighboring DRC.

By 1998 Laurent Kabila was no longer following the script written for him by the Rwandans. Maybe the speed of his accession had gone to his head. He was now president of a country the size of Western Europe, after all, a leader to be reckoned with. Why should he take orders from the pip-squeak that was Rwanda, a scornful and disrespectful pip-squeak, at that?

Rwanda would later let it be known that it was Kabila's flirtation with the battered remnants of the *interahamwe* and ex-Habyarimana military that finally poisoned relations with their former protégé, but the explanation reverses the order of events. Kabila only reached out to the *génocidaires* once the relationship with his former backers had irreparably broken down, depriving him of military backup.

"Kabila wanted the Rwandan troops in Congo out. Their presence made him look like a puppet. He wanted to assert his authority," recalls the General. "But Kagame wanted them to stay. He had certain expectations in terms of resources. He felt Rwanda had lost a lot [during the fighting] and deserved compensation. Promises were seen as not being realized." What form of compensation Kagame regarded as appropriate would later become abundantly clear.

On July 13, 1998, Kabila fired James Kabarebe as his army chief of staff. Two weeks later he ordered all Rwandan troops out of the country.

At a key meeting, an impatient Kagame asked his inner circle how to respond to this insult. He wanted to show the uppity Kabila that he could be dumped and replaced with someone more compliant just as ruthlessly as Mobutu had been. Kabarebe, humiliated in front of his own men, anxious to impress the boss, was itching to go into action. What he had delivered once, he could deliver a second time, the former chief of Congo operations told Kagame at the meeting.

Both Patrick and General Kayumba, in contrast, counseled a more conciliatory approach. Patrick was convinced Kabila could be managed—whether by flattery, threats, or encouraging regional players to apply pressure. "I expressed to President Kagame privately and later on in a meeting with other senior officers that Rwanda's invasion of Congo was quite unnecessary, as it would result in the loss of innocent lives and resources of which we could not afford at the point in time."

The General was similarly skeptical, remembering how quickly Tanzania's invading troops turned from admired heroes to loathed predators in the eyes of Ugandans in the 1970s. "I saw what happened when the Tanzanians ousted Amin, the way so-called liberators, who were cheered at the start, swiftly became resented occupiers. I told Kagame, 'You will never win it. The Congolese will never accept Rwandan occupation. We cannot occupy Congo, it has never successfully happened in African history.'"

Quite apart from the question of how to fund a fresh conflict, Rwanda's army was weary, the two men told Kagame. The younger generation of fighters had been in a state of constant battle readiness since the early 1990s, and older commanders had seen action since the early 1980s—they deserved a break, the chance to stop, remove their uniforms, buy land, start families. The trials of war only make sense if warriors can enjoy the fruits of peace.

Another consideration was the impact a second Rwandan assault would have on DRC's Banyamulenge community, already regarded by the Kinshasa government as treacherous fifth columnists. They risked paying a high price for their ethnic allegiances.

And as Rwanda's leading diplomatic envoy during the preparations for the First Congo War, Patrick was well aware of a key difference in the 1996 and 1998 scenarios. A huge amount of preparatory legwork had gone into pulling together the pan-African coalition that had backed the AFDL, ensuring its stunning success. The second time around there had been no time. To intervene without first getting the region on board would be immensely risky, both politically and strategically.

"We were saying, 'Where is the political benefit?'" says the General. "We were looking at all the issues and saying, 'Let's talk to Kabila, and if he won't listen, mobilize the other governments so we don't go it alone.' We were looking at a belligerent foreign policy none of us thought worthwhile."

"Let me try and talk the Mzee round," Patrick urged his employer. As ever, Kagame was studiedly noncommittal in front of his peers. "I'll think about it," was all he would say. Two weeks later, the most daring operation ever attempted by the RPF—a movement that already boasted an impressive track record in that area—began. Kabarebe had won the day.

"Patrick wasn't in support of the war, but once it began, he did his bit," says the General. As the military men readied to go into action, Patrick reached out to the former rebels whom the Rwandans had nurtured and called them to heel. "Throughout the country, AFDL politicians began mysteriously dropping off the radar," write political scientists Philip Roessler and Harry Verhoeven.[6] Deogratias Bugera secretly crossed the Congo River to Brazzaville, his colleague Azarias Ruberwa stayed on after a wedding in Bukavu and drove across the border, and Bizima Karaha rerouted his return from an OAU summit in Mozambique.

Once again, the renegades mustered in a house in Kigali's suburbs, to once again be given their orders by Patrick, Emmanuel Ndahiro, and their colleagues. What would become known as the Rassemblement Congolais pour la Démocratie (RCD) must be presented as a Congolese uprising, not a Rwandan insurgency, they were told. Kagame himself picked Ernest Wamba dia Wamba, a mildly spoken Congolese professor of political science who had spent years in exile in the United States and Tanzania, as its political head.

"It was a strange bunch," Wamba dia Wamba, who looked—and would increasingly come to behave—like an absentminded Oxford don, later told Stearns. "You had capitalists and socialists. You had Mobutists and those who had thrown them out of power. You had academics and people who apparently had never read a book."[7]

If the fiction had strained credulity the first time around, it looked even more threadbare the second. But the tatty "cover story" would have to do. "We thought we would take Kinshasa within a month at the most," Patrick told Stearns. As ever, what mattered was the military situation, not the politics, and that was moving at lightning speed.

The Second Congo War[8] was a multipronged affair. On August 2, 1998, the Tenth Brigade of the Congolese army—the force's best-equipped and most disciplined troops—mutinied against the Kabila government. Hundreds of Rwandan soldiers, supported by Uganda's armed forces, simultaneously poured into North and South Kivu. In a few days the Rwandans and local Banyamulenge were in control of Congo's eastern border. Farther north, the Ugandan army went on the attack, invading Ituri Province and setting its sights on the key river city of Kisangani.

The third prong, involving a 1,200-mile air bridge, was intended to culminate in Kinshasa's strategic encirclement. Commandeering four civilian airliners parked on the tarmac at Goma's airport, Kabarebe flew 3,500 Rwandan and Congolese fighters to Kitona, a little-used air base 200 miles west of the capital, where the vast Congo River spills into the Atlantic Ocean.

Leapfrogging half a continent to the western Bas Congo Province, where DRC's key ports are located, Kabarebe shuttled fighters and supplies to Kitona until he had a column capable of taking on Kinshasa. Then they marched east, capturing town after town. Once they'd seized the massive Inga Dam, the rebels shut down the turbines, plunging the Congolese capital into darkness.[9]

Kabila fled to Katanga, his home province in southern DRC, but it was at this point that Rwanda's failure to lay the necessary diplomatic groundwork came home to roost. In mid-August, Zimbabwe,

Angola, Namibia, and Chad agreed to join the Second Congo War. Only this time, they chose the government side, flying in soldiers and turning their formidable air power on the Rwandans, the Ugandans, and their Congolese proxies. It was one thing, as far as a swath of the region was concerned, to rid Central Africa of a past-his-sell-by-date dictator who specialized in hosting rebel groups. It was another for Rwanda—and to a lesser extent its ally Uganda—to make a habit of high-handedly deciding who ran their giant neighbor.

Marooned on the wrong side of Africa, without hope of resupply— "Kitona was a logistical nightmare," remarks the General—Kabarebe was forced to retreat down the path he had already beaten. As Congolese Tutsis were lynched in the streets of Kinshasa, he searched desperately for an escape route. After capturing a small Angolan regional airport at Maquela do Zombo, Kabarebe spent two months flying in generators and construction equipment. His men worked round the clock to extend the air strip until it was long enough to take the cargo planes, being scrambled by General Kayumba back in Kigali, required to evacuate his trapped troops.

Operation Kitona was Rwanda's version of the World War II Allies' "Bridge Too Far," in which 35,000 US and British troops were dropped behind enemy lines in the Netherlands, a textbook case of military overreach. "Today the operation is studied for its daring initial aerial assault as well as the intelligence failures on the Rwandan side," reads the relevant Wikipedia entry.

Exhausted, stressed, Kabarebe collapsed toward the end of the operation. It was Patrick, who had flown to Luanda to persuade the Angolans not to bomb Maquela do Zombo during the evacuation, who arranged for his colleague to be airlifted to South Africa for medical treatment. The spy chief also did his best to cover Kabarebe's tracks in the media. When rumors were circulating but still unconfirmed, Patrick invited the press corps in Kigali to a reception. There they found a strangely sheepish-looking Kabarebe. He'd been absent, they were told, because he'd been busy "milking his cows"—an appropriately Tutsi pastime. A raid on Kitona? What raid on Kitona? He'd been in Rwanda all the time. "We all went away and dutifully wrote our stories," remembers AP's Hranjski. "But I don't think any of us believed the official explanation for a minute. Patrick laughed about it later."

While the dispute over tactics in DRC was kept behind closed doors, members of Kigali's press pack were starting to pick up the odd tremor of dissonance. "Patrick never criticized Kagame, he never said anything bad, but there were always hints," remembers Hranjski. "You sometimes got the sense from Patrick's body language that he wasn't that happy with decisions being taken."

Visitors registered a marked disinclination to be cowed. "It wasn't that Patrick was hostile to Kagame," recalls *Africa Confidential* editor Patrick Smith. "But what was striking was his lack of obvious deference—everyone else had it, that touch of deference—the diplomats, the politicians, but not Patrick."

Patrick possessed many qualities, but modesty was not one of them. "All those RPF guys were super-smart," recalls Lara Santoro, then Africa correspondent for the *Christian Science Monitor*. "But Patrick was definitely the smartest, the most worldly of the bunch, and I think he had a profound sense of intellectual superiority toward the rest." That very much included the man who had attended his old school, but dropped out. "Patrick was too smart to be openly contemptuous, but he definitely wasn't a fan. Not because he wasn't a fan of the regime, but because he wasn't a fan of Kagame."[10]

The Kitona operation marked the moment when Kabarebe's and Patrick's destinies seesawed into a new configuration. The one who had been up was now down; the one who had been down was up. Kagame never forgot, or forgave, Patrick's skepticism. As the ex–spy chief wrote in his US affidavit, "[Kagame] later told me, while I was in jail, he kept this in his mind as another attempt by me to stand up to him."

•

At the turn of the century the story reached an extraordinary apotheosis, one few analysts would have predicted a few years earlier. Rwanda's repeated interventions in DRC had split apart the coalition that had ousted Mobutu, alienating a handful of previously friendly regional states, but at least its nearest neighbors, Uganda and Burundi, remained on its side. Then, to diplomatic astonishment, Uganda and Rwanda went to war with one another.

The immediate trigger was a split in the RCD, which saw Wamba dia Wamba fleeing to Kisangani, where he was hailed by Uganda as the rebellion's legitimate leader. Behind him in Goma, Emile Ilunga took over the rump movement, with the Rwandans offering support.

The two allies' troops, busy establishing lucrative trading networks in DRC's northeastern and eastern provinces, found themselves eyeball to eyeball in Kisangani's streets, markets, and airports. The setting of V. S. Naipaul's *A Bend in the River*, the city of 600,000 inhabitants feels terminally sleepy and run-down, but it is the country's biggest inland port after Kinshasa and a gateway to the country's equatorial heart. Who controls it matters.

In August 1999, reporter Hranjski was in a taxi driving away from Kisangani's Bangoka Airport, where the Ugandans controlled one side of the runway and the Rwandans the other, when the mounting tensions between Ugandan brigadier James Kazini and Rwandan commander Patrick Nyamvumba finally exploded. "Suddenly all the artillery opened up," Hranjski told me. "The ground literally shook beneath our feet, so much was being fired off. It was incredible." That night he crouched indoors as stray bullets bounced off the corrugated iron roof of his lodging. "If you closed your eyes it sounded like raindrops."

The following day, Hranjski went to interview Nyamvumba. He had just left the commander's villa when the event every war correspondent dreads occurred. "One moment I was chatting to the Rwandan soldier and the next I was on the ground, looking straight at his boots." He'd been shot.

His Rwandan escort dragged him behind a wall, flipping Hranjski onto his back. "It was a beautiful day and there was this amazing, clear sky above. Your senses become heightened at those moments, and I can still remember the exact green of the grass and the precise blue of that sky. 'I'm dying,' I thought. 'This is it.' I couldn't feel anything below my waist. And there was a terrible pain where the bullet had gone in."

The bullet had tunneled through his right lung, lodging near his spine. That night, grinding his teeth in agony as he lay in Kisangani's deserted hospital, Hranjski had last rites administered by an old Belgian priest. "I was in a bad way by then," he recalls.

It was Patrick who came to the rescue. The man on whose sofa Hranjski had so often sprawled arranged for the reporter to be driven to the airport under Red Cross escort and flown to Kigali, where he was met by Kagame's personal doctor before being airlifted to Nairobi for surgery.

Behind the reporter, the fighting continued, the nadir touched when Uganda's head of military intelligence Noble Mayombo and Kahinda Otafiire found themselves pinned down by Rwandan fire in a Kisangani textile factory. Both were NRM stalwarts, old RPF friends. When Patrick heard his former bush companions were in acute danger, he called the General, appalled. "They are going to kill these guys," he exclaimed. General Kayumba called Kabarebe, a cease-fire was ordered, and the Ugandan commanders made their humiliating escape.

•

What made the violence in Kisangani so poignant was the intimacy between the two armies. During lulls in fighting, soldiers hobnobbed at Gentry's, the most popular nightclub in town, Rwandans in pristine camouflage rubbing shoulders with Ugandans in their green uniforms. The two groups' behavior—quietly reserved on the Rwandan side, noisily jocular with the Ugandans, who liked their *waragi*—might be starkly different, but sometimes the men put aside their differences and danced together.

Alexandre Liebeskind, from the International Committee of the Red Cross, found himself acting as a go-between for the men who couldn't quite grasp why their bosses were suddenly no longer on speaking terms. "Rwandan soldiers were saying to me, 'Will you say hi to so-and-so,' or 'Please tell so-and-so hello.' They'd give me notes to pass to officers on the Ugandan side. All these guys had served together in the UPDF."[11]

The strands of that brotherly scrap weave in and out of one another, as fiddly to unpick as the plaited fibers of a mat. All the more so as beneath the explanations both sides offered their Western allies—as a UN investigation would later witheringly reveal—stretched layers of crude, unacknowledged self-interest.

At its most philosophical, the occupation of DRC had exposed a widening ideological rift between the two former rebel movements. True to their political roots, the Ugandans believed their Congolese partners should build revolutionary consciousness from the ground up. "We are interested in empowering the Congolese," Museveni told Uganda's parliament when he explained the Kisangani crisis, "and it seems the Rwandese do not like it."[12]

The Rwandans, drippingly dismissive of their Congolese allies' capacities, weren't too bothered about the DRC's long-term political transformation. Always quick to cite the survival of the Tutsi community as their focus, their priority was establishing a buffer zone between Rwanda and the exiled *génocidaires* hiding in the Congolese forests.

And then there was the question of the allocation of DRC's spoils. Uganda saw Ituri Province and the northeastern Congolese towns of Butembo, Beni, and Bunia as part of its natural sphere of influence. Let the Rwandan troops stick to Goma, Bukavu, and Uvira down south, where they belonged. It was not a view the Rwandans shared.

But sibling rivalry was clearly a key factor, too. Like so many fights, it all boiled down to respect, or the perceived absence of it, and the visceral need felt by a younger, subservient partner to shift a relationship onto a more equal footing. The Ugandan military elite's language when referring to their brothers-in-arms was a giveaway. "Museveni used this whole 'My children, my boys' line when he talked about the RPF," remembers John Nagenda, Museveni's former official spokesman. "And at a certain stage, Kagame said, 'Rubbish. We're not your boys.' Having gone through what they had, it really irked the RPF, to be called 'boys.'"

The habit many Ugandan officers had acquired of referring to Kabarebe as a "small corporal," jarred with the Rwandans. The ten-year age gap between Patrick Nyamvumba, a mere lieutenant-colonel at the time, and the swaggering James Kazini didn't help, either. "Patrick? Patrick is just a boy. I am a brigadier. Who is he to discuss anything with me?" Kazini would tell Ugandan journalists.

When recalling the past, the Ugandans dwelled on the way the NRA had welcomed the Banyarwanda into its ranks, and the ranks and responsibilities showered upon them once peace came. "We taught them how to fight," Ugandan officers would say. Some gratitude was surely in order. What the Rwandans remembered, instead, was the NRA's reliance on the Banyarwanda to do its dirtiest fighting, Museveni's failure to win them the right to return, and the sense of having always been unwelcome in alien territory.

"The son rebels against the father," says Liebeskind. "The Ugandans still believed the Rwandans owed them their victory. The Rwandans, for their part, didn't have much respect for the UPDF. They saw it as a degenerate army, old-fashioned and without much purpose."

If Fred Rwigyema—who really *did* regard Museveni as a surrogate father—had lived, it's a safe bet the Kisangani war would never have occurred. But Fred was gone, and his successor, the sidekick the Ugandan president had never warmed to, was not the respectful type. Adjustment, in Paul Kagame's eyes, was long overdue. As he told his former colleagues in Kampala, "The trouble with you guys is you can't accept that the president you wanted for Rwanda died."

•

Like all key developments, Rwanda's adventures in the Congo took place without the input of its civilian government. As Theogene Rudasingwa writes in his memoir, "The decisions to go to war in the DRC had, as usual, been solely taken outside constitutional powers. Rwanda's parliament had not been consulted. President Bizimungu as well as other senior leaders in RPF had been informed after the fact."[13]

Kagame's campaign to concentrate power in his hands, removing any civilian politicians disinclined to parrot his views, reached fruition in the early months of 2000.

Despite the emasculating Forum of Political Parties, Rwanda's parliament had gradually established an impressive reputation for independence. Encouraged by Sebarenzi, it had set up a public accounts committee, an auditor general's office, and a national tender board. It had called upon serving ministers to justify their actions and explain missing funds—including embezzled donor aid—and in some cases had censured them.

Such feistiness, and the possible ambition of the popular speaker, presented a problem for a control-freak vice-president, and in late 1999 Sebarenzi realized the RPF smear machine had turned its attention to him. Rumors began circulating that he was working with the exiled *Mwami* to overturn the government. Then he learned the RPF was circulating a petition among the political parties asking for him to be removed for "threatening national security."[14]

When he confronted Kagame, he got a bald denial. "I have no problem with you at all," the latter insisted. "It's your own people in the Liberal Party." A few years earlier, Sebarenzi would have believed him. Now he knew better. One by one, the lawmakers whose work he had championed signed the petition. "Don't think I am against you," one parliamentarian pathetically admitted. "We have accepted to be dogs and I have signed it."

Hoping to retain, at least, his parliamentary seat, Sebarenzi agreed to resign as speaker. But a few days later he learned this would not suffice. As his resignation had triggered alarmed speculation both at home and internationally, a confession of guilt and public apology—that ritual of self-abasement—was required.

"This is ridiculous, I can't confess to something I haven't done," was his response, a refrain that would be echoed by so many others picked up by the Rwandan security forces. Then a message from a female relative with a friend in intelligence arrived.

"I've heard that an assassination is being planned," she told him.

"Assassinate who?" asked the speaker, although he already knew the answer.

"You."

And so Sebarenzi found himself in his underpants—trousers and shoes clutched to his chest—wading the river separating Rwanda from Uganda, off to start a new life in the United States. He had lost almost more relatives than he could count in 1994, including a father who had been beheaded. As a Tutsi *rescapé*—genocide survivor—he was, in theory, exactly the kind of citizen the regime was devoted to nurturing, yet here he was, joining the long list of notables taking the *subway*.

In February 2000, it was Hutu prime minister Pierre-Célestin Rwigema's turn to resign, victim of yet another RPF-orchestrated campaign whose innuendos parliament had already investigated and discounted.

Then, on March 5, Assiel Kabera, President Bizimungu's adviser, was assassinated. Another Tutsi *rescapé* and Sebarenzi's close friend, he'd been a driven campaigner for ethnic reconciliation. He was shot with professional neatness outside his own house—a villa near the closely guarded presidential palace—by three men in military uniform.[15]

Noble Marara, presidential bodyguard, heard the shots while sitting in his car, waiting for the First Lady to emerge from her mother's house. Back at base, he was reassured by an intelligence officer that Kabera, "one of the enemies," as the man put it, had been "sorted." "He . . . behaved like someone who was giving me some good news or sounding like it was saving the whole nation. . . . For the first time, I realised they could kill anyone," Marara later wrote.[16]

The murder deeply disturbed Patrick. Not just because he had respected Kabera as an individual, but because it illustrated how Kagame operated, using different tracks to covertly get his way. "It really bothered Patrick," recalls David Himbara, who befriended the spy chief after flying into Kigali to take up a new post as economic adviser. "The man was well educated, idealistic, he was assassinated in his house—and just imagine, Patrick, head of intelligence, didn't even know." The topic came up between the two because as a new arrival in need of accommodation, chillingly, Himbara was allocated the dead man's house.[17]

In late March Bizimungu finally accepted the inevitable and stepped down, overwhelmed by accusations so petty—he had registered two trucks in DRC to avoid paying Rwandan taxes, it was said, and had failed to pay adequate compensation to people evicted from land he was developing—they seemed almost laughable.

Bizimungu delivered a blistering final speech to parliament, in which he laid out exactly how and where, in his view, the RPF had lost its way. It was a magnificent eulogy, but General Frank Rusagara, one of the drafters of the RPF's constitution, was the only party member to stand and applaud. No one outside the building heard it, as neither Rwanda state radio nor television broadcast Bizimungu's words. By the time Rusagara, a well-known iconoclast, had arrived back home, his own firing had already been announced.

One month later, in what Patrick would simply describe to the US Department of Homeland Security as "a coup," Kagame was officially sworn in as Rwanda's new president.

"Any pretence of power-sharing was now gone," later wrote Theogene. "Paul Kagame was the Chairman of the ruling RPF, the head of all the security institutions and now the President of the Republic. Previously he had ruled from behind-the-scenes but now he had formally assumed all the powers."[18]

Total control did not turn Kagame magnanimous. When Bizimungu tried to set up his own party, it was immediately banned on the grounds of fomenting ethnic hatred, and the former president was eventually jailed for fifteen years, accused of creating a militia and embezzling state funds. He was released after three years by presidential pardon, after showing the required degree of abnegation.

Kagame had silenced any dissenting voices in Rwanda's civilian government, parliament, judiciary, and human rights movement. He had also, in his critics' eyes, divided the RPF into two opposing factions.

At one extreme, says General Kayumba, sat cadres who wanted a party and a country based on "freedom of expression, a vibrant media, an independent civil service, and a nonpartisan army": Fred's old vision. "And then there was another group, whose members thought issues of reconciliation and reconstruction should be put on the back burner and we should focus on building Kagame's image as the source of all wisdom." That group included Tito Rutaremara, James Musoni, Jack Nziza, and James Kabarebe.

"They were looking for positions. That's how Kabarebe, who was just a bodyguard to Kagame, was catapulted to the top and Musoni became a super minister."

Perhaps, though, that first faction was simply naive. As US ambassador to Uganda in the early 1990s, Johnnie Carson got to know and like most of the RPF's key members. Today he sees the rifts that opened up during these years as a case of ambitious colleagues fundamentally misconstruing the nature of the system crystallizing around Kagame and overestimating their own strengths.

"I've seen it before in other countries, with other African leaders," says Carson, who later served four years as US assistant secretary of state for African affairs. "There were half a dozen to a dozen Rwandans around Kagame who genuinely felt that they had the capacity to lead the government and be president.[19]

"They believed they were part of a small, democratic party, and over time they'd be given a chance to serve in the highest office of the land. Many of them were just as gifted as Kagame and some were perhaps more articulate and intelligent, but none of them had his political cunning," according to Carson.

"They all overestimated Kagame's egalitarian nature, his willingness to share leadership and to have his vision challenged. And when they challenged him in hard and substantive ways, he recoiled and then rebounded, in the way of a green mamba, lashing out to bite another snake."

It was never the case, in Carson's view, that Kagame was a primus inter pares. "There was no question that Kagame was the leader," he says. "He was focused, committed, unflinching. Paul Kagame is without doubt the most ruthless politician operating in Africa today."

•

Kagame was now free to focus on the battlefield.

Western donors who had funded both Uganda's and Rwanda's postwar development programs had been appalled by the falling-out between the two allies and done their best to separate the now feuding armies. In May 2000, under a UN-supervised agreement, Uganda and Rwanda were meant to pull their troops 60 miles back from Kisangani, leaving the city demilitarized. Instead, the Ugandan army, camped on the north side of the Congo River, sent its forces storming south across the Tshopo Bridge, a rickety wrought-iron crossing. Rwandan troops who had marched out of the city did a smart about-face and marched straight back.

Fighting for control of the river's southern bank, the two armies knocked holes in the walls of intervening houses, then opened fire. "They were using weapons meant to be fired at long distance—mortars and antiaircraft guns—as infantry weapons. So civilian casualty numbers were very, very high," recalls Liebeskind.

Slowly, the Rwandans closed in on their former friends. Whenever the RPA captured a Ugandan position, its soldiers would continue firing in the direction of their own Rwandan forces, thereby concealing just how much ground they had captured. The flanking tactic ensured that Ugandan troops controlling the bridgehead failed to register just how disastrously they had been encircled until they were overrun.

What was nicknamed Congo's "Six-Day War," because it coincided with the anniversary of the 1967 Israeli-Arab conflict, left 600 dead. Most were Congolese civilians, but a few days later, shocked Ugandan officers took delivery of the bodies of at least 140 of their own soldiers. Many of them appeared to have been blindfolded with elephant grass and shot in the back of the head.

Despite its troops massively outnumbering Rwanda's at the conflict's outbreak, Uganda had clearly lost the Kisangani battle. But Rwanda's victory came at a price. The two countries' relationship would never be the same again.

When Clare Short, Britain's secretary of state for international development, called Kagame and Museveni to London for a summit in November 2001, worried about murmurings of a looming new Ugandan-Rwandan clash, feelings still ran so high that former old friends on the delegations could not make eye contact across the conference table.

In ending the fight, the Rwandans had applied unnecessary levels of brutality, confirming every Ugandan stereotype regarding what was seen as an RPF readiness, even appetite, for taking human life. "I'm convinced there was a conscious decision to over-kill, to humiliate," one Great Lakes analyst told me. Maximum pain had been deliberately inflicted on a former friend, the better to leave a lasting impression.[20]

Once the guns had gone quiet, Red Cross representative Liebeskind went to meet Lieutenant General Karenzi Karake, known as "KK," who had assumed command of the Rwandan troops from Nyamvumba. He found the general—in true Tutsi style, carton of milk in hand—matter-of-factly contemplating his triumph with his colleagues.

"We wanted to send a message," KK told Liebeskind. "If you shoot at us, we shoot back." He paused and coolly took a sip of his milk. "I think they got it."

Liebeskind would never forget the image. "On one side you had a group of officers who had won a war from an incredibly weak position, against the odds, sitting sipping milk. On the other you had an army whose commanders broke open the whisky at 10 a.m., mourning its losses."

Having humiliated the Ugandans, the Rwandan army and the RCD in December crushed the Congolese army and its Zimbabwean allies in Pweto, southeastern Congo. One month earlier, Kabila had ordered Anselme Masasu, the former Rwandan army sergeant who had made up the AFDL's fourth leg, executed for mustering his own militia. The fighting at Pweto was vicious, with the *kadogos* who had joined the army at Masasu's bidding ordered to shoot wounded comrades rather than let them be captured alive.

Such mistreatment swiftly boomeranged back on the DRC president. On January 16, 2001, when Kabila was sitting in his office in the presidential palace in Kinshasa, a *kadogo* bodyguard, Rashidi Kasereka, walked up and shot him in the back of the head.

The murderer's identity is not in doubt, but theories as to why he acted at that precise moment have circulated ever since. Was he prodded, and if so, by whom? Fingers have pointed at both Kigali and Luanda, where the Angolan authorities, already exasperated at Kabila's intransigence, had been outraged to discover that the man whose skin they had saved was busy trafficking in diamonds with the UNITA rebel movement.

What's certain is that while the panicking DRC authorities were still pretending Kabila was alive, flying his corpse to Harare for medical "treatment," Rwandan intelligence knew exactly what had happened. At least twenty-four hours before the news hit the BBC, Fabienne Hara of the International Crisis Group received an unexpected call at her Brussels office. It was Patrick. "Kabila's dead," he told her. When she put the obvious question—"Who did it?"—his response was typical. "He didn't say the Rwandans were responsible," she recalls. "'Well, they say it was his bodyguard,' he told me—but he was laughing."

With Belgian scholar Filip Reyntjens, years later, he was more direct. Reyntjens, who had met Patrick when he was at the height of his powers, regularly bounced queries off him via Skype once he'd rebased in South Africa. At one point the topic of Kabila's assassination came up.

"I said, 'You were head of ESO so I assume you know who killed Kabila.' And he laughed. Laughed, you know, Patrick Karegeya–style, and said, 'Of course I know, because we did it!'"

"That's not quite good enough," protested the academic. "Can you provide any detail to back that up, any background, information about chain of command?"

"Just ask them in Kinshasa to check Rashidi's cell phone," Patrick replied. "They'll find that in the days running up to Kabila's murder there were a series of phone calls between Rashidi and Kabarebe."

Using a well-placed political contact in Kinshasa, the terrier-like Reyntjens did exactly that, only to be told—after a long silence— that DRC's new leadership considered the dossier far too sensitive to reopen.

Was Patrick shooting his mouth off? He was certainly by that stage a man with a grievance, in a mood to lash out at his former employer. But he was also one of only a tiny handful of Rwandans in a position to know exactly what had happened inside Kabila's study that day, and there was no reason, now, for him to remain silent.

•

The DRC had been effectively dismembered, its neighboring states playing the part of bickering hyenas. The north was controlled by Jean-Pierre Bemba's Movement for the Liberation of the Congo (MLC), new militia kid on the block; the east by different RCD factions; and the west and south lay in government hands. The nation would only be nominally reunited after peace talks in South Africa's Sun City casino resort in 2002.

That narcissistic contest between the region's military elites indirectly claimed a staggering number of victims. The International Rescue Committee estimates that up to 4.7 million Congolese died in the civil war in eastern Congo: civilians for the most part killed not by gunshot, shrapnel, or bombing—for this was a low-impact conflict—but by diarrhea, malaria, and malnutrition, classic blights of underdevelopment.

The entire episode altered forever how many outsiders viewed Uganda's and Rwanda's regimes. Hranjski, who today bears a thick red weal snaking around his torso—the scar left by a Kenyan surgeon— was not untypical. For him, the conflict marked the end of an already floundering intellectual love affair.

He had certainly entertained doubts about the morality of his Rwandan hosts before then. "I was there when the RPF death squads were hunting Hutus down in the forests in 1996, so even then I realized these guys were capable of anything. But there was a moral plausibility to the argument that they were 'killing the killers,'" he says.

By the time the two armies clashed in Kisangani, all that was over. "The feeling among outsiders was, 'You're literally destroying another country for nothing. What are you even *doing* here?' This wasn't about hunting down *génocidaires*, it was about money and who controlled what. It exposed the ugly side of all that pure Rwandan revolutionary ideology."

A bigger concept also expired: the belief that the end of Cold War superpower meddling meant that a coalition of progressive African governments, championed by like-minded "Renaissance leaders," could drive corrupt one-party rule from Central Africa. "Pan-Africanism died on the Tshopo Bridge," grunted a morose Salim Saleh when I interviewed him.

For Patrick, though, in charge of external intelligence, Kisangani represented a disaster of a different, very personal nature.

Ever the pragmatist, he'd seen no reason to fight when a deal suiting everyone—well, all DRC's occupying powers—could surely be reached. "I told the Rwandan High Command," he later confided in Emmanuel Habyarimana, former defence minister. "If you want DRC's spoils, why can't you coordinate, work together to exploit them in a civilized way?"[21]

The violence, when it exploded, put Patrick in an excruciating position. Sitting tantalizingly on the fence, he had always played it all ways, emphasizing his Rwandan essence when in Kigali, but playing down his Rwandan nationality when hanging out with Ugandan family. "Patrick would say, 'I'm not a Rwandan,'" remembers a cousin. "'I may be working for the Rwandan government, but I'm a Ugandan.'" He was still micromanaging the family farm in Biharwe and sending money to the border, destined for his mother.

Now, his biggest selling point—his instinctive understanding and intimate connections with both regimes—had become a massive reputational question mark. "Patrick was extremely, extremely troubled by that war. He knew he'd be the one under suspicion, as he'd always been seen as a Ugandan by the Rwandans," says Hranjski.

Western officials trying to knock Ugandan and Rwandan heads together would come to regard Patrick as a hawk during negotiations, but the hard-line stance they detected may well have been prompted by simple panic. He could no longer afford to show a hint of pro-Ugandan bias. His Janus-like personal history had been a unique selling point. Now he couldn't win: both sides saw him as a potential traitor. Tellingly, Kagame would later cite the supposed discovery that Patrick was working for a foreign power when quizzed about his murder by a British journalist.[22]

It was only once Patrick had fallen from grace that he could afford to admit his real feelings over the episode. Interviewed by a young European journalist while hovering between detention and arrest, he was so outspoken she became alarmed. "We were sitting on the terrace of the Hotel Mille Collines, and yes, it was quiet that day, but there were still people around and he was talking very loud.[23]

"When did you stop believing in what Rwanda was doing in Congo?" she asked.

"In Kisangani," he told her. "That's when things changed for me."

As candid as ever, Patrick did not bother shedding crocodile tears. "He had a strange sense of morality," the journalist says. "Before Kisangani, all crimes found justifications from him. He had no problems with killing Hutus in DRC because, in his view, Rwanda was still at war then. But RDF [Rwanda Defence Force] and UPDF blood, that was another story." Nothing could excuse the slaughter meted out to former brothers-in-arms.

"Those kids died for nothing," Patrick told her. "Too much blood was shed. And it was just greed. Ground control. It no longer had anything to do with Rwanda's security. Kisangani was a war of egos, triggered by Kagame's temper."

CHAPTER FIFTEEN

SPOILS OF WAR

Those who work for me are kept faithful,
not so much because of their pay as because they know
what might be done with them if they broke faith.
—Al Capone

One weekend in late July 2000, an intelligence official from one of the Western embassies in Kigali strolled onto the terrace of the Lac Kivu Lodge in Goma and admired the view.

Before him, the choppy lake waters stretched to the dreaming, gray-blue hills of Rwanda, a volcanic mountain range traced in watercolor tints behind. He was looking forward to some fresh tilapia. The hotel, located not far from Mobutu's old villa, was known for its fish restaurant.

Then he froze. He'd just spotted Patrick, with whom he often socialized, locked in intense conversation at a table with a middle-aged Congolese woman. He knew her, too. She was one of the Great Lakes' most notorious diamond traders. As Patrick carefully ignored him, the intelligence official and his date discreetly backpedaled and took a table out of their line of sight. It wouldn't do to interrupt Rwanda's head of ESO when he was busy clinching a major gem deal.[1]

Rwanda's intervention in DRC had morphed into something rich and strange. While Kigali never ceased talking up the *génocidaire* threat lurking in Congo's forests, security was no longer the main reason for maintaining troops there. Using their local rebel allies as fronts, Rwanda's and Uganda's militaries were vacuuming up Congo's diamonds, gold, cobalt, columbo-tantalite, cassiterite, and iron. Tropical timber, cattle herds, elephant tusks, quinine, and tea were being trucked across the border, then exported abroad, miraculously rebranded as Rwandan and Ugandan produce.

The proceeds propped up the occupying countries' treasuries—allowing them to win glowing, undeserved praise from the World Bank, the IMF, and their bilateral donors—but DRC did get something in return: the arms and military equipment that allowed its rebel groups to continue the civil war. Congo's riches were being used to fund its own destruction.

The pillaging had become so blatant—and had so outraged aid organizations, human rights groups, and the government in Kinshasa—that the UN Security Council finally felt obliged to react. Applying a format used in Angola, Liberia, and Sierra Leone, it appointed an international panel of experts to investigate.

Their preliminary report, published in April 2001, tracked the way DRC's exploitation by its two neighbors progressed and changed.[2] In the early years it had been a simple case of "mass looting." Stockpiles of minerals, coffee, and wood in eastern DRC had simply been removed from factories, farms, and storage facilities by occupying armies and their rebel allies. Manufacturing plants and machinery had been dismantled, private cars driven across the frontier, banks emptied of their cash.

The quantities involved were not small. In one Rwandan operation, seven years' of stockpiled coltan, the metal used in making cell phones, was removed from one Kivu mining company. "A very reliable source informed the Panel that it took the Rwandans about a month to fly this coltan to Kigali," the report said. Uganda, instead, had focused on timber and coffee beans.

Once that phase was over, the Rwandans and Ugandans shifted to "active extraction." Their soldiers controlled the mines in which locals—often children—dug the gold and coltan first trucked and later flown across the border. Not only were the put-upon Congolese being "taxed" by the local rebel authorities, who passed a major share of that revenue to Kigali and Kampala, but they were often paid in counterfeit banknotes.

In Rwanda's case, the looting was so "systematic and systemic," a special administrative body had been set up to oversee it: "the Congo Desk." "The unit has been the cornerstone of the financial transactions of the RPA," wrote the authors. The UN report did not name its director, but every diplomat in Kigali knew his identity: Patrick Karegeya.

In a fascinating cable sent back to Washington, a political officer at the US embassy explained how Rwanda's new diamond trade worked: "In Kigali, businessmen go first to 'the Congo Desk' which, they say, is operated by the Rwandan external security services. The men mentioned most frequently as the Congo Desk representatives are chief of external services Colonel Patrick Karegeya, Major Dan Munyuza, and Gatete. . . . (Gatete is believed to be an RPA major who works directly for RPA chief of staff Bg Kayumba Nyamwasa).[3]

"Typically," it went on, "a five percent 'tax' must be paid to the Congo Desk in Rwanda for permission to export diamonds located in the RPA/RCD-Goma sector of the DROC. We have also heard that a flat fee, ranging from USD 20,000 to USD 100,000 must be paid."

Moreover, the cable said, "upon arrival in Kigali, RCD-Goma sources claim that the diamond exporter is protected and/or escorted from the tarmac by Rwandan external security agents and no additional duties or other fees are paid in Kigali. . . . Some of the diamond exporters claim that prior to travel on Sabena airways (the only European air carrier operating from Kigali), they hide their diamonds in filled shampoo bottles to avoid paying customs duties in Europe."

The exposure of the Congo Desk's existence marked "a turning point," recalls Jim Freedman, a Canadian expert on the Great Lakes who worked on the final UN report. "It was a huge discovery, and then it became a major scandal. We knew the Rwandans had been committing massive human rights violations in eastern Congo, but the panel of experts' report showed that an equally important concern was to make as much money as possible."[4]

The notion that Rwandan forces remained inside DRC solely to protect the country's twitchy Tutsi—a justification the US State

Department and British DFID, among others, were happy to swallow—collapsed. "We haven't fought much with the RPA in the last two years," the report quotes an *interahamwe* fighter saying. "We think they are tired of this war, like we are. In any case, they aren't here in the Congo to chase us, like they pretend."

Freedman recalls interviewing "a lot" of *interahamwe*. "And they were just as involved with the extraction of minerals as the Tutsis—in fact, sometimes they were working together." Notwithstanding an ALIR offensive in mid-2001, he pooh-poohs the notion that the *génocidaires* still posed any substantial existential threat to Kigali. "These were straggling groups of rebels making their own little living as pirates or plunderers. The idea they might threaten the Rwandan state was just absurd."

Not all looting is alike. What struck the UN investigators was the contrast in the rationale and hence the style of Ugandan and Rwandan operations. "There was a remarkable difference between Rwanda and Uganda, it was night and day," recalls Freedman. "With Ugandans, it was all catch-as-catch-can, there was a happy-go-lucky element. They could give a damn if it filled Uganda's coffers; they were in it for themselves."

With Rwanda, things were different. Army officials certainly allowed family members to take advantage of the many opportunities their presence in DRC presented—"If you'd set up a noodle bar in Kisangani airport at that time, you'd have made money," laughs a Western journalist, and taxi drivers in Kigali took to labeling the brand-new suburbs springing up *Merci Congo* (Thank you, Congo). But individual enrichment was never the point. War is expensive, and Rwanda was poor. Kagame had said Rwanda's DRC operation needed to be "self-financing." "Profit-making" would have been the more accurate term.

"The guys were doing it for the same reason the Chinese do it, to aggrandize the nation. It was a clean asset-stripping operation, very puritanical and unscrupulous, for a higher purpose," says Freedman.

Might that, I ask, explain why the exiled Patrick hardly lived a life of luxury? "If Patrick didn't get rich, it doesn't surprise me," Freedman replies. "There probably wasn't a great deal of leakage on the Rwandan side, because they were on a mission. It wasn't about personal corruption—this was a *national* money-making effort."

The radically different approaches prompted very different responses to the UN investigators' findings. Caught with their hands in the till, the Ugandan government set up a commission of inquiry, presided over by a British judge. There was no question of Rwanda doing likewise. "Rwanda would never have set up a commission to investigate these iniquities because far from being seen as something bad, this was regarded as a noble and exalted part of their mission to rule the Congo," comments Freedman. "The difference came across in the Rwandans' immense secrecy. Uganda was never secretive.

"The Rwandans knew they were doing something atrocious," he adds, "and it was very difficult to get information from them. This was basically a mafia and its members had taken the oath of Omertà."

But as Patrick Smith, one of the panel investigators, discovered, while the head of the Congo Desk might be scrupulously professional, he had little appetite for his role. Over a beer in the gardens of the Umubano Hotel, one of Patrick's favorite places to hold court, greeting a succession of army officers and ministers as they strolled across the lawns, the spy chief shared his misgivings. "The Congo intervention is a mistake," Patrick told Smith. "We have to pull out. It's really hurting us in the region."

"He knew from his travels," recalls Smith, "just how disliked Rwanda had become, how much resentment there was from neighboring countries. He wanted the message to get back to Kagame."

Patrick invited Smith to address a group of youngsters he was training up as intelligence officers. "These were young guys just out of college, wet behind the ears and keen to learn. Patrick wanted me to explain to them exactly why it was that other African countries were hostile to Rwanda. They were saying, 'We're doing a really good job of building up the country after the genocide. Why aren't they more supportive?' So I said that Rwanda was seen as looting the DRC, which got them all outraged."

As the UN panel continued its investigations, Patrick played a risky game. When its authors presented their report in Nairobi, it was Patrick who flew to Kenya to present an impervious brass face. But in Kigali, he was using the investigators' findings—which named specific companies, high-profile Rwandans, their Western collaborators, the flights and export routes used, tonnages, truckloads, and percentages—to highlight the reputational risks of what Rwanda was doing.

"Basically, he'd triangulate our research. He wasn't giving us any material we didn't already have, but the evidence wasn't hard to find. So we would collect all this information and then take it to Patrick, who could then use it to point out to Kagame the folly of Rwanda's policy. He could tell his boss, 'These guys have so much evidence on us, we need to act,'" recalls Smith.

The final UN report came out in October 2002.[5] By then, with their governments facing prosecution at the International Court of Justice in The Hague, Uganda and Rwanda had begun withdrawing their troops. Delving deeper than its precursor, the report made clear that they weren't the only offenders. Both President Laurent Kabila and his son Joseph had bartered mines for Zimbabwean military support and shifted large chunks of what had once been state-owned mining assets into the private sector.

Taking a swipe at the World Bank and bilateral donors for their complicity, the authors recommended making future aid to Burundi, Rwanda, Uganda, and Zimbabwe conditional on their governments pulling out all troops and putting a halt to the looting. Baring its teeth, it recommended that financial sanctions and travel bans be slapped on twenty-nine businesses and fifty-four individuals. Another eighty-five companies were cited as being in violation of Organisation for Economic Co-operation and Development guidelines.

Non-Africans singled out included Russian arms dealer Victor Bout, Zimbabwean businessman John Bredenkamp, and Belgo-Congolese magnate George Forrest. On the Ugandan side, Salim Saleh, his wife Jovia Akandwanaho, James Kazini, and Kahinda Otafiire were all named, while on the Rwandan side the list included Kabarebe, Munyuza, and Nziza—three men who would later attempt to kill Patrick.

Patrick himself is not mentioned in either of the key UN panel's reports. It's a hugely puzzling omission, given that he was widely identified as the Congo Desk's boss—a label he himself always carelessly laughed off. Why not?

The obvious man to turn to for an explanation, panel chairman Mohamed Kaseem, has since died. Freedman's view is that while Patrick, mostly Kigali-based during this period, was nominally head of the Congo Desk, key decisions were being made in DRC by Kabarebe and his underlings. "If Patrick Karegeya's name isn't on the list, it's because it didn't deserve to be." That analysis would fit with Kagame's well-established management technique of assigning the same job to competing players.

Smith's view, shared by diplomats I've spoken to who served in Kigali at the time, is that Patrick was so well known and liked in foreign embassies and in Washington, New York, and London—a man seen, what was more, as having a helpful moderating influence on Kagame—that naming and shaming him in public would be counterproductive.

Whatever the reason, Patrick's omission from the reports could not have gone unnoticed among the men emerging as Kagame's new favorites. Sometimes the very worst thing for an underling is to be proved right. Those involved in drafting the report sometimes ponder the extent to which publication added to the growing distance between the spy chief and an inner circle over which he had once held sway.

"I have this terrible feeling," admits Freedman, "that maybe we were partly responsible for what happened to Patrick Karegeya."

Shortly before the final report came out, under the watchful eye of the UN peacekeeping force dispatched to DRC to separate the key players, the last of the 23,400 Rwandan troops who had illegally occupied the country for four years marched across the frontier at Goma. The exploitation of DRC's resources certainly did not end then, but the days of the Congo Desk were over. "After that," reckons Freedman, "Rwanda became much more discreet. They didn't stop extracting resources, but they made sure it was much less obvious."[6]

CHAPTER SIXTEEN

THIS MAN IS AN EMPEROR

It is a deadly but common misperception to believe that
by displaying and vaunting your gifts and talents, you are
winning the master's affection. He may feign appreciation,
but at his first opportunity he will replace you with someone
less intelligent, less attractive, less threatening.
—**Robert Greene,** *The 48 Laws of Power*

B y the turn of the century, the RPF was a very different crea-
ture from the movement that had once awed and inspired
foreign dignitaries, guilt-ridden policymakers, and Western
journalists.

Whatever crimes the movement had or hadn't committed inside
Rwanda, its interventions in DRC had exposed a casualness to human
life, cavalier ruthlessness, and shocking levels of greed. And at home,
the steady elimination of one civilian politician after another—most
of them Hutus—had removed any convenient fiction as to who, exactly, ran Rwanda and which ethnic community was in pole position.

The collegiate character of the RPF had leached away, and with it
a commitment to bracing self-criticism. "In the early days it was very
normal during meetings to debate openly, to correct fellow cadres

by stating where they had gone wrong," recalls a ministry official.[1] Now even the most mischief-free comment—pointing out failings in Rwanda's health-care system, for example, or mentioning that electricity supplies did not meet the population's needs—meant you risked being branded "an enemy of the state."

Many drew the obvious conclusion: either keep quiet or limit yourself to glowing expressions of admiration for President Kagame. Of course the concentration of power in one man's hands was deeply worrying, the Tutsi elite told itself, "but if he goes, we all go." Unity was vital, Kagame was both champion and mascot.

Returning from Washington, where he had served as ambassador, Theogene Rudasingwa spotted copies of Robert Greene's best-selling *The 48 Laws of Power* lying on the desks of more than one senior RPF officer. "Never outshine the Master" was Law 1. Was that the message on how to deal with Kagame? he wondered.

It was not a rule likely to foster excellence. Indeed, in Kagame's entourage, the adjective "ambitious," which Western graduates will proudly claim during job interviews, was not meant as a compliment. Rather, it was code, Theogene concluded, "for anyone who takes a principled stand and is confident. Interpreted, it means that you are a competitor for the job of President."[2]

A great consumer of gossip and none-too-fussy about its credibility or source, Kagame claimed the right to interpose himself in every aspect of his aides' lives, including their marriages, with at least one senior RPF member told that he was expected to divorce a wife not deemed "pro-Rwandan" enough.

The president's capacity for personalized intimidation usually escaped Western outsiders. When philanthropists, celebrities, pastors, and rabbis met Kagame in Davos, Washington, Brussels, or Addis, what struck them was the hermit-like austerity of Kagame's appearance, the monkish simplicity of his dark shirts and high-collar tunics.

Listening to that quavering voice, they concluded this was no bullying Idi Amin, dependent on sheer physical girth to cow others. Slender as a sheet of paper, the man was virtually two-dimensional, a breeze might lift him off his feet. This was clearly someone who relied on his intellect rather than his fists.

They were mistaken. While Kagame was certainly never regarded as a man of action by his military contemporaries, once he attained the presidency he readily resorted to physical violence to impose his will. Careful to rein in his temper when in polite, international company, he had no compunction about letting fly with colleagues, preferably juniors many grades below him who dared not respond.

With civilians, the treatment was more humiliating than painful. When a cabinet meeting was called, Kagame would often wait behind the door, and anyone who dared arrive late would receive a kick to the buttocks, sending them sprawling. They learned the importance of punctuality.

With members of the armed forces, punishment was more severe. Bodyguard Noble Marara dates his first beating at Kagame's hands back to 1995, when he was driving Fred Rwigyema's jeep, a colleague called Bosco at his side.[3] Reckoning that the vehicle was too old and historically precious to be in active service, he had decided to drive it to Kigali's national museum for safekeeping. On the road, the two men met Kagame's convoy.

He's still not sure what triggered the outburst, but anything involving Fred, the superhero to whom so many RPF officers constantly compared Kagame, could spark unpredictable reactions. Spotting the jeep, Kagame stopped the two men, ordered them out, and started kicking Marara, then beating him with a stick, before instructing his escorts to take over. The beating went on so long, an RPF officer who was passing actually stopped to remonstrate.

"At one point Bosco was struggling to breathe," says Marara. "Kagame got scared. So he tried to justify himself by saying that we weren't properly uniformed. I was covered in bruises and bleeding. Bosco had to go to hospital."

The next occasion was three years later, in 1998, when Museveni was due to visit Rwanda and Marara was allotted responsibility for vetting the district in which the Ugandan president would be spending the night. The evening before, an army driver had reversed into a street lamp lining the route, and Kagame immediately spotted the damage on inspection the following day.

"He asked who was in charge of road safety and I was pointed out. 'You call yourself head of transport and you didn't see this?' he said. He told me to kneel. And then he started kicking me."

Marara couldn't quite believe what was happening. "I had a pistol on me, and he was kicking me! I said, 'This guy is not right in the head! I have a gun on me, I'm the one who drives his convoy, I'm loyal to him, and he's kicking me.'" The punishment seemed to last forever. When Kagame finally stopped, he told Marara to repair the street lamp, and then he left.

Kagame's behavior seemed almost calculated to lose him the support of the army rank and file. How could Marara help but compare that incident with his last encounter with Fred, who had spoken so compassionately to his brother as he lay dying in a Ugandan hospital?

There was always a sense with Kagame that he was tamping down some roiling, inexplicable fury, barely reining in something vast and vicious. "He can't control his anger," says General Kayumba. "You can see it in the media interviews he gives—he becomes almost mad with rage."

James Kabarebe, who, like Marara, started off as one of Kagame's bodyguards but rose to become Rwanda's army chief of staff, would regularly be slapped across the face by Kagame when the latter was disappointed with his force's performance. He would do it in front of Kabarebe's men, heedless of the impact such public humiliation would have on discipline or morale.

"I have seen Kagame beat James Kabarebe countless times," the General told me. "Hitting him, punching him, throwing things at him, all in full view of the troops. James was a force commander at the time. If Kagame was doing that to his aide de camp, imagine what he was doing to the others."

When the insurgency in northwestern Rwanda was at its height and security forces in the Ruhengeri area were being caught off guard by Hutu infiltrators, Kagame personally set out to stiffen backbones. Around 1,500 soldiers and gendarmes were ordered to assemble at Mukamira barracks, and the then defence minister drove in, followed by a Tata lorry under military police escort. It was loaded with whips. As the troops watched in stunned silence, Kagame systematically whipped his senior commanders, while his military police meted out the same punishment to the junior officers.

"Some fifty to sixty commanders were whipped," says former major Jean-Marie Micombero. An RPF stalwart working as a trainer at the Nyakinama Gendarmerie School at the time, he witnessed the whole ugly incident. "It took the entire afternoon. Officers beaten in front of their own subordinates. . . . It went against every principle of leadership."[4]

Close colleagues grew so accustomed to Kagame's rages that they came to seem almost normal behavior, a personal quirk. But when those outside the charmed inner circle first encountered it, they wondered if he was completely sane.

Emmanuel Habyarimana—no relation to the former president—was one of the precious group of Francophone Hutu officers who switched allegiances following the genocide, taking to heart the RPF's message of ethnic integration. Joining the new Rwandan army, he rose to the position of brigadier general and in 2000 was appointed minister of defence. That year he accompanied Kagame to one of the army's regular meetings in Ruhengeri, get-togethers at which members of the top brass were meant to exchange notes, air problems, and discuss strategy.

The episode is engraved on his memory. Kagame, who was supposed to chair the get-together, arrived in an inexplicably filthy temper. "He got up, addressed the first man: 'You, Third Battalion Commander, what have you done?' and then he kicked him," says Habyarimana. "With the next man it was, 'You, Brigade Commander, what's your name?' and he was kicked, too. He worked his way across the room, kicking and punching each one."[5]

Kagame was flanked by armed Republican Guards while the generals and commanders had all, following protocol, handed in their weapons at the door. Not daring to lift a finger to defend themselves, these battle-hardened senior military men backed off. As each blow landed, they were herded like frightened sheep into a corner of the room.

"Then Kagame reached a sturdy, beefy major, a really big man, and tried to shove him," recalls Habyarimana. "But he wasn't going anywhere. At that point I intervened. I said, 'This is too much.'" Kagame seemed to come to his senses, the meeting was abruptly canceled, and Kagame and Habyarimana left together.

As they headed out, the shocked Habyarimana admonished his boss, telling Kagame he had been within a hair's breadth of getting them all killed. "If that big guy had reacted, then the Republican Guard would have opened fire, an officer might well have decided to go down fighting, seized a Republican Guard weapon, and everyone could have died in the resulting chaos, yourself included," he said.

"Ach," replied the disgusted Kagame, "they won't do anything unless you beat them."

"But is it right to beat them even when they're off-duty?" remonstrated Habyarimana. "There's a legal procedure for punishing officers who have committed misdemeanors."

"Yes, even then, that way they know when they go into action that if they retreat they will be either killed or beaten," replied his unrepentant boss.

A year later, in November 2002, Habyarimana was removed from his post. Accused by the government of "extreme pro-Hutu views," he fled to Switzerland. He still marvels over what he witnessed. "Backing battalion commanders, brigade commanders into a corner . . . " he shakes his head. "What I saw in Ruhengeri was abnormal, unacceptable, unjustifiable." Some might call it extreme bullying. Habyarimana applies another term: "It was a form of internal terrorism."

Habyarimana, like Marara, still wonders what triggered Kagame's outburst, but a behavioral psychologist might suggest such questions are a waste of time. The utility of such violence lies in its very unpredictability. For the autocrat, like the corporate bully, soccer coach, or abusive husband, the aim is to become their victims' fixation. Browbeat a subordinate relentlessly enough, keep them constantly off-balance, and their curiosity dries up and confidence shrivels, replaced by a single concern: avoiding censure.

•

In 2001, Patrick took the plunge. "I've done my part and I want to go back to school," he told Kagame.

What he had failed to appreciate was that membership of the RPF was a one-way affair. Like the guests in the Eagles' Hotel California, you could check out anytime you liked, but you could never, *actually*, leave. As with Museveni's NRA, the Mafia, or many a secret society, once you went in, you did not come out.

"Until I find someone to replace you, you stay," Kagame told Patrick. No question of being inside or outside the tent: the flap had been zipped up in his face. "I'm resigning, but this man is not allowing me," Patrick complained to his wife. "So he stayed there," Leah recalls, "but you could see he was bitter."

The final point of contention between the two former school-mates would involve neither domestic nor foreign policy. Its well-spring would be Kagame's abiding terror of being deposed, and its focus, this time, was General Kayumba.

In August of that year, the General, now army chief of staff, left Rwanda on a yearlong training course in military strategy and security at the Royal Military College of Science in Shrivenham, taking up an offer made to the Rwandan government by the British Ministry of Defence.

He had been offered similar training opportunities before, but, busy fighting the insurgency in the northwest and then sucked into DRC, had repeatedly postponed. Now Kagame encouraged him to take up the offer, and he was relieved to take a break from Kigali's febrile, unhappy climate. That year in Oxfordshire, which he shared with his youngest son, would be one of the happiest of his life.

His departure suited both men, for General Kayumba, like Patrick, was making the torturous journey from trusted comrade to suspected challenger. Kagame had not forgotten his chief of staff's stance on Pasteur Bizimungu's removal, or his skepticism concerning Congo's Second War. The General's departure followed hot on the heels of an argument over army operations in DRC.

Rivals—mostly Kabarebe, Nziza, and Ndahiro—were whispering in Kagame's ear. The commander who would later effortlessly charm his South African bodyguards was immensely popular in the ranks. Too popular. The General had been building his own structures within the armed forces, they told Kagame, forming relationships with officers loyal to him and him alone.

When Kagame's personal helicopter pilot flew his aircraft to Kampala in March 2002, never to return, it was said he had declared he would take orders only from the General. It was exactly the kind of behavior Kagame had made it his business to root out back in the Ugandan bush, the kind that might well signal the buildup to a future military coup. It would hardly be the first time in African history a charismatic army chief of staff had developed ideas above his station.

Kagame did the obvious thing and turned to his super-smart head of external intelligence, Patrick, for both corroboration and a plan to neutralize the supposed threat.

"They wanted to take Kayumba to an island, throw away the key, and let him die of hunger," recalls Leah. But her husband was not playing ball. "Patrick was adamant. He didn't believe it. 'Where did you get that?' he told Kagame. For Kagame to think he should eliminate Kayumba, that was beyond Patrick."

The General was completely loyal, Patrick assured his president. Anything he'd been hearing to the contrary was simply malicious gossip by envious colleagues. Why should the RPF inflict such damage upon itself? "Why turn on our own people?" Patrick protested.

In the normal course of events, the coup plot story should have ended there. The man whose day job was to spot and preempt threats to national security had dismissed as nonsense one of the more fantastical of the many rumors that crossed the president's desk. Instead, Kagame reached for an explanation that fed his incipient paranoia. Since Patrick had denied the coup story, Patrick must be in on the plot, too.

●

Today the exiled General Kayumba is doing exactly what Kagame once suspected he would: training a militia in eastern Congo and gathering around him a loose coalition of both Hutus and Tutsis determined to oust his former boss. But at the turn of the century, were Kagame's suspicions well founded? Or did he, in the ultimate of ironies, inadvertently bring about exactly the outcome he feared?

Researching this book, I asked serving and dissident members of the RPF, Rwandan and Western journalists, diplomats, intelligence officers, and military attachés whether they had ever stumbled across concrete evidence the General plotted in the late 1990s and early 2000s to challenge and oust Kagame. The answer I got was always no.

Kigali's presentation of the General and Patrick as Rwanda's equivalent of Brutus and Cassius, turning unexpectedly on their employer and friend—high-profile players inexplicably turned rogue—is undermined, first and foremost, by the simple record of events.

The series of official reprimands, punishments, and humiliations handed out to the two men over time doesn't gel with the scenario of a suddenly exposed plot. Kagame's response to that would have been sudden and crushing. Instead the slow escalation speaks of a leader's determination to administer a painful lesson to uppity subordinates, demonstrating exactly who was boss. A slow war of attrition, cuff after cuff, spelling out a message: "Know your place."

A telling, if intangible piece of evidence in their defense is a certain tone of voice. Interviewing Patrick or the General after they fell from grace, you heard the same distinctive, plaintive note, one echoed over lunches and coffees by their wives and close relatives, still stunned by their sidelining. It's the sound of baffled personal hurt. "We were loyal," it says. "You were our friend." "How could you do this to us?"

Would a colleague caught in the act of plotting his boss's overthrow feel wounded in this way? Wouldn't the tone be different: self-justificatory, defiant, a tad shamefaced?

Other elements undermine the treason scenario. The very ingredients that made the two men potentially formidable opponents ensured they were unlikely to break with the system. From the tactics Kagame had used to rise to the top of the RPF to the invasions of DRC, their itineraries were so closely woven with Kagame's that it was almost impossible to separate one from the other. As Noble Marara told me, "If there are two men who made Kagame, it's Kayumba and Karegeya." They were implicated, up to the hilt, and they knew it.

Finally, no one was better placed than the heads of ESO and the NISS to grasp just how certain Kagame was to detect the merest whisper of treachery. "They may have harbored doubts, nursed ideas, but they would not have been such fools as to think they could aim for Kagame and survive," says a Western intelligence operative who spent years in Kigali.[6]

"I still know some of the guys in Rwandan intelligence, and even in the depths of the Congolese forests they have never been heard to utter a word of criticism of the boss. They know it would be back at headquarters within seconds. These were smart guys. They knew exactly how effective the Rwandan intelligence network was, what they would be risking, and what the price would be."

Why, then, given the paucity of incriminating evidence, did Kagame nonetheless target both men?

There are echoes of Macbeth, the Scottish warlord whose rise to power leaves a trail of blood, in the tale. In Shakespeare's play, one of the most insightful studies of power ever written, Banquo is unfortunate enough to be present when three witches articulate his friend's

darkest secret: his vaulting ambition. Ha
murderous hunger, Banquo is doomed.

Patrick and the General had known Kag
demigod at home and abroad, when he wa
unpopular one at that. At the back of their
memory of a gawky school dropout who had be
becoming a street boy. For that, he could not forgive th
venting himself as a visionary leader who had liberated Rwanda
sis virtually single-handedly, he increasingly wanted to be surrounded
by impressionable young acolytes who had no memory of his falter-
ing early steps. "It's not good to know a lot of things about people,"
Leah recalls Fred Rwigyema's mother once telling Patrick.

One can't help wondering whether the coup plot was just something Kagame wanted to believe of two contemporaries blessed with
the easy assurance that came with being better educated, from more
prosperous backgrounds, happier families, men who had spent
childhoods at ease in their joint Ugandan-Rwandan identities. He
had always felt twitchy and insecure compared to the General and
Patrick; now they would learn their place.

In revealing his readiness to target the General, what was more,
Kagame had exposed the full extent of his monstrous insecurity to a
confidant. "It became a complicated thing," recalls Leah. "Kagame
became afraid because Patrick knew his intentions." Eliminating the
General would not suffice; Patrick would also have to go.

My intelligence source sees something more calculating at work,
too. Kagame, he says, is the past master of what he calls "the Beria
method of rule," in memory of Stalin's ruthless secret police chief,
Lavrentiy Beria. "Show me the man and I'll find you the crime," was
one of Beria's catchphrases. Nothing sowed terror in the inner circle
quite as effectively as targeting men and women everyone had believed loyal, forcing them to publicly confess their crimes.

"If you want to keep everyone on their toes, you make sure they
never know who is in or out of favor," he explains. "And if you want
to remain in power a *very* long time you have to go after not just your
enemies, but also your friends, and you even go one step further by
going after people who haven't done anything, who are beyond reproach, models of behavior."

...d goes out: No one is safe. "People end up afraid of their
...ows, suspicious of their oldest friends. It's a very cynical tac-
...e acknowledges. "And it works very well indeed."

•

Patrick seized the opportunity of a trip to London to visit General Kayumba at his training course in Shrivenham. As his friend
showed him round the large British army compound, Patrick briefed
him on the rumors circulating in Kigali. Both men grew somber.

"When I come home I'll ask for retirement," said the General.

"Maybe I'll beat you to it and retire before you do," said Patrick,
with a sad laugh.

But on his return to Kigali in August 2002, the General had exactly the same experience as Patrick. "I came back from the UK and
said, 'I want to retire.' But Kagame said, 'You can't go.'"

Instead the discontents found themselves working together. Bent
on distancing the General from his adoring troops, Kagame appointed him head of the newly established National Intelligence and
Security Service. As the long-standing director general of Rwanda's
external intelligence, Patrick now answered to him. The move seems
counterintuitive, but Kagame, the General believes, a genius of
divide-and-rule, was confident he could undermine the friendship.

"He thought he could play us against each other," says the General. "He tried to build a wedge during this period, trying to frame
Patrick on a number of occasions, bad-mouthing him, telling me he
was disloyal, had misused money—yet Patrick was not in control of
finances. It never worked."

Within days, the two men committed a social faux pas that
lodged in the presidential mind under the category of "Unforgivable
Slights." They made the mistake of throwing a party for Fred Rwigyema's widow.

Following Fred's death, the senior cadres of both the NRM and
the RPF had clustered protectively around Jeannette Gisa and her
children. Bathed in her husband's retrospective glow, Jeannette was
venerated by some of the younger officers, hungry for heroes. As
one of Fred's closest friends, Kagame might have been expected to
show special interest in her welfare. Instead, he seemed threatened
by Jeannette's very existence, convinced she was encouraging the

birth of a personality cult that could only reflect badly on him. And he suspected Salim Saleh, Fred's old friend in Uganda, of using her as his "eyes and ears" in Kigali.

Soon after moving to Kigali, Leah had set up an international travel agency with Jeannette, and it had proved popular with government departments and ministries. Then Leah received a call from Kagame that surprised her. He complained that her business partner was bad-mouthing him.

"I know some soldiers are making her think she's very important," he said. "I'm going to step on your business because she is talking about me."

Alarmed, hoping this was just a joke, Leah appealed for leniency. "This woman has been widowed at a young age. Give her a chance," she begged.

The response was flat. "No, I can't. She's been talking about me. When I think about her it gives me heartburn."

The party General Kayumba and Patrick threw was staged to celebrate Jeannette's graduation from the Kigali Institute of Science and Technology. Leah issued the invitations, with the president's name top of the list. He did not attend. Kagame would have guessed that any event thrown in Jeannette's honor would blur into an emotional commemoration of Fred. "He was annoyed that we had created a platform for her and encouraged other people to honor her," says the General. "His policy was always to isolate her."

A party snubbed, a celebration ignored. It should have been a trivial incident, but it underlined just how thoroughly out of favor the two men had fallen.

Western friends who dropped in to see Patrick around this time noticed a change in his appearance. The sleek, professional suits had been replaced by garish, loose-fitting Hawaiian shirts unbuttoned to the breastbone. The new look would have been appropriate for a vacationer sipping a piña colada on a Brazilian beach. In the somber Rwandan context, where individualism and ostentation were frowned upon, it represented a covert "fuck you" gesture to authority.

"He certainly didn't look the RPF part," remembers *Africa Confidential*'s Patrick Smith. The heavy drinking, too, jarred. "In a country where the head of intelligence is drinking quite a lot, and has friends like me, there's going to be trouble." Patrick's laughter had acquired a bitter edge. His lippiness no longer sounded like a bit of fun, excitingly risqué. It felt positively self-destructive, a verbalized form of self-harm.

•

In 2003, Rwanda was due to hold its first presidential elections since the genocide, the first multiparty polls in its history. It was heralded as a fragile, post-conflict state's initial tentative step on the democracy ladder, but for RPF cadres increasingly skeptical about the regime's trajectory, the episode was hardly reassuring.

A few weeks before the vote, General Kayumba was invited by Theogene Rudasingwa to Kagame's office for a meeting. There he found a group of RPF heavyweights—Patrick, Ndahiro, Rutaremara, Kabarebe, and Kayonga, plus the chairman of the National Electoral Commission, Professor Chrysologue Karangwa.

No one present, according to the General, bothered to pay so much as lip service to the notion of noninterference in the results. "The topic of the meeting was, 'What should the percentage of the elections be?' The chairman of the electoral commission brought the question up. 'What do you want us to have?' he asked. 'We' as in 'We, the RPF.'"

Patrick piped up. "We should get 65 percent," he said. "We need an opposition and we need the electoral process to have credibility."

Kabarebe, predictably, disagreed: "You're talking nonsense," he told Patrick. "*Afande*"—the boss—"should get 100 percent."

The arguments raged this way and that. "But by the time we left the office we had all agreed to settle for 70 percent," says the General. Patrick had largely won the argument. It was the canny thing to do. "But later I bumped into Kabarebe and he was hemming and hawing and saying, 'Oh, 100 percent is just a number.'"[7]

After former prime minister Twagiramungu announced he was returning from Brussels to run as a candidate, his political party, the Republican Democratic Movement (MDR), found itself banned on the grounds of "divisionism," and Twagiramungu publicly accused of sharing the *génocidaires'* ideology of extermination. The party had been in coalition with the RPF for years, but apparently no one had noticed until then.

Twagiramungu was forced to run as an independent, and his campaign leaflets were seized; his provincial campaign managers were arrested and paraded on television, where they denounced their former leader. On the eve of the election, Twagiramungu showed *The Economist*'s reporter in Kigali a letter he'd received from one of them: "I'm so sorry, but I have to stay alive," it read.[8]

Notwithstanding all the pressure, when the votes came in they gave Twagiramungu a bigger share than the RPF was willing to concede. And so an urgent call was put through to the Ministry of Defence: vote-stuffers needed. One of those involved was Major Jean-Marie Micombero.

"The problem was that the computer was saying Kagame had won so many votes, but the actual votes kept coming in and they didn't tally. A lot of soldiers were called in to sit issuing fake votes."

"Did you take part?" I ask Micombero.

"All the soldiers did, because a lot of votes were required. And at a certain point, these fake votes had been loaded into a truck and they were being taken to headquarters when there was an accident: the truck was upset and the fake votes spilled all over the tarmac. The road had to be closed and a military barricade set up, to stop anyone noticing. *C'était comique.*"

The General recalls that in certain areas, soldiers did their job too well. "In some places we were registering final tallies of 110 percent for Kagame, because of all the vote-stuffing and because people were repeat-voting two, three, as many as four times."

The final total gave Kagame 95.1 percent, leaving Twagiramungu—who might have been expected to benefit from sharing the ethnicity of most of the population—with less than 4 percent. Many Hutus would have voted for Kagame, Twagiramungu acknowledges, "not because they like him but because they fear him," but he still dismisses the results as a joke. "They ritually humiliated me by saying I'd only won 3 percent overall and 0.6 percent in my own district."

Patrick's advice had been ignored, and Kagame had given himself a tally only a handful of percentage points short of the 98.9 percent his predecessor, Habyarimana, had routinely claimed in the polls.

A Western ambassador who had befriended Patrick before being reassigned rang from his new posting to offer entirely ironic congratulations. "But only 95 percent, Patrick?" he quipped. "Next time, I'm sure you'll do better." Patrick's response was equally sardonic, the humor of the not-funny-at-all variety. "And next time you come to Kigali, we'll kill you."[9]

Foreign donors were well aware of what had transpired. But they allowed themselves to be convinced by the RPF argument that a society struggling to heal the genocide's wounds was simply not ready for majority rule. The Tutsi minority's safety came first. "After failing Rwanda in 1994, the international community did so again in 2003 by allowing a dictatorship to take hold," commented Reyntjens.[10]

•

Ironically, that meeting to get everyone to agree on the extent of Rwanda's electoral rigging had been called by a player who was also reaching the end of his tether. His career—like General Kayumba's and Patrick's—was also about to go into screeching reverse.

Among the RPF stalwarts who ended up in opposition, no one can quite rival Theogene Rudasingwa for his combination of suavity and elegance. "Le beau Theogene," Francophone reporters dubbed him at the height of his powers, while their American counterparts preferred "the Gucci Guerrilla."

Softly spoken, surprisingly pale skinned, and gently melancholic, he is a man with a track record of passionate affiliation often regretted and painfully renounced. A lapsed doctor who only recently rediscovered the joys of medicine, he is a dedicated Marxist who came to relish the perks of high office, a Christian who lost his faith but was Born Again, a man who swore off politics only to end up wading back into the fray.

The elegance must be innate, because Theogene's upbringing could scarcely have been tougher. His youth was spent in a refugee camp set up in a stretch of land in western Uganda that was later semi-abandoned because it was infested with tsetse flies.

Having lost their father in grotesquely violent circumstances—all Theogene ever knew was that his father had been crucified from a post during Muyaga—he and brother Gerald Gahima were raised by their widowed mother, who at one stage walked the family all the way from western Uganda to Burundi in search of a better life, only to decide things were tougher there and trudge all the way back. The first time Theogene ever wore shoes, or slept on a mattress, was at secondary school.

He did well enough there to qualify for a medical course at Makerere, a place he could only take up by pretending to be a Ugandan citizen: a friend of a friend agreed to stand in as fictional father. Such humiliations lingered. "Being a refugee dehumanises and therefore politicizes," he later wrote. An angry young man, he hung pictures of Lenin and Mao on his bedroom wall, picturing himself as an African Che Guevara, another doctor turned revolutionary.

When the Obote regime began persecuting Rwandan refugees and Ugandan citizens of Banyarwanda origin in the early 1980s, the newfound Marxist fantasized—like many other Banyarwanda—about joining Museveni's NRM. But he had a widowed mother to care for and a medical course to complete.

Since his brother Gerald had been one of RANU's founding members, strenuous attempts were made to recruit him to the RPF. But Theogene, by temperament an outsider, found the movement's expectation that every refugee would join "militaristic, condescending, and overbearing." He was viewed in the diaspora, he recalls, as "an eccentric dissenter."

It was only when "the boys" crossed over in October 1990 that he relented, one of the many Banyarwanda youngsters inspired by Fred Rwigyema, a man he'd never met. The last of three siblings to sign up, he joined a group of similarly minded refugees driving to the border. After a few weeks of rushed military training in the Akagera Park, he was recruited by an RPF medical unit administering rough-and-ready treatment to the wounded fighters pouring in.

Once the RPF moved to the Virunga Mountains and began notching up its first serious victories, his articulacy ensured that he became a de facto rebel diplomat. He flew, for instance, to Addis Ababa, to convince African delegates at OAU headquarters that the RPF was a multiethnic movement bent on a peaceful resolution to Rwanda's long-running refugee problem. Theogene was also a member of the RPF's negotiating team in Arusha, becoming aware in the process that both sides nursed profound misgivings about the pledges they were making.

With the fall of the Habyarimana government, Theogene was appointed RPF secretary-general and then dispatched to Washington as ambassador—a key position for a movement that needed, in light of Francophone hostility, to make a friend of the United States. He remembers, with a rueful laugh, loyally peddling to a series of US and UN officials in Washington and New York the line that the RPF had heroically intervened to stop a genocide started by Hutu extremists who had killed their own president. "I was a very effective salesman of that narrative. I charmed them all."

Playing the guilt card to silence criticism of Kigali's foreign and domestic policy was always a key part of his diplomatic tool kit, he acknowledges, and it was not—as I'd assumed—inspired by Israel's example. "That one, I was very much responsible for," Theogene says. "We didn't learn that from anyone, it was an instinct. For years we've done it very effectively, because it really intimidates people. The Americans, the Brits, they become cowed by guilt."

He adds, "There's the genocide and 'Never Again'—therefore we have a passport to do whatever we can to prevent a repeat—and then there's 'Where were you?' It's really a very cynical ploy."

When the time came to justify breaking up the refugee camps in Zaire, while adamantly denying Rwandan involvement, he did that, too, although there was always a nudge-nudge wink-wink quality to those conversations: "There was a kind of unspoken and unwritten understanding among the people I dealt with, like Susan Rice, Gayle Smith, John Prendergast, Ted Dagne, that we all knew what the truth was."

Recalled to Kigali in 1999, he was appointed Kagame's chief of staff. Like many of his colleagues, he'd been experiencing misgivings for years, but had suppressed his doubts in the name of ethnic solidarity. The systems and institutions being established, they told themselves, would rein in Kagame's burgeoning autocratic tendencies.

"'It was in all our interest,' we used to say. The Tutsi had to rally behind Kagame. His habits would gradually decline as the institutions grew stronger," Theogene recalls. And there was an element of the Emperor's New Clothes about the relationship between Kagame and his coterie. "The question you put to yourself at the time was, 'Will I be the first person to rock the boat?'"

But the time at Kagame's side made it impossible to continue harboring any illusions about the nature of the regime. "There wasn't a particular moment when I lost faith in the RPF project, it was over a period. The run-up to the 2003 elections left me with a very bad appetite." Frantz Fanon's *The Wretched of the Earth*, with its description of how the party becomes entrenched, the leader unchallengeable, kept coming to mind. "I said in my heart, 'We've become like all the things we used to read about.'"

He examined his own behavior and did not like what he saw. The punishing hours he and other RPF cadres put in—up at dawn, attending meetings until late into the night, on permanent standby for "the Boss's" call—he realized, had served to keep awkward questions at bay. "You remember Boxer, the horse, in Orwell's *Animal Farm*, who says, 'I work hard'? We were like him. We worked hard, and while we were working, Kagame was plotting."

At the end of 2003, his brother was forced to resign. Gerald Gahima's involvement in high-profile cases involving requisitioned Hutu estates had made him deeply unpopular, with accusations flying that he had abused his position to get rich. Theogene also found himself accused of corruption, in a quasi-comic case centering on new bathtubs for the presidential villa.

He was eventually cleared, but knew it was time to leave. It would take three humiliating trips to the airport in Kigali before the authorities allowed him to board a flight. He headed with his family for the United States. His first time there, he'd been a rebel envoy, and then he had returned as ambassador. Now he was a refugee again.

•

In March 2004, Patrick was removed as head of external intelligence—the job, painfully, went to his nemesis, Emmanuel Ndahiro, and Patrick was appointed lowly "army spokesman." It was a vertiginous, dizzying demotion for a man on first-name terms with almost every senior intelligence official, defence minister, and head of state in sub-Saharan Africa.

"You have to work hard now, as things are going to be tough," Patrick warned his wife.

Rwandans call what he was experiencing *agatebe*—"being placed on your stool," "benched." A previously high-ranking official is given what is clearly a non-job, a token position, in which he or she might have to report to work each day, but actually has nothing of any significance to do.

"They'd bring him his papers and he'd work from home," recalls Leah. "But you could see he'd lost morale." *Agatebe* can last for months, or for years, and it's the moment when many a feisty government official learns to swallow his pride and turn dutiful sycophant. But not Patrick.

In January 2005, General Kayumba was appointed ambassador to India. Recognizing the posting for what it was—a luxury-embossed version of *agatebe*—the General accepted that his brilliant military career lay behind him and that, in the way of his Tutsi forefathers, he had become homeless once more.

"When I became ambassador I thought I'd never go back," he says. The General had been a promising student once, star of his university cohort, and he toyed now with the notion of returning to academia. While there was a sense of relief—the game was over—his departure from Kigali was laced with menace. "When you go to India I'll arrest your friend," Kagame told him before he boarded his flight.

•

Instead Patrick was sent on a four-month field training course at the military college in Ruhengeri. Run by Robert Higiro, the course was designed to prepare junior officers for positions of command, so Patrick, as a full colonel who had already held some of the highest intelligence posts in the land, was senior to those teaching him.

Patrick would have been the first to admit he had received only the sketchiest military training in his youth, thanks to his trajectory from Luzira prison straight into the bush. But as Robert acknowledges, "It was a form of punishment. He was way past the right rank and age to be on that course. If he'd still been on good terms with Kagame, he wouldn't have come." Kagame was underlining how low in the hierarchy Patrick really sat.

Someone with a bigger ego might have staged a sustained sulk. Not Patrick. The least natural of soldiers, he had nonetheless always enjoyed the company of military men and was ready to absorb new skills. Robert was impressed by Patrick's determination to knuckle down and do a good job.

"All military courses are testing, and on those courses, everything comes out. There are nights with no sleep, lots of planning strategy and developing tactical concepts while keeping watch—it puts you on your mettle," says Robert. "Patrick didn't throw his weight around, he took it all in good spirits and didn't lose his motivation. I saw how hardworking he was, how he didn't like to fail."

"He was a brilliant student," he adds. "That's when we became friends."

But the course coincided with a devastating personal loss. Patrick received news that his father, the man who had prophetically warned his son against getting embroiled in Rwandan politics, had died. Patrick asked for permission to travel to Mbarara for the burial. As an outspoken patriarch respected in his local community, John Kanimba's send-off would be a major event, and the son who had most obviously "done good" would be expected to preside over ceremonies. The request was refused.

On his return to Kigali from Ruhengeri, where he graduated in the top three of the class, Patrick fell sick with malaria. It was at this moment of vulnerability that the authorities chose to move in. On April 30, 2005, Leah was out buying plane tickets for her elder children to fly to South Africa, where they were due to attend school, when Patrick phoned. "Come back home," he told her. On arrival, she found a military truck at the gate and soldiers inside the house. While Patrick sweated in bed—"he was very, very sick," Leah recalls—the soldiers had made themselves at home, settling down to watch soccer on the family's giant television set.

"They've come to take me to prison," Patrick told Leah.

"What, prison, when you're sick?" She was stunned.

"I'm going and I don't know when I'm coming back," he told her. "Pack me a bag, some jackets and some books."

Leah panicked, uncertain what to tell the children, aged between seven and thirteen at the time. "My mind went completely blank. I told the driver to take the kids to a relative's house. I didn't want them to see Patrick being loaded onto a military truck."

There was more than a touch of ritual humiliation about the style of Patrick's arrest. A civilian car would have sufficed. The decision to dispatch, instead, a military truck and army unit underlined that as far as the authorities were concerned, there was no difference between Patrick and one of the homeless regularly scooped up and taken to "reeducation centers" for littering Kigali's neat streets.

"I never thought Dad *could* be arrested," Patrick's youngest son, Richard, told me. And that was precisely the point. "You're just like everyone else," Kagame was effectively telling his old friend. And in modern Rwanda, being "just like everyone else" meant you could be taken away at any moment.

"Dad is on a course," Leah told Portia, Elvis, and Richard. But after a week the story was in the newspapers, and Richard, attending primary school in Kigali, came home crying: "Mummy, Mummy, my friends say Daddy is in prison."

Leah called General Charles Kayonga, an old family friend. Kayonga was a former Makerere graduate who had fought with the NRA in the Ugandan bush, like Patrick, and Patrick had once been legal guardian to Kayonga's wife. The response chilled Leah to the bone: "You have nothing to do with Patrick. Patrick belongs to us," Charles Kayonga told her. "This is our soldier. Take care of your children." The RPF system was claiming its own.

When the Western media expressed astonishment at the arrest, the response exposed just how much irritation at Patrick's entire attitude, rather than any serious misdemeanor, lay at the core of his problems. "He has persistently been indisciplined and crossed the expected line of the RDF disciplinary Code of Conduct," James Kabarebe told local journalists. Patrick, he said, had used an authorized trip to South Africa as a chance to make an unexplained stopover in Kenya. On more than one occasion he had been warned about his behavior and advised to change, but had failed to comply. "We do not believe in heroism or untouchables."[11]

A few days later, Leah was contacted by a military official, who told her Patrick was not eating: his mouth was full of ulcers. She was allowed to take provisions to her ailing husband, and in the process discovered where he was being held: a safe house up in the mountains without electricity or running water. The guards had taken away his precious books—even newspapers were forbidden. "He was sitting there in the bush, with just a small radio. He would listen to comedy plays on the BBC World Service," Leah says.

It was to be the only marital visit allowed. Desperately worried about Patrick's health, Leah asked to see the president. But only Jeannette Kagame would meet with her. During their conversation, a curious grievance suddenly broke the surface of the vast sea of presidential pique. As Leah pleaded with the First Lady for clemency, her business relationship with Jeannette Gisa, Fred's widow, came up once again.

"You people deserve it," Jeannette told Leah. "We tried to warn you about Fred Rwigyema and you didn't listen to us. If my husband wasn't a tolerant man, you could be dead by now." Leah attempted to placate her: "I didn't realize it was this serious," she said. "If Patrick has done wrong, I'll ask him to make amends." As for the partnership with Fred's widow, she promised to end it.

Leah had paid ritual obeisance, just as the Kagames wanted, but she had not consulted Patrick beforehand, and he was furious. Her husband's jokey exterior, she was beginning to register, concealed a core almost as steely and implacable as the president's own. "I passed on the First Lady's message and Patrick sent me a note saying, 'Please don't ever go to beg on my behalf. If you do that I'd rather not find you at home when I return.'"

Patrick's mother, Jane Keshoro, also did what she could, traveling from Mbarara to Kigali to appeal to Kagame's mother, Asteria, asking her to persuade the boy who had never made eye contact when he'd come visiting to relent. It was a fruitless mission. The mother was as nonplussed by Kagame's behavior as his colleagues, and there was a hint of genuine fear about her response. "This one, I cannot call him and he comes," said the old lady. "I cannot control him."

As the weeks passed without news, many in the Rwandan elite assumed Patrick had been killed. In fact, this was Kagame's version of a light rap across the knuckles. In September, after five long months, completely out of the blue, Patrick came home. "He was okay," recalls Leah. "He had accepted the situation and while he was there had made friends with his guards, the boys looking after him."

No charges were pressed, no explanation given. Patrick had simply undergone a common experience in post-genocide Rwanda in which citizens suddenly "disappeared." Some were released without a scratch; others were beaten, tortured, or executed. Unpredictability was precisely what made the technique so effective: it kept everyone permanently on edge.

Patrick was called to the presidential office, where he found both Kagame and Kabarebe. The head of state, it emerged, had been surprised and irritated to discover just how many times visiting African dignitaries or Western envoys, once their business was complete, would ask after Patrick, notable by his absence.

"Who do you think you are?" Kagame said. "Everywhere I go, people are asking about you."

"I was not there," Patrick replied. "So how can I answer for it?"

"We hope you have learned a lesson," said Kagame.

"What lesson?" replied Patrick.

It was not, Leah admits, the required response. "Such answers made Kagame think, 'You're not understanding why you were detained.'"

Later James Kabarebe invited Patrick to his residence. To Kagame's Bad Cop, he now played Good Cop. "Look, all of us are suffering. Give me something to tell him," he begged. Patrick, he said, should write Kagame a groveling apology, simultaneously requesting a job. "If I were you I would crawl down and apologize."

The contest had entered a new stage in which pure ego, rather than loyalty, was at stake: Kagame required acknowledgment of his absolute mastery. It was Rwanda's version of the confessions Stalin demanded from old Bolshevik party leaders during the Moscow show trials. Eat crow, in public, and some modicum of mercy might be shown.

"Kagame has that method," says Leah. "You are imprisoned and then you are released and then you apologize and you are allowed to go away and take a small job and submit. But Patrick wouldn't do that. Patrick was not shaken at all; if anything, he was even more firm."

"That is you, that is not me," he told Kabarebe. "There is nothing I have to say to him."

Such sustained defiance signaled more trouble ahead. The massively insecure Kagame had never believed that Patrick, smarter and funnier than himself, could accept him as a president, says Leah: "When he didn't apologize, it confirmed it. After that there were no more jobs."

Personal dignity comes at a price in Rwanda. Kagame would devote a surprising amount of energy to demonstrating just how high that price could go, and into what tiny shards a totalitarian state—relentless as a tarmac tamper—can crush the individual.

In Britain, "being sent to Coventry" is a euphemism for society's decision to ostracize a disruptive individual. In France they talk about "*mettre quelqu'un en quarantaine*" (placing someone in quarantine). In Eritrea, when a former party member has fallen from presidential grace, it's called "being frozen." Rwandans talk, instead, of *akato*—a boating term—"to be afloat, adrift." A slim canoe buffeted on an ocean of community fear.

When you are *akato*, relatives no longer come by. The nervous among them write open letters distancing themselves from you. Neighbors walk briskly by on the street, eyes lowered. Your business goes mysteriously quiet, contracts dry up. Your schedule empties. You have become a social leper.

"It eats you away," the wife of someone currently enduring *akato* told me. "Anyone who attends your wedding or calls round to express condolences is deemed to be showing 'negative solidarity.' So no one comes near you. Even close relatives, old friends, won't speak to me now. And the worst impact is on your children, because *akato* extends to them. Your children are no longer invited for birthday parties or sleepovers."[12]

And so it was for the Karegeyas. There would be no more play-dates with the Kagames' four children, no more elegant dinners at Aux Caprices. "People had come to know that things were bad between us and Kagame," Leah recalls. "Neighbors would keep away from you. You start being careful. Because you don't know who to trust."

A former head of intelligence's family now learned what it felt like to be tracked day and night. Leah no longer worked with Jeannette Gisa, but her own picture-framing business became a focus of interest. "They used to monitor us all the time. I'd have a motorbike following me on the road and one would ride around my shop, going round and round." She bought herself a second cell phone, and then a third, to try and confuse her shadows.

While Patrick was training in Ruhengeri, she had moved into a brand-new hillside estate called Vision 2020, where she had bought a plot and was having a house built. She hoped to rent it out, a source of future income now that Patrick's earnings could no longer be counted upon.

Unemployed, listless, Patrick remained under a loose form of house arrest. "He would just take Richard to school and back and inspect the new house," Leah says. With its fate hanging on a president's whim, the family adopted the habit of ironically sprinkling "Kagame willing," rather than "Inshallah"—God willing—into the conversation.

In April 2006, I met up with Patrick in Kigali. I was acting as a guide for the writer David Cornwell, better known as John le Carré, who was putting the final touches to a novel set in DRC,[13] and I'd suggested transiting through Rwanda. In my email, I'd told Patrick I'd be traveling with a well-known author, without identifying him. Until the pair of us met Patrick on the terrace of the Hotel Mille Collines, no one in officialdom had registered that the "David Cornwell" whose hand they were shaking was a literary celebrity. Patrick clocked him immediately—he'd read many of his books—and was delighted.

So was le Carré. The presidential favorite fallen from grace, the intelligence supremo who knew too much to ever be granted freedom, the iconoclast being painfully masticated in the jaws of a system he had helped create. . . . Patrick could have walked straight from the pages of one of his novels. He felt he'd met his East European equivalent many a time.

We ate in an Indian restaurant, and throughout our meal, a man—presumably Rwandan intelligence—sat silently at a nearby table, carefully keeping us in view. Patrick was in casuals and looked flabby and not particularly healthy. What had been the hardest thing about his detention? I asked. "They took away my books," he said. "*My books.* That was the worst." He was trapped, he said. "They keep paying my salary and they won't let me resign, travel, or study abroad. So I am just here, rotting."

He'd been rereading my history of Eritrea, he told me.[14] "There are so many resonances with Rwanda," he said. "It became a system in which it became more and more impossible to say, 'This is bullshit' to the powers-that-be. And that's what has happened here. I stood up and said, 'This is bullshit,' and I'm paying the price. He won't allow that."

He had acquired a very Eritrean habit, or rather, a habit characteristic of regimes where state surveillance has become ubiquitous, of never identifying the head of state by name. Kagame was always either "He" or "Him." You never know, after all, who might be listening: in this case, a man on the other side of an Indian restaurant. Self-censorship enters the very fabric of the language.

"Your friend smiled and joked but did you notice that it never reached his eyes?" le Carré asked me, back at the Hotel Mille Collines. "I fear he will be rubbed out. There's a darkness gathering over him."

One month later, the second shoe dropped, as the Karegeyas had always known it must. Leah got the news flying in from South Africa. "My driver came to pick me up and said, 'Patrick has been taken again.' I started ringing the military police. Later Patrick sent a message telling me to look for a lawyer, and then we started getting the dates and going to court."

This time Patrick was actually charged, with insubordination and desertion from the army—bitterly ironic, given his previous attempts to resign. Kabarebe, the man he'd had medevaced out of Congo to South Africa, had twisted his refusal to apologize and request a job into dereliction of duty. A military rather than a civilian court would hear the case, and military courts in any country, but particularly in Rwanda, usually take a brisk line on human rights. The prosecution was seeking a seven-year sentence.

In aiming for a substantial sentence, Kagame was looking far ahead, Patrick believed. Rwanda had passed a law stating that anyone sentenced to more than six months in prison was barred from political office unless cleared or pardoned by the president. "He was making sure I would never be able to oppose him politically," Patrick wrote in his account for the US authorities.

A member of the Tutsi elite, veteran RPF stalwart, a man who knew where all the bodies were buried and boasted a network of friends in the army, intelligence services, Western embassies, and foreign ministries across the globe, Patrick would make a formidable enemy if he went into opposition politics. That wasn't going to be allowed to happen.

The tribunal's outcome was decided well in advance. "The RPF official at the court, out [of] fear of the president could not question my reasons of being charged; and no comments or views on the case were allowed. . . . No single witness or document was presented in evidence to prove my guilt," he wrote in his affidavit. Leah's memory is of an RPF prosecutor who kept saying, aggressively, "We can't hear, we can't hear you," to Patrick's testimony, when, Leah said, "we could all hear just fine."

A confidential cable sent to Washington by a staffer at the US embassy supports Patrick's description of the tribunal as "a kangaroo court." "There was little hard evidence provided in the trial to substantiate the charges other than cell phone bills that confirmed contact was made between Kabarebe and Karegeya—but not the subject matter of the calls," the staffer wrote. "The desertion and insubordination charges came down to a 'he said / he said' argument, unfortunately for Karegeya, the other 'he' in this equation is the most senior ranking General in the [armed forces]."[15]

After a one-day hearing, the court found Patrick guilty, sentenced him to eighteen months, and stripped him of his military rank.

So Patrick did his time. Just as he had made a go of the Ruhengeri training course and his mountain rustication, he somehow made the jail experience his own. It was his second stint in prison, after all, and he knew about the importance of structuring the days, not giving in to depression, retaining a sense of humor.

Held in a twelve-room detention center, he was initially its only inmate. Leah and Richard would visit on Saturdays and Sundays. "We'd take lunch and it became our picnic spot, we'd laugh and eventually it became fun, it was his place. Eventually the authorities saw it was not having much effect, so they reduced our visits to once a week."

De facto solitary confinement ended when two old friends, generals Frank Rusagara and Sam Kaka, joined him in jail. Blessed with some of Patrick's irreverence, they had fallen afoul of the regime for preventing police from arresting Assinapol Rwigara, a high-profile Rwandan businessman who had fallen out with the RPF, while he was attending a funeral.

"Have you come to destroy my peace?" joked Patrick when he spotted them. "You have invaded me, so now you owe me rent."

"He *owned* that prison," Leah recalls. "People would go to visit him just to laugh. He'd tell them, 'You're more in prison than I am. You can't say what you like: I can.'"

As the date of Patrick's release approached, Leah's family began to fret. "My sister told me to tell Patrick to apologize if I wanted to keep living in the country." But Leah remembered Patrick's reaction when she had relayed the First Lady's message. "I knew I couldn't do that. I told her she was wasting her time."

Her sister insisted, and went to see Patrick in prison: "I know you love your children," she told him. "For the sake of your kids, go and apologize. You're in trouble because you refuse to bow. This man is an emperor and you have to bow to an emperor."

Patrick laughed and said, "After eighteen months in jail you want me to apologize? For doing nothing? Over my dead body."

And so, mulish, steadfast, defiant, Patrick served out his sentence. On his release on November 15, 2007, his exchange with the army generals underlined, for both sides, how far they had drifted apart. The subsequent warning phone call merely served as confirmation. When he told Leah he was going, she did not demur. "If you don't agree with this man, you have to leave," she told him.

"If he'd stayed he'd have been killed. I always say those extra years were a bonus from God."

Patrick had surrendered his passport on detention, but if there's one skill an ex-intelligence chief possesses, it's the ability to conjure up forged travel papers at short notice. Patrick swiftly acquired a new Ugandan passport under a fake name: Byayesu—"He belongs to Jesus"—Serapio. An ironic choice for a confirmed atheist: it caused hilarity in the family.

Once in Kampala, his old stomping ground, he headed, perhaps surprisingly, for the British High Commission, which had moved from the dusty city center to a modern new building near Uganda's national museum. There he asked to see the resident intelligence official. There'd been a change of the guard, and the young staffer who showed him to a private room had only just arrived in Kampala.

He knew Patrick by reputation only, but noted that the spy chief was sweating, despite the building's crisp air-conditioning. He seemed jumpy, ill at ease. What he told the British official came as a total shock.

"I was part of the team that brought down the plane."

THE MISSILE

RPF soldiers inspect the wreckage of President Juvénal Habyarimana's plane in Kigali, May 1994.

Corinne Dufka.

Advocates Gerrie Nel and Kennedy Gihana discuss Patrick Karegeya's inquest in Randburg court.

Michela Wrong.

Former comrades turned regional rivals: Museveni and Kagame.

Peter Busomoke, Getty Images.

CHAPTER SEVENTEEN

THE PLANE AND OTHER SECRETS

They were too deeply woven into their own past, caught in the web they themselves had spun . . . ; they were all guilty, just not of those particular deeds to which they were confessing.

—**Arthur Koestler,** *Darkness at Noon*

The plane, ah, the plane. It is the other massive secret that squats like a giant toad at the heart of the RPF story, even uglier and more poisonous than the question of who killed Fred Rwigyema or organized the assassination of Laurent Kabila, because its consequences claimed so many hundreds of thousands of lives.

Within hours of the Falcon 50 explosion above the Habyarimanas' villa in Kigali on the evening of April 6, 1994, a host of rival theories began to sprout.

It was initially claimed that white men had been spotted running from the possible missile launch site: Belgian UN peacekeepers, French paratroopers, or simply mercenaries in the pay of God Knows Who? But soon the theories divided along a simple major schism. Either the jet had been downed by the RPF, greedy for more than the Arusha Accords were about to yield and well aware that the elections envisaged would favor Hutu parties and reduce the movement to a cameo role in Rwandan politics, or it had been attacked by radical members of the Akazu clustered around Agathe Habyarimana. Raging at the president's overly generous concessions, the notion ran, the extremists had fired the opening salvo in an internal coup, offering Habyarimana up as sacrificial lamb in order to crush both the RPF and Hutu moderates.

Support for the second theory came from the many hints dropped in extremist newsletters and radio broadcasts predicting "something very big" in the first days of April, the casualness with which the notion of a genocide had been being bandied about for several years in Kigali, and the speed with which the first *interahamwe* roadblocks went up after the plane's downing.

As for the alternative explanation, of RPF culpability: "It was not in the political interest of the RPF to kill President Habyarimana," historian Gérard Prunier initially argued. "It had obtained a good political settlement from the Arusha agreement and could not hope for anything better."[1] Once the Hutu government had fled, leaving the evidence of its ghastly handiwork scattered across the land, Western donors piling in to help the RPF had no difficulty accepting that version of events.

It was, though, a slightly counterintuitive theory. Embracing it meant the opposite of applying Occam's razor, which states that the simplest answer is likely to be the correct one. It required one to believe that Agathe Habyarimana and her allies had plotted the deaths of not only her husband—father of her six children—but her half brother Elie Sagatwa and the Rwandan army chief of staff Deogratias Nsabimana, who were also on the doomed Falcon and hardly ranked as political "moderates."

Many have certainly depicted the First Lady as an African Lady Macbeth, ice cold and calculating, but this course of action was not only emotionally repellent, but wildly risky. Would even the most ruthless extremists sacrifice both head of state and army chief, with all the disarray entailed, when power-hungry rebels sat camped inside the capital?

As the years passed, the question of RPF responsibility for the plane showed a stubborn refusal to go away, and some analysts, journalists, aid workers, and diplomats who had accepted the new government's account without a murmur began to doubt.

Witnesses claiming firsthand testimony kept coming forward, and all had one characteristic in common: they were ex-RPF. "Isn't it interesting," comments Filip Reyntjens dryly. "Since 1994 there have been a steady drip, drip of leaks and semi-disclosures about the downing of the plane from insiders within the RPF, while not a single one of the Hutu extremists blamed for it by the government has ever leaked or disclosed anything."[2]

One was Aloys Ruyenzi, a former Kagame bodyguard who claimed to have been present at a meeting in Mulindi between Kagame and his closest commanders at which the decision was made to shoot down the plane. The other was Abdul Ruzibiza, a former RPF lieutenant who said he'd been given the task of surveying possible sites to be used for the missile launch.[3]

Over drinks late at night, Western journalists based in Kigali would occasionally be disconcerted to hear a friend in the RPF let his guard down long enough to say that *of course* they had done it, it had been a war, a fight to the finish, and Habyarimana's death represented the definitive, knockout blow every combatant craves—why, a roar of collective joy had gone up in Mulindi, where the rebels had all been crowded around a TV set watching soccer when the news of the plane going down came through on Kagame's radio set.

The reporters knew better than to draft articles quoting their contacts: try that, and their friend would be taken in for questioning, the assignment ended abruptly. "Everyone knows" does not count as proof, after all. The topic was off limits, *verboten*.

Put simply, too many people had died. There's an obvious difference between suggesting that a power-hungry rebel movement inadvertently triggered the slaughter of its own ethnic support base by killing a head of state, and arguing that the RPF *intended* between 500,000 and 1 million *petits Tutsis* to die because—so one extreme theory goes—the more massive the bloodletting, the better the rebels could position themselves as rescuers. But that nuance quickly, and very deliberately, was lost. To suggest the RPF might have brought down the plane became synonymous with arguing it was responsible for the genocide.

And even setting aside the issue of intentionality, killing a president returning from peace talks—a leader who on paper had agreed to share power, even if few believed Habyarimana could ever follow through—would make the rebels guilty not only of bad faith, but a war crime. Once a guilt-ridden United Nations established the International Criminal Tribunal for Rwanda (ICTR) in Arusha to identify the perpetrators of one of the worst human rights outrages of the twentieth century, criminal charges became a concrete possibility.

Any admission of RPF guilt, what's more, would undermine the new Rwandan government's image as a blameless victim rising like a phoenix from the ashes of toxic ethnicity and international indifference. The RPF elite had put a lot of work into building the brand. Entertaining the possibility that, whether through rashness or ruthlessness, the leader routinely labeled in the West as "the Man Who Ended the Genocide" might actually also have *started* it, would not do.

And so the debate rumbled on, with article after article, book after book, and investigation after investigation (Belgian, French, Spanish, Rwandan, then French again)—sifting through the evidence of launch site, line of fire, acoustics, ballistics evidence, witness testimonies—in search of a nugget that would provide final, definitive proof. "Who downed the plane?" joined "Who shot Kennedy?" and "How did Dag Hammarskjöld die?" as one of the great unanswered questions of modern political history.[4]

As the cement of the RPF's redemption narrative hardened, where you stood on the question became the litmus test of moral decency among the many "Friends of Rwanda" the RPF was making in political, religious, and diplomatic circles abroad. Doubt would not be tolerated. Query the credibility of the Hutu extremist thesis and you were likely to be labeled a "revisionist," on a par with Holocaust deniers.

In his prime, Patrick scrupulously toed the official line, hard and implacable when anyone dared query the government's version of events. "That's a taboo subject," he told one young researcher working for an international think tank. "Keep well away from it if you want to keep working in the Great Lakes."[5]

When reporter Lara Santoro tried in 2000 to provoke a reaction by telling Patrick ICTR investigators were talking about the plane's downing, she found she had touched a nerve. She was used to joshing with Patrick: not this time. "I don't care what people are saying," Patrick spat out, before effectively conceding the principle. "So what? So what if He shot down the plane? Those people were going to kill anyway. What does it matter who started it?" He was shaking with rage.

Patrick's fury at that moment was probably a reflection of the effort he and his colleagues had expended, pulling every diplomatic string they had at their disposal, to ensure the tribunal's scope of responsibility remained focused exclusively on crimes committed by the previous Hutu administration, not those now in power.

When it was first established with respected South African judge Richard Goldstone as chief prosecutor, the ICTR certainly saw probing the plane's downing as well within its scope. So when ICTR investigators Jim Lyons and Michael Hourigan, a former FBI staffer and an Australian lawyer, respectively, were approached in 1997 by three former RPF fighters claiming direct knowledge of Kagame's responsibility, they excitedly called Goldstone's successor, Canadian Louise Arbour, to say they had compiled a dossier outlining grounds for prosecution.[6]

But Arbour's approach swiveled unexpectedly from initial enthusiasm to frosty hostility. During a tense meeting, she ordered the investigation terminated, pooh-poohed the credibility of the men's sources, and queried their mandate to investigate the plane. Shocked investigators speculated that Kigali's various Western "friends"—most likely, the US government—had applied pressure. What prompted her about-turn remains unclear.

"Louise Arbour just did a 180-degrees turnaround. Someone above her was telling her this was not a good idea, to be investigating Paul Kagame," Lyons later told the BBC.[7]

Arbour's feisty successor, Swiss prosecutor Carla Del Ponte, insisted that her jurisdiction did indeed extend to the plane and secretly set up a Special Investigations Unit to probe that and other RPF crimes. Word must have gotten out: no surprise, given that Rwanda's intelligence services had placed informants among the ICTR's Rwandan translators and were also, thanks to equipment helpfully provided by the United States, monitoring the court's telephone, fax, and Internet traffic.[8]

When Del Ponte's joint contract at both the ICTR and the International Criminal Tribunal for the former Yugoslavia expired, she was forced by UN secretary-general Kofi Annan to focus on the latter, and a Gambian took over her Rwanda duties. "It is clear that it all started when we embarked on these Special Investigations," Del Ponte later said. "Pressure from Rwanda contributed to the non-renewal of my mandate."[9]

Human Rights Watch investigator Alison Des Forges, often called as a prosecution witness by the ICTR as trials of the genocide's suspected masterminds got underway, had left the question of who brought down the plane open in *"Leave None to Tell the Story": Genocide in Rwanda*, her magisterial investigation. But her views, like those of many experts—including Prunier—changed over time. Interviewed by Lara Santoro in Arusha in 2001, she told the journalist—off the record—that she had always suspected the RPF might be responsible for the plane's downing, but had recently become convinced of it. She died without making her suspicion public, killed when her own domestic flight crashed on approach to Buffalo, New York, in February 2009.

Yet even as one tribunal was being successfully hobbled, other prosecutors emerged to challenge Kigali's official version of events.

In November 2006, French antiterrorist judge Jean-Louis Bruguière, who had been asked by the families of the dead French pilots and flight engineer aboard to investigate, caused a diplomatic shock wave by announcing that he was issuing international arrest warrants for nine of Kagame's closest aides, including General Kayumba, Kabarebe, Kayonga, and Nziza.

"For the RPF, the physical elimination of President Juvénal Habyarimana was the necessary precondition for seizing power by force and was inscribed in a vast plan worked out to this end," said Bruguière. "The final order to attack the presidential plane was given by Paul Kagame himself during a meeting held in Mulindi on March 31, 1994."[10]

As head of state, Kagame enjoyed immunity under French law, but the warrants, if acted upon, would have marked the effective decapitation of the RPF. "I was eating in the officers' mess in Kigali when the news came through on the BBC and it was a massive, massive shock," recalls Major Jean-Marie Micombero. "It changed everything."

Outraged, Kigali immediately cut diplomatic ties with France. Denouncing Bruguière as "an imposter," Kagame railed against the notion that a country that had propped up Habyarimana's despotic regime should dare pronounce judgment on his own. "They should first try themselves because they killed our people," he said.[11]

The RPF presented Bruguière's prosecution as a distasteful act of political vindictiveness: a jab-in-the-eye by a French state incapable of accepting marginalization in a former African client state. And by then, enough had been revealed about Paris's support for Habyarimana's security forces, its military experts' training of the *interahamwe*, for many to agree.

Rwanda would counter with its own inquiry. Dubbed "the Mutsinzi Report" after the chairman Jean Mutsinzi, its January 2010 findings—to no one's surprise—laid the blame squarely on the Akazu.[12] "To no one's surprise" because, while it interviewed over 500 witnesses and commissioned a ballistics report from a British defense academy, every member of its "committee of independent experts" was an RPF member, appointed by Kagame.

Given this background, why was one of Patrick's first acts on winning his freedom to slap a jaw-dropping mea culpa onto a young MI6 officer's desk in Kampala, an admission that, if widely accepted, would call for the revision of the entire history of the genocide?

He was hardly being original, one British intelligence official I spoke to pointed out. "Every military official from Rwanda who defected in those years was claiming that they knew who brought down the plane and were part of it. They knew the French were investigating the matter and they knew it was exactly what the French wanted to hear."[13]

But Patrick wasn't any run-of-the-mill Rwandan official. This was the former head of external intelligence speaking out on the single most controversial issue in RPF history. And he hadn't gone to the French. Jason Stearns sees Patrick's "walk-in," as embassies label such unscheduled visits, as far more significant. On the run and in need of friends, Patrick, he reckons, was making sure his friends in the Western intelligence agencies took his departure seriously.

"His defection was a really massive thing, everyone was wondering what had happened. Here was a guy who was known for being slippery, evasive. So he needed to show that he was serious this time. So he put that on the table to show that there was no going back."

Was the claim true, or an example of Patrick adroitly placing himself at the center of events when it served his purpose?

Patrick had not been included in Bruguière's list of suspects or an even more ambitious indictment unveiled in February 2008, three months after his departure from Rwanda, by a Spanish judge fired up by the principle of universal jurisdiction. Judge Fernando Andreu Merelles's rambling indictment involved arrest warrants for forty Rwandan army officers—including General Kayumba and Kabarebe, once again—for genocide, terrorism, and crimes against humanity, including the plane's downing—but Patrick only got a mention as head of the Congo Desk.

His absence from the various warrants makes, on the surface, logical sense. At the time of the jet's downing, after all, Patrick was still officially employed by the Ugandan government based in Kampala, playing the role of liaison between Museveni and the RPF.

But he constantly shuttled across the border, and according to a Ugandan intelligence source who knew Patrick well, was in Mulindi the weekend before the plane went down.[14] It would have been natural, given how highly Kagame and his colleagues valued his intellectual input, to include Patrick in any key discussion about Habyarimana's elimination. He would be able to assess, better than anyone, the likely impact on key ally Uganda, the wider region, and Western donors.

Many of the facts recounted by Abdul Ruzibiza—one of the first RPF insiders to break cover—have been contested, but his 2005 memoir includes an interesting detail. Patrick, he says, was part of the Ugandan delegation sent to the summit Habyarimana attended in Dar es Salaam on April 6. So when the Falcon took off from the airport with two doomed presidents aboard, Patrick was perfectly placed to call James Kabarebe and notify him that the aircraft was headed their way. That, certainly, would have made Patrick "part of the team" that brought down the plane.[15]

So it's possible Patrick's confession was sincere. But he did not repeat it to Stearns when they met in Dar—"Jason, it's too early to talk about that," he told the writer—and when I raised the topic in London, he also failed to mention any personal involvement. But he wasn't expecting me to accept the "Hutu extremist" line, either. As we tucked into Lebanese *meze* on the Edgware Road, he marveled that anyone had been credulous enough to fall for it.

"I've never been able to understand why there is any speculation about that at all, why you're always reading, 'It could have been so and so, or it could have been so and so,'" he said, one eyebrow raised.

"It's obvious. All you have to do is look at who supplied the missiles and there you have your answer," he continued. "They had to come from somewhere." The surface-to-air missiles that downed the Falcon were Soviet-made. They had been sold to Uganda by Russia, he said. And only one side in the Rwandan conflict had ready access to Ugandan weaponry: the RPF.[16]

I wasn't the only Western journalist with whom Patrick, once in exile, abandoned his previous pose of innocence. Lara Santoro, now based in New Mexico, found herself chatting to Patrick while researching a book. Both their lives, by then, had changed beyond recognition: she was raising a child while writing novels, he was an unemployed enemy of the state. Once again, she asked about the plane: the episode haunted her. They spoke in hypotheticals, but this time the question was not whether the RPF had brought it down—both took that as a given—but Kagame's motivation.

"Do you think He knew?" she asked him.

"Knew what?"

"That half a million would die."

"No," said Patrick. "But it didn't matter. He didn't give a damn."

Voiced in private to old contacts and long-standing friends, the hints and nudges by disenchanted RPF stalwarts could only last so long. At some point, the four heavyweights in the newly created Rwanda National Congress (RNC) came to realize they were going to have to state their position.

The "Rwanda Briefing" published by the movement's future founders in August 2010—essentially its manifesto—made no mention of the plane's downing and did not go into the detail of RPF atrocities against the Hutu civilian population inside Rwanda, while recognizing massive loss of life in DRC. "It was a consensus document," explains Theogene Rudasingwa.

The RNC was pitching itself as a movement for ethnic reconciliation. It had managed to recruit a smattering of Hutu politicians who had served in Habyarimana's administration, but if it was to transform Rwandan society, it would need to strike alliances with exiled

Hutu groups simmering with anti-RPF grievances—movements that remembered all too well the brutal effectiveness of General Kayumba's army, groups embittered by the *génocidaire* label that had been applied to them all too often by the very men now reaching out.

If the Tutsi community needed to hear expressions of genuine regret from Hutus for the genocide, Hutus also needed to hear public acknowledgment of RPF atrocities, and that included the truth about Habyarimana's assassination.

Theogene, who had rediscovered his Christian faith, was haunted by the memory of conversations he had overheard in his formerly privileged position. During the many trips they had made together, Kagame's senior officers had let their guard down in front of the president's chief of staff, and hair-raising reminiscences had flowed.

"I listened and made mental note. I became like a detective," Theogene said.[17] Hearing officers of what was supposed to be a revolutionary army laughing as they discussed the most controversial episodes of RPF history—episodes he had either misrepresented, defended, or lied about in public—he was mortified.

The details of the downing of Habyarimana's plane, how the massacre of Kibeho was carried out, how the army had killed Hutus in DRC "until they simply got tired," how they had helicoptered the bodies of victims of the Northern Insurgency to the Akagera Park for secret burial, the assassinations of Sendashonga, of Lizinde, of Kabila. . . . The unsavory disclosures came unbidden, one after the other.

The RNC, he felt, would have to own up. "For years we'd been saying, my brother and I, 'How long will we keep quiet? We owe people some explanation.' I was driving the process. My position was that we have to say what we know, so Rwandans know we're serious and want to take remedial action. I approached it from a doctor's point of view, from the perspective of healing a patient. If you don't tell a patient the truth, he can't heal."

But Theogene was lucky. His various positions allowed him to place a convenient distance between himself and a range of toxic executive decisions. For those who had been singled out for judicial pursuit—or were likely to be—admissions were harder to make.

"If you are the head of intelligence, where does your confession start and where does it stop?" he acknowledges. Yet Patrick, he says, came to accept the inevitable. "Patrick had crossed the chasm. He had realized how much damage had been caused on each side and felt strongly that there had to be justice. . . . He had no problem with the idea of reaching out and telling the truth. But [General] Kayumba did."

The RNC's founders were still working on a joint position when Theogene forced their hands. In the autumn of 2011, he checked into an airport hotel in North Carolina, where he was due to address a meeting. For months, he had been agonizing over the text of a collective apology. "I felt that my second conversion to Christianity demanded that I come out with all the truth." Pulled this way and that that night—"One voice would keep on telling me that I should release it; another would tell me to wait"—he went onto his Facebook page shortly after midnight on October 1 and posted it.[18]

Kagame, he said, had told him, "with characteristic callousness and much glee," in July 1994, that he was responsible for shooting down the plane, deliberately derailing the Arusha peace process because he was bent on "absolute power." While insisting that he had never personally been party to the plot, Theogene begged forgiveness from the families of those who had died on the plane and the entire Rwandan nation, acknowledging his role as one of the regime's propagandists-in-chief.[19]

"Like many others in the RPF leadership," he said, "I enthusiastically sold this deceptive storyline, especially to foreigners who by and large came to believe it, even when I knew that Kagame was the culprit of the crime." He was revealing all this, he said, because only the truth could set Rwanda free.

Having posted the text, he fell sound asleep, conscience finally clear: "My chains were gone, and I could rely only on God as my shield," he wrote in his memoir. "I have lied too long," he told the BBC when one of its journalists contacted him.

•

Once Theogene had taken that first step toward expiation, it seemed the RPF's former general secretary could not stop. The following April, he flew to Paris to give six hours of testimony on the episode to Judge Marc Trévidic, who had been appointed to probe the plane's downing afresh by a French administration keen, under President

Nicolas Sarkozy, to put relations with Rwanda on a new, less confrontational footing.

The following year, in October 2013, Theogene flew to Madrid to tell Judge Merelles what he knew about the plane; about the role that Tri-Star Investments, which he set up, had played as a money launderer for the RPF; and about the deaths of nine Spanish citizens in Rwanda.

By then General Kayumba, too, recognizing the inevitable, had gone public. The trial in Johannesburg of the six men accused of his attempted murder was heard in June 2012. Sensing that France, always swayed by realpolitik in Africa, was determined to bury the controversy, he used that opportunity to publicly accuse Kagame of responsibility for the plane's downing as well as for Laurent Kabila's murder.

Granting a series of press interviews, he denied any personal involvement in the plane's destruction, but said he stood ready to formally present his evidence to French investigators. "I was in a position to know," he said.[20]

The following year, it was Jean-Marie Micombero's turn to testify. Now living in Brussels and a prominent RNC member, Micombero had worked in intelligence and risen to number two in Rwanda's Ministry of Defence. He'd also spent a year in jail in Kigali on embezzlement charges, a fact used to discredit him. He told Judge Trévidic how, as one of the 600 elite troops guarding Rwanda's parliament building in 1994, he had attended meetings where the logistics of the presidential attack were discussed. "When the boss is killed, everything will go ahead more smoothly," his senior officers remarked. "No one in the military believed in Arusha," Micombero told me.[21]

A road ambush on Habyarimana's presidential convoy had initially been envisaged, but RPF commanders could not work out how to safely extract the team afterward, so focus shifted to the air. The missiles were smuggled into Kigali hidden in a pickup truck stacked with wood—the method tried and tested many times at Patrick's house on Muyenga Hill. A morning attempt had to be postponed because of fog. A bout of malaria put Micombero out of action, but he could effortlessly identify the members of the five-man team who had driven off that evening to carry out the operation, changing the history of the Great Lakes forever.[22]

•

The plane was not, however, the only issue upon which Theogene believed the RNC needed to unburden itself.

In May 2012, the Brussels-based Institut Seth Sendashonga pour la Citoyenneté Démocratique, set up in the Hutu government minister's memory, was due to hold its annual commemoration of his murder. Theogene reached out to Cyrie, asking if he could use the occasion to publicly apologize for the assassination.

"In the end he addressed the conference via Skype," Cyrie told me. "He apologized to me, my children, and Sendashonga's family for serving a system that had killed this man. He said he took moral responsibility as a member of the regime that had killed Sendashonga, even though he did not have any personal involvement. It was very moving. After that, we kept in touch."

Going one step further, Theogene raised the possibility of a meeting with Patrick.

Cyrie had not forgotten the rumors that had swirled around the spy chief. She wanted to know the truth, but she was also afraid. Then, by sheer coincidence, her NGO scheduled a get-together in Johannesburg—on Patrick's new home turf—and the opportunity seemed too good to miss. "I told Rudasingwa I was going to be there and said, 'Can you fix up a meeting? There are still many questions I want answering,'" Cyrie said.

Jittery with nerves, she agreed to meet Patrick at the Premier Hotel, a nondescript conference hotel near the airport booked by her employers. She took basic precautions. "I still had my suspicions," she said. They would talk in the bar, she stipulated, next to the lobby, to ensure there were plenty of people milling around. "I asked two colleagues to keep an eye on the situation. They sat in the corner of the bar and pretended to be just having a drink."

Her first reaction on spotting Patrick—a gap-toothed, boggle-eyed, middle-aged man accompanied by two South African minders who took up position at a nearby table—was to burst out laughing.

"You don't look like I imagined," she told him.

He was curious. "How did you imagine me?"

"Like KGB or something." The ice was broken.

Patrick reiterated Theogene's apology. "He was absolutely clear that the RPF as a system did it, and that Kagame had ordered it," Cyrie told me. "Your husband was a good man," he said. "If we had kept him and allowed him to do what he wanted to do, maybe Rwanda would be a different place today. I'm really very sorry for the loss you and your children suffered."

But when it came to the details of the second, fatal hit, the message was more complex. Patrick insisted he had not been the one to arrange it.

"So how did your name come up?" countered Cyrie. Why had David Kiwanuka, the Rwandan informer arrested immediately after Sendashonga's murder, mentioned Patrick?

"I never met that young man. I don't know him at all. I had nothing to do with your husband's death, but I can tell you what I know."

He'd explained Kagame's methodology, the parallel tracks set up to ensure competition and loyalty from employees who were never entirely certain who else had been assigned any particular task. "He told me, 'There are people in official positions, like me, and then there are people behind doing the same job, known as the "technicians." Every institution has a shadow person following it.'"

Patrick said he'd heard about the hit while on a fence-mending trip to the DRC. Back in early 1998, tensions between Kigali and President Laurent Kabila were about to explode into the Second Congo War. In Kinshasa, he'd taken a cryptic call from a Kenyan opposition politician, a prominent lawyer and businessman.[23]

"I have delivered what your boss asked me. Now I need to be paid," the caller said.

"Why are you asking me?" said the puzzled spy chief. "Why are you calling?" The Kenyan clearly assumed he was in the loop. Then the story came out.

The three men who had ended up in the dock in Nairobi had been no more than convenient scapegoats. Kenya has no shortage of crooked local policemen and army officers happy to hire themselves out—along with their weapons—for freelance work. Kagame, Patrick told Cyrie, had commissioned the Kenyan politician to recruit a few such men. The politician had been offered $100,000. "He agreed, saying he was used to those kind of tasks." Patrick couldn't explain why his own name had been planted, but guessed it was to muddy the waters, shifting blame to an employee Kagame wanted to keep to heel.

As for proving RPF responsibility, he told Cyrie, the trail left by that payment from one of the RPF's many Swiss bank accounts to the opposition politician's account at the Kenya Commercial Bank would suffice. "If you reopen the case and there is a judicial process, I will come and testify," he volunteered.

It was the same stance Patrick had taken on the shooting down of Habyarimana's plane—"I want to say these things in a court of law"—and it came replete with poetic irony. After Patrick's own murder, Spanish lawyers representing a group of alleged Spanish, Congolese, and Rwandan victims of RPF crimes would reveal that they had been investigating Patrick over Sendashonga's murder. Because they had been working on potential charges, the investigators had never taken up his offer of cooperation.[24]

Did Cyrie believe Patrick, ultimate practitioner of the Rwandan art of *ubwenge*? It didn't take a genius to see that this complicated version of events conveniently shifted responsibility from Patrick as an individual onto a former boss turned enemy. Reporter Lara Santoro, who interviewed David Kiwanuka, scoffs at Patrick's claim that he "never met that young man." The late Kiwanuka told her he met Patrick on many occasions, she says.

Cyrie understood, too, that just as the RPF had once reached out to recruit Sendashonga, treasuring his ability to reconcile ethnic communities, the RNC now hoped to win a Hutu martyr's posthumous blessing, with all that it implied in terms of useful political capital.

But she was nonetheless half-convinced. "I do believe him, yes, although my instinct tells me he didn't tell me everything. If he was lying, why bother meeting me? He probably told me the truth, but not the whole truth."

How the execution was carried out was only one of her questions, though. Why was it, she asked Patrick, that Kagame, who had once seemed on excellent terms with Sendashonga, had come to want him dead?

"Your husband was a very intelligent man," Patrick replied. "Someone who stood up for what he believed, and Kagame was not comfortable with that. He was afraid Sendashonga could bring Hutus and Tutsis together on common ground. That was obviously a threatening prospect, and so he was killed."

Nothing personal, just an example of tall poppy syndrome: a reaction any Roman emperor or Mafia boss would understand.

As the punishing light of the veldt began to soften and the traffic whooshed past a far less plush hotel than the one in which the spy chief would himself die, the widow and the man she'd always believed had killed her husband began to relax. At some point, he took out his phone and called General Kayumba, to allow him, too, to apologize. "We were cowards, Sendashonga was right," the General told Cyrie.

It was vindication for her husband, if coming too late. "Why didn't you guys who are now in the RNC stand up to Kagame at the time?" she asked Patrick. He tried to explain the peculiarly beleaguered perspective of the RPF, and how it justified the most egregious acts. "We saw it coming. But we were made to believe that we must stick together or die together, that we were a small minority, surrounded by *interahamwe*, and that if we ever became divided they would come back and slaughter all of us."

"So why did you break with him?" she said.

Patrick grimaced. "It had reached a point where he would treat us as though we were his slaves," he told her. "I told him once, 'You know, I'm a man, and so are you.'" It was the *auriga*'s refrain: "Remember you're just a man."

Not every family member approved of her readiness to meet with these former top RPF officials. But as anyone who has been bereaved in shocking circumstances can attest, not knowing the details, wondering what really, *really* happened, is a slow acid that corrodes the soul. In hearing this account, Cyrie did herself some good.

"It made me feel better," she said. "Because now I could join the dots. That question of who had killed him and how, whether it had been Rwandans or Kenyans, it had bothered me."

Cyrie herself will never forget the long years of silence. "I told Rudasingwa, 'Why did it take you so long? You guys could have come out earlier and said something.' She also still smarts, retrospectively, at how the allegation that Sendashonga had stolen $54 million was planted in the Rwandan newspapers, a false lead taken up by the Kenyan police who questioned her. "Kill a man, but don't kill his reputation."

She told Patrick and the General that she would not join their opposition movement. "I don't trust them, coming from where I do," she told me. She would never pretend to be friends, and would continue to comment as she saw fit on the RNC's actions. But she did bestow on them something for which anyone who has claimed a life hungers: "I told them, 'I forgive you personally, but it's only me. It doesn't imply my family's forgiveness.'"

That reckoning, in part a tribute to Patrick's extraordinary capacity to connect, represents a generosity of heart few of us could attain. Remembering the encounter with the doomed ex–spy chief now, she says something so magnanimous it takes my breath away: "I felt sorry for them. Because I could see that Patrick was trying, more or less, to do what Sendashonga tried to do, only later on."

CHAPTER EIGHTEEN

DO NOT DISTURB

"You're not going to use the story, Mr. Scott?"

"No sir. This is the West, sir. When the legend becomes fact, print the legend."

—*The Man Who Shot Liberty Valance*

The Rwanda National Congress had begun the process of lancing a boil. Theogene's admissions, apologies, and testimony sent shock waves through the Rwandan community. But as far as large sections of the international community were concerned, the former senior members of the RPF might have never spoken.

One of the most curious aspects of this story was the way in which academic researchers, diplomats, journalists, and—above all—development officials in the West who had once regarded the likes of Patrick Karegeya, Theogene Rudasingwa, Gerald Gahima, and General Kayumba Nyamwasa as key sources, hanging on their insights and relaying their remarks back to headquarters, suddenly had remarkably little interest in what they had to say.

In business, the executive turned whistleblower grabs headlines—with good reason. Nondisclosure agreements are drafted precisely to prevent these players finding a voice. For who, after all, can provide more devastating, more credible insights into a system's workings, a business's dirty underbelly, than the high-profile insider?

Who, in Rwanda, was better placed to spill the beans on Kagame's regime than its former head of external intelligence, ruling party secretary-general, attorney general, and army chief of staff? Yet curiosity proved in astonishingly short supply. It was, perhaps, a case of "Tread softly, for you tread on my dreams." Rwanda's story had the international community so thoroughly by the emotional and intellectual throat, it could not, now, wrest free.

Some elements of that stranglehold were entirely self-serving. Rwanda's most prized twenty-first-century export was not coffee, but its well-trained military. Kigali's readiness to contribute troops to African peacekeeping forces meant one less headache for Western policymakers, who knew that their own publics—in the wake of the Black Hawk Down debacle in Somalia—would balk at sending young men to die on the continent.

Others were expressions of guilt.

There was the specific guilt associated with the international community's behavior during the genocide, which representatives like Theogene learned to exploit brilliantly, even while marveling, he says, at its effectiveness. "I get shocked when people succumb to it," he told me. "Because at the end of the day it's Rwandans who killed Rwandans. We wreaked damage on one another, so this whole notion of the Americans and the international community and the British saying, 'Mea culpa, mea culpa,' I just don't see the basis for that."

But there was also the amorphous sense of guilt felt by white liberals toward the entire history of colonial oppression, embracing not just Tutsis but also Native Americans, Tasmanians, Armenians, Crimean Tartars, black and brown people generally: shamefaced feelings that stretched back through the generations and were associated with any community that had been victimized or gone ignored as the pampered West turned its stony face away.

Beneath this rich mix ran a sluggish river of intellectual torpor. No one, after all, enjoys constantly querying past assumptions. "*Homo sapiens* is a storytelling animal," writes Israeli philosopher Yuval Noah Harari, "that thinks in stories rather than in numbers or graphs, and believes that the universe itself works like a story, replete with heroes and villains, conflicts and resolutions, climaxes and happy endings.

"Once personal identities and entire social systems are built on the top of a story," he adds, "it becomes unthinkable to doubt it, not because of the evidence supporting it, but because its collapse will trigger a personal and social cataclysm."[1]

And so it was with Rwanda. Few narratives possess the seductive power of the RPF's redemptive tale of humiliated-refugees-reborn-as-crusaders, righteous warriors returning to a lost motherland to save their brothers from the forces of Absolute Evil and then, on the toxic ruins of a racist society, building a spotless, disciplined, tech-friendly African Utopia. There were echoes of antiquity in this classic Quest saga: the Exodus of the Bible and Torah, Virgil's *Aeneid*, with Plato's idealized *Republic* as its culmination.

Having broadly decided at one point that Kagame and the RPF were "the Good Guys" in Rwanda, "Good Guys" who had stopped what was self-evidently "A Very Bad Thing," many an academic, diplomat, development official, and businessman would cling with a sloth's viselike grip to that view, pretty much irrespective of events on the ground or any suggestion that the RPF had, in fact, played a part in bringing that Very Bad Thing about.

"Do Not Disturb," read the sign Patrick's killers hung on the door handle of his hotel room. The injunction was one Western outsiders were all too ready to embrace.

•

By 2010, a major debate about the viability and nature of foreign aid was underway in the West. The words "Rwanda" and "poster child" had been twinned for more than a decade, and for a host of NGO workers, development officials, and billionaire philanthropists, criticizing Kagame's regime meant toppling the pillars on which they had constructed their careers.

When George H. W. Bush declared a New World Order in 1991, Western confidence was at its height. The Berlin Wall had come down, capitalism had obviously trumped communism, and governments in the industrialized north thought they were rich and magnanimous enough to "fix" societies emerging from war, dictatorship, and famine.

In the United Kingdom, under the inspirational leadership of Clare Short, the altruistic Department for International Development (DFID) was born. Bono and Bob Geldof turned from rock stars into aid advocates, and the campaign to Make Poverty History won enthusiastic backing from the G8 at the Gleneagles summit.

That aid poured mainly into African governments' education and health sectors but also funded civil society groups bent on increasing political participation and entrenching human rights. As private radio stations multiplied across Africa, the spread of cybernet cafés and cell phones ensured that ordinary Africans knew their civic rights just as well as any voter in Sweden or New Mexico.

Then came September 11 and the botched invasions of Afghanistan and Iraq. A fearful West went into self-defense mode. The superpower that had once been bighearted enough to send troops to distribute food in Somalia now turned into a country preoccupied with its own survival, and mainly interested in Africa as a breeding ground for Islamic jihad.

Public belief in aid wavered, undermined by a steady stream of scandals exposing ministerial fraud that seemed to vindicate the quip that foreign aid amounted to "poor people in rich countries giving money to rich people in poor countries."

Increasingly, development experts and Africa's ruling elites looked for inspiration to China, where a system no one could ever mistake for a democracy had lifted 850 million people out of poverty. A vibrant civil society in Africa no longer seemed a priority, nor did first-past-the-post democratic systems seen as fomenting ethnic rivalry. Strong leaders promising law and order—Kagame's great selling point—appealed.

The field of possible heroes was smaller than it had once been. One by one the shine had come off Africa's "Renaissance" leaders, leaving only an ailing Meles Zenawi in Ethiopia and Kagame to play the role of "donor darlings." Desperate for success stories, the donors were ever more tempted to turn a blind eye to the repressive side of the two presidents' regimes.

"There's that phrase attributed to Franklin D. Roosevelt," says Phil Vernon, veteran aid analyst. "'He may be a son of a bitch, but he's our son of a bitch.' There's been a palpable shift from the New World Order, with its commitment to entrenching human rights and democracy, back to that. It's full circle, back to the Cold War."[2]

Only, this time around, winning classification as "our son of a bitch" did not rely solely on being on the "right" side in the global fight against radical Islam. "The emphasis now," says Vernon, "is on making places more stable, not necessarily better. Establishing law and order. One thing you always hear about Kagame is, 'He's effective. He gets stuff done.'"

The British Conservative minister Andrew Mitchell illustrated how far the new thinking had come: "It's all very well talking about human rights but the fundamental, primary human right is the right to be free from the threat of violence," he told me. "As far as I'm concerned, Kagame is a hero for ending the violence."

Rwanda was situated in one of the most violent districts on the planet, the new realists argued, a country prone to coups, wars, epidemics, and refugee crises. The leadership deserved to be cut some slack.

"If you live in a country in which a million people have been murdered in a genocide the international community did nothing to stop, inherited an economy in which there wasn't even a typewriter and everything had been smashed, you tend to look at criticisms by the West and of course you consider them," said Mitchell. "But this is a very tough government that makes up its mind on the basis of its own self-confidence."

The comparison most frequently made was to Lee Kuan Yew, and Rwandan officials traveling abroad could be spotted in their plane seats perusing chunky copies of the Singaporean prime minister's memoirs, hoping for clues as to how tiny little Singapore had pulled off its three-decade transformation.[3]

The stance justified a hard-nosed attitude toward the odd army massacre, journalist's disappearance, or opposition leader's assassination. Yet it was premised on a peculiarly cockeyed view of recent history. For if Africa's Great Lakes remained a turbulent region, Rwanda, with its constant interventions in DRC, its cynical support for militias across its borders, its covert meddling in Burundi and Uganda, and its ruthless elimination of presidents with whom it failed to see eye to eye, had played a major role in keeping it that way. But for those accustomed to stripping the political ingredients from their assessments of African nation-states, Rwanda's incredible statistics made it easy to overlook that inconvenient fact.

Impressive growth rates in the wake of a civil war or massive national trauma are no surprise: there is nowhere for a shattered economy to go but up. But Rwanda's post-genocide economic recovery showed extraordinary staying power: from 2000 to 2010, annual gross domestic product (GDP) grew by an average of 8.4 percent, more than three times sub-Saharan Africa's 2.8 percent average. According to the government's household living conditions survey, 1 million Rwandans had been lifted out of poverty between 2008 and 2011.[4]

Back in 2000, the UN's member nations had pledged to meet eight Millennium Development Goals (MDGs)—basic targets on education, child mortality, maternal health, and gender equality—by 2015. Embarrassingly, by 2005 it was clear that Africa was the only continent likely to miss every single target.[5] Not Rwanda, though, where there's a saying that goes, "An order is heavier than a stone." The top-down administrative structure dating back to the Mwami responded with instinctive efficiency to checklists, deadlines, and targets. Rwanda's figures on under-five mortality, vaccination, and the percentage of children sleeping under mosquito nets were the stuff of dreams. On a macho continent, it scored on gender issues, too: women accounted for 64 percent of its parliamentary seats in 2010—never mind if said parliament had virtually no real power.

The World Bank has devised an Ease of Doing Business index comparing times taken to register a business, win a trading license, or get connected to the electricity grid across the world. In 2011 Rwanda's ranking stood at 58 out of 174 countries, suggesting—somewhat surprisingly—that it was a more corporate-friendly environment than either the Czech Republic (63), Italy (80), or Greece (109).[6]

During these years I seemed to be invited to one presentation after another in the City of London—the kind of events where pretty young women in short black dresses take your coat on arrival and pretty young men circulate with trays of white wine—where analysts would with great fanfare unveil the country they reckoned to be the most exciting investment prospect in Africa. Plucky little Rwanda won every time.

Concern about sleaze's corrosive impact on emerging economies was rife in the West, and Rwanda scored superbly there, too: just as long as the focus was kept conveniently tight. In 2010 the NGO

Transparency International (TI) judged it the least corrupt country in East Africa.[7]

One afternoon I listened, slightly bemused, as an official from Rwanda's Office of the Ombudsman, seen as a model of its kind, explained his work to an admiring audience in Oslo. While you were certainly unlikely to be shaken down by a customs officer with whisky on his breath, I reflected, did the systematic looting of DRC's minerals not count as corruption? Sure enough, a TI investigator, Gustave Makonene, was shot dead in Rwanda in 2013 by two policemen after showing an unhealthy interest in mineral smuggling.[8]

Like the RPF stalwarts who ended up in exile, Rwanda's supporters convinced themselves institutions were what mattered long term, and there again, the nation scored superbly. The National Electoral Commission, the Office of the Ombudsman, the Rwanda Development Board, the Kigali Institute of Science, Technology and Management, the National Institute of Statistics . . . the bodies sprang up like pristine white mushrooms in the forest, bodies that would—surely, inevitably—become healthy checks and balances.

Rwanda ticked all the boxes, even if actual foreign investment remained puzzlingly modest, something perhaps explained by the global perception that Crystal Ventures, the holding company set up by the RPF as a successor to Tri-Star Investments, had already sewn up most of Rwanda's juicy economic opportunities—from furniture-making to milk-processing, quarrying to road construction, private security to finance. Economists might regard Rwanda as a case of successful "developmental patrimonialism," as this near-monopoly arrangement was labeled, but international investors seemed a lot less enthusiastic.

And so Kagame ended up performing one of the cleverest, most ironic of modern balancing acts. Admired by African heads of state for telling the West to take a hike whenever it dared challenge his policies, a champion of feisty African self-reliance on countless public platforms, he remained dependent on foreign aid to balance his budget, year in, year out. He had perfectly calibrated Western donors' need to be needed.

The support of the World Bank and International Monetary Fund could be taken for granted. On top of that, the philanthropic foundations set up by the world's most influential retirees adored his regime. Bill Clinton, whose foundation invests in the fight against malaria, hailed Kagame as "one of the greatest leaders of our time"; Tony Blair, whose charity placed paid experts inside the president's policy unit, praised him as "a visionary."

The messianic US economist Jeffrey Sachs had chosen Rwanda as the site for his third Millennium Village, an experiment in integrated development; the Bill and Melinda Gates Foundation was investing in Rwandan farmers; Howard Buffett considering sinking $500 million of his father's money into the agriculture sector; and Harvard Medical School professor and health campaigner Paul Farmer was so won over he moved his family to Rwanda.[9]

It helped that Kigali—so clean, so efficient, so safe—was such a pleasant place for an expatriate to operate.

Western reporters fresh to Kigali wrote admiring articles so similar they could almost have been photocopied. The correspondents would always marvel at the absence of litter on the smoothly tarmacked streets. In 2008 Rwanda became the first African country to ban the manufacture and use of plastic bags; seven years later it banned smoking in public, doing away with ugly cigarette butts; and two years after that, the smoking of the hookah.

The absence of another form of litter—beggars, street urchins, street vendors, petty criminals, and the homeless—also always got an approving mention, even after a Human Rights Watch report explained the reason: the indigent were routinely rounded up and taken to "rehabilitation centers," where regular beatings were the main form of education, according to those who emerged.[10]

They might also have been struck at the near-silence of the city streets. Rwandan culture has never been known for raised voices, and the police enforced noise pollution controls in the city's well-heeled suburbs so assiduously, local musicians sometimes wondered how their work would ever be heard.

On my last visit to Kigali, I walked out of my hotel and nearly stumbled upon an old woman hunched over the ground, paintbrush in hand. She was part of a team, all sporting matching vests, hard at work refreshing the faded black-and-white-striped curbs. No doubt another team was responsible for the flower beds planted in the traffic islands. I'd never seen a tidier city center.

I flagged down one of the *boda boda* scooters, the quickest way of beating the traffic. In Uganda *boda boda* drivers are both fearless and lawless, weaving between car bumpers, mounting pavements, and shooting lights, a menace to pedestrians and their passengers, who nonetheless climb aboard with toddlers in arms, nary a helmet in sight. In Rwanda, *boda boda* drivers sported numbered vests and were obliged not only to wear helmets, but to carry spares for passengers.

Later, talking to a US adviser on contract to Rwanda's Foreign Ministry, I asked about the black-clad commandos, state-of-the-art rifles cradled in their arms, antennaed radio packs on their backs, patrolling Kigali's streets. Once you clocked their presence, you also noticed they were situated at precise ten-meter intervals along the thoroughfares.

"Oh yes, that's the army," said the expatriate. "The public likes seeing the army deployed. Makes them feel safe."[11] I was careful not to let my skepticism show. In a country where so much violence had been meted out, often by men in uniform, it was hard to believe Rwandan civilians found their presence reassuring.

On that same visit, I bumped into a Western journalist I had last crossed paths with covering the 1994 refugee exodus into what was then Zaire. I'd heard he had married a local, put down roots, and stayed. We ended up sharing a pizza on a terrace looking out over the lights of Kigali as he summarized the neat intellectual bargain so many outsiders make on behalf of Rwandan citizens.

"Back when you and I were covering the genocide, Michela, when the corpses were lying by the sides of the street and neighbor was killing neighbor, if someone had shown us Kigali today, with its high-rise buildings and its safe streets, wouldn't we have thought that counted as a pretty good outcome, if we're absolutely honest?"[12]

Historian Gérard Prunier regards such attitudes as a lingering form of racism, in which violence is seen by the international community as "normal for Africa," and a firm hand on the tiller a sadly necessary corrective to keep barely civilized inhabitants in control.

"Kagame is seen in the West as a mixture of Franklin Roosevelt, General Eisenhower, and General Patton for putting an end to the genocide," Prunier says. "And now on top of that he managed to get all these backward Africans not to use plastic bags and urinate on the sidewalks. There's a refrain that runs, 'Yes, he can be rough on the natives. But can you really expect anything else?'"

"Progressive dictatorship," he comments sardonically, "is a new political category of regime which is spreading worldwide."

The worrying thing about the West's current gushing enthusiasm for strongman rule in Central Africa is its historical naivete. That can in part be traced to the comparative youthfulness of so many of those interacting with Rwanda. As an older generation of historians and analysts retires or dies off, post-genocide Rwanda has become one of the "sexy" African countries for Western research.[13] Academic conferences are packed with the fresh faces of first-time researchers.

But any researcher under the age of forty has no personal memory of the country before the RPF. History, for them, began in 1994, and the country's pristine infrastructure and clockwork bureaucratic efficiency are inevitably seen as Kagame's handiwork, admirable work at that. But those, like me, who ventured into Habyarimana's Rwanda also marveled at the ribbon-like smoothness of the roads, the sobriety of customs officers, the surreal fact that it was still possible, even as horror engulfed the country, to be fined by an overly punctilious policeman in Kigali for running a red light.

As Peter Uvin points out in his book *Aiding Violence*, Habyarimana's Rwanda was also a "donor darling"—"there was no *colline* and no public service where one did not find the four-wheel-drive vehicles of foreign experts"—only the bilateral donors in question were Switzerland, Belgium, Germany, and France, rather than today's United States, United Kingdom, Denmark, and Germany.[14]

If development economists rave today about the efficiency of the Rwandan state, their European predecessors, tellingly, said the same of its genocidal predecessor, choosing to overlook the administration's appalling record on the treatment of Tutsis because the figures on vaccinations and primary education were so damn impressive.

The strong, overbearing state was no Kagame invention; rather, it's a Rwandan specialty dating back to the days of the Mwami. "State collapse," as Gerald Gahima once told me, "was never an option."

But World Bank, DFID, and US Agency for International Development officials ensconced in the capital, under pressure from headquarters to "push money out the door," were not inclined to look back that far. Prey to the groupthink that comes with meeting like-minded colleagues twenty-four hours a day, they were working too hard to venture very often outside Kigali, where they would have registered that conditions in Rwanda's dirt-poor rural areas were a far cry from the images on the government's glossy brochures.

However important their message, the RNC stalwarts' timing in 2010 was distinctly "off."

CHAPTER NINETEEN

SONG OF THE STOOL PIGEON

You get used to killing. Human life becomes
something plain, easy to dispose of. You spend 15–20
minutes on who to kill. On how to kill him: two, three days.

—**Ami Ayalon,** former head of Shin Bet[1]

T he discovery of Patrick's body in Room 905 of the Michelangelo left the RNC reeling.

In one fell swoop, the organization had lost one of its smartest minds, his vast contacts book, his diplomatic skills, and above all, an emollient temperament that had helped the movement bridge the glaring differences in its ranks between Hutus and Tutsis, former Marxists and instinctive capitalists, Francophones and Anglophones, military men and civilians.

"It was a massive blow," the former diplomat Gervais Condo told me. "A major, major loss. We have no one, now, who can deliver on Patrick's areas of expertise. Some old contacts, people we knew twenty years ago, but now he's dead we're really struggling."

The next few years would be spent trying to regroup, even as Rwandan intelligence, the wind in its sails, sought to press home its advantage.

In early March 2014, two months after Patrick's murder, yet another attempt was made on General Kayumba's life. This time an armed commando raided the safe house where he was staying with Rosette and the family. South Africa's elite unit, the Hawks, was tipped off ahead of time. It appears to have allowed the raid to take place during the family's arranged absence, in order to secure the necessary incriminating evidence, which pointed in the usual direction.

"It was very clear that they were intelligence personnel attached to the Rwandan embassy," a diplomatic source told Reuters.[2] "It's not an embassy, it's an operation center for planning missions to kill innocent civilians," scoffed Patrick's nephew David Batenga. "It should be closed." The South African government finally snapped, expelling three Rwandan diplomats and one Burundian. Unabashed, Rwanda responded by ordering six South African diplomats in Kigali out of the country.

Rwandan intelligence's focus was not restricted exclusively to the RNC. In early April, two days after President Kagame and an official delegation flew into Belgium to attend an EU-AU summit, four police cars, one of them armored, drew up outside the Brussels home of former prime minister Twagiramungu.[3]

Informing Twagiramungu that his life was in imminent danger, they placed him under armed guard. The police would not reveal how they had acquired this information, saying only it was provided by "a third country"—probably a euphemism for "US intelligence"—but it was clearly both detailed and urgent. "They talked emotionally," said Twagiramungu. "They said this was very serious."

The police detail was withdrawn four days later, leaving Twagiramungu with the distinct impression that a high-profile attack had been planned to coincide with Kagame's visit, but abandoned in light of the security measures taken by the Belgian police. As ever, the Belgian authorities did Kigali the massive favor of not telling the media what they knew.

By the year's end, Rwandan intelligence was at it again in South Africa. This time the plot came to light by sheer fluke, the random arrest of a motorbike driver delivering pizzas. The fascinating details tumbled out during court hearings held to decide whether or not Alex Ruta, a former Rwandan army lieutenant working for the NISS, should be deported.[4]

By Ruta's own account, his boss had in October 2014 given him a special assignment: he was to travel to South Africa, where he was to "befriend" members of the RNC. He was given a new passport and told to take a complicated meandering route—first Tanzania, then Zambia, Mozambique, Zimbabwe—in order to muddy his tracks.

Arriving in South Africa in the run-up to Christmas, Ruta hooked up with another agent who installed him in a safe house in Johannesburg's Regents Park suburb and introduced him to a go-between who would link him up with the RNC. It was only when the NISS agent mentioned he was finding him a gun, Ruta claimed, that he realized his assignment was not to "befriend," but to execute.

Panicking, Ruta began avoiding the go-between. After an incident in which gunfire was aimed at his house, he was briefly placed under the Hawks' Witness Protection Scheme. Stopped on his motorbike while delivering pizzas in Pretoria, he'd been arrested for being in possession of a fraudulent asylum seeker's permit and driving without a license. His extraordinary assignment only came to public light when, having served three months in jail, he appealed against his return to Rwanda, where, he told the court, "I will face certain death," presumably for balking at a professional assignment.

•

But the most precious insights into Rwandan intelligence operations in the years that followed Patrick's murder come from Eric Ruzindana, a former Rwandan army officer who moved to Belgium, where he was determined to secure the passport that would allow him to legitimize his status and access regular work.

In Brussels, Eric joined the immigrant population that accumulates around any cosmopolitan European city: a community whose members drive late-night taxis, work strictly cash-in-hand, and occasionally trade drugs, sharing digs with Russian ex-spies, Kazakh former soldiers, Polish truck drivers, Romanian petty thieves, and Turkish middlemen, all on the same hustle.

After being seen attending an anti-Kagame demonstration, he'd been approached by Rwandan intelligence, with a job offer. It was the usual deal. Kigali knew that Theogene Rudasingwa often passed through Brussels, where he hooked up with other exiled Rwandans and tried to mobilize support. Eric was to wheedle his way into the former RPF secretary-general's confidence and devise a foolproof method for killing him during one of these visits. Rwandan intelligence was also keen to eliminate senior RNC member Jean-Marie Micombero and Robert Higiro, now based in Brussels. But the main target this time was Theogene.

But Eric was not quite what he seemed. During his time in uniform, he'd become disgusted by the atrocities he'd seen the RPF commit. "I hate that government because of all the innocent people I saw them kill. I wasn't going to work for them again," he told me.[5] He'd been deliberately dangled under military intelligence's nose by RNC member Jonathan Musonera, in a classic entrapment exercise. Once Kigali took the bait, Musonera flew to Belgium to sit patiently at Ruzindana's side, coaching him in how to string out communications as long as possible while taping the conversations on his cell. It was yet another sting.

If the tapes are authentic—and three Rwandan sources whom I asked to listen believe they recognize the voices—these were rich pickings. Eric's initial handler was René Rutagungira, Rwanda's top intelligence agent in Kampala and the man blamed for Lieutenant Joel Mutabazi's kidnapping and Aimé Ntabana's mysterious disappearance. Once Eric moved to Brussels, Dan Munyuza, who had been promoted to head Rwanda's external intelligence, Patrick's old job, took over.

To anyone who had listened to the tapes the General and Patrick released in mid-2011 or read the transcripts in the Swedish "Bananas" case, the tone and content of the "Rukara Files," as Theogene eventually labeled the transcripts of these forty-five separate phone conversations, are strikingly familiar.[6]

There's the same sloppy use of code. Having revealed early on that the plot involves himself, "James," and Munyuza, Rutagungira is easily tricked into spelling out the fact that the light-skinned Theogene's code name will be "Rukara"—a heavy-handed joke, as *rukara* means "black" in Kinyarwanda. Micombero's will be "Kanyombya," and Robert's "Number One." Rutagungira had sent the codes separately by SMS, but when Eric claims not to remember them, Rutagungira talks him through them over the phone, an elementary blunder.

Kigali shows the same striking absence of curiosity regarding Eric's supposed motivation, surely a key issue for any spymaster, as it did with would-be assassins Robert, Emile, and Jennifer. The emphasis is strictly pragmatic: access, likelihood of success, possibility of exposure, and—most important—cost. The two men could be haggling over the price of a new kitchen rather than a man's life.

There's the same readiness to contemplate the most lurid elimination techniques, with the various scenarios put forward by Eric—usually enthusiastically agreed to by his handlers—reminiscent of a Jason Bourne movie, only with even less concern shown than Hollywood filmmakers for possible collateral damage. If killing Theogene requires the deaths of several close companions, so be it.

But there was a key difference, too. In contrast with Emile, Jennifer, and Robert, who were trusted by Patrick and the General, Eric never won Theogene's full confidence. Throughout the operation his intended victim was uncertain whether Eric was a double agent taking Kigali for a ride, or actually a triple agent playing both Kigali and the RNC. "I never trusted him, so I never let him get close," Theogene said.

First Eric and his handlers consider poisoning, that tried and tested Rwandan technique. "I am the one who serves him with drinks," Eric assures Munyuza. "If we had something to put in, it would be simple. René told me you have it."

Later, Eric suggests having a collaborator bundle "Rukara" into a van and inject him, presumably—in light of later conversations—with heroin. One advantage of this technique, one assumes, is that Theogene might then appear to have had a drug habit and simply overdosed. Eric discusses going to Poland to identify a hit squad.

By mid-July 2015, Eric has moved on to discussing how Theogene could be surprised in the apartment he uses when visiting Brussels. "It is better to look for a key and it is done in his own home," Munyuza tells Eric. "It is better so that they find a very high concentration in his body."

Eric later calls Munyuza to say he has met the hit squad. "They have shown me all their tools. They are professional. They have like those of the scientific police." For 140,000 euros, the team will wait for Theogene inside the apartment. "Three of them would already be in the house and we find them there when we go home. They have 80 mg of heroin and a syringe. They would inject him, even if he screams it wouldn't go far."

Chillingly, Munyuza opens up the possibility of plenty of future work—"Tell them you are going to work with them on many other operations because the business is long"—and reminds Eric to take Theogene's iPad and remove the battery—a de facto tracking device—from his smartphone.

The following day, Eric is all set. He tells Munyuza he plans to spend the day with Theogene in a Belgian village and will then return to the apartment, at which point, "I will pretend that I forgot my cell in the car so that he enters his house alone. The team will be ready for him. They will inject him with heroin, 80 mg on his right arm. They already have masks, gloves, and different number plates they will use. They have established there are no cameras where he lives." As for Eric, he will make a point of being seen in a few bars in Brussels equipped with CCTV that evening, in order to provide an alibi.

But then comes a key detail. Each killer wants 50,000 euros, Eric tells Munyuza, 150,000 euros in all. "That is a lot, tell them 100,000 only," says Munyuza. Eric warns him, "I doubt they will accept. They are crooks who take cocaine." Munyuza stands firm, telling Eric to dangle a second hit—on "Kanyombya" (i.e., Micombero)—as bait.

Momentum seems to peter away. In late August 2015, Eric raises another possibility: "I have a plan of using an ex-KGB man," he tells Munyuza. "Be quick and give me the whole plan," Munyuza urges him. Then Eric raises another problem: What is to be done with the "boys"—presumably members of the Rwandan diaspora—who provide security whenever Theogene visits? "Should we also put them to sleep?" Eric wonders aloud. "There is one who loves Rudasingwa very much. It is better to do away with all of them." Munyuza casually agrees, but asks for a plan. "Work with foreigners but look at all the options."

When the conversation next resumes, Eric gives more detail. His "ex-KGB" friend used to be a doctor in the military, he says, and is familiar with such operations. "He would come with two collaborators from Kazakhstan." It seems Theogene is no longer planning to stay in a hired apartment, because the focus moves to "doing it in the hotel."

Eric explains the ex-KGB doctor's methodology. "He said they would use three types of drugs: the first one would paralyze him; the second would stop his heart. He would check in the hotel adjacent to ours. He has some equipment that would disorganize the cameras so that his identity is not revealed." The drugs, which are used for prisoners on death row, Eric explains, would be sourced in Russia.

"If they inject him wouldn't he fight?" asks Munyuza.

"No he has no strength," Eric assures him. "Once he goes to bed I would check if he is asleep, then I would alert them to come in to do their job." As for the entourage: "He told me there is a drug we can give the boys to sleep for ten hours."

But Eric is worried about costs. The Russian hit squad is charging 400,000 euros, he says, "because of the expensive drugs he has to get." Munyuza is shocked. "Eeeh, that is a lot of money!" Eric is instructed to bargain the price down.

The operation seems to have been put on hold, because by the end of August 2015, Eric is back in touch to say that Theogene is definitely flying into Brussels. No talk of using the Russian team, now; instead Eric suggests a staged traffic "accident." "There is a Romanian truck driver who was my neighbor. He is a demobilized soldier from Romania who does transport from Amsterdam to Brussels. I have asked him without confirming because he had asked for two trucks. That gave me some energy to plan."

"How would you do it?" asks Munyuza.

"I had thought of doing it on the highway. It will be at night with little traffic. I would be in the front car, and he would be behind with my security boys. . . . From the front I would signal the Romanian to be behind me. He would go on the man's side and bump them off the road. I would organize to go and check if [Theogene] is still breathing, and if not finish the job."

"I will get back to you," replies Munyuza. "Keep it as you told me and do not fail."

"It is not possible to fail on the highway," Eric assures him. This time the price is lower, just 80,000 euros. "Accept the price," Munyuza instructs him.

Just as everything seems set, the operation is dealt a major blow. Theogene, Eric claims, has called at the last moment to say his travel documents need to be renewed and he has been unable to travel.

Later in September, Eric mentions yet another Russian ex-KGB friend. This time the plan involves a toxic spray—the disastrous gassing by Russia's special forces of Moscow's hostage-filled Dubrovka Theater in 2002 comes to mind. Eric says, "He told me he would spray the room with a gas that would put him to sleep and would then inject into him a drug that would stop his heart."

Munyuza tells him to "plan quickly," adding, "There are only two days left."

The following day, Eric says inspection of the premises has prompted a different plan. The team will use an elevator that runs down into the basement, bundling the target into a vehicle. "We shall also use a system that disrupts the CCTV cameras, so that my guys gain entry. . . . He would dump the body in Lille in France, close to Belgium." The two then discuss payment—the truck driver wants 200,000 euros, with 150,000 up front, while Munyuza insists on 150,000, with a 100,000 deposit.

As he wavers, Munyuza reminds Eric of the importance of prepping for a nice, clean operation. "Do not forget to buy bedsheets and towels so that you do not stain the carpets."

"One of his people is an expert in all that," Eric assures him. "They have to protect themselves."

Theogene tells me that he found that part of the conversation, with its reminder of the way Patrick's killers used bedcovers and towels to conceal their handiwork, the most disturbing section of the exchange. "The bit where Dan is saying, 'Buy lots of sheeting so you don't stain the carpet.' Isn't that a glimpse into the mind of a psychopath? But that's what Dan is."

The last tape released dates to October 7, 2015, when whatever plans were hatched have collapsed. "I can see Rukara still has some days to live," Munyuza comments dryly.

"It did not work out?" asks Eric.

"It did not work out," Munyuza confirms. "Tell him that your people found the price too high." But Eric should remain in contact with the hit man. "Tell him once money is available the business will be his."

The constant chatter must have drawn the attention of more than one intelligence service, because in late 2015, Robert Higiro was warned by the State Department in Washington that his life was in danger and advised to leave Belgium. He rebased in the United States, and the relationship between Eric and Rwandan intelligence came to a close.

The most shocking thing about these conversations is not, in fact, their content, but that they took place at all, after the exposure Rwanda's assassination program had already received. Munyuza had clearly learned neither caution nor sophistication with the passage of the years; nor was he any more skilled at choosing his agents. "Dan keeps doing the same thing, over and over again," comments Theogene. "It shows you the impunity and the arrogance of the man."

Theogene gave copies of both the tapes and the transcripts to the FBI as well as to the Belgian and Ugandan embassies in Washington, so that they could be relayed to Belgium's and Uganda's respective police and intelligence services. The response, he says, was disappointing.

"The FBI told me they would look at them and be in touch if they needed any more. After that, nothing." As for his personal security arrangements: "They just said, 'If you see anything suspicious, call 911.' That's useless to me. By the time they respond, I'll be dead."

But by then, Kagame's former chef de cabinet had other things on his mind. The great irony was that the next major blow to the RNC—which was to prove nearly as devastating as Patrick's assassination—would come not from Kigali but from Theogene himself.

•

In African postindependence history, the biggest challenge confronting opposition movements is not the regime they denounce but their own comrades, the tendency to squabble, fall out, and divide over points of principle playing disastrously into the hands of the government of the day. The RNC was no exception.

On July 1, 2016, Theogene, the perennial iconoclast, published a letter announcing his departure from the RNC and the creation of a rival movement, "New RNC." While his critics accused him of not wanting to contest overdue internal elections, he presented the split as a principled stand against a militaristic drift he blamed on General Kayumba, who he said was bent on installing "puppet subordinates" to head the RNC's various branches.[7]

Having left the RPF after its capture by a Tutsi military clique, he was not about to sit back and watch the RNC being sabotaged in the same way, he told me. Since both the General and Kagame shared the same Tutsi supremacist mindset, the existing RNC could not offer Rwandans a way out. Deciding to leave had been an "agonizing" process, but removing Kagame was not enough, "unless the pursuit and exercise of power in Rwanda by cliques is uprooted decisively and completely." Jonathan Musonera, who had overseen Eric Ruzindana's taping operation, was one of those to join Theogene in the New RNC.

It was a bitter, personalized split, and it played marvelously into Kigali's hands. Had Patrick, the great mediator and supreme persuader, lived, it's hard to imagine he'd have allowed it to happen.

CHAPTER TWENTY

THE INQUEST

The longer it takes to deal with a matter,
the harder it becomes.

—Magistrate Mashiane Mathopa,
at Patrick Karegeya's inquest

"This is not one of those cases where no one will ever be charged," the first police investigator assigned to the Patrick Karegeya murder case had assured a shell-shocked David Batenga. That pledge had calmed him at the time. But for five long years, nothing happened.

The witnesses gave their statements, fingerprints were taken from the two hotel rooms, the body was autopsied, DNA samples sent to the forensics laboratory and . . . nothing. The postmortem results remained confidential. Patrick's laptops, iPad, and papers, all removed by the police from his Ruimsig house, were not returned. No charges were brought, no arrests made, no inquest date announced.

The police referred the case to the Hawks, who interviewed all the witnesses again. And then again. David was questioned five times in all—"They asked the same questions each time, so that's just incompetence"—and then the Hawks simply stopped returning

403

his calls. Even prosecutor Shaun Abrahams, appointed director of public prosecutions, went mysteriously silent on him.

There seemed to be no appetite for pursuing the matter. Not surprising, perhaps, because, from a political and diplomatic perspective, it was a cringe-makingly awkward case.

Kagame was transforming himself into one of Africa's most high-profile statesmen. His capital was being successfully marketed as a glossy international conference center, network hub, and showcase of successful development. In 2014, Kigali hosted the African Development Bank's annual general meeting; two years later the World Economic Forum chose it for an "African Davos"; the Commonwealth agreed to hold its Heads of Government meeting there in 2020.

VIPs and finance ministers heading for the brand-new high-rise hotels marveled at the cleanliness of Kigali's streets, the availability of Wi-Fi in the airport bus, and quietly agreed that if a touch of repression was the price for all this, it was probably worth paying. To the aspirational authoritarian leader, "iron rule" is not exactly a term of abuse.

In January 2018 Kagame assumed the rotating chairmanship of the African Union—another international stage. His term was the most dynamic for decades, with the man who got stuff *done* pushing for tariff-free, continent-wide trade and lambasting his peers for their dependency on Western aid with the same unforgiving vigor as he berated his own officials.

The RPF also patched things up with its old foe, France. In October 2018, Louise Mushikiwabo, the foreign minister who had relished Patrick's murder, was appointed secretary-general of the Organisation Internationale de la Francophonie, giving Rwanda huge clout in the vast swath of the globe that speaks French.

Given Kagame's soaring international status, it was awkward for South Africa, the continent's largest economy and self-assigned moral arbiter, not to have diplomatic dealings with Rwanda. Kigali should have been the party finding the situation discomfiting, given the event that had triggered the crisis. Instead, Pretoria seemed on the defensive, its ANC ministers and diplomats, so ideologically wedded to the principles of negotiation and compromise, uncertain how to deal with quite such a macho regime.

Cyril Ramaphosa's election as South African president gave the two nations a chance to reboot the relationship. They grabbed it. In March 2018 the two presidents held a tête-à-tête on the fringes of an AU summit in Kigali and pledged to "normalize" ties.

Matters, for the RNC, were not helped by the publication that December of a UN panel of experts' report alleging that General Kayumba had established a guerrilla force up on the high plateau south of Uvira in the DRC, a militia supported by Burundi and Uganda and dedicated to Kagame's overthrow.[1]

The report's main thrust surprised no one—the fact that the RNC had a military wing was common knowledge—but it made General Kayumba's presence in South Africa all the more awkward. Two South African human rights groups had been pushing since 2011 for the General's refugee status to be rescinded on the grounds that he was wanted for crimes against humanity.[2] RNC members urged David Batenga to let the matter of Patrick's inquest quietly drop. "You'll get us all expelled," was the message.

But something in David jibbed. Sure, he read the local newspapers just like everyone else, and he heard the mounting laments about South Africa's collapsing criminal justice system. But like so many African exiles starting new lives down south, he held this adopted system to a higher standard than his own. "South Africa isn't some banana republic," he insisted. "The rule of law applies here."

On his side he had lawyer Kennedy Gihana.[3]

Persistence has been Gihana's leitmotif, dogged determination the spine running through his extraordinary trajectory. It was what had prompted him, a refugee raised in Uganda's Ankole region, who fought for the RPF in some of the most hair-raising episodes of Rwanda's civil war, to *walk* most of the 3,500 miles from Kigali to Johannesburg when he'd become disillusioned with the post-genocide government.

The trek through five countries had taken him six months. Cadging food, sleeping outside, taking the *panya* roads to avoid thugs and muggers, he managed to talk his way across border points, despite owning neither passport nor visas.

Once in South Africa, Kennedy had slept on the streets until winning a job as a security guard at the Rwanda High Commission in Pretoria. While carrying out those duties, he'd scraped together the funds to study for a South African law degree. On graduation in 2006, he'd become both an immigration lawyer and the RNC's pro bono legal representative, a role he believed had immediately made him a target for Rwandan agents in South Africa.

The car accident that had shattered his thigh had confirmed that suspicion, as had a conversation with Gustave Tuyishime, a Rwandan refugee working as a bouncer and taxi driver in Pretoria. Tuyishime was yet another one of the DMI's hapless would-be assassins. He had contacted Kennedy to tell him he'd been wired $16,000 by a Rwandan intelligence agent with instructions to buy a gun and kill first the General and then, when he'd failed to deliver on that first assignment, to target Kennedy while he was being treated in the hospital. Appalled, Tuyishime had instead warned Kennedy, who had moved to a different hospital.[4]

Clearly, Kennedy was not the type who gives up easily. When he sensed that Patrick's case had stalled, he started approaching South African human rights groups, asking them if they could kick-start the process. He knocked on the doors of seven separate organizations—all refused. Apart from one: AfriForum.[5]

Mention the word "AfriForum" to a white liberal, or a member of South Africa's growing black middle class, and they'll screw up their faces in distaste. "I really don't like what that organization is doing," a white journalist told me when I raised the name. The group describes itself as a minority rights group, but it has been called a "Fascist organisation" by at least one newspaper columnist: the "minority" it is chiefly concerned with, critics claim, are Afrikaans farmers who benefited from apartheid and live in fear of seeing their property redistributed by a black majority government.

Founded in 2006, AfriForum had become more radical with the passing years, making headlines when its members met populist politicians in Australia, Europe, and the United States to lobby support for its campaign against ANC plans for land expropriation. The crusade prompted a characteristically over-the-top tweet from President Donald Trump, who announced the United States would be investigating the South African government's "large-scale killing" of white farmers, while Australian home affairs minister Peter Dutton stepped forward with an offer of special visas for this "persecuted" group.

But Kennedy wasn't interested in AfriForum's headline-grabbing domestic politics. This NGO, he realized, was the only organization in the country capable of launching an independent criminal investigation and prosecution. That was thanks to Gerrie Nel, the high-profile former public prosecutor who had resigned from his post at the National Prosecuting Authority (NPA) in 2017 to set up a special unit at AfriForum dedicated to redressing glaring miscarriages of justice.

Nel is famous in South Africa. During the televised trial of "Blade Runner" Oscar Pistorius for the shooting of model girlfriend Reeva Steenkamp, he acquired an awestruck fan following.[6] They called him "the Bulldog" and raved on social media about his terrier-like interrogation of the paraplegic sprinter. You can watch clips on You-Tube of Nel asking Pistorius, who vomited with nerves during the trial and repeatedly burst into tears, "Now, why are you crying?" The question is posed with distant, almost scientific curiosity. Reading up on Nel, I wasn't surprised to discover he taught wrestling as a hobby. "Do you ever get hurt?" I asked him at one point. "No," he said, looking faintly amused. "I hurt other people."

Nel had surprised and in some cases appalled his admirers by joining AfriForum. He'd spent thirty-six years working for the state, after all, during which time he'd not just led the Scorpions—the Hawks' formidable predecessors—but prosecuted the killers of black activist Chris Hani, and sent corrupt policeman Jackie Selebi to jail. But if he refrained from publicly spelling out his grievances, it wasn't hard to see what lay behind the shock career move.

Determined to escape prosecution on more than 700 corruption charges, previous president Jacob Zuma had eviscerated the judicial system, appointing men and women with criminal records to head key institutions and departments. Underfunded, mismanaged, and demoralized, the NPA hemorrhaged staff, most of whom ended up in the corporate sector. In choosing instead to set up his private prosecutions unit, staffed by ex-policemen he knew and trusted, Nel was basically appointing himself ombudsman of the service he'd once proudly served. South Africa's legal system had always theoretically catered for private prosecutions, but before Nel's move, there had only ever been two.

The cases Nel chose on AfriForum's behalf seemed designed to pique public interest, and they certainly weren't confined to dispossessed Afrikaans farmers. When the Porsche driven by Dudu-zane Zuma, the then president's son, plowed into a taxi in 2014, kill-ing a young mother, the NPA decided not to prosecute the young man on the grounds of insufficient evidence. After AfriForum got involved, it reinstated charges of culpable homicide.[7]

AfriForum also took on the case of a Johannesburg model who said she'd been hit in the face with an extension cord by Grace Mu-gabe, allegedly furious at the young woman's liaison with her sons. Nel called for Zimbabwe's former First Lady's diplomatic immunity to be lifted so she could be prosecuted. "His bark and his bite are both equally terrifying," a South African news website warned the irate Mrs. Mugabe.[8]

"When we started out doing this, most South Africans would have predicted our clients were going to be mostly white," Nel told me. "In fact, most have been black. It's a principled thing we're doing with people who have been failed by the system."[9]

At first glance, Nel's decision to represent Patrick's family seemed out of kilter. Here was a country many ordinary South Afri-cans would struggle to locate on a map. The victim's family was so cash-strapped that Nel, like Kennedy, would be working for free. But in other ways it was classic Bulldog territory. There was simply no plausible explanation for the failure to hold an inquest, stage a prosecution, or launch extradition proceedings. Instead there was a strong whiff of political meddling about events, of cozy deals done behind closed doors, and that got Nel's muzzle twitching.

"I have an absolute problem with selective prosecution," he said. "The fact that some people get prosecuted and others don't for the same kind of crimes. I had it as a state prosecutor, and I have it now." If, on top of that, the victim was a black African, that certainly wouldn't do AfriForum's image any harm, either.

Nel's involvement in Patrick's case had a swift, galvanizing effect. However committed Kennedy might be, he was a foreigner working in an alien environment. He simply didn't possess the profile, the network, or professional clout, established over the decades, of his new collaborator. In November 2018, to general surprise, a date for a hearing was announced, with at least thirty witnesses lined up to give testimony and sixteen working days blocked off in the court calen-dar. Curiously, this would be an inquest, not a murder trial. But on

January 16, 2019, almost exactly five years after Patrick's death, the family was finally to get its day in court.

Why did it matter? The Rwandan public was certainly in no doubt about who had killed Patrick Karegeya. The government's position was to deny all responsibility while in the same breath stating that as a well-known "terrorist," Patrick obviously deserved to die. If the Americans had seen fit to assassinate Osama bin Laden and never apologized for it, why shouldn't the Rwandan government take out high-profile members of the RNC? It was the usual Kagame double-speak, all the more effective, as far as the domestic audience went, for its internal inconsistency. What the donors got was a token "We're innocent." What the Rwandan audience heard was, "We can and will say any old thing to please those fools in the international community. But *of course* we killed him. We're proud of it. And remember: we'll do this to anyone else who stands in our way."

But a court ruling appointing responsibility to Kigali might matter to those westerners—to the officials at the World Bank, IMF, DFID and USAID, who kept Rwanda's Treasury afloat with aid; to staff at the Gates, Blair, and Clinton foundations; and to admirers such as Paul Farmer, Howard Buffett, Pastor Rick Warren, and Rabbi Shmuley Boteach—who were keen to focus on the first part of Kagame's two-pronged message while ignoring the second.

Given the stakes involved, it was a surprisingly modest venue. Randburg Magistrates' Court is a low-slung, ugly red-brick building that squats inside a fenced compound off one of the long, tree-lined avenues traversing Johannesburg's northern suburbs. Access is up two shallow flights of stairs, through a scanner operated by police officers, and then through an old-fashioned metal turnstile. Inside, white-kerchiefed advocates stride along the corridors, black gowns flying, while beleaguered-looking defendants stage huddled conversations on functional benches. "No Guns Beyond This Point" reads a sign on the wall, immediately prompting you to wonder how many of the men and women milling around are packing. Other posters advertise the services of Narcotics Anonymous.

In Courtroom No. 13, Patrick's small army of supporters gathered. Leah had flown in from Washington and was looking poised and elegant in a chartreuse dress. She sat next to David, de facto man of the family in Patrick's absence. General Kayumba's attendance would have required a special deployment by his security team, so his absence came as no surprise, but his wife, Rosette, and their eldest daughter were there. Behind them sat a dozen RNC supporters, including Jennifer Rwamugira, sporting yellow T-shirts printed with an image of Patrick, in the military uniform he so disliked, looking heavy-lidded and suitably sardonic. "We Stand With Our Hero" read the slogan. Slightly surreally, a couple of white AfriForum supporters—their sun-frazzled skins the color of copper, hair curly and uncombed—had donned the T-shirts in solidarity.

I scoured the faces. Somewhere in the courtroom there was bound to be someone—probably several "someones"—paid by the Rwanda High Commission to log what was said and who turned up, but there was no telling who.

A very small cluster of international and South African journalists sat on the left side of the courtroom. In the months running up to the inquest, global news had been dominated by lurid details of the murder and dismemberment of Jamal Khashoggi in the Saudi consulate in Istanbul, and the year before, the nerve-agent poisoning of double agent Sergei Skripal had caused a diplomatic row between Moscow and London. Here was another example of an authoritarian state reaching blithely beyond its own borders to eliminate a perceived enemy, indifferent to issues of legality or sovereignty.

The BBC, CNN, Reuters, Associated Press, AFP, RFI, Al Jazeera, and Voice of America all have newsrooms in Johannesburg, as does any serious South African newspaper, radio station, or television channel. Given that the inquest was taking place a ten-minute drive away from many of their regional offices, turnout seemed surprisingly low. I hadn't expected any other journalist to bother flying all the way from London for the event, but I was still surprised. A local gangland stabbing would have attracted more attention.

That might be a measure of widespread cynicism about the South African judicial process. "You can rest assured that nothing of any interest will emerge," a local political analyst had blithely assured me. Over lunch in the Rosebank mall, one of the few reporters following the case was equally skeptical, musing aloud that there was surely nothing to prevent a magistrate from conveniently finding that yes, Patrick had been murdered, but as for motive, men like Patrick made enemies, and perhaps some private vendetta or a business deal turned sour was to blame. . . . The very fact that this was an inquest, presided over by a lowly magistrate rather than a judge, seemed indicative. "It's easier to get to magistrates than judges," a veteran South African legal hand had warned me. "They're paid less."

But that wasn't the only explanation for the modest media presence—or, for that matter, the telling absence of any academic, policy analyst, or researcher who had built their professional reputation on an in-depth knowledge of Rwanda. "If you make the *slightest* criticism of Rwanda, you can rest assured that Kigali will see it, make a note of it, and when you or one of your colleagues next applies for media accreditation, some official will make you absolutely crawl through the dirt to get it," a veteran news editor later explained.[10]

Magistrate Mashiane Mathopa entered from a back door, and the court rose as he took his seat high up on the dais. Disconcertingly, Mathopa spoke so softly his words barely registered on the microphone at all. The handful of reporters craned forward, eyes glued to the odd couple standing before him. Well over six feet, Kennedy could never be mistaken for anything other than a Tutsi. He towered, tall and dark, over the sandy-haired, surprisingly petite Nel, who nonetheless managed to radiate a sense of suppressed menace. Standing alongside a stolid-faced AfriForum colleague, somehow instantly recognizable as an ex-cop, the two could easily have been mistaken for a pair of grizzled ex-mercenaries, back from some covert operation in Angola.

Facing them was Yusuf Baba, the affable young public prosecutor, who kept wiping sweat from his brow. January is the height of the South African summer, and the air in the courtroom was torpid and soupy. In a vain attempt to get a breeze circulating, the clerks had propped open the doors, and snatches of conversation gusted over from the corridors, cutting across the exchanges between magistrate and advocates.

At a press conference at a Centurion hotel the previous day, David had whispered to me, "Gerrie is not happy with the way things have been done, not happy at all." Some kind of explosive showdown, he'd warned, was in the offing.

And sure enough, once the initial formalities were over, Nel, in best attack-dog mode, went for the jugular. Why had the NPA decided on an inquest rather than a prosecution? "This matter was not properly investigated, and definitely not investigated with a view to arresting and prosecuting those responsible," he said. Given the contents of the case docket, the five-year delay was "inexplicable," he added, denouncing both "abuse of a process" and "a cover-up." "One is left to make the irresistible inference of political meddling."

Inquests are held to establish just four things: the identity of the deceased, how and when he died, and whether an offense had been committed. In Patrick Karegeya's case, Nel told the magistrate, all these details were already known. As reporters' pens scurried across their notebooks, he read out the names of the four Rwandans responsible—Appollo Ismael Kiririsi [*sic*], Alex Sugira, Samuel Niyoyita, and Nshizrungu Vianney—identifying the suspects in court for the first time. He appealed to Magistrate Mathopa to halt the inquest while the South African Police Service explained its failure to institute criminal proceedings. Counterintuitively, a family that had fought to see action was now asking for everything to stop.[11]

As Mathopa adjourned to consider the application, a cluster of reporters huddled around first Kennedy, then Nel. The former prosecutor, his face bleached by the cameramen's spotlights, gave a series of interviews peppered with the punchy sound bites beloved of television editors. He seemed supremely at his ease.

Mathopa gave his answer the following Monday. I had been expecting the magistrate to neatly sidestep Nel's land mine, acknowledging his concerns, perhaps, while proceeding smoothly with a process intended to bury the truth. Instead, he shocked Courtroom No. 13 by not only agreeing with Nel that the Karegeya family were owed an explanation—he gave the Sepedi-language equivalent of "Justice delayed is justice denied"—but for the first time revealing the existence of a damning letter sent by the public prosecutor's office to the Hawks. In what the magistrate helpfully flagged up as "a letter of vital importance," South Africa's director of public prosecutions on June 5, 2018, justified the decision not to prosecute on the grounds that the suspects had all returned to Rwanda, and, "furthermore, close links exist between the suspects and the current Rwandan government."[12]

Written just three months after Ramaphosa and Kagame publicly announced their determination to normalize ties, the letter exposed to withering view what lay behind the failure to make judicial headway. With that one line, South Africa's conviction that the Rwandan government was responsible for Patrick's murder, along with its obliging readiness to conceal that fact, had been exposed. To Nel, it felt like the ultimate gift. "I was amazed when the magistrate read out that letter," he later told me. "The prosecutor was saying, 'We know there's political interference, therefore we're doing nothing.' I would never have written something like that. But that's what they said."

Mathopa accordingly ordered Inquest No. 0001/2019 struck from the roll, on the grounds that it was "not enjoying public confidence," and gave the Hawks two weeks to explain in writing what, if any, steps they had taken to arrest the Rwandan suspects.

In early March Kennedy messaged me in London with a new court date: April 18, 2019, just before the start of the Easter holiday. I flew to a Johannesburg teetering on the edge of winter. The trees lining the avenues of Randburg were tinted with gold and auburn and there was a distinct chill in the air. With offices and shops already closing—Easter is almost as serious a break as Christmas in South Africa—there were even fewer journalists present. Just five foreign correspondents and only one South African reporter, who left halfway through proceedings to catch a flight to join his vacationing family in Durban.

The "informal inquest," as Mathopa dubbed it, was staged not in court but in a boardroom hidden down a narrow corridor. Lawyers and family members, including Leah and David, took up position around a conference table. There had been initial, eyebrow-raising talk of excluding the press, but at a gesture from Kennedy the journalists slipped into a row of chairs propped against the wall.

Stripped of his puff-sleeved black robes and seated at ground level, Mathopa looked far less imposing. He briskly read out his formal findings, stamped, signed, and dated, which established that "PATRICK KAREGEYA, A 53 YEARS OLD ADULT MALE PERSON," died on "01 JANUARY 2014," and that the cause was "CONSISTENT WITH FEATURES OF LIGATURE STRANGULATION." As to the question whether the death "was brought about by any act or omission *prima facie* involving or amounting to an offence on the part of any person," Mathopa had typed "YES AND KNOWN." As in, a crime had been committed and likely perpetrators identified.[13]

Once again, South Africa's police had provided a host of embarrassing detail. Ordered to explain what action he had taken to arrest the perpetrators, the Hawks' investigating officer, one Lieutenant Colonel Kwena Motlhamme, had submitted a five-page statement, in which he said that Patrick's murder and attempts on the General's life "were directly linked to the involvement of the Rwandan government." The Hawks, he wrote, had told a security committee as much when summoned to parliament to brief its members: "The involvement of the Rwandan Government was brought to their attention." Diplomats of the respective countries had been expelled, but there was no extradition treaty between the two nations. "These facts made it very impossible for any attempt to locate the suspects from their country of origin," Motlhamme insisted. The addition of the word "very" somehow gave his statement an authentic South African flavor.[14]

It was an explanation that carefully failed to specify exactly which individual, or body, had decided to kick Patrick's case into the long grass. But it left no doubt on one point, at least: incompetence, underfunding, bureaucratic mix-ups, or staff shortages were not to blame. A political decision had been made.

After all the years of waiting, it had taken just twenty minutes to whack the ball straight back at the National Prosecuting Authority. Crudely speaking, the magistrate had presented the authority with a "Shit or get off the pot" choice when it came to prosecuting Patrick's killers, however awkward.

As far as the Karegeya family were concerned, little of substance had been revealed. The insights into how the South African authorities had tried to bury the case had caused not a flicker of surprise—this was what they had always instinctively known. Nonetheless, there was a sense of suppressed gaiety, of heady relief, in Randburg Magistrates' Court. Family members and RNC supporters sitting on the corridor benches smiled and quietly squeezed one another's hands. Despite all the procrastination, despite the media's semi-indifference, the international community's rose-tinted vision of Kagame had taken a knock. Damning things had been said that could never now be unsaid, and all of them on the record.

From the United States, Patrick's eldest son, Elvis, tweeted his elation with a banner headline: "GOOD FUCKING MORNING! HOW

IS EVERYONE DOING???"—followed by four giant smiley faces. "I'm extremely happy," Leah told journalists. "To hear this judgment from the court is something we're thankful for. It proves we were right." The response from Kigali, and its High Commission in Pretoria, was a resounding silence.

Nel gave the NPA three months. Since the court hearings had exposed abuse of process, he said, it had no choice but to have warrants authorized and proceed with the extradition process. If the authorities still refused to prosecute, he would steam ahead with his specialty: a private prosecution.

It took a little longer than that, but in August 2019, South Africa's Justice Department finally issued warrants for Ismael Gafaranga—Apollo—and Alex Sugira, the man who booked the room down the corridor from Patrick's. The following June, the NPA advised Nel it had transmitted extradition requests to Kigali, paving the way for "red notices" to be issued, logging the suspects on Interpol's list of wanted individuals.[15]

Two out of four. There was a plethora of evidence against the other two men, Kennedy told me, but extradition requests are premised on "overwhelming" rather than "circumstantial" evidence. He was satisfied. For the Tutsi former soldier who had so painstakingly taught himself South African justice, here was proof that the wheels of justice might turn slowly, but they move to an inexorable conclusion. "It can be thirty years or forty years, but these people will be prosecuted in the end."

No one in the RNC thinks Kigali will be in any rush to cooperate. "You can be absolutely sure that Kigali will drag things out as long as it can," predicts David Batenga. Every legal brake and diplomatic lever will be applied, just as the question of who brought down Habyarimana's plane has been successfully obfuscated, dodged, and sidelined for decades now.

But continuing is a point of principle. For Nel, it's about signaling that despite the misfortune that has befallen South Africa's entire justice system, his country will never be a haven for assassins. For the RNC, on top of the desire to do right by Patrick and train a spotlight on Kigali's extraterritorial assassination program, there are pragmatic reasons for pressing on. Alex Sugira, Samuel Niyoyita, and Nshizrungu Vianney, the three professionals in that four-man

hit squad, may well be given fresh assignments. The Rwandan officials who facilitated the Michelangelo operation remain at large in
the region, enjoying the privileges, protection, and access routinely
granted diplomats.

Former Rwanda High Commission first secretary Claude Niko-
bisanzwe, who was among those expelled from South Africa in 2014,
has certainly not suffered any professional damage. He was made permanent secretary at the Ministry of Foreign Affairs in Kigali, and in
September 2018 named Rwanda's first ambassador to Mozambique.

His colleague and fellow expulsee Didier Rutembesa, who the
RNC believes actually coordinated the attack on Patrick, has been
appointed first counsellor at the same High Commission in Maputo.
Given Mozambique's semipermeable borders with South Africa, Es-
watini (Swaziland), Zimbabwe, Zambia, Malawi, and Tanzania, that's
a prime spot from which to target members of the Rwandan diaspora
in southern Africa deemed to be nurturing treacherous intentions.

CHAPTER TWENTY-ONE

REGRET IS AN UNDERSTATEMENT

There is no such thing as a good death,
Be it by genocide or war,
Slaughtered in revenge,
Vanished in an accident or by illness.
Those loved ones are praying for us,
There is no worse thing than death.
—**Kizito Mihigo,** *"The Meaning of Death"*

South African archbishop Desmond Tutu was probably the man who brought the Bantu term *ubuntu* international recognition. "Our common humanity," is one translation, "interconnectedness" another. It captures a worldview radically at odds with Western individualism. "I am because we are": individuals only find meaning by dint of their place in society.

But *ubuntu* can also have a dark side. Nowhere in Africa better demonstrates that than incestuous, densely populated Rwanda, where the peasant tilling the exposed hills gazes into his neighbor's fields, officialdom divides the community into bite-sized, easily monitored chunks, and decades of land shortage have reduced agriculture to a grim battle for survival.

"Everyone knows you," wrote former parliamentary speaker Joseph Sebarenzi. "Everyone knows your family. Everyone knows if you are sick. Everyone knows if you need help. And they will help. They will take turns carrying you on a stretcher for the two-hour walk to the hospital. They will give you milk from their cow if yours is dry."[1]

But the peasant who helps carry you to hospital also knows your wife is from the "wrong" ethnic group. He remembers that you said something rude about the president when you'd drunk too much banana wine. If instructed to kill you, he may well pick up a machete, because the value of obedience has been impressed on him since birth and, above all, no one wants to stand out from the crowd.

As a boy, Sebarenzi noticed how in the rural areas, local drums, transmitting orders from on high, would direct the killing of Tutsis, with Hutu neighbors dropping their machetes, as if waking from a trance, the moment the drums ceased. "Rwandans kill when they are asked and stop as soon as they are told. . . . The very thread that knits Rwandans so closely together is the same one that can so quickly unravel the country."

This was not, one senses, the side of Rwandan society that inspired Fred Rwigyema growing up in Uganda's refugee camps. "You have to let people breathe," the "Late Fred" used to tell his comrades.

Letting people breathe. . . . It's a concept his old friend has proved incapable of putting into practice, so contrary does it run to Kagame's experience, training, and personality. The ultimate control freak, the class geek has created a state in his own image: introverted, suspicious, unaccountable, and a prey to sudden violence.

In theory, Rwanda has put ethnicity behind it. *Gacaca*, a community-based justice system in which *genocidaires* confessed their crimes to fellow villagers, allowed Hutus and Tutsis to live alongside one another again, however uneasily. The ID cards which condemned many Tutsis to their deaths in 1994 were scrapped by the new government, which decreed that neither "Hutu" nor "Tutsi" exist, everyone is "Rwandan."

But privately, Rwandans will tell you ethnicity is a national—if now hidden—obsession and everyone knows their neighbors' or friends' lineage. Noble intentions are in any case undermined by the painfully-extended, salt-in-the-wound genocide commemorations staged each April, which remind the Hutu population of their community's never-to-be-expurgated guilt. So does the fact that 1994 has been officially labelled "the genocide *of the Tutsis*," terminology condemning to oblivion thousands of Hutus murdered for opposing Habyarimana or calling for political reform. It is comparable to failing to mention that homosexuals, gypsies, blacks, the disabled, Communists, and Jehovah's Witnesses died in the Holocaust alongside Jews. "That phrase puts the blame on the entire Hutu community," says Jean-Marie Vianney Ndagijimana. "It's been fake reconciliation process from the get-go."

As for the Hutus slaughtered during the RPF's invasion of Rwanda or the army's invasion of eastern DRC, their stories are officially ignored. When a reporter for Slate interviewed an old Hutu woman who had survived the refugee camps of DRC, losing family members and fighting off rape attempts, she was corrected by the translator for describing herself as a *rescapé*—a survivor. "Maman, survivors are only Tutsis," the interpreter told her.[2]

RPF past crimes, tellingly, were ruled to lie outside the *Gacaca* courts' jurisdiction. And the fate of those who raise the issue makes clear only one interpretation of history will be tolerated.

When Victoire Ingabire, the exiled head of the main Hutu opposition movement, flew back to Rwanda in January 2010, intent on standing in the elections, her first act was to visit the official Genocide Memorial in Kigali and question why the remains of Hutu victims were not displayed alongside those of the Tutsis. She was swiftly arrested, then sentenced to eight years for "belittling" the genocide and funding the FDLR—a sentence later increased to fifteen years—making it impossible for her to run for office.[3]

Gospel singer Kizito Mihigo, a Tutsi *rescapé* who had rebased in Rwanda in 2011, was for a while the regime's favorite performer, singing the national anthem at official ceremonies and hosting a television program. All that ended with his release of "The Meaning of Death," a song recognizing with its mention of revenge killings that Rwanda's Hutus had also been slaughtered: "They too are human." Eyes closed, rosary clutched in one hand, the baby-faced singer called on Rwandans to recognize their common humanity.[4]

Despite his celebrity profile, Mihigo was arrested, accused of collaborating with the FDLR and the RNC—the prosecution claimed the singer was out to avenge Patrick Karegeya's murder—and whipped

419

across the buttocks in the Senate president's office. Kagame, he was told, had not appreciated his song. Confessing to all charges, Mihigo begged for forgiveness—a concession Patrick and the General knew better than to make—and was sentenced to ten years in prison, but released alongside Ingabire under a presidential amnesty. In February 2020, he was spotted by villagers trying to cross into Burundi. Re-arrested, he died a few days later in a police cell, supposedly hanging himself: a version of events few of his fans accept.

Genuine ethnic reconciliation would undermine a regime that, in truly Orwellian tradition, depends for its survival on the concept of perpetual war, requiring the existence of a never-to-be-vanquished foe.

The number of militias operating in eastern DRC has mushroomed from some 25 in 2008 to between 100 and 150 today, but most analysts agree that the FDLR is now a spent force, posing no real challenge to Rwanda's army, probably the best in Africa. As for RNC hopes of joining forces with its erstwhile enemies, they are constantly undermined by the conflicting agendas of the extremist Hutu groups based in the Kivus. "I don't think Kigali sees them as a military threat anymore," says Congo expert Christoph Vogel. "In private, no one pretends they think 40,000 Hutu fighters are about to move into Rwanda."[5]

Notwithstanding, the old generation of RPF fighters never stops warning the new that constant vigilance is vital. "We are confronting other genocides which can happen again," General James Kabarebe warned Rwandan students in a 2019 speech that brutally undermined the government's official stance on reconciliation. Just as expelled Tutsis had reorganized in the refugee camps, he said, Hutu *génocidaires* had prospered in exile and now controlled the economies of Mozambique, Zambia, Malawi, South Africa, and even Europe. And the children of these *génocidaires* shared their parents' mentality.[6]

Rwanda's government did not have a problem with political opposition "as such," he added. "But what appears to be opposition in Rwanda harbours an ideology. . . . When they talk of democracy, it comes with that ideology, when they talk of freedom of the press, human rights. . . . all of these have a genocide ideology in the background." And so a once well founded fear of extermination is exploited to extinguish basic freedoms.

The vocabulary routinely adopted by Rwanda's politicians, government officials, and newspaper columnists betrays an instinctively totalitarian mindset. Orwell's Ministry of Truth, where Winston Smith worked, could have coined the "negationist tendencies" said to afflict Rwanda's dissidents and the "divergent views" they promote. Anyone who questions the official history is a "genocide-denier," even when the individual concerned—like Kizito Mihigo—is a Tutsi who lost close family members during the genocide.

That is no trivial accusation, because in Rwanda, "minimizing" or "denying" the genocide is an offense that carries a ten-year prison sentence. The vaguer charge of "divisionism" can in theory get you five years, although it's more often used as a deterrent, stifling criticism by NGOs and civil society organizations, or, in the case of the MDR opposition party—once Rwanda's biggest—getting it disbanded.

And with typical ambition, these concepts are being given international reach. In October 2019 Rwandan senators called on the government to appoint an ambassador-at-large with special duties to track down individuals and organizations spreading "revisionism" abroad, identifying academic Filip Reyntjens and former prime minister Faustin Twagiramungu as obvious offenders. Ever since I began writing this book, I've been grimly aware the same accusation would one day be leveled against me.

This totalitarian system, like so many, is strongly militaristic. The government's decision to revive *Itorero,* which in precolonial times produced the Mwami's warrior elite—his *intore*—is part of this philosophy of keeping a country in constant combat readiness. Officially labeled a "civic education programme," *Itorero's* true nature is revealed in photos that show serious-faced Rwandan youngsters in camouflage, drilling and marching, just as their RPF parents did.

Even that definition requires nuancing. Discussing Rwanda with a British academic in London, I referred to it as a "military state." He corrected me: "Kagame's not just a president with a military background, he's one with a background in *military intelligence.* He comes from the world of spooks, of secrets and informants, a world in which you never have to deal with democracy or dissent. It's quite different."[7]

"The entire country is a spying machine," says Rwandan economist David Himbara, who twice worked by Kagame's side before leaving and becoming one of his most virulent critics. "The army, the police, they come to his office to tell him things. He doesn't govern, he collects rumors. Rwanda is one vast rumor mill."[8]

Distrustful of his own elite, Kagame requires senior military officers and civil servants to apply for presidential permission prior to any foreign trip. He was always known to monitor the army radio network, on the prowl for whispers of incriminating information. The advent of social media has provided him with a far larger stage on which to apply his covert skills, silently eavesdropping on global discussions of his presidency, dipping into conversations, and anonymously lambasting critics.

His Facebook interest was exposed by Portia's experience of having her passport seized in Kampala. The Twitter habit came to light in the wake of Patrick's death. RFI journalist Sonia Rolley, who had been tweeting about the murder, found herself being abused by someone using the handle @RichardGoldston. The account was being followed, curiously, by more than forty Government of Rwanda users.[9]

It specialized in vitriolic attacks, berating South African president Zuma as "a black retard," calling the AU "a toothless dog," and tweeting support for the M23 rebellion in DRC, from which Kigali has always distanced itself. When it accused Rolley of being a "Delilah" to Patrick's "Samson," US reporter Steve Terrill asked @RichardGoldston to stop.

Until then an unabashed Kagame admirer, Terrill had tried to create an online newswire dedicated to unbiased reporting on Rwanda. Intrigued by the anonymous websites and social media accounts that dominated the debate, he had already contacted the president's office about the mysterious @RichardGoldston handle, asking who was behind it.

The reply to Terrill's March tweet defending Rolley came not from @RichardGoldston but from President Kagame's official account. When Terrill pointed this out, the account was deleted and the president's office announced that @RichardGoldston was "an employee in the Presidency" who had been reprimanded.

Was Kagame himself the author of @RichardGoldston? Surely no junior staffer would dare pen such controversial messages, tweets whose content often contradicted official policy, had Kagame not approved, and the fact that so many government offices followed the account suggested its provenance was an open secret.

As for telephone and email conversations, Rwandan opposition members, human rights activists, and journalists assumed for years their communications were being monitored by Kigali. No one trusted Facebook, most stayed off email. As time passed, many started avoiding Skype, and finally WhatsApp also came under suspicion.

When, in December 2017, Citizen Lab, a unit based at the University of Toronto that specializes in digital espionage, published an investigation into how the Ethiopian government had used spyware made by an Israel-based company called Cyberbit to target dissidents, my thoughts immediately turned to Rwanda. Given Rwanda's links with Israel's military intelligence, it seemed logical to assume any cybersecurity company selling wares to Addis Ababa would also have approached Kigali. Sure enough, Citizen Lab identified Rwanda as one of the customers to have been provided a demo.[10]

Two years later, WhatsApp, working in partnership with Citizen Lab, publicly acknowledged that its platform had been abused. This time the Israeli company identified was NSO Group, based in Tel Aviv, and the program, dubbed Pegasus, was so powerful that the Israeli government—which NSO asks to approve its customers—classifies it as a weapon, the *Financial Times* reported.[11]

Cyberbit's system had worked by sending malware posing as Adobe Flash updates and PDF plugins to WhatsApp users. NSO went further. The user didn't even have to answer the call for the phone to become an eavesdropping device, transmitting location, encrypted chats, and travel plans. Reading this detail made me think, with a shiver, about Apollo and the shiny silver cell phone Emile spotted in Patrick's kitchen.

NSO insisted it only sold its technology to vetted customers. But WhatsApp said there had been "an unmistakeable pattern of abuse" and that it was contacting the 1,400 victims scattered across the world to notify them. "On the list of targeted individuals identified by WhatsApp, a considerable number were from Rwanda," wrote the *Financial Times*.

The newspaper tracked down six, including RNC member Faustin Rukondo, based in Leeds; Frank Ntwali, the RNC dissident stabbed by the freeway in South Africa; a Rwandan army officer who had testified before French judge Marc Trévidic; and—no surprise here—General Kayumba in South Africa.

So what outsiders had been tempted to dismiss as Rwandan exiles' persecution complexes turned out to be entirely justified. Once WhatsApp had closed the vulnerability, the *Financial Times* reported, NSO switched to new methods to deliver its spyware. In the suspicious, nervy world of African civil society, dissidents must keep jumping from one system to another, trying to keep ahead of their better-equipped, better-funded trackers.

No African government curates its public image more assiduously than Rwanda. Despite being one of the world's poorest countries, it spends hefty sums on Western lobby firms specializing in reputation management. It's impossible to know if they are responsible for the small army of trolls that systematically swoops down on anyone criticizing Rwanda on social media, but the uniformity of language and the anonymous handles do not suggest spontaneous emotion.

In his report to the US Department of Homeland Security, Patrick cited the intimidation of the Rwandan press as one of the areas where he'd parted company with Kagame. "There is no story that should make the government kill or force a journalist into exile," he wrote. Rwanda's critical journalists today live outside the country, its domestic newspapers and websites serving as mere megaphones of His Master's Voice. Rwanda ranks a miserable 155 out of 180 on the World Press Freedom Index published by Reporters Without Borders.[12]

It's harder to control the international media, but Rwanda does its best. It operates a de facto blacklist, noting which reporters are responsible for negative coverage and punishing organizations deemed to have stepped out of line.

Researching this book, I found it hair-tearingly difficult to get a range of mainstream Western newspapers and news agencies to show a smidgeon of interest in revelations of Rwanda's extraterritorial espionage and assassination program. Dissidents offered them the proof, the story was of undoubted interest, they would not run the articles. Bullying, sadly, works.

Some of the most heartrending coverage of Rwanda's genocide came from the BBC. But the relationship between Kigali and the corporation soured when its World Service launched a Kinyarwanda current affairs program giving Rwandan citizens a platform on which to air their grievances. Kigali set out to infiltrate the broadcaster, repeatedly approaching several employees with requests for uncut, pre-broadcast interviews with government critics, along with regular updates on what the BBC planned to transmit on the Great Lakes.

When in October 2014 the BBC broadcast *Rwanda's Untold Story,* a television documentary that broke every taboo by challenging the generally accepted Tutsi death toll, interviewing both General Kayumba and Theogene, and airing the notion that Habyarimana's plane might have been brought down by the RPF, the outraged Rwandan government suspended the Kinyarwanda service.[13]

Most foreign visitors to Kigali remain blind to this hydra-headed operation to choke off criticism and mold opinion, but occasionally one gets an inkling. At an international conference in Italy, I was chatting to a former Western ambassador who had gone into consultancy work. In tribute to his former role, he'd received a helpful briefing from what he called "our intelligence guys" before a scheduled working trip to Kigali.

"'On arrival,' they told me, 'You'll be met at your hotel by a very good-looking young woman or man. That's a honeytrap—don't touch the local fruit. During your stay, don't go onto the local Wi-Fi system with either your laptop, smartphone, or iPad, as they'll use that to get into your system and hoover up your information. You should take it as read that your room is being bugged. Don't say anything important or personal over the phone. Never leave your laptop or your phone out of your sight. And during the duration of your stay, you should assume your luggage will be gone through not once, but twice.'"[14]

It was the kind of warning a Western diplomat might have received visiting East Germany under the Stasi, Iraq during Saddam Hussein's rule, or North Korea today. In sub-Saharan Africa, perhaps only Ethiopia and South Africa would have merited a similar briefing. Patrick would, I reflected, have been proud.

If passing visitors enjoy that level of attention, expatriates actually based in Kigali—especially those working in the all-important development sector—are subject to far more intense scrutiny, even if some are too naive to register the fact.

"All the drivers and interpreters at the embassies, DFID, and USAID offices are reporting back to intelligence," says the General.

As former head of military intelligence and the NISS, he would know. "Even when a member of the so-called opposition goes to have a private chat with a diplomat at an embassy, what he says will have first been vetted and agreed by us."

Sometimes the Rwandan system inadvertently reveals what squirms beneath the rock to outsiders who can't quite believe what they have glimpsed. Over a dinner in Washington, I once found myself sitting next to a young graduate who had been unnerved by the four months she'd spent in Kigali researching China's growing investment in Rwanda—not a topic she'd expected to attract controversy.

Academic researchers need government approval before starting work, but once the permit is issued in Kigali, it's usually smooth sailing after that. Not for this student. "After I'd been there a couple of weeks I noticed a plainclothes guy, always the same guy, waiting outside my house," she told me. "Each morning he'd follow me as I walked to the nearest coffee shop. He never spoke to me, but would follow me for an hour or two. There was nothing covert about it."[15]

Several soldiers were always positioned on the corner of the building, and they would greet her by name whenever she left the house. "That seemed pretty strange as I'd never introduced myself," she said. Then one day, one of the soldiers spoke up: "It's not fair, what you're saying about Kagame." She wasn't aware of having said anything controversial about the president: it was a remark deliberately calculated to induce anxiety.

Then the calls began. "I'd bought a local SIM card and my phone would ring in the middle of the night, supposedly from Rwandans I'd recently interviewed," she said. "When I picked up, it would either be a dead line or I'd just hear sounds of movement on the other end. When I later asked those contacts about the calls, they'd tell me they hadn't made them."

The final straw came when the cell phone display showed an incoming call from her mother. "By then she'd been dead for eight years," she said. "When I picked it up, a voice said, 'It's time for you to go.' I was due to leave soon in any case, but I pulled my trip forward by a week. And I broke the SIM card under my heel and threw it away."

•

Despite all the manicuring and monitoring, there are signs that the wheels are beginning to come off Rwanda's "development miracle" story. Over the past five years, a small group of jaundiced former insiders and increasingly vocal development experts have begun challenging the country's statistical record. The angriest dismiss Rwanda as a Potemkin village, a sophisticated con trick, with the donors cast in the role of useful idiots.

David Himbara, who ran Kagame's strategic policy unit in the 2000s, and is largely responsible for Rwanda's extraordinary ranking on the World Bank's Ease of Doing Business index, is one such figure. In 2008, the year after Patrick's departure, the economist was offered a graphic insight into the kind of personalized intimidation that might prevent competent Rwandan officials from telling the truth.[16]

What prompted the incident was never entirely clear, but it centered on the new curtains hanging in the presidential office. Himbara believes his former boss might have been annoyed that the order did not go to a business in which the RPF, which controlled so much of the economy via Crystal Ventures, held a stake.

"He calls his senior staff into the office," Himbara recalls. "Then he asks the finance director and an army captain in charge of security where they bought the curtains—they give him the name of the shop—and Kagame says no, and mentions a rival shop. 'I'm asking you to admit you bought these curtains there.' 'No, Your Excellency,' they say, insisting it was the first shop."

But then, he says, "Kagame picks up the phone and five soldiers come in carrying thin sticks. Kagame asks the finance director and army captain to lie on the floor and he takes a stick and beats them for five minutes. Then, when he gets tired, he asks his men to take over."

"While they were being beaten, what did you do? What did everyone do?" I ask. Himbara places one long, slim finger to the corner of his eye and tracks the course of a single tear down one cheek. "I cried," he says simply. "It was so ugly.

"They beat those people in front of us for half an hour. Then Kagame said, 'Get up!' One stood up but immediately fell down. I went to help him and Kagame shouted, 'Sit down!'" The incident so haunted Himbara that he kept track of what happened to its two luckless protagonists. In September 2019, former finance director

Kalisa Mupende died in jail, having shuttled in and out of prison ever since that career-destroying incident.[17] The captain left the army and became a peasant farmer.

On another occasion, Himbara was passing the office where Rwanda's cabinet was meeting when he heard the door suddenly open, and then Foreign Minister Rosemary Museminali, a short, dignified woman who had served as ambassador to the United Kingdom, flew across the portal. The door was slammed shut, then immediately yanked open again, and a handbag followed its owner. "She had been told to remove her 'fat arse' and she delayed moving her 'fat arse,'" says Himbara. "So he physically ejected her."

In a context where a head of state beats a subordinate in public and kicks a female minister out of a room, Himbara can't have been surprised when he, too, was called to heel. The incident involved Rwanda's GDP growth, a figure regarded with a certain skepticism by economists, who have wondered for years what—other than illegal mineral exports from DRC—could justify its year-on-year buoyancy.

"His ministers were telling him that the economy had grown by 11 percent in 2008, just like China," he says. "I listened in silence and then he asked me what I thought. 'Mr. President,' I said, 'It's just not possible in 2008, when demand for coffee and tea declined, to have 11 percent growth. Our partners will have problems believing this. Especially the IMF, as they have people on the ground. This won't be an easy sell.'"

Kagame's patience snapped. "You know, you're an arrogant son of a bitch," he told the economist. "Look around you. What do you see?"

"Ministers," stammered Himbara.

"These are the cadres who brought the likes of you back to Rwanda, and you come here with your papers and criticize. Without them, you'd be a peasant on a farm in Ruhengeri." He fired Himbara on the spot, but the order came with a characteristic kicker: "That doesn't mean you can go anywhere. You sit and I tell you what to do."

Himbara made his escape notwithstanding, using the occasion of a trip to South Africa. He called in his resignation on landing in Johannesburg only to have an aide relay the following message from Kagame: "Tell that dog to come back, whether he wants to or not." His response was, "You can tell the president, 'This dog will never work for another dog again.'" Despite Himbara making this story public, Rwanda's GDP growth for 2008 is today officially recorded as 11.2 percent.

Rwanda's GDP figures are not the only target for growing skepticism. The country's stunning record on poverty reduction, measured using a detailed household survey conducted by the National Institute of Statistics Rwanda (NISR)—one of Kagame's spanking new institutions—has also been challenged.

The most contentious finding came in 2015, when Kagame was preparing for a constitutional referendum that would allow him to keep standing for election, and needed to demonstrate success. Oxford Policy Management (OPM), a UK-based consultancy, had helped the National Institute of Statistics on three previous surveys. But on examining the statistics, it found poverty had actually *increased* by at least 6 percent between 2010–2011 and 2013–2014. Rejecting the finding, the government asked OPM to look again. After weeks of to-and-fro, OPM terminated its contract, and its experts did not sign off on the final report.[18] "It reminded me a lot of what it was like in the Soviet Union," commented one of those involved. "People wanted to get the approved results, at any cost."[19]

The NISR accordingly found that poverty had fallen by 6 percent during the period in question: another extraordinary Rwandan win! But it was a conclusion only reached, several Western researchers and academics argue, by changing the inflation estimates on which calculations were routinely based.

A statistician who has dedicated five increasingly incensed articles to the topic believes that, in fact, poverty now stands at over 60 percent, up 15 percent since 2011—a result that in itself raises questions about the constant years of GDP growth. "Of all the countries in the world for which there is data, we could only find one (South Sudan) that has experienced a faster increase in poverty," he writes.[20]

Tellingly, his articles in the peer-reviewed *Review of African Political Economy* are always anonymous.[21] Such is the strength of the development industry's consensus, such the fear of a vengeful Pilato.

Highly technical, the debate has been largely confined to a group of economists and academics who grasp the rarefied jargon, but it's a debunking of international significance, undermining as it does the notion that top-down dictatorship beats messy democracy when it comes to delivering basic services to the poor. It also matters intensely to Kagame, as once Rwanda is not seen as some global inspiration, just an African state that has put high aid flows to effective—but not miraculous—use, support for his repressive style of rule becomes far harder to justify.

"There's only terror keeping it all together in Rwanda," says the anonymous statistician. "And that only works if you have growth. Once you don't have growth, it all collapses."[22]

The World Bank, which has invested more than $4 billion in Rwanda since the genocide, sticks loyally in public to its portrait of Rwanda as a remarkable success story. But internally, disquiet simmers. In December 2015 an anonymous group of World Bank employees calling itself "Professionals for Truth in Aid" wrote a letter to the then bank president and vice-president for Africa, warning that by ignoring Kigali's manipulation of statistics and failure to provide reliable data, the institution was running "serious reputational risks."[23]

"I used to be one of those pushing for more budget support to Rwanda," the letter's drafter, who has since left the bank, told me. "I can't believe it now. How is it that we believe statistics produced by a regime like this? Would we believe Stalin's statistics, Hitler's statistics?"[24]

Given the fate awaiting any government official rash enough to challenge the president, it's no surprise Rwandans have actually coined a term for successful data doctoring. *Guteknika*, they call the faking of statistics to support a dubious official narrative. "People say what they are expected to say," comments a veteran economist. "In fifteen years of going to Rwanda, I think I've heard people talking openly and freely only two or three times."[25]

The self-censorship practiced by such doubting international experts highlights the compromised nature of developmental oversight.

If an institution such as the World Bank, the DFID, or a UN agency commissions an "independent" assessment of a country like Rwanda, the consulting firm concerned will turn to retired DFID officials, ex-ambassadors, and academics who specialize in the Great Lakes. But these players know their names will be on the final report, that donors partner up with the government when commissioning analysis, and that Kigali neither forgives nor forgets. How honest, then, will their judgment be? "No names, please, I expect to do consultancy work there in future," was a response I became very used to hearing.

When I raised the conflict-of-interest issue and its insidious role in distorting perceptions of Rwanda with a young academic in London—yet another expert who didn't want to be quoted—he was philosophical: "Oh, I suspect there's no donor out there anymore who doesn't think there's a problem with the Rwandan model." Not quite good enough, I thought. The contents of those corridor conversations only occasionally reach the public platforms, the television studios, or the magazine articles, where Rwanda is still lauded as "the Switzerland of Africa," just as it was in Habyarimana's time.

•

As a more complex economic picture emerges, attention will inevitably swing to the area that has always been the RPF's weak spot: its human rights record.

Rwandan human rights groups, constantly harassed by the authorities and infiltrated by government agents, do their best to keep lists of dead, tortured, and disappeared. Given that no international human rights organization maintains an office in Kigali today—Human Rights Watch's Lewis Mudge, last man standing, was expelled in 2014—checking their allegations is never easy. But it's hard, scrolling through the lists of names, not to reach the conclusion that today's RPF has assassination in its very DNA.

In 2014, Human Rights Watch issued a report detailing thirteen cases of former RPF politicians, military figures, intelligence agents, and journalists who had fled Rwanda and been assassinated, kidnapped, or attacked in Kenya, Uganda, South Africa, or the United Kingdom. Patrick had provided researcher Carina Tertsakian with some of the names, only for his own, shockingly, to join the final list.[26]

The organization took an extremely conservative approach in "Repression Across Borders," Tertsakian told me, listing only the cases in which the evidence of state involvement seemed undeniable: the files of myriad less-well substantiated but still suspect deaths sat on her desk.

It did not include, for example, Theogene Turatsinze, the former managing director of Rwanda's Development Bank, who fled the country and rebased in Maputo. Young and brilliant, he was said to have learned far too much about the president's personal business interests in his time at the bank. In October 2012 his body was found floating at sea, hands trussed. Mozambique's police force initially attributed the murder to the Rwandan government only to later retract the accusation—echoes of the Hawks' behavior here—and characterize it as a common crime.[27]

The Human Rights Watch report was swiftly overtaken by events. While it's possible that Camir Nkurunziza, a former Rwandan military officer who was killed in Cape Town in May 2019, fell victim to a run-of-the-mill botched carjacking, the death of Louis Baziga, head of the Rwanda diaspora association in Mozambique, who was shot by three men in his car in Maputo three months later, had all the hallmarks of a state execution.[28]

Some killings get more attention than others, because they involve high-profile Tutsi insiders: in theory, the very group Kagame is there to nurture and protect.

One was Emmanuel Gasakure, a cardiologist who abandoned his career in France to return to post-genocide Rwanda, where he focused his energies on rebuilding Rwanda's health system and played a key role in setting up the country's universal health insurance. As Kagame's personal physician, he fell afoul of the First Lady and was eventually arrested on suspicion of leaking the contents of the presidential couple's medical files. Detained at the infamous Remera Police Station—where singer Kizito Mihigo would later die—Gasakure supposedly assaulted the officer on guard and was shot dead during a scuffle in February 2015. His friends, who remember a gentle, dedicated workaholic overwhelmed by the pressures of his job, find it impossible to believe that scenario.[29]

Another was Assinapol Rwigara, a Tutsi tobacco and real estate tycoon who had loyally financed the RPF. Following a business dispute, Rwigara died in a suspicious traffic accident the same month as Gasakure. The family have never accepted the police account, claiming the truck that supposedly crushed him only lightly struck the car on the passenger's side, that witnesses spotted him trying to run from the crash site, and that he was still breathing when police zipped him into a body bag.[30]

After the "accident," Rwigara's brand-new hotel was bulldozed by the Kigali City Council, which claimed it had been built without a permit; the family was billed for the demolition, reinforcing the impression of a very personal feud.[31] The killing so appalled the tycoon's young daughter, Diane, that she decided to run in the 2017 presidential elections. She was promptly jailed—alongside her mother—and charged with forging electoral documents. The family's tobacco company was auctioned off, allegedly to recover unpaid back taxes.

But there have been many Hutu victims, too, particularly among those who might be seen to represent an electoral challenge. While the now-released Ingabire is allowed, at least, to live, members of her unregistered coalition have come to grisly ends. The party's national coordinator was stabbed to death in 2019 at his workplace, the body of one of Ingabire's aides was found on the edge of a forest, and another has been missing since July 2019, presumed dead.[32]

What's particularly chilling is the regime's belief in collective punishment. In an echo of the days when the Mwami's *intore* would routinely put to the sword the wives, children, and slaves of a vanquished chieftain, distant relatives and passing acquaintances of high-profile targets—a cousin of a cousin, a name on a confiscated cell phone's contact list—are deemed guilty by association. "There's not a single member of Patrick's extended family left in Rwanda now," says Leah.

Because Rwandans know this, they rush to distance themselves. One of the saddest experiences is reading the groveling apologies to Kagame penned by Rwandans at home and abroad, who just want to be left in peace, or the graceless "to whom it may concern" letters in which Rwandans publicly distance themselves from friends and relatives.

The sinister role played by Rwandan embassies has become even clearer. In 2019 the anti-government website Jambonews published an investigation into a cell dubbed "the Intervention Group," which it said had been operating out of the Rwanda High Commission in Brussels for five years. Tasked with infiltrating Rwanda's European diaspora, the cell's 100 or so members took pictures of anyone attending opposition meetings, broke up civil society get-togethers, and pressured Rwandans working for NGOs or international bodies active in their country to turn informant.[33]

Exploiting contacts at the airport in Zaventem, in Belgium, the cell logged Rwandan citizens' departures and arrivals, Jambonews reported, and sent agents fanning out across Europe and into the

United Kingdom. It was an Intervention Group member, for example, who was picked up at Folkestone by the Metropolitan police in May 2018, heading for an RNC meeting in London, and put on a coach back to Brussels.

One of the cell's targets was Canadian journalist Judi Rever, who spent years researching atrocities committed by the RPF for her book *In Praise of Blood*, a damning indictment of the rebel movement. She flew to Brussels in July 2014 to conduct research, only to be met, much to her surprise, by Belgian police, who assigned her a team of armed escorts and an armored car for the duration of her stay. "We have reason to believe that the Rwandan embassy in Brussels constitutes a threat to your security," she was told.[34]

Another was journalist Serge Ndayizeye, who not only ran the RNC's radio station, but acted as a one-man crowd mobilizer, flying out ahead of any official Kagame visit to a Western city—whether London, Paris, Boston, or Toronto—to organize anti-government demonstrations.

In October 2015, he'd been beaten up by five men while waiting outside the Amsterdam Convention Center, where Kagame was due to speak, losing his cell phone, along with all its precious contact numbers. His assailants had looked like ordinary homeless, street beggars, but were clearly on a mission. "When I tracked my phone I could see that it went into the convention center," he told me. "Then it was taken to Schiphol airport and then it flew to Kigali."

In June 2017, Ndayizeye flew to Brussels, where Kagame was due to attend an EU Development Day. This time he received a call from Belgium's intelligence services, telling him to report to headquarters immediately. When he got there he was told his life was in danger.

"I could either accept official protection, which meant moving into a hotel and being under round-the-clock surveillance, or return immediately to the US," he said. Rounding off his meetings, he flew home. "On that trip, I hadn't stayed in a hotel, I'd stayed with a Rwandan family. I later heard that a member of that family had been reporting my movements to the Rwandan embassy all along."

Kigali's geographical ambitions extend even further, an investigation by the Australian Broadcasting Corporation reveals. In August 2019, ABC broadcast an exposé of the spy network being run out of

Rwanda's High Commission in Singapore, which involved placing agents in any Australian city with a sizable Rwandan population—Sydney, Perth, and Brisbane—to infiltrate the communities and silence dissent (Rwanda has no High Commission in Australia).

Many of those used were Rwandan students. Others had been granted political refugee status in Australia but were being threatened or blackmailed by the High Commission, offered assurances that their assets back home wouldn't be touched, for example, or told they would be allowed to fly back to visit relatives if they spied for the Rwandan government.[35]

The amount of effort expended in such cases may at first glance seem disproportionate to the level of threat posed by the exiles concerned. But that is to misunderstand the devastating impact these long-distance operations have on those back home. "It demonstrates the reach of the RPF beyond borders and has a chilling effect," says HRW's Mudge.

Kagame is a great one for threats. There was a time he confined them to his Kinyarwanda speeches, knowing no Western audience would pick them up. With his sophisticated minders now gone, Kagame has become ever more explicitly brutal, in any language. Videos circulating on YouTube capture the many occasions on which Kagame, admonitory finger raised like some Old Testament prophet, sometimes quivering with rage, promises to bring destruction down upon the heads of his foes.[36]

Human rights groups campaign against impunity because, they argue, it encourages perpetrators to behave ever more outrageously. It's certainly hard to watch footage of Kagame effectively boasting of Sendashonga's murder at a *filmed* government retreat without marveling at the arrogance of the performance. Cyrie Sendashonga found it so objectionable she wrote to Kenyan president Uhuru Kenyatta, copying in Kenya's attorney general and director of investigations, saying that since Kagame's statements amounted to an "admission of guilt," those responsible needed to be indicted, arrested, and prosecuted.

"God created me in a very strange way," Kagame once told a sympathetic interviewer.[37] One of his regime's most extraordinary characteristics is the relentlessness of the vindictiveness it demonstrates, in a region where other heads of state have turned the readiness to forge pragmatic friendships, to strike alliances of convenience with former enemies, into an art form.

Like the cyborg running down its assigned victim, this vengeful Terminator never stops, even when pursuit comes across as bizarrely self-defeating. Portia Karegeya marvels aloud at Kagame's inability to empathize or forgive, bend or reconcile. "What is wrong with you, that you can't let anything go?" she questions. "All my family's properties have gone, everything has been seized. Why do people have to die? You've *won*."

In theory, the regime would have everything to gain from allowing disillusioned former insiders to build new lives elsewhere. Instead, when the regime hears that an exile has been offered a job, it does all it can to stymie the opportunity, virtually ensuring that these frustrated former employees funnel their energies instead into opposition activism.

It happened to Patrick after his Somalia consultancy, it has happened to Theogene Rudasingwa, and David Himbara also experienced this when he won a job in 2012 at the African Development Bank (AfDB) headquarters in Tunisia, having fled Rwanda a few years earlier.

When an opening came up at the bank, he hesitated and called AfDB president Donald Kaberuka, Rwanda's former finance minister and an old friend, to ask if applying might cause problems. "Absolutely not," Kaberuka reassured him. Himbara got the job. On arrival in Tunis, he went straight to his new office, hung up some pictures, and shook hands with new colleagues. Then the Zimbabwean economist who had originally encouraged him to apply summoned him.

"You have to leave," he told him. "At 8 a.m. I began my new job, by midday I'd been sacked," Himbara says. He suspects he'd been spotted by one of the Rwandan employees at the AfDB, who had promptly called Kigali.

Struggling to nail down consultancies, unable to continue lecturing —he canceled a course he was teaching in Toronto when suspiciously high numbers of Rwandans enrolled—Himbara has found that his enforced inactivity gives him more time to focus on a series of books lambasting the Kagame administration and questioning its economic credentials.[38]

That same relentlessness surfaced in September 2020, when Paul Rusesabagina, a man credited with saving the lives of over 1,200 Tutsis during his time running Kigali's Hotel Mille Collines in 1994, was lured from exile in Texas. Boarding a private jet at Dubai airport he believed to be bound for Burundi, Rusesabagina was flown instead to Kigali, to be handcuffed on arrival and charged with terrorism.[39]

A long-running critic of the RPF, Rusesabagina stands accused of founding and financing the National Liberation Front (FLN), an armed group blamed for a series of attacks in southwestern Rwanda, and whose leader, Callixte Sankara, was extradited to Kigali from the Comoro Islands in 2019.

The Oscar-nominated film *Hotel Rwanda* had probably made Rusesabagina the second most famous Rwandan in the West after Kagame, with President George W. Bush hanging the American Medal of Freedom around his neck. By renditioning a man who had hobnobbed with Hollywood stars, Kagame was taking a reputational risk, with the arrest likely to prompt a reexamination of not only Rusesabagina's record, but his own.

But the operation succeeded in one key regard: it sent a cold chill down the back of every government critic based abroad, hammering home the "You can run but you can't hide" message Kagame voiced at that prayer breakfast after Patrick's murder. "If the Rwandan government can do this in the United Arab Emirates, it changes everything," acknowledged a worried Charlotte Mukankusi, the RNC's head of outreach. "When we travel, many of us go through Addis Ababa and through Dubai. If we aren't safe there, we can't go anywhere."[40] And that, for Kagame, trumped every other consideration.

•

Rwanda's post-genocide constitution originally limited Kagame to two terms as president. But as the deadline for his departure approached it became clear that despite professing exhaustion, he wasn't going anywhere. After 4 million Rwandans "spontaneously" signed petitions, an amendment approved by 98 percent of voters in a December 2015 referendum allowed Kagame to keep running for election until 2034. Rwandan lawmakers, apparently unaware of how ludicrous they sounded, said they had conducted nationwide consultations but found only ten people who opposed the idea.[41]

If Kagame keeps running for office as long as the constitution now allows, he will have been in control of Rwanda for forty years, winning a series of elections so lacking in credibility that most of the organizations that routinely monitor African elections tactfully pass on Rwanda. Like many an African strongman, including Museveni, Kagame has been careful to groom no obvious successors. Instead, he recycles the same familiar names—Appointed, Promoted, Fired, Arrested, Appointed Again—ensuring that no potential rival stays long enough in any one post to build up a following.

The cult of personality continues to build. Rwandan newspapers, radio stations, and news sites broadcast one long paean of praise, with Kagame seemingly never short of opinions on Rwanda's correct path, his views ranging from the big picture to the personal minutiae of his citizens' daily lives.

Abroad, the Rwandan president enjoys the kind of uncritical adulation once lavished on Myanmar's Aung San Suu Kyi or the Dalai Lama, and he is a regular speaker on American university campuses, where he is often bestowed with a symbolic degree. If the Wikipedia page set up by a fan listing "awards and honours bestowed upon Paul Kagame" is to be believed, the man who never completed high school now boasts more honorary degrees than Barack Obama.[42]

Outsiders seem ready to accept the view that Rwanda's achievements are his personal handiwork and that his exiled critics are simply envious rivals who left because they were caught with their hands in the till. Reading Kagame's various biographies and interviews, one gets a sense of the major figures of the RPF—men and women like the late Fred Rwigyema, Peter Bayingana and Chris Bunyenyezi, Stephen Ndugute, Pasteur Bizimungu, Seth Sendashonga, General Kayumba, Sam Kaka, Frank Rusagara, Patrick Karegeya, Patrick Mazimpaka, Donald Kaberuka, Aloisea Inyumba, and Rose Kabuye—being steadily edged out of the picture. The black-and-white faces of the 1980s bleach, curl, and shrivel away in history's acid bath, leaving a technicolor, iconic image of just one hawk-faced leader.

A US diplomat friend of mine, a man I assume worked for the CIA, once mused aloud over the behavior of the Zairean army, notorious for rape and pillage. In a moment of either biting cynicism or seasoned realism, he said, "People always wonder why armies in these situations behave so appallingly. But the answer's so simple: 'Because they *can*.'"

They *can*, so they *do*. Kagame's regime, whose deplorable record on human rights abuses at home is beyond debate, has also been caught red-handed attempting the most lurid of assassinations on the soil of foreign allies, not once but many times. Western funding for his aid-dependent country has not suffered, the admiring articles by foreign journalists have not ceased, sanctions have not been applied, and the invitations to Davos have not dried up.

The harshest responses have been the occasional diplomatic admonishments made behind closed doors, and the odd, discreet police visits to targeted individuals. On the rare occasions when charges have been brought, prosecutions have been mysteriously delayed and verdicts left unenforced.[43]

Caught in similarly embarrassing situations, would any other African state be shown such indulgence, year in, year out? Russia, Saudi Arabia, and China have certainly not been granted such leniency: their plots were exposed to withering public view, with redress angrily demanded. Kagame *can*, so he *does*.

Obsessed with its dreadful past, the Rwandan population has struck the classic Faustian pact—trading freedom for peace. But most analysts wonder if the deal can survive Kagame's departure.

When diplomats or aid officials speculate as to the form that might take, they somehow manage to miss the obvious issue blocking voluntary retirement. Every charge ever leveled against General Kayumba and his fellow RPF officers would have been leveled first against Kagame, too, had he not been president and enjoyed immunity at the time. That's a powerful disincentive to quitting.

But no man lives forever, as Rwanda was reminded when the president's prolonged absence from the public stage in September 2020 prompted reports that he had a brain tumor and had been medevaced to Britain for emergency surgery. A Rwandan pastor went so far as to solemnly announce Kagame's death in a videotaped speech, calling on Rwandans to remain calm and implement the constitution.

Kagame quickly scotched the rumors by staging a press conference, but the transmission focused minds on a pressing question: What is the long-term plan? Whether or not one believes Rwanda's developmental program was inspirational and transformative, what happens when its founder goes? And in that area, there's plenty of room for concern.

"It's about resilience versus brittleness," says veteran aid expert Phil Vernon. "When you have a very centralized power system, it's incredibly brittle. The technocratic approach is to look at the buildings that have gone up, schools and hospitals for example, and see that as progress. But institutions and buildings are two different things. Setting one up doesn't mean the norms and values making it effective are internalized. What you've got in Rwanda is an organization—the army—which occupies the commanding heights of a very small economy, with all the perverse incentives that creates. That suggests a very brittle future."

In the region, Rwanda has few friends. Rwanda and Uganda have repeatedly come close to the brink of all-out war in recent years, with each president bitterly convinced that his counterpart wants him dead. While Kagame seems to have reached a modus vivendi with DRC president Félix Tshisekedi, who allows his elite forces to penetrate the Kivus to target militias there, history suggests such collaboration never lasts very long. As for Burundi, President Pierre Nkurunziza, who died in 2020, certainly didn't see Kagame as a benign influence, accusing him of backing a foiled coup.

But Kagame's true challenge lies at home. By never admitting moral fault and constantly harping on the wickedness of the previous regime, the RPF has created a tense, tightly repressed society whose two biggest communities, Hutu and Tutsi, both see themselves as victims of monstrous injustice. As political scientist René Lemarchand comments, "Where two communities within the same state believe themselves to be victims, the stage is set for endless conflict."[44]

A development economist I spoke to, a man advised by his employers not to visit the region, ruefully pointed me to one index on which Rwanda scores extremely badly, year after year. It's the index compiled as part of the UN's World Happiness Report, on which Rwanda routinely ranks among the bottom six countries. In 2020 Rwanda was ranked 150th out of 153, only marginally happier than South Sudan, a country recovering from civil war. "It suggests people are very unhappy," he commented. "But it's a society in which that's taken as a given, regarded as normal, and people just get on with their lives as best they can."[45]

"I tell my wife," says Theogene, "Rwanda is a bit like a painted grave. Nice on the outside, nothing but bones on the inside."

•

The Fourways cemetery in Johannesburg was full of birdsong the day I visited Patrick's grave, one of the last duties I'd set myself. Consulting a map that detailed the occupants of the cemetery, a woman at reception helped me locate the general sector where Patrick's plot was likely to be. Gardeners who trimmed the neat pathways pointed me to the individual grave.

Patrick's tomb is marked with a gray marble slab adorned with a photo of him in the military uniform he preferred never to wear. It bears one quote from Maya Angelou—"A great soul serves everyone all the time, a great soul never dies. It brings us together again and again"—and another from Malcolm X—"I am for truth no matter who tells it. I am for justice no matter who it's for or against."

There were plenty, I knew, who would scoff at such lofty words on the grave of a man who departed with so many dark secrets. Patrick himself would probably have raised a quizzical eyebrow. The men who set up the RNC were too intelligent, too self-critical, not to know what they had done and how they would be judged by posterity.

Asked by a journalist if he regretted working for the system he now opposed, General Kayumba's answer was simple: "Regret is an understatement." Theogene is even more direct: "When they say these dictators and monsters are created by those around them, I think it's true. That exaggerated respect, the way we treated one man as royalty. . . . We had a hand in the making of a monster."

The former comrades' revenge is to become the ghosts that haunt Kagame, striking a chill to the presidential heart, their names alone grim harbingers of that most commonplace of African scenarios: the abrupt dawn arrest, the discontented army on the streets, the mutineers' matter-of-fact radio announcement.

While General Kayumba insists he is too old now to aspire to high office, Kagame clearly does not share his view. The constant references to the General in Rwanda's media, the fretful denunciations of the "terrorists" who make up the Rwanda National Congress, and the relentless pressure applied to Uganda and South Africa to hand over the movement's ringleaders betray a deep sense of trepidation.

One other specter torments Kagame: the friend who continues to outshine him in death as he did in life, more valiant, better loved, acutely missed. Fred may lie buried in Kigali's Heroes Corner, but his memory possesses a life of its own. When a Rwandan professor in California, writing in the tradition of dynastic Tutsi poetry, penned a rolling, 126-line eulogy to his country's "guiding light," "the great pillar that our homes can stand on and our precious jewels hang," the leader he addressed was not Kagame, but Fred.[46]

Beret-sporting and ironically smiling, his image regularly pops up on the Twitter accounts, WhatsApp profiles, and Facebook pages of Tutsi millennials. Unblemished by age or the corruption of office, beyond the reach of any presidential rewriting of the national narrative, he is the hero who was taken before the genocide that poisoned everything it touched. Forever young, forever handsome, forever brimming with unfulfilled promise, Fred Rwigyema is that most dangerous of things, the future the RPF promised but failed to deliver, a symbol of the Utopia for which Rwandans still pine.

ACKNOWLEDGMENTS

On top of the sterling work done by Clive Priddle, my forbearing editor, and my literary agents Charles Buchan and Sarah Chalfant, my thanks go to Gerard Prunier, for his encouragement and background knowledge; Fiona Leney, for her precious editorial input; Vicki Mabon, who sorted out the maps; Miles Morland, who helped keep me solvent; Caroline Moorehead, source of wise advice; Peter Chappell, for television archive material; Peter and Penny Fabricius, who hosted me in Johannesburg; and the late Susan Linnee, much-missed friend and surrogate auntie, who encouraged so many writers and journalists throughout her life. Finally, I am grateful to the many Rwandans and Ugandans who generously shared their insights, experiences, and memories. In an ideal world, I would be able to identify more of them here. But this is not an ideal world.

ACRONYMS

AFDL   Alliance of Democratic Forces for the Liberation of Congo-Zaire. Congolese rebel coalition pulled together, funded, and armed by Rwanda, which toppled Mobutu Sese Seko in 1997.

ALIR   Army for the Liberation of Rwanda. Hutu rebel force set up in DRC in 1997 by combined *interahamwe* and ex-FAR. It was replaced by the FDLR in 2001.

ANC   African National Congress. South African political party that fought apartheid. Initially banned by the white regime, its members were forced into exile or imprisoned. It now governs the country.

DFID   Department for International Development (United Kingdom). Governmental department responsible for foreign aid.

DP   Democratic Party (Uganda). Popular in southern Uganda and among Catholics.

DRC   Democratic Republic of Congo (formerly Zaire).

EPLF   Eritrean People's Liberation Front. Rebel group that seized power in Eritrea in 1991.

ESO   External Security Organisation (Rwanda), which Patrick Karegeya ran for ten years.

FAR   Forces Armées Rwandaises. Rwanda's army under President Juvénal Habyarimana, referred to as "the ex-FAR" once it went into exile in 1994.

FDLR   Forces Démocratiques de Libération du Rwanda. Hutu rebel group based in eastern DRC, made up of former members of the *interahamwe*, ex-FAR, and members of Habyarimana's presidential guard and committed to restoring Hutu power in Rwanda.

FRELIMO   Mozambique Liberation Front.

FRONASA   Front for National Salvation. Short-lived left-wing Ugandan rebel movement set up by Yoweri Museveni to fight the regime of Idi Amin.

ICRC   International Committee of the Red Cross.

ICTR   International Criminal Tribunal for Rwanda. Court set up in Arusha, Tanzania, to put those suspected of involvement in the genocide on trial.

ISO   Internal Security Organisation (Uganda).

MPLA   Popular Movement for the Liberation of Angola.

NISS   National Intelligence and Security Service (Rwanda).

NPA   National Prosecuting Authority (South Africa).

NRM/NRA   Yoweri Museveni's rebel group, which seized power in Uganda in 1986. The liberation movement was called the National Resistance Movement; the National Resistance Army was its armed wing.

RANU   Rwanda Alliance for National Unity. Banyarwanda refugee organization, precursor of the RPF.

RCD   Rassemblement Congolais pour la Démocratie. Congolese rebel group created with Rwandan support to challenge Laurent Kabila. It splintered into various factions.

RFI   Radio France Internationale. Publicly funded French radio.

RNC   Rwanda National Congress. Opposition movement set up by Patrick Karegeya, Kayumba Nyamwasa, Theogene Rudasingwa, and Gerald Gahima.

RPA   Rwanda Patriotic Army, armed wing of the RPF (sometimes given as *Rwandese* Patriotic Army). Rebaptised as RDF (Rwanda Defence Force) in 2002.

RPF   Rwandan Patriotic Front (sometimes given as *Rwandese* Patriotic Front). FPR, Front Patriotique Rwandais, is the French version.

TPLF   Tigrayan People's Liberation Front. Rebel movement that seized power in Ethiopia in 1991. Ethiopian prime minister Abiy Ahmed sent troops to oust its leadership from Tigray in November 2020.

UNAMIR   United Nations Assistance Mission for Rwanda. Under the command of Brigadier General Roméo Dallaire of Canada, its mandate was originally to assist in the implementation of the Arusha Accords. After the genocide began, its numbers were belatedly increased.

UNHCR   United Nations High Commissioner for Refugees.

UNITA   União Nacional para a Independência Total de Angola. Angola rebel movement led by Jonas Savimbi, supported during the Cold War by the United States and South Africa.

UNLA   Uganda National Liberation Army. Armed wing of the Uganda National Liberation Front (UNLF). The UNLF was a Tanzania-supported umbrella group uniting various Ugandan rebel groups, including FRONASA, that were opposed to Idi Amin. After Milton Obote took power and gradually sidelined Museveni, the UNLA effectively became Obote's army, dominated by members of the Acholi community.

UPC   Uganda People's Congress. Political party founded by Milton Obote.

UPDF   Uganda People's Defence Force. The new army unveiled by Museveni after his 1986 capture of power in Kampala.

WFP   United Nations' World Food Programme.

A NOTE ON TERMINOLOGY

Some readers may find the various terms used to describe different regions, ethnic communities, and their members confusing. This chart is intended as a simple guide:

INDIVIDUAL	COMMUNITY	REGION	LANGUAGE
Munyarwanda	Banyarwanda	Rwanda and its neighbors	Kinyarwanda
Munyankole	Banyankole	Ankole	Runyankole
Muganda	Baganda	Buganda	Luganda

REFERENCE NOTES

Many of my interviews were with eyewitnesses who have themselves written books from which I quote. When this happens, I spell out the two different sources—personal interviews versus their own works. With witnesses who *aren't* authors, having identified them a first time in the reference notes, I do not go on to spell out the fact that we spoke directly every time they are quoted. It is assumed.

Introduction

1. Jacques-Roger Booh Booh, *Le Patron de Dallaire Parle: Révélations sur les dérives d'un général de l'ONU au Rwanda* (Paris: Editions Duboiris, 2005).

2. Richard Kandt, *Caput Nili: Eine empfindsame Reise zu den Quellen des Nils* (Berlin: Dietrich Reimer, 1904).

3. Ewart S. Grogan and Arthur H. Sharp, *From the Cape to Cairo* (Fairford, UK: Echo Library, 2014).

4. Author's interview with Gérard Prunier.

5. Author's interview with Patrick Karegeya.

6. Frantz Fanon, *Black Skin, White Masks* (New York: Grove Press, 1967).

7. Author's interview, anonymity requested.

Chapter 1: An Incident at the Michelangelo

1. Author's interview with David Batenga.

2. Author's interview with Portia Karegeya.

3. Author's interview with Leah Karegeya.

4. "Rwandan Foreign Affairs Minister Louise Mushikiwabo Chastises Patrick Karegeya's Orphans," AfroAmerica Network World, January 7, 2014, www.afro america.net/Africa/News/Entries/2014/1/7_Rwandan_Foreign_Affairs,_Louise _MUshikiwabo,_Scolds_Patrick_Karegeyas_Orphans.html.

5. "Gen Kabarebe on Karegeya: 'When You Choose to Be a Dog, You Die Like a Dog,'" *News of Rwanda*, January 11, 2014, www.newsofrwanda.com/featured1/21824/gen-kabarebe-on-karegeya-when-you-choose-to-be-dog-you-die-like-dog.

6. "Paul Kagame's Speech at Rwanda Leaders Fellowship Prayer Breakfast," Kigali, January 12, 2014, http://paulkagame.com/?p=2955. Extracts of the speech were broadcast on several Rwandan radio stations. Kagame did not refer to Patrick by name, but the target of his comments was clear.

7. Matina Stevis and Thorold Barker, "Rwanda President Denies Role in Ex–Spy Chief's Death," *Wall Street Journal*, January 23, 2014, www.wsj.com/articles/rwanda-president-denies-role-in-exspy-chief8217s-death-1390506556.

8. "Family Stranded with Karegeya's Body in South Africa," *Daily Monitor*, January 5, 2014, www.monitor.co.ug/News/National/Family-stranded-with-Karegeya-s-body-in-South—/688334-2134390-luvbckz/index.html.

9. Author's interview, anonymity requested.

10. Author's interview with Thembi Majola.

11. Gene Sharp, *From Dictatorship to Democracy: A Conceptual Framework for Liberation* (Boston: Albert Einstein Institution, 1994).

Chapter 2: Chronicle of a Death Foretold

1. Imfunsi is the website set up by Rwandan journalists in exile that published the tapes. It now appears to be defunct. The audio is available on YouTube, however. See "Gen. Kayumba Assassination Attempts—Recording 2 (English)," YouTube, posted by Imfunsi, July 10, 2011, www.youtube.com/watch?v=JpO6BmTd1SE&t=2s.

2. Author's interview, anonymity requested.

3. Patrick Karegeya's 2012 signed submission to the US Department of Homeland Security, which he wrote and presented in support of Leah Karegeya's application for political asylum in the States.

4. Author's interview, anonymity requested.

5. Author's interview, anonymity requested.

6. Author's interview with Jason Stearns.

7. Author's interview, anonymity requested.

8. Author's interview with Emile Rutagengwa. Emile's story was first told by Jacques Pauw in *Rat Roads: One Man's Incredible Journey* (Cape Town: Zebra Press, 2012).

9. "UN Hires Fugitive Karegeya to Train Somali 'Mercenaries,'" *Editions Sources du Nil*, February 4, 2011. When the Rwandan government belatedly heard about the consultancy, Kigali's media covered the story in sensationalist style, claiming that Patrick, General Kayumba, and Salim Saleh were jointly training a mercenary force bent on destabilizing Rwanda. Kagame called UN secretary-general Ban Ki-moon to accuse his organization of employing mercenaries, and the UN felt obliged to launch an internal investigation. The response made future work of this kind unlikely.

10. IGIHE website, www.igihe.com.

11. Author's interview with Kayumba Nyamwasa.

12. Author's interview with Fred Muvunyi.

13. Author's interview with Rosette Kayumba.

Chapter 3: If at First You Don't Succeed

1. Author's interview with Theogene Rudasingwa.

2. "The State vs. Amani Uriwane [Uwimani], Hassan Mohammedi Nduli, Sady Abdou, Richard Bachisa, Hemedi Dendengo Sefu, Pascal Kanyandekwe," Case No. 41/1325/2010, Date 22/02/2014.

3. The trial's outcome surprised many observers. On August 29, 2014, magistrate Stanley Mkhari found three Tanzanians and one Rwandan guilty of attempted murder, sentencing them to eight years. While accepting that the plot was politically motivated, emanating "from a certain group of people from Rwanda," the magistrate astonished the prosecution by acquitting Bachisa, the driver, and Kanyandekwe, the suspected ringleader. RNC members pointed out that the two men—who both flew back to Rwanda—could have publicly made the link between Kigali and the shooting, so their departure averted an awkward international incident. Despite being repeatedly cited in court by the prosecution, Vincent Ngendo, who left South Africa shortly after the shooting, was never among the defendants. When I asked the General why he thought Bachisa had betrayed him, he said, "Stupidity and greed. He was safe here." The young man had been spotted in a popular Kigali barbecue joint, he told me, since his return. He shrugged, reverting to revolutionary terminology: "He's just a lumpen."

4. Theogene Rudasingwa, *Healing a Nation: A Testimony. Waging and Winning a Peaceful Revolution to Unite and Heal a Broken Rwanda* (North Charleston, SC: CreateSpace, 2013).

5. Author's interview, anonymity requested.

6. "Rwanda 'Assassins' Kill Reporter Jean Leonard Rugambage," BBC, June 25, 2010, www.bbc.co.uk/news/10413793.

7. Xan Rice, "Rwandan Opposition Leader Found Dead," *The Guardian*, July 14, 2010, www.theguardian.com/world/2010/jul/14/rwanda-opposition-politician-found-dead.

8. Robert Mukombozi, "Patrick Karegeya, Exiled Rwanda Colonel, Calls for War on Kagame," *La Tribune Franco-Rwandaise*, August 3, 2010, www.france-rwanda.info/article-patrick-karegeya-exiled-rwanda-colonel-calls-for-war-on-kagame-54866207.html.

9. General Kayumba Nyamwasa, Dr. Theogene Rudasingwa, Col. Patrick Karegeya, and Gerald Gahima, "Rwanda Briefing," August 2010, www.afroamerica.net/pages/KayumbaKaregeyaRudasingwaGahimaRwanda_Briefing_August2010_ConsolidatedVersion2.pdf.

10. Rudasingwa, *Healing a Nation*.

11. "Proclamation Establishing the Rwanda National Congress," December 12, 2010, www.rwandanationalcongress.org.

12. James Karuhanga, "Kayumba, Rudasingwa Get 24-Year Prison Terms," *New Times*, January 15, 2011, www.newtimes.co.rw/section/read/27640.

13. Author's interview with Robert Higiro. His explosive story was first broken in Geoffrey York and Judi Rever, "Assassination in Africa: Inside the Plots to Kill Rwanda's Dissidents," *Globe and Mail*, May 2, 2014, www.theglobeandmail.com/news/world/secret-recording-says-former-rwandan-army-major-proves-government-hires-assassins-to-kill-critics-abroad/article18396349. A year later, on May 20, 2015, Robert gave evidence about the Rwandan government's assassination plan to the US House of Representatives' Subcommittee on Africa, detailing

his conversations with Dan Munyuza. The footage is available online at https://docs.house.gov/meetings/FA/FA16/20150520/103498/HHRG-114-FA16-Wstate-HigiroR-20150520.pdf.

14. "Bourbon Coffee Finance Manager Killed," *New Times*, November 14, 2010, www.newtimes.co.rw/section/read/82958.

15. Recording of Jack Nziza talking to anonymous go-between, June 2010, at "Gen. Kayumba Assassination Attempts—Recording 1 (English)," YouTube, posted July 4, 2011, by Imfunsi, www.youtube.com/watch?v=20PzbJOVYQc; recording of Dan Munyuza talking to anonymous go-between, September 2010, at "Gen. Kayumba Assassination Attempts—Recording 2 (French)," YouTube, posted July 11, 2011, by Imfunsi, www.youtube.com/watch?v=WMwkcyFMpto; recording of Jack Nziza talking to anonymous go-between, June 19, 2010, at "Gen. Kayumba Assassination Attempts—Recording 3 (French)," YouTube, posted August 6, 2011, by Imfunsi, www.youtube.com/watch?v=VHQ7g1DZDmg.

16. Author's interview, anonymity requested.

17. Author's interview with Filip Reyntjens.

18. Geoffrey York, "Rwandan Officer Who Leaked Assassination-List Evidence Becomes a Target," *Globe and Mail*, November 19, 2015, www.theglobeandmail.com/news/world/rwandan-officer-who-leaked-assassination-list-evidence-becomes-a-target/article27382007.

19. In June 2018 Kale Kayihura was arrested in Kampala. He was later charged with aiding and abetting the kidnapping and illegal repatriation by subordinate police officers of Rwandan exiles in Uganda between 2012 and 2016. Stuart Yiga, "Kayihura Co-accused Arraigned in Military Court," New Vision, January 9, 2019, www.newvision.co.ug/news/1492361/kayihura-accused-arraigned-military-court. Released on bail, he was awaiting trial when this book went to press.

20. "Charles Ingabire: Inyenyeri News | Killed in an Area Near Kampala, Uganda | December 01, 2011," Committee to Protect Journalists, https://cpj.org/data/people/charles-ingabire.

21. "Man Imprisoned in Sweden for Spying on Rwandans," AP, October 23, 2013, https://apnews.com/5f49700ff4d84572ab5e2ba14988e7c9.

22. Andrew Meldrum, "Rwanda News: Sweden Expels Rwanda Diplomat for Spying," *Global Post*, February 13, 2012, www.pri.org/stories/2012-02-13/rwanda-news-sweden-expels-rwanda-diplomat-spying.

23. Tom Rhodes, "Rwandan Exiled Journalist Comes Out of Hiding," Committee to Protect Journalists, February 16, 2012, https://cpj.org/2012/02/rwandan-exiled-journalist-comes-out-of-hiding.

24. Author's interview with René Mugenzi.

25. In July 2020, nine years after these events, Mugenzi was sentenced to twenty-seven months in prison for stealing £200,000 from the Norwich cathedral where he worked as treasurer. Friends said he had become addicted to online financial trading, an addiction exacerbated by the stress of his work as a human rights activist. Sending Mugenzi to jail, the judge acknowledged he had pleaded guilty at the first opportunity and hailed him as a man of "active good character," notwithstanding his crime.

26. Jenny Cuffe, "Call to Stop Rwandan Aid over Death Threats to Exiles," File on 4, Radio 4, BBC, August 2, 2011, www.bbc.co.uk/news/uk-14217337.

27. Author's interview, anonymity requested.

28. Author's interview with Andrew Mitchell.

29. Author's interview, anonymity requested.

Chapter 4: Plots Thicken

1. Author's interview, anonymity requested.

2. Author's interview with Jennifer Rwamugira.

3. Jennifer's family has paid a high price for her defiance. She moved her children to South Africa after Rwandan intelligence made repeated attempts to track them down at their school in Uganda, but her husband was not so lucky. Arrested in 2014, he was held without charge for four years. On his release he was in such bad shape that he had to use a wheelchair. Rearrested in 2018, he has not been heard from since.

4. "Karegeya's Daughter Caught in Rwanda-Uganda Passport Fix," *East African*, July 16, 2012, www.theeastafrican.co.ke/news/Karegeya-s-daughter-caught-in-Rwanda-Uganda-passport-fix/2558-1456420-view-printVersion-h12p6hz/index.html.

5. "Repression Across Borders: Attacks and Threats Against Rwandan Opponents and Critics Abroad," Human Rights Watch, January 28, 2014, www.hrw.org/news/2014/01/28/rwanda-repression-across-borders.

6. Author's interview with Gervais Condo.

7. Author's interview with Serge Ndayizeye.

8. "Final Report of the Group of Experts on the DRC Submitted in Accordance with Paragraph 4 of Security Council Resolution 2021 (2011) (S/2012/843)," November 15, 2012, https://reliefweb.int/report/democratic-republic-congo/final-report-group-experts-drc-submitted-accordance-paragraph-4.

9. Chris McGreal, "Rwanda's Paul Kagame Warned He May Be Charged with Aiding War Crimes," *The Guardian*, July 25, 2012, www.theguardian.com/world/2012/jul/25/rwanda-paul-kagame-war-crimes.

10. Mark Tran, "Andrew Mitchell: 'Restoring Rwanda Aid Not the Act of a Rogue Minister,'" *The Guardian*, November 8, 2012, www.theguardian.com/global-development/2012/nov/08/andrew-mitchell-rwanda-aid-rogue-minister.

11. Author's interview, anonymity requested.

12. Author's interview, anonymity requested.

13. Mutabazi was subsequently tried in Kigali, charged with terrorism and the president's attempted murder, and sentenced to life. In Kampala, eight Ugandan officers—one military colonel and seven police officers—were later charged with Mutabazi's abduction, a case seen as marking an end to Museveni's tolerance of Rwandan security operations conducted on Ugandan soil. See "Ugandan Officers Charged with Abducting Rwanda Refugees," *East African*, January 9, 2019, www.theeastafrican.co.ke/tea/news/east-africa/ugandan-officers-charged-with-abducting-rwanda-refugees-1410110.

14. Author's interview with Hrvoje Hranjski.

15. Author's interview with Jonathan Clayton.

16. Author's interview, anonymity requested.

17. Author's interview, anonymity requested.

18. Author's interview with Carina Tertsakian.

19. Author's interview with Kennedy Gihana.

20. Author's interview, anonymity requested.

Chapter 5: My Roots Are Buried Here

1. John Hanning Speke, *The Discovery of the Source of the Nile* (Edinburgh: William Blackwood and Sons, 1863).

2. Sheila Rule, "Rebel Sworn in as Uganda President," *New York Times*, January 30, 1986, www.nytimes.com/1986/01/30/world/rebel-sworn-in-as-uganda-president.html.

3. Sam Amanyire and Felix Basiime, "I Am Going Nowhere—Museveni," *Daily Monitor*, February 4, 2008, www.monitor.co.ug/News/Education/688336-728862-ke2cwt/index.html.

4. "Uganda's Parliament Votes to Scrap Presidential Age-Limit," Deutsche Welle, December 12, 2017, www.dw.com/en/ugandas-parliament-votes-to-scrap-presidential-age-limit/a-41874961.

5. Author's interview with Ernest Mugabo.

6. Author's interview with Jane Keshoro.

7. Alison Liebhafsky Des Forges, *Defeat Is the Only Bad News: Rwanda Under Musinga, 1896–1931* (Madison: University of Wisconsin Press, 2011).

8. Richard Kandt, *Caput Nili: Eine empfindsame Reise zu den Quellen des Nils* (Berlin: Dietrich Reimer, 1904).

9. Jason Stearns, *Dancing in the Glory of Monsters: The Collapse of the Congo and the Great War of Africa* (New York: PublicAffairs, 2012). Ugandan academic Mahmood Mamdani also dissects the various academic theories explaining the Tutsi-Hutu divide, then explores how that divide was politically racialized under Belgian rule. See his *When Victims Become Killers: Colonialism, Nativism, and the Genocide in Rwanda* (Princeton, NJ: Princeton University Press, 2001), chaps. 2 and 3.

10. Catherine Watson, "Exile from Rwanda: Background to an Invasion," Issue Paper, US Committee for Refugees, February 1991.

11. One of the key characters in Ugandan writer Jennifer Makumbi's bestselling novel *Kintu* (Oakland, CA: Transit Books, 2017 [Kenya, 2014]), is an aggrieved Banyarwanda herdsman who casts a curse on the eighteenth-century Baganda king who employs him.

Chapter 6: Hiding in Plain Sight

1. Raymond Baguma and Bizimungu Kisakye, "President Kagame Rehabilitates His Former School," *New Vision*, October 30, 2007.

2. Author's interview with Sylvester Singila.

3. François Soudan, *Kagame: Conversations with the President of Rwanda* (Enigma Books and Nouveau Monde editions, 2015).

4. Author's interview with James Bigirimana.

5. Jean-Paul Kimonyo, *Rwanda Demain! Une Longue Marche Vers la Transformation* (Boulder: Karthala, 2017).

6. Author's interview, anonymity requested.

7. The *busuti* or *gomesi* is traditional attire for women in Buganda, a floor-length dress with a low waist, a square neckline, puffed sleeves, and a wide sash. Involving up to six meters of material, it covers most of the body. Usually only donned for special occasions in the cities, it is still widely worn on a daily basis in rural areas.

8. Elijah Dickens Mushemeza, *The Politics and Empowerment of Banyarwanda Refugees in Uganda 1959–2001* (Kampala: Fountain, 2007).

9. Ambassador Thomas Patrick Melady, telegram to State Department, January 2, 1973.

10. Author's interview with Kizza Besigye.

11. Pecos Kutesa, *Uganda's Revolution, 1979–1986: How I Saw It* (Kampala: Fountain, 2006).

12. Author's interview with Pecos Kutesa.

13. Stephen Kinzer, *A Thousand Hills: Rwanda's Rebirth and the Man Who Dreamed It* (Hoboken, NJ: John Wiley and Sons, 2008).

14. Yoweri Kaguta Museveni, *Sowing the Mustard Seed: The Struggle for Freedom and Democracy in Uganda*, ed. Elizabeth Kanyogonya and Kevin Shillington (London: Macmillan, 1997).

15. Author's interview with Kahinda Otafiire.

16. Museveni, *Sowing the Mustard Seed*.

17. Author's interview with Kenneth Kakuru.

18. Kutesa, *Uganda's Revolution*.

19. Author's interview, anonymity requested.

20. Robert Astles, "Forty Tribes: A Life in Uganda," private publication by the Robert Astles Estate, 2015.

Chapter 7: The Bush War

1. Author's interview with Samuel Sawaye.

2. William Pike, *Combatants: A Memoir of the Bush War and the Press in Uganda* (self-published, 2019).

3. Pauline Bernard wrote on the uses to which the bone displays were put and the emotions evoked in "The Politics of the Luweero Skulls: The Making of Memorial Heritage and Post-Revolutionary State Legitimacy over the Luweero Mass Graves in Uganda," *Journal of Eastern African Studies* 11, no. 1 (2017).

4. Yoweri Kaguta Museveni, *Sowing the Mustard Seed: The Struggle for Freedom and Democracy in Uganda*, ed. Elizabeth Kanyogonya and Kevin Shillington (London: Macmillan, 1997).

5. These include Pecos Kutesa, *Uganda's Revolution, 1979–1986: How I Saw It* (Kampala: Fountain, 2006); Odonga Amaza, *Museveni's Long March: From FRELIMO to the National Resistance Movement* (London: Pluto Press, 1998); Matayo Kyaligonza, *The Agony of Power* (Kampala: n.p., 2006); Gilbert Gumoshabe and Elly Tumwine, *Uganda Since 1986: The Achievements of the NRM Revolution* (Kampala: n.p., 2015); Muhoozi Kainerugaba, *Battles of the Ugandan Resistance: A Tradition of Maneuver* (Kampala: Fountain, 2010). John Kazoora, *Betrayed by My Leader: The Memoirs of John Kazoora* (self-published, 2012), is at odds with the tradition. Critical of Museveni's leadership, it can only be bought on the black market. Sam Njuba, *The Betrayal: As Ugandans Are Taken for a Ride Again* (self-published, 2014), falls into a similar category. Daniel Kalinaki, *Kizza Besigye and Uganda's Unfinished Revolution* (Kampala: Dominant Seven, 2014), is a different kind of book. While obviously written with the opposition leader's collaboration, it is more than just a firsthand account.

6. Pike, *Combatants*.

7. Kutesa, *Uganda's Revolution*.

8. Stephen Kinzer, *A Thousand Hills: Rwanda's Rebirth and the Man Who Dreamed It* (Hoboken, NJ: John Wiley and Sons, 2008).

9. Author's interview, anonymity requested.

10. Author's interview with Jim Muhwezi.

11. Author's interview, anonymity requested.

12. Kutesa, *Uganda's Revolution*.

13. Chris Rwakasisi, who ran Obote's feared National Security Agency, was arrested in 1985 and sentenced to death on six counts of kidnapping with intent to murder. He spent twenty-four years in Luzira prison before being pardoned by Museveni in 2009.

14. Catherine Watson, "Exile from Rwanda: Background to an Invasion," Issue Paper, US Committee for Refugees, February 1991.

15. Author's interview, anonymity requested.

16. Author's interview, anonymity requested.

17. Author's interview, anonymity requested.

18. Clifford D. May, "Ugandan Disputes US over Killings," *New York Times*, August 20, 1984, www.nytimes.com/1984/08/20/world/ugandan-disputes-us-over-killings.html.

19. Milton Obote, "Notes on Concealment of Genocide in Uganda," April 1990, Uganda People's Congress, www.upcparty.net/obote/genocide.htm.

20. Britain's *Observer* ran "The Killing Fields of Kapeka," by William Pike, on its front page on August 19, 1984. Syndicated abroad, it was also a front-page story in France's *Liberation* a few days later.

21. Author's interview with Patrick Bracken and Joan Giller.

22. Author's interview with Winnie Byanyima.

23. Andrew Rice, *The Teeth May Smile but the Heart Does Not Forget: Murder and Memory in Uganda* (New York: Metropolitan Books, 2009). One of the weaknesses of the Commission of Inquiry into Violations of Human Rights, chaired by Oder and made up of six commissioners, was its overambitious terms of reference. It was authorized to investigate abuses going back to independence. After government funding dried up, it depended on support from the Ford Foundation and Denmark, publishing its findings to very little fanfare in 1994.

Chapter 8: On to Kampala

1. Author's interview with Ali Porteous.

2. Author's interview with Jim Muhwezi.

3. Pecos Kutesa, *Uganda's Revolution, 1979–1986: How I Saw It* (Kampala: Fountain, 2006).

4. Daniel Kalinaki, *Kizza Besigye and Uganda's Unfinished Revolution* (Kampala: Dominant Seven, 2014).

5. Interviews conducted for *Africa in Pieces: The Tragedy of the Great Lakes*, 1999, television documentary produced by Capa; Mahmood Mamdani, *When Victims Become Killers: Colonialism, Nativism, and the Genocide in Rwanda* (Princeton, NJ: Princeton University Press, 2001); Gérard Prunier, *The Rwanda Crisis: History of a Genocide* (Kampala: Fountain, 1995). Frank Rusagara, in *Resilience of a Nation: A History of the Military in Rwanda* (Kampala: Fountain, 2009), estimates that by the end of 1986, nearly a quarter of the NRA's force of 14,000 fighters—3,000 men—were Rwandans.

6. William Pike, *Combatants: A Memoir of the Bush War and the Press in Uganda* (self-published, 2019).

7. Dan Vittorio Segre, *Memoirs of a Fortunate Jew* (Bethesda, MD: Adler and Adler, 1987).

8. Robert Mukombozi, "What Col Karegeya Said About Rwanda," *Observer*, January 2, 2014, https://observer.ug/index.php?option=com_content&view=article&id=29425%3Awhat-col-karegeya-said-about-rwanda.

Chapter 9: Band of Brothers

1. Author's interview, anonymity requested.
2. Author's interview, anonymity requested.
3. Author's interview, anonymity requested.
4. Author's interview, anonymity requested.
5. Author's interview, anonymity requested.
6. Author's interview with Charles Onyango-Obbo.
7. Author's interview, anonymity requested.
8. Author's interview with John Nagenda.
9. Author's interview with Amama Mbabazi.
10. Mahmood Mamdani, *When Victims Become Killers: Colonialism, Nativism, and the Genocide in Rwanda* (Princeton, NJ: Princeton University Press, 2001).
11. Author's interview with Gerald Gahima.
12. Gérard Prunier, *The Rwanda Crisis: History of a Genocide* (Kampala: Fountain, 1995), 70.
13. Teddy Seezi Cheeye, *Weekly Topic*, October 19, 1990.
14. Author's interview with Salim Saleh.
15. Stephen Kinzer, *A Thousand Hills: Rwanda's Rebirth and the Man Who Dreamed It* (Hoboken, NJ: John Wiley and Sons, 2008).
16. Author's interview, anonymity requested.
17. Author's interview, anonymity requested.
18. Author's interview, anonymity requested.
19. Tito Rutaremara, interviewed by British researcher John Burton Kegel, November 2018.
20. Author's interview, anonymity requested.
21. Author's interview, anonymity requested.
22. Author's interview, anonymity requested.

Chapter 10: Exodus

1. William Pike, *Combatants: A Memoir of the Bush War and the Press in Uganda* (self-published, 2019).
2. Author's interview, anonymity requested.
3. Author's interview with John Kazoora.
4. Author's interview with William Pike.
5. Author's interview with David Bashaija.
6. Author's interview, anonymity requested.
7. Author's interview with Pecos Kutesa.
8. Author's interview, anonymity requested.
9. Author's interview, anonymity requested.
10. Author's interview, anonymity requested.
11. Frank K. Rusagara, *A History of the Military in Rwanda: Resilience of a Nation* (Kampala: Fountain, 2009).
12. Author's interview with Sheila Kawamara.

13. "Rwigyema Death: Details Revealed," *New Vision*, November 5, 1990.

14. James Kabarebe, "Rwanda Invasion: Kagame Breathes Life into Collapsing Struggle," *Daily Monitor*, October 6, 2013, www.monitor.co.ug/Magazines/People Power/Kagame-breathes-life-into-collapsing-struggle/689844-2019896-3qen4vz /index.html.

15. Author's interview, anonymity requested.

16. There is a further, Machiavellian twist to this version of events, one historian Prunier endorses. This states that Fred was murdered by Bayingana and Bunyenyezi acting on behalf of the ambitious, absent Kagame, who was bent on the top RPF post. The problem with this theory is that it ignores Bayingana and Kagame's mutual rivalry and dislike, which made collaboration unlikely. Gérard Prunier, *From Genocide to Continental War: The "Congolese" Conflict and the Crisis of Contemporary Africa* (London: C. Hurst, 2009).

17. Bayingana and Bunyenyezi were interviewed in the Mirama Hills, just inside Rwandan territory, on October 4, 1990, by Cathy Watson, Aidan Hartley, and Sam Mukalazi.

18. Author's interview, anonymity requested.

19. Theogene Rudasingwa, *Healing a Nation: A Testimony. Waging and Winning a Peaceful Revolution to Unite and Heal a Broken Rwanda* (North Charleston, SC: CreateSpace, 2013).

20. Stephen Kinzer, *A Thousand Hills: Rwanda's Rebirth and the Man Who Dreamed It* (Hoboken, NJ: John Wiley and Sons, 2008), 69.

21. Kinzer, *A Thousand Hills*, 179.

22. Mahmood Mamdani, *When Victims Become Killers: Colonialism, Nativism, and the Genocide in Rwanda* (Princeton, NJ: Princeton University Press, 2001).

23. Kinzer, *A Thousand Hills*, 79–80.

24. Author's interview, anonymity requested.

25. Alison Des Forges, Human Rights Watch, and Fédération international des droits de l'homme, *"Leave None to Tell the Story": Genocide in Rwanda* (New York: Human Rights Watch, 1999).

26. Gérard Prunier, *The Rwanda Crisis: History of a Genocide* (Kampala: Fountain, 1995).

27. Cathy Watson, "Rebels at the Ready in Fragile Rwanda Truce," *The Guardian*, September 8, 1992.

28. Author's interview with Theogene Rudasingwa.

29. Author's interview, anonymity requested.

30. Elijah Dickens Mushemeza, *The Politics and Empowerment of Banyarwanda Refugees in Uganda, 1959–2001* (Kampala: Fountain, 2007).

31. In *Rwanda and the New Scramble for Africa: From Tragedy to Useful Imperial Fiction* (Quebec: Baraka Books, 2013), Robin Philpot expounds the French perspective of events in the Great Lakes in detail.

32. Aloisea Inyumba was appointed Rwanda's minister of gender and family protection in the post-genocide transitional government. She was given a state funeral on her death from throat cancer in 2016 and Kagame delivered the eulogy.

33. Author's interview, anonymity requested.

34. John Burton Kegel, "The Road to Genocide: A Short Military History of the Rwandan Civil War" (BA diss., University of Kent, 2014).

35. Author's interview, anonymity requested.

36. Mamdani, *When Victims Become Killers*.

37. Noble Marara, *Behind the Presidential Curtain: Inside Out of Real Paul Kagame from His Former Bodyguard* (North Charleston, SC: CreateSpace, 2017).

Chapter 11: The Genocide and Its Aftermath

1. Jacques-Roger Booh-Booh, deposition for International Criminal Tribunal for Rwanda, November 21, 2005.

2. "Primo Levi's Heartbreaking, Heroic Answers to the Most Common Questions He Was Asked About 'Survival in Auschwitz,'" *The New Republic*, February 16, 1986, https://newrepublic.com/article/119959/interview-primo-levi-survival-auschwitz.

3. "Statement by the Political Bureau of the Rwandese Patriotic Front of the Proposed Deployment of a U.N. Intervention Force in Rwanda," Rwandese Patriotic Front, April 30, 1994, at Document Cloud, www.documentcloud.org/documents/1687041-footnote-12-pt-rpf-statement-april-30.html.

4. Theogene Rudasingwa, *Healing a Nation: A Testimony. Waging and Winning a Peaceful Revolution to Unite and Heal a Broken Rwanda* (North Charleston, SC: CreateSpace, 2013).

5. Author's interview with David Mugenyi.

6. "Rwigyema Buried—But Spirit Lives On," *The Monitor*, October 2–4, 1995.

Chapter 12: The Best President Rwanda Never Had

1. Author's interview with Cyriaque Sendashonga.

2. Author's interview with Seth Sendashonga.

3. Author's interview with Faustin Twagiramungu.

4. André Guichaoua, ed., *Seth Sendashonga, 1951–1998: Un Rwandais pris entre deux feux. Témoignages et propos* (Paris: Harmattan, 2013).

5. Author's interview with Jean-Marie Vianney Ndagijimana.

6. Theogene Rudasingwa, *Healing a Nation: A Testimony. Waging and Winning a Peaceful Revolution to Unite and Heal a Broken Rwanda* (North Charleston, SC: CreateSpace, 2013). This arrangement remains in force, with non-RPF government ministers routinely assigned Tutsi members of the RPF as permanent secretaries.

7. Gérard Prunier, *The Rwanda Crisis: History of a Genocide* (Kampala: Fountain, 1995), 43.

8. "Leaders in Africa Disappointed Me," in *The Africanists*, July 11, 2018, www.janpronk.nl/interviews/english-and-other-languages/leaders-in-africa-disappointed-me.

9. Rakiya Omaar and Alex de Waal, "Rwanda: Who Is Killing; Who Is Dying; What Is to Be Done," African Rights, May 1994.

10. Author's interview, anonymity requested.

11. Judi Rever's book *In Praise of Blood: The Crimes of the Rwandan Patriotic Front* (Toronto: Vintage Canada, 2018) details alleged atrocities committed by the RPF during this period. She and colleague Benedict Moran later released a cache of thirty-one sworn testimonies, many given by former RPF soldiers, collected by the ICTR's Special Investigations Unit. When the ICTR wound down in 2015, not a single indictment of the RPF had been issued, its more than sixty convictions all related to Habyarimana's regime. "Exclusive: The top-secret testimonies that implicate Rwanda's president in war crimes," *The Continent*, November 2020, https://mg.co.za/africa/2020-11-29-exclusive-top-secret-testimonies-implicate-rwandas-president-in-war-crimes/.

12. Gersony is profiled in Robert D. Kaplan, *The Good American: The Epic Life of Bob Gersony, The U.S. Government's Greatest Humanitarian* (New York: Random House, 2021).

13. Author's interview with Tony Jackson.

14. "Summary for UNHCR Presentation Before Commission of Experts, 10 October 1994: Prospects for Early Repatriation of Rwandan Refugees Currently in Burundi, Tanzania and Zaire," United Nations High Commissioner for Refugees, http://rwandinfo.com/documents/Gersony_Report.pdf.

15. ICTR-98-41-T Defense Exhibit DK-112, October 14, 1994, Outgoing Code Cable MIR, from Shaharyar Khan to Kofi Annan, regarding "The Gersoni [*sic*] Report Rwanda" (admitted November 16, 2006), United Nations Assistance Mission for Rwanda, at Rwanda Documents Project, www.rwandadocumentsproject.net /gsdl/collect/mil1docs/index/assoc/HASHc166/6f755cde.dir/doc84106.PDF.

16. Gérard Prunier, *From Genocide to Continental War: The "Congolese" Conflict and the Crisis of Contemporary Africa* (London: C. Hurst, 2009).

17. Alison Des Forges, Human Rights Watch, and Fédération international des droits de l'homme, *"Leave None to Tell the Story": Genocide in Rwanda* (New York: Human Rights Watch, 1999).

18. In 2008 she was declared persona non grata in Rwanda.

19. Author's interview with Noble Marara.

20. Author's interview, anonymity requested.

21. Ambassador Robert Krueger's cables were declassified in October 2016. See PDFs at the following URLs at the Internet Archive: https://ia600204.us.archive .org/7/items/GenocideInRwanda/Documents%20Atrocities%20Perpetrated%20 or%20Permitted%20by%20RPF%20Forces%20in%20Southern%20Rwanda%20 and%20Burundi%20169229.pdf; https://archive.org/stream/GenocideInRwanda /Documents%20Atrocities%20Perpetrated%20or%20Permitted%20by%20 RPF%20Forces%20in%20Southern%20Rwanda%20and%20Burundi%20 169229#page/n0/mode/2up; https://ia600204.us.archive.org/7/items/Genocide InRwanda/Documents%20Atrocities%20Perpetrated%20or%20Permitted%20 by%20RPF%20Forces%20in%20Southern%20Rwanda%20and%20Burundi%20 169229.pdf; https://archive.org/stream/GenocideInRwanda/Documents%20 Atrocities%20Perpetrated%20or%20Permitted%20by%20RPF%20Forces%20 in%20Southern%20Rwanda%20and%20Burundi%20169229#page/n0 /mode/2up. The book Krueger later wrote with his wife, *From Bloodshed to Hope in Burundi: Our Embassy Years During Genocide* (Austin: University of Texas Press, 2007), both corroborates and amplifies Gersony's findings, leaving little doubt about RPA brutality in the border region between Rwanda and Burundi.

22. "Rwanda: Reports of Killings and Abductions by the Rwandese Patriotic Army, April–August 1994," Amnesty International, October 19, 1994, www.amnesty .org/en/documents/afr47/016/1994/en.

23. A detailed account of what happened at Kibeho was provided by Terry Pickard, an Australian army medic, in *Combat Medic: An Australian's Eyewitness Account of the Kibeho Massacre* (Wavell Heights, Australia: Big Sky Publishing, 2008).

24. Susan Thomson, *Rwanda: From Genocide to Precarious Peace* (New Haven, CT: Yale University Press, 2018).

25. Author's interview, anonymity requested. Museveni made a similar point in his 1986 inauguration speech, saying his men pressed him to assassinate Obote and army commander Bazilio Okello. He refused, he said, because "if you kill Bazilio there are other Bazilios who are also there."

26. In *Another Fine Mess: America, Uganda, and the War on Terror* (New York: Columbia University Press, 2017), US writer Helen Epstein exposes the dark underbelly of Museveni's regime.

27. A strong motive for Lizinde's assassination was provided by RPF intelligence officer Aloys Ruyenzi, one of Judge Bruguière's key witnesses, who claimed to have kept guard as Kagame and five aides, including Lizinde, discussed the logistics of the plane downing. Lizinde's knowledge of the terrain meant his advice was priceless, Ruyenzi said. "President of Rwanda Blamed in Assassinations," *Los Angeles Times*, February 17, 2007, reprinted in *Mercury News*, www.mercurynews .com/2007/02/17/president-of-rwanda-blamed-in-assassinations. Lizinde's son Flavien, whom I interviewed, is skeptical of the notion that his father played a significant role in the plane's downing, but believes his network of contacts and links with the ex-FAR made him someone worth eliminating. "He knew all the RPF's secrets. Kagame was afraid of him because of that. He always hated him talking to outsiders."

28. Prunier, *From Genocide to Continental War*.

29. Author's interview, anonymity requested.

30. "Rwanda: Resolve Disappearances, Assassination," Human Rights Watch, May 4, 2014, www.hrw.org/ku-so/node/224118.

31. The RPF has long looked to Israel for inspiration and support. The admiration is mutual: the late David Kimche, Mossad's deputy director, became an investor in Rwanda's telecommunications sector after retirement and was an ardent Kagame fan, comparing the Rwandan president to David Ben-Gurion. But René Lemarchand is one of many academics and writers to highlight the dangers of drawing overly close analogies between the Holocaust and Rwanda's genocide. The differences between the Jews and Tutsis are as significant as the similarities. "To put it baldly: Jews did not invade Germany with the massive military and logistical support of a neighbouring state; nor did they once rule Germany as the political instrument of an absolute monarchy; nor were they identified with a ruling ethnocracy; nor did Jewish elements commit a partial genocide of non-Jews in a neighbouring state 22 years before the Holocaust. Again, Jews did not stand accused of murdering the head of state of a neighbouring state (as happened in Burundi with the assassination of Melchior Ndadaye in October 1993). And while Jews were insistently accused by the Nazi propaganda mill of working hand in hand with Bolshevism to subvert the state, at no time did their actions, within or outside Germany, lend the slightest credibility to these accusations. Immensely more threatening was the military posture of the RPF on the eve of the Rwanda genocide." René Lemarchand, "Disconnecting the Threads: Rwanda and the Holocaust Reconsidered," *IDEA* 7, no. 1 (2002).

Chapter 13: I Was James Bond

1. Author's interview, anonymity requested.

2. Author's interview with Abdulkarim Ali.

3. Philip Gourevitch, *We Wish to Inform You That Tomorrow We Will Be Killed with Our Families* (New York: Picador, 1998). The book won Gourevitch a bevy of awards. Samantha Power, *A Problem from Hell: America and the Age of Genocide* (London: Flamingo, 2002), examining US policy response to the genocide, was awarded a Pulitzer.

4. Author's interview with Fabienne Hara.

5. Author's interview with Susan Linnee.

6. Author's interview, anonymity requested.

7. Author's interview, anonymity requested.

8. Linda Melvern, *Intent to Deceive: Denying the Genocide of the Tutsi* (London: Verso, 2020).

9. Henry Samuel, "Petty Disputes Led to Nazi Denunciation in WWII France," *Daily Telegraph*, December 2, 2008.

10. Anna Funder, *Stasiland: Stories from Behind the Berlin Wall* (London: Granta, 2002).

11. Ernesto Che Guevara, *Congo Diary: The Story of Che Guevara's "Lost" Year in Africa* (Melbourne: Ocean Press, 2012).

12. Jason Stearns, *Dancing in the Glory of Monsters: The Collapse of the Congo and the Great War of Africa* (New York: PublicAffairs, 2012).

13. Author's interview with Anderbrhan Welde Giorgis.

14. Philip Roessler and Harry Verhoeven, *Why Comrades Go to War: Liberation Politics and the Outbreak of Africa's Deadliest Conflict* (London: Hurst and Company, 2016).

15. Gourevitch, *We Wish to Inform You.*

16. United Nations Human Rights Office of the High Commissioner, "Democratic Republic of the Congo: Report of the Mapping Exercise Documenting the Most Serious Violations of Human Rights and International Humanitarian Law Committed Within the Territory of the Democratic Republic of the Congo Between March 1993 and June 2003," August 2010, www.ohchr.org/Documents/Countries/CD/DRC_MAPPING_REPORT_FINAL_EN.pdf.

17. Roberto Garretón, "Report on the Situation of Human Rights in DR Congo, Submitted by the Special Rapporteur, Mr. Roberto Garretón (E/CN.4/2001/40)," February 1, 2001, https://reliefweb.int/report/burundi/report-situation-human-rights-dr-congo-submitted-special-rapporteur-mr-roberto. For more on Rwandan atrocities in Eastern Congo, read Stearns, *Dancing in the Glory of Monsters,* and Judi Rever, *In Praise of Blood: The Crimes of the Rwandan Patriotic Front* (Toronto: Vintage Canada, 2018).

18. Author's interview, anonymity requested.

19. Interview conducted for the documentary *Africa in Pieces: The Tragedy of the Great Lakes,* 2000, directed by Jihan El-Tahri, produced by Capa, written by Peter Chappell and Hervé Chabalier.

20. Author's interview with Rick Orth.

21. Richard Orth, "Rwanda's Hutu Extremist Insurgency: An Eyewitness Perspective," in *Genocide in Cambodia and Rwanda: New Perspectives*, ed. Susan E. Cook (London: Routledge, 2017).

22. Amnesty International, "Rwanda: The Hidden Violence: 'Disappearances' and Killings Continue," June 22, 1998; Amnesty International, "Rwanda: Extrajudicial Executions / Fear for Safety. Several Thousand Unarmed Civilians in a Cave," December 5, 1997.

Chapter 14: We Have Accepted to Be Dogs

1. Author's interview with Theogene Rudasingwa.

2. Patrick Karegeya's affidavit to the US Department of Homeland Security, 2012.

3. Filip Reyntjens, *Political Governance in Post-Genocide Rwanda* (Cambridge: Cambridge University Press, 2013).

4. Joseph Sebarenzi, with Laura Ann Mullane, *God Sleeps in Rwanda: A Journey of Transformation* (Oxford: Oneworld, 2009).

5. Augustin Cyiza, a Hutu former lieutenant colonel who persuaded some 800 FAR soldiers to serve in Kagame's new post-genocide army, disappeared in April 2003. His family says he was kidnapped by the security services; they believe he was tortured and killed at an army camp, his body then buried in a mass grave in the Akagera National Park. SAPA, "Rwandan Ex-Judge's Family Want Answers," IOL, April 10, 2013, www.iol.co.za/news/africa/rwandan-ex-judges-family-want-answers-1498481.

6. Philip Roessler and Harry Verhoeven, *Why Comrades Go to War: Liberation Politics and the Outbreak of Africa's Deadliest Conflict* (London: Hurst and Company, 2016).

7. Jason Stearns, *Dancing in the Glory of Monsters: The Collapse of the Congo and the Great War of Africa* (New York: PublicAffairs, 2012).

8. The Second Congo War was misleadingly dubbed "Africa's First World War" by Madeleine Albright, then US secretary of state, as she attempted to capture the international nature of the conflict, which was unprecedented in African history. The label is unhelpful, however, because Congo's second war never involved more than eight of the continent's fifty-three countries, and the staggeringly high civilian death toll was not the result of trench warfare or aerial bombing, but starvation and treatable diseases, with children disproportionately affected. The International Rescue Committee, responsible for the mortality studies, always made this clear, but its figures were routinely misunderstood and misreported.

9. Comer Plummer, "The Kitona Operation: Rwanda's African Odyssey," *The Rwandan*, May 13, 2013, www.therwandan.com/the-kitona-operation-rwandas-african-odyssey-by-comer-plummer.

10. Author's interview with Lara Santoro.

11. Author's interview with Alexandre Liebeskind.

12. "Rwanda Wanted to Dominate, We Wanted to Empower Congolese," *The Observer* (Uganda), July 27, 2014, https://observer.ug/features-sp-2084439083/57-feature/33002-rwanda-wanted-to-dominate-we-wanted-to-empower-congolese.

13. Theogene Rudasingwa, *Healing a Nation: A Testimony. Waging and Winning a Peaceful Revolution to Unite and Heal a Broken Rwanda* (North Charleston, SC: CreateSpace, 2013).

14. Sebarenzi, *God Sleeps in Rwanda*.

15. "Rwanda: The Search for Security and Human Rights Abuses," Human Rights Watch, vol. 12, no. 1 (April 2000), www.hrw.org/reports/2000/rwanda/Rwan004.htm#TopOfPage.

16. Noble Marara, *Behind the Presidential Curtain: Inside Out of Real Paul Kagame from His Former Bodyguard* (North Charleston, SC: CreateSpace, 2017).

17. Author's interview with David Himbara.

18. Rudasingwa, *Healing a Nation*.

19. Author's interview with Johnnie Carson.

20. Author's interview, anonymity requested.

21. Author's interview with Emmanuel Habyarimana.

22. John Carlin, "Rwanda's Paul Kagame: saviour or dictator?" *Sunday Times* August 26, 2017, www.thetimes.co.uk/article/rwandas-paul-kagame-saviour-or-dictator-bjdhp22nv.

23. Author's interview, anonymity requested.

Chapter 15: Spoils of War

1. Author's interview, anonymity requested.

2. "Report of the Panel of Experts on the Illegal Exploitation of Natural Resources and Other Forms of Wealth of DR Congo," United Nations, April 12, 2001, https://reliefweb.int/report/democratic-republic-congo/report-panel-experts-illegal-exploitation-natural-resources-and.

3. Cable from US embassy in Kigali to US Department of State, Subject: Rwanda: Organized Crime Involvement in Diamond Industry (C-CNO-00829), available at US Department of State, Freedom of Information Act, Virtual Reading Room Documents Search, https://foia.state.gov/Search/Search.aspx.

4. Author's interview with Jim Freedman.

5. "Plundering of DR Congo natural resources: Final report of the Panel of Experts (S/2002/11460)" October 16, 2002, https://reliefweb.int/report/burundi/plundering-dr-congo-natural-resources-final-report-panel-experts-s20021146.

6. The DRC sued Uganda, Rwanda, and Burundi at the International Court of Justice (ICJ) in The Hague in June 1999 "for acts of armed aggression," demanding compensation for "intentional destruction" and "looting." In 2005 the court ordered Uganda to pay $10 billion in reparations, but the ICJ has no powers to enforce its findings, and Uganda has yet to pay a penny. In 2019 the ICJ reopened the case after an appeal by Kampala, which argued the award was "excessive." The case against Kigali has been stymied by the fact that Rwanda is not an ICJ signatory. Current close relations between President Félix Tshisekedi and Kagame suggest a compensation case is unlikely to be brought in any other court. "Armed Activities on the Territory of the Congo (Democratic Republic of the Congo v. Uganda)," International Court of Justice, www.icj-cij.org/en/case/116.

Chapter 16: This Man Is an Emperor

1. Author's interview, anonymity requested.

2. Theogene Rudasingwa, *Healing a Nation: A Testimony. Waging and Winning a Peaceful Revolution to Unite and Heal a Broken Rwanda* (North Charleston, SC: CreateSpace, 2013).

3. Author's interview with Noble Marara.

4. Author's interview with Jean-Marie Micombero.

5. Author's interview with Emmanuel Habyarimana.

6. Author's interview, anonymity requested.

7. Rudasingwa gives a similarly critical account of the 2003 elections in *Healing a Nation*: "The chairman of the National Electoral Commission, Professor Chrysologue Karangwa, an over-zealous Tutsi, wanted to give RPF maximum victory by any means necessary" (p. 259).

8. "Rwanda's Presidential Election—Kagame Won, a Little Too Well," *The Economist*, August 28, 2003, www.economist.com/middle-east-and-africa/2003/08/28/kagame-won-a-little-too-well.

9. Author's interview, anonymity requested.

10. Filip Reyntjens, *Political Governance in Post-Genocide Rwanda* (Cambridge: Cambridge University Press, 2013).

11. "Nothing Strange About Colonel Patrick Karegeya's Arrest (General James Kabarebe)," Ugandanet, May 13, 2005.

12. Author's interview, anonymity requested.

13. John le Carré, *The Mission Song* (New York: Little, Brown, 2006).

14. Michela Wrong, *I Didn't Do It for You: How the World Betrayed a Small African Nation* (New York: HarperCollins, 2005).

15. "Former Intel Chief Karegeya Sentenced for Desertion and Insubordination," US Confidential Cable, July 13, 2006, available at Wikileaks, https://wikileaks.org/plusd/cables/06KIGALI687_a.html.

Chapter 17: The Plane and Other Secrets

1. Gérard Prunier, *The Rwanda Crisis: History of a Genocide* (Kampala: Fountain, 1995).

2. Author's interview with Filip Reyntjens.

3. Few men better personify the Epimenides paradox than Ruzibiza. In 2005 he released *Rwanda: L'histoire secrète* (Paris: Éditions du Panama), a denunciation of RPF human rights abuses, including the attack on the plane. His testimony was heavily relied on by Judge Bruguière in his 2006 indictment. In 2008 Ruzibiza recanted parts of his account, saying the book had in fact been written by several people and that Bruguière had distorted his words. In 2010 he recanted that retraction, saying he had felt his personal security to be at risk. He died of cancer in Norway later that year, having thoroughly muddied the waters. Senior ex-RPF figures have told me that while much of the material in his book is correct, he did not personally witness or take part in many of the key incidents—a similar charge to that leveled at Noble Marara.

4. In 1997, the Belgian Senate issued a report that sat on the fence, concluding there was not enough information to determine culpability. In 1998, France's National Assembly came out with another, positing two possible explanations: Hutu extremists on the one hand, the RPF on the other. In 2006, after eight years of investigation, France's Jean-Louis Bruguière issued arrest warrants for nine RPF officials. In 2008, Spain's Fernando Andreu Merelles issued warrants against forty current or former Rwandan military officials. In 2010 the Rwandan government released the Mutsinzi Report implicating Hutu extremists. In 2012 France's Marc Trévidic and colleague Nathalie Poux identified Kanombe's military barracks as the likely site from which the missiles were launched, suggesting Hutu extremists were to blame.

5. Author's interview, anonymity requested.

6. Sebastian Rotella, "Genocide Findings Cause an Uproar," *Los Angeles Times*, February 17, 2007.

7. *Untold Story: Rwanda*, directed by John Conroy, presented by Jane Corbin, BBC, October 2014.

8. Carla del Ponte, *Madame Prosecutor: Confrontations with Humanity's Worst Criminals and the Culture of Impunity* (New York: Other Press, 2009).

9. "Del Ponte Says UN Caved to Rwandan Pressure," Global Policy Forum, September 2003, www.globalpolicy.org/component/content/article/163/29047.html.

10. Piotr Smolar, "Attentat de Kigali en 1994: Jean-Louis Bruguière accuse Paul Kagamé," *Le Monde*, November 21, 2006, www.lemonde.fr/afrique/article/2006/11/21/rwanda-le-juge-bruguiere-met-en-cause-le-president-kagame_836769_3212.html.

11. Arthur Asiimwe, "Rwanda's Kagame Lambasts French Judge over Warrants," Reuters, January 20, 2007, www.reuters.com/article/us-rwanda-france/rwandas-kagame-lambasts-french-judge-over-warrants-idUSL2292236620061122.

12. Philip Gourevitch, "The Mutsinzi Report on the Rwandan Genocide," *New Yorker,* January 8, 2010, www.newyorker.com/news/news-desk/the-mutsinzi -report-on-the-rwandan-genocide.

13. Author's interview, anonymity requested.

14. Author's interview, anonymity requested.

15. Ruzibiza, *Rwanda.*

16. In October 2020, after years investigating exactly this issue, Filip Reyntjens published a paper that included new evidence regarding the serial numbers of the two missiles used, part of a consignment bought by the Ugandan army. He concluded all evidence pointed to RPF involvement. "Retour sur l'attentat de Kigali, l'étincelle qui a allumé le feu du génocide," Working Paper 2020.04, Institute of Development Policy, University of Antwerp, www.uantwerpen.be/en /research-groups/iob/publications/working-papers/wp-2020/wp-202004.

17. Author's interview with Theogene Rudasingwa. The personal crisis is also covered in his book *Healing a Nation: A Testimony. Waging and Winning a Peaceful Revolution to Unite and Heal a Broken Rwanda* (North Charleston, SC: CreateSpace, 2013).

18. Rudasingwa, *Healing a Nation.*

19. Theogene Rudasingwa, "A Confession," Facebook, October 1, 2011, www.facebook.com/notes/theogene-rudasingwa/a-confession/275694929121550.

20. Donna Bryson, "General Says Kagame Hunted Him, Others," IOL, July 12, 2012, www.iol.co.za/news/africa/general-says-kagame-hunted-him-others -1340475; David Smith, "Exiled Rwandan General Attacks Paul Kagame as 'Dictator,'" *The Guardian,* July 30, 2012, www.theguardian.com/world/2012/jul/30 /exiled-rwandan-general-paul-kagame; "Kagame Wants Me Dead," *City Press,* July 29, 2012.
In 2016, Kayumba's testimony to French investigating magistrate Jean-Marc Herbaut, who replaced Marc Trévidic, was leaked to Geoffrey York and Judi Rever of the Canadian *Globe and Mail.* The General recalled being summoned to RPF headquarters just two hours after the plane came down on April 6, where he saw Kagame and two aides listening to radio reports on the assassination. "We kept listening to the announcements and comments for about five minutes, until Paul Kagame reduced the volume of the transistor portable radio and told us that President Habyarimana's aircraft had been shot down by our troops," his twelve-page deposition read. "He explained that he had kept it secret within a small group under his direct command to avoid any leakage." Kagame and the two aides described how the missiles were smuggled to Kigali under a load of firewood on a truck, according to General Kayumba. The attack had first been planned when the presidential jet flew to Tanzania, but was postponed because of heavy fog, he said. It was then authorized for the return flight, according to the newspaper. Geoffrey York and Judi Rever, "Probe Revisits Mystery of Assassination That Triggered Rwandan Genocide," *Globe and Mail,* April 3, 2017, www.theglobeandmail.com /news/world/probe-revisits-mystery-of-assassination-that-triggered-rwandan -genocide/article32316139. See also Judi Rever, *In Praise of Blood: The Crimes of the Rwandan Patriotic Front* (Toronto: Vintage Canada, 2018), 193.

21. Author's interview with Jean-Marie Micombero.

22. The various testimonies given by General Kayumba, Micombero, and Theogene did not prevent the French judiciary from dismissing the case in December 2018, citing a "lack of irrefutable material evidence." A lawyer representing Agathe Habyarimana said the ruling was "a disappointment but it doesn't come as

a surprise," given the drive to improve diplomatic relations between France and Rwanda.

23. The Kenyan politician Patrick identified was active in the struggle to force President Daniel arap Moi to accept multiparty politics in the 1990s. In her essay in André Guichaoua, ed., *Seth Sendashonga, 1951–1998: Un Rwandais pris entre deux feux. Témoignages et propos* (Paris: Harmattan, 2013), Cyrie gives a strong set of clues to his identity.

24. Judi Rever, "Amid Attempts to Seek Indictments Against Rwanda's Regime, Spain's Pursuit of International Criminals Under Threat," *Foreign Policy Journal*, February 27, 2014.

Chapter 18: Do Not Disturb

1. Yuval Noah Harari, *21 Lessons for the 21st Century* (London: Jonathan Cape, 2018).

2. Author's interview with Phil Vernon.

3. Lee Kuan Yew, *From Third World to First: Singapore and the Asian Economic Boom* (New York: HarperCollins, 2000).

4. World Bank Open Data, www.data.worldbank.org.

5. Commission for Africa, "Our Common Interest: Report of the Commission for Africa," March 2005, https://reliefweb.int/report/world/our-common-interest -report-commission-africa, 64.

6. "Ease of Doing Business Rankings," World Bank, www.doingbusiness.org /en/rankings.

7. "Rwanda Has Negligible Corruption—Transparency," BBC, July 22, 2010, www.bbc.co.uk/news/world-africa-10726324.

8. Clement Uwiringiyimana, "Killers of Rwandan Anti-Corruption Activist Jailed for 20 Years," Reuters, January 23, 2015, www.reuters.com/article/uk-rwanda -corruption/killers-of-rwandan-anti-corruption-activist-jailed-for-20-years-id UKKBN0KW0RD20150123.

9. Millennium Promise Alliance, www.millenniumpromise.org; "Rwandan Farm-ers to Benefit from Bill Gates Funding," *New Times*, October 16, 2009, www.new times.co.rw/section/read/12286; Tim Gaynor, "Philanthropist Howard Buffett Backs Brown Revolution in Africa," *Al Jazeera*, February 1, 2015, http://america .aljazeera.com/articles/2015/2/1/philanthropist-howard-buffett-backs-brown -revolution-in-africa.html; Bella English, "In Rwanda, Visionary Doctor Is Moving Mountains Again," *Boston Globe*, April 13, 2008, http://archive.boston.com/lifestyle /articles/2008/04/13/in_rwanda_visionary_doctor_is_moving_mountains_again.

10. "Rwanda: Rounded Up Off the Streets," Human Rights Watch, September 24, 2015, www.hrw.org/news/2015/09/24/rwanda-rounded-streets.

11. Author's interview, anonymity requested.

12. Author's interview, anonymity requested.

13. Belgian historian and anthropologist Jan Vansina, who specialized in re-cording the oral history of Central Africa, died in October 2017 at the age of eighty-seven; René Lemarchand, Franco-American political scientist who had done groundbreaking work on ethnic conflict in the Great Lakes, turned eighty-eight in 2020.

14. Peter Uvin, *Aiding Violence: The Development Enterprise in Rwanda* (Boulder: Lynne Rienner Publishers, 1998).

Chapter 19: Song of the Stool Pigeon

1. Ronen Bergman, *Rise and Kill First: The Secret History of Israel's Targeted Assassinations* (London: John Murray, 2018).

2. Pascal Fletcher and Helen Nyambura-Mwaura, "South Africa, Rwanda Expel Diplomats in Row over Rwandan Exiles," Reuters, March 7, 2014, www.reuters.com /article/us-safrica-rwanda/south-africa-rwanda-expel-diplomats-in-row-over-rwandan -exiles-idUSBREA261BS20140307.

3. Geoffrey York and Judi Rever, "Rwandan Dissident in Belgium Warned of Suspected Targeted Attack," *Globe and Mail*, May 14, 2014, www.theglobeand mail.com/news/world/rwandan-dissident-in-belgium-a-suspected-target /article18653424.

4. Ruta v. Minister of Home Affairs (CCT02/18) [2018] ZACC 52; 2019 (3) BCLR 383 (CC); 2019 (2) SA 329 (CC) (20 December 2018), South Africa, Constitutional Court, at South African Legal Information Institute, www.saflii.org/za /cases/ZACC/2018/52.html.

5. Author's interview with Eric Ruzindana.

6. Theogene Rudasingwa, *President Paul Kagame's Plot to Assassinate Me: Top Secret Rukara Files Revealed* (self-published, 2020). Theogene sent me four digitalized audiotapes of the Rukara cell phone exchanges, which I played to three Rwandan sources, individuals familiar with Dan Munyuza's voice. They all three identified the main caller as Munyuza.

7. "A New RNC Under Dr Theogene Rudasingwa," *The Rwandan*, July 1, 2016, www.therwandan.com/a-new-rnc-under-dr-theogene-rudasingwa.

Chapter 20: The Inquest

1. "Letter Dated 18 December 2018 from the Group of Experts on the Democratic Republic of the Congo Addressed to the President of the Security Council," United Nations Security Council, December 31, 2018, https://reliefweb.int/sites /reliefweb.int/files/resources/Midterm%20report%20of%20the%20Group%20 of%20Experts%20on%20the%20Democratic-31dec2018.pdf.

2. Siyavuya Mzantsi, "Appeal over Refugee Status for 'War Crime' General Granted," IOL, May 31, 2017, www.iol.co.za/capetimes/news/appeal-over-refugee -status-for-war-crime-general-granted-9456786.

3. Kennedy's extraordinary personal story is the focus of Jacques Pauw, *Rat Roads: One Man's Incredible Journey* (Cape Town: Zebra Press, 2012).

4. Geoffrey York and Judi Rever, "Assassination in Africa: Inside the Plots to Kill Rwanda's Dissidents," *Globe and Mail*, May 2, 2014, www.theglobe andmail.com/news/world/secret-recording-says-former-rwandan-army-major-proves -government-hires-assassins-to-kill-critics-abroad/article18396349.

5. See AfriForum, www.afriforum.co.za.

6. Nick Thompson, "Gerrie Nel: 'Bull Dog' Prosecutor Sinks Teeth into Oscar Pistorius at Murder Trial," CNN, April 14, 2014, https://edition.cnn.com /2014/04/10/world/africa/oscar-pistorius-trial-gerrie-nel/index.html.

7. "AfriForum Satisfied That Duduzane Had His Day in Court," AfriForum, July 12, 2019, www.afriforum.co.za/en/afriforum-satisfied-duduzane-day-court.

8. "Gerrie Nel Sets Sights on Grace Mugabe," *Sunday Times*, August 17, 2017, www.timeslive.co.za/news/south-africa/2017-08-17-gerrie-nel-sets-sights-on-grace -mugabe.

9. Author's interview with Gerrie Nel.

10. Author's interview, anonymity requested.

11. Peter Fabricius, "SA Is 'Covering Up' the Assassination of Rwandan Dissident Patrick Karegeya—Gerrie Nel," *Daily Maverick*, January 17, 2019, www.dailymaverick.co.za/article/2019-01-17-sa-is-covering-up-the-assassination -of-rwandan-dissident-patrick-karegeya-gerrie-nel.

12. Magistrate Mashiane Mathopa's seven-page ruling, inquest serial number 0001/2019, January 21, 2019; three-page letter from G. L. Roberts, deputy director of public prosecutions, Gauteng Local Division, Johannesburg, to the senior public prosecutor, June 5, 2018, placed on record January 16, 2019.

13. Magistrate's ruling, J56 (81/804249) No. 01, April 18, 2019.

14. Five-page statement by investigating officer Lieutenant Colonel Kwena George Motlhamme, South African Police Service, under oath, April 18, 2019.

15. Geoffrey York, "South Africa Seeks Arrest of Murder Suspects with Alleged Links to Rwandan Government," *Globe and Mail*, September 19, 2019, www.theglobeandmail.com/world/article-south-africa-seeks-arrest-of-murder -suspects-with-alleged-links-to.

Chapter 21: Regret Is an Understatement

1. Joseph Sebarenzi, with Laura Ann Mullane, *God Sleeps in Rwanda: A Journey of Transformation* (Oxford: Oneworld, 2009).

2. Michael J. Kavanagh, "Rwanda's Latest Ethnic Cleansing," *Slate*, April 7, 2004, https://slate.com/news-and-politics/2004/04/rwanda-s-latest-ethnic-cleansing .html.

3. "Rwanda: Eight-Year Sentence for Opposition Leader: Victoire Ingabire Found Guilty of Two Charges in Flawed Trial," Human Rights Watch, October 30, 2012, www.hrw.org/news/2012/10/30/rwanda-eight-year-sentence-opposition-leader.

4. Kizito Mihigo, "Igisobanuro Cy'urupfu (English Subtitles)" [The Meaning of Death], YouTube, posted by RDI-Rwanda Rwiza, April 15, 2014, www.youtube .com/watch?v=WcGC3eFuDAc&list=RDWcGC3eFuDAc&start_radio=1.

5. Author's interview with Christopher Vogel.

6. "General James Kabarebe Incites and Encourages Young Tutsis to Hate and Discriminate as Well as Hostility Against Hutus," Mouvement Rwandais pour le Changement Démocratique, https://mrcd-ubumwe.org/archives/46976.

7. Author's interview, anonymity requested.

8. Author's interview with David Himbara.

9. Steve Terrill, "Taking Sides in Rwanda," African Arguments, May 6, 2014, https://africanarguments.org/2014/05/06/taking-sides-in-rwanda-by-steve-terrill.

10. Bill Marczak, Geoffrey Alexander, Sarah McKune, John Scott-Railton, and Ron Deibert, "Champing at the Cyberbit: Ethiopian Dissidents Targeted with New Commercial Spyware," Citizen Lab, Munk School, University of Toronto, December 6, 2017, https://citizenlab.ca/2017/12/champing-cyberbit-ethiopian -dissidents-targeted-commercial-spyware.

11. Mehul Srivastava and Tom Wilson, "Inside the WhatsApp Hack: How an Israeli Technology Was Used to Spy," *Financial Times*, October 30, 2019, www .ft.com/content/d9127eae-f99d-11e9-98fd-4d6c20050229.

12. "World Press Freedom Index," Reporters Without Borders, https://rsf.org /en/ranking.

13. It's an indication of how thoroughly the RPF narrative has taken hold abroad that while a state-appointed committee in Kigali urged the government to institute criminal proceedings for "genocide denial" against the BBC for broadcasting *Untold Story*, thirty-eight "scholars, scientists, researchers, journalists and historians" in the West also addressed an open letter of protest to the corporation.

14. Author's interview, anonymity requested.

15. Author's interview, anonymity requested.

16. Jeffrey Gettleman, "The Global Elite's Favorite Strongman," *New York Times*, September 4, 2013, www.nytimes.com/2013/09/08/magazine/paul-kagame -rwanda.html. When Gettleman asked Kagame about this episode during an interview, Kagame offered a watered-down alternative version, saying he had only "shoved" one of the men so hard he fell to the floor. "It's my nature. I can be very tough, I can make mistakes like that," he said. Hitting people, he added, was not "sustainable," which struck Gettleman as a strange word to use, "as if the only issue with beating your underlings was whether such behavior was effective over the long term."

17. David Himbara, "Kagame Imprisoned Mupende in 2009 After Viciously Beating Him. Mupende Is Dead," *Medium*, September 21, 2019, https://medium .com/@david.himbara_27884/kagame-imprisoned-mupende-in-2009-after -viciously-beating-him-mupende-is-dead-761e085de0a7.

18. Tom Wilson and David Blood, "Rwanda: Where Even Poverty Data Must Toe Kagame's Line," *Financial Times*, August 13, 2019, www.ft.com/content/683 047ac-b857-11e9-96bd-8e884d3ea203; "Has Rwanda Been Fiddling Its Numbers?," *The Economist*, August 15, 2019, www.economist.com/middle-east-and-africa/2019 /08/15/has-rwanda-been-fiddling-its-numbers.

19. Author's interview, anonymity requested.

20. Anonymous, "The Rwandan Debacle: Disguising Poverty as an Economic Miracle," *Review of African Political Economy*, September 2, 2019, http://roape .net/2019/09/02/the-rwandan-debacle-disguising-poverty-as-an-economic-miracle.

21. "Rwandan Debacle" is cited above; other articles by the same writer published anonymously in *Review of African Political Economy* include the following: "A Straightforward Case of Fake Statistics," April 18, 2019; "Revealing Lies, Questioning Complicity," January 29, 2019; "The Cover Up: Complicity in Rwanda's Lies," November 21, 2018; and "Rwanda's House of Sand: Brutality, Lies and Complicity," July 26, 2018. See www.roape.net.

22. Author's interview, anonymity requested.

23. Tom Wilson and David Blood, "Rwanda: Where Even Poverty Data Must Toe Kagame's Line," *Financial Times*, August 13, 2019, www.ft.com/content /683047ac-b857-11e9-96bd-8e884d3ea203.

24. Author's interview, anonymity requested.

25. Author's interview, anonymity requested.

26. "Repression Across Borders: Attacks and Threats Against Rwandan Opponents and Critics Abroad," Human Rights Watch, January 28, 2014, www.hrw.org /news/2014/01/28/rwanda-repression-across-borders.

27. Jennifer Fierberg, "A Little Knowledge Is a Dangerous Thing. So Is a Lot," *Salem News*, October 16, 2012, www.salem-news.com/articles/october162012 /danger-rwanda-jf.php.

28. Carien Du Plessis, "Shooting Death of Rwandan Exile in Cape Town Could Be Pandor's First Big Diplomatic Test," *Daily Maverick*, June 3, 2019, www.daily maverick.co.za/article/2019-06-03-shooting-death-of-rwandan-exile-in-cape-town

-could-be-pandors-first-big-diplomatic-test; "Head of Rwandan Diaspora in Mozambique Shot Dead," Club of Mozambique, August 26, 2019, https://clubofmozam bique.com/news/head-of-rwandan-diaspora-in-mozambique-shot-dead-140247.

29. "He Knew Too Much: The Life and Death of Dr Emmanuel Gasakure and the Corruption of the Kagame Regime," *The Rwandan*, May 4, 2015, www.the rwandan.com/he-knew-too-much-the-life-and-death-of-dr-emmanuel-gasakure -and-the-corruption-of-the-kagame-regime.

30. "Family of Deceased Tycoon Assinapol Rwigara Petitions President Kagame," *East African*, March 14, 2015, www.theeastafrican.co.ke/rwanda/News /Family-of-deceased-tycoon-Rwigara-petitions-President-Kagame/1433218 -2653598-myixcwz/index.html.

31. "Rwanda: Kigali City Authority Demolishes Late Rwigara's Hotel," *The Rwandan*, September 12, 2015, www.therwandan.com/rwandakigali-city-authority -demolishes-late-rwigaras-hotel.

32. Jason Burke, "Rwanda Opposition Leader Says Ally's Killing Was Act of Intimidation," *The Guardian*, September 25, 2019, www.theguardian.com/world /2019/sep/25/rwanda-opposition-leader-victoire-ingabire-ally-killing-act -intimidation.

33. "Belgique: Les activités obscures de l'ambassade du Rwanda à Bruxelles," Jambonews, June 30, 2019, www.jambonews.net/actualites/20190630 -belgique-les-activites-obscures-de-lambassade-du-rwanda-a-bruxelles.

34. Judi Rever, *In Praise of Blood: The Crimes of the Rwandan Patriotic Front* (Toronto: Vintage Canada, 2018), 205.

35. Amy Greenbank, "Spies in Our Suburbs," Australian Broadcasting Corporation, August 24, 2019, www.abc.net.au/news/2019-08-25/spies-in-our-suburbs -alleged-spy-web-silencing-rwandan-refugees/11317704.

36. "Kagame avuga uko bishe Seth Sendashonga yarenze umurongo ko nta nimbabazi," YouTube, posted by juka ce, March 10, 2019, www.youtube.com /watch?v=Ob3f9OhQ7kw&t=152s.

37. François Soudan, *Kagame: The President of Rwanda Speaks* (Enigma Books, 2016).

38. Himbara, who set up an NGO called Democracy in Rwanda, has published *Kagame's Economic Mirage* (North Charleston, SC: CreateSpace, 2016), *Kagame's Killing Fields* (North Charleston, SC: CreateSpace, 2017), and *Rwanda's Stillborn Middle-Income Economy* (Author House, 2020). He is a vigorous critic of Kagame and his regime on Facebook, and in May 2015 he testified about the regime's human rights record before a subcommittee of the US House of Representatives. See "Testimony by Dave Himbara on Developments in Rwanda," House Committee on Foreign Affairs, Subcommittee on Africa, Global Health, Global Human Rights, and International Organizations, May 20, 2016, https://docs .house.gov/meetings/FA/FA16/20150520/103498/HHRG-114-FA16-Wstate -HimbaraD-20150520.pdf.

39. "How the Hero of 'Hotel Rwanda' Fell Into a Vengeful Strongman's Trap," New York Times, September 18, 2020, https://www.nytimes.com/2020/09/18/world /africa/rwanda-paul-rusesabagina.html.

40. Author's interview with Charlotte Mukankusi.

41. "Only 10 Rwandans Against Paul Kagame's Third Term, Says Lawmakers' Report," Agence France-Press, August 11, 2015, available at *Nation*, https:// nation.africa/kenya/news/africa/only-10-rwandans-against-paul-kagame-s-third -term-says-lawmakers-report-1118754.

42. "List of Awards and Honours Bestowed upon Paul Kagame," Wikipedia, https://en.wikipedia.org/wiki/List_of_awards_and_honours_bestowed_upon _Paul_Kagame.

43. In June 2015 NISS director Karanzi Karake was arrested on arrival at Heathrow in a case triggered by the 2008 Spanish indictment of 39 RPF military officers accused of war crimes in Rwanda and DRC in the 1990s. The makeup of his defence team, which included Tony Blair's barrister wife, Cherie, illustrated what powerful connections Rwanda's leadership enjoys abroad. KK was released two months later. No charges, in contrast, have ever been brought in the West against senior Rwandan officials repeatedly accused by dissidents of masterminding Kigali's extraterritorial assassination program.

44. René Lemarchand, "Rwanda: The State of Research," SciencesPo, Mass Violence and Resistance—Research Network, June 25, 2018, www.sciencespo.fr /mass-violence-war-massacre-resistance/en/document/rwanda-state-research .html.

45. World Happiness Index 2020, Reporters Without Borders, https://rsf.org /en/ranking.

46. Alexandre Kimenyi, "A Tribute to Gisa (General Fred Rwigema), a Young Man with an Indescribable Beauty," December 2, 1990, www.kimenyi.com. A translation is available at Hungry for Truth, Peace and Justice, https://hungryoftruth .blogspot.com/2009/07/tribute-to-gisa-general-fred-rwigema.html.

INDEX

Kagame, Paul, (*continued*)
  Rwanda's progressive dictatorship,
    391–392
  Sendashonga's death, 276, 377–378
  social media attacks, 421–422
  taking over RPF leadership,
    216–221, 223
  targeting dissenters, 79–82, 103–104,
    320
  targeting Karegeya and the General,
    50–54, 342–346
  tracing the assassination attempt
    back to, 73–77
  2010 election, 67–69
  undercover NRA work, 147–148,
    151–152
  vindictiveness, 435–436
  Western view of the genocide, 38
  . *See also* Rwandan Patriotic Front
Kakuru, Kenneth, 140, 170, 186, 247
Kalinaki, Daniel, 172–173
Kalisa, Innocent, 101
Kandt, Richard, 2, 116
Kanimba, John, 112–113, 123,
    155–156, 248, 353
Kanyandekwe, Pascal, 64
Kanyarengwe, Alexis, 191–192, 218
Kanyarwanda, 130
Kanyemera, Kaka, 179
Karaha, Bizima, 310
Karake, Karenzi "KK," 89–90, 322
Karangwa, Chrysologue, 346
Karegeya, Elvis (son), 31, 34–35,
    87–88, 113, 414–415
Karegeya, Leah (wife), 36, 170
  exile, 43, 47, 88, 100–101
  inquest, 409–410, 415
  Kagame targeting dissenters, 343,
    345
  Kagame's character, 179
  Ntabana's disappearance, 97–98
  Patrick's assassination, 23, 26–27,
    30–32, 34–35, 41
  Patrick's contacts and informants,
    48–49
  Patrick's imprisonment, 351–361
  return to Rwanda after the RPF
    victory, 247–248
  RPF Akazu, 286–287
  RPF invasion, 208

Karegeya, Patrick, 116(fig.)
  Apollo's arrest, 96–97
  Arusha Accords, 231–232
  assassination plot, 18–23, 25–38,
    56–61, 70–75, 77–78, 342–346
  assault on RNC members, 93–94
  attempt on the General, 63
  burial, 32–35
  contacts and informants, 47–49
  diamond deal, 327–328
  DRC mineral looting, 329–333
  early connection with Kagame,
    134–136
  education, 123
  election fraud, 346–348
  emotional and physical decline,
    100–104
  exile, 40–47, 66–67, 86–87, 89,
    100–101, 112
  extramarital liaisons, 292–293
  Falcon 50 explosion, 368, 371–372
  family and upbringing, 112–116,
    123–124
  First Congo War, 297
  the General's loyalty, 53
  government intimidation, 39–41
  Habyarimana overthrow, 199–200
  Hranjski shooting, 314–315
  ideology and philosophy, 35–36
  imprisonment, 142, 352–361
  indictment in absentia, 69
  inquest, 403–404, 406–412, 414–416
  joining the revolution, 170–171
  Kabila's assassination, 323–324
  Kagame benching, 351–352
  Kagame's collective punishment,
    433, 436
  Kagame's election interference,
    347–348
  Kagame's postwar shift in behavior,
    180
  law school, 139–142
  leaving the RPF, 339–341
  "marriage," 181
  Ntabana's disappearance, 95–96
  Obote's disappeared rebel
    sympathizers, 141–142
  opposition group plans, 61–62
  opposition radio station, 94
  the political lie, 4–6

MICHELA WRONG is a writer and journalist with more than twenty years' experience covering Africa. She joined Reuters news agency in the early 1980s and was posted as a foreign correspondent to Italy, France, and Ivory Coast. She became a freelance journalist in 1994, when she moved to then-Zaire and found herself covering both the genocide in Rwanda and the final days of dictator Mobutu Sese Seko for the BBC and Reuters. She later rebased in Kenya, where she spent four years covering East, West, and Central Africa for the *Financial Times*. She is the author of three other books of nonfiction and a novel.

PublicAffairs is a publishing house founded in 1997. It is a tribute to the standards, values, and flair of three persons who have served as mentors to countless reporters, writers, editors, and book people of all kinds, including me.

I. F. STONE, proprietor of *I. F. Stone's Weekly*, combined a commitment to the First Amendment with entrepreneurial zeal and reporting skill and became one of the great independent journalists in American history. At the age of eighty, Izzy published *The Trial of Socrates*, which was a national bestseller. He wrote the book after he taught himself ancient Greek.

BENJAMIN C. BRADLEE was for nearly thirty years the charismatic editorial leader of *The Washington Post*. It was Ben who gave the *Post* the range and courage to pursue such historic issues as Watergate. He supported his reporters with a tenacity that made them fearless and it is no accident that so many became authors of influential, best-selling books.

ROBERT L. BERNSTEIN, the chief executive of Random House for more than a quarter century, guided one of the nation's premier publishing houses. Bob was personally responsible for many books of political dissent and argument that challenged tyranny around the globe. He is also the founder and longtime chair of Human Rights Watch, one of the most respected human rights organizations in the world.

⋅　　⋅　　⋅

For fifty years, the banner of Public Affairs Press was carried by its owner Morris B. Schnapper, who published Gandhi, Nasser, Toynbee, Truman, and about 1,500 other authors. In 1983, Schnapper was described by *The Washington Post* as "a redoubtable gadfly." His legacy will endure in the books to come.

Peter Osnos, *Founder*